UNDERSTANDING
HOMEOPATHY
and
INTEGRATIVE MEDICINE

By

Jose Miguel Mullen,

Medical Doctor and Homeopathic Physician.

FIFTH EDITION

ISBN: 0-7596-9718-3 (e-book)
ISBN: 0-7596-9719-1 (Paperback)

This book is printed on acid free paper.

1stBooks - rev. 6/7/02

DISCLAIMER

This book is not intended to treat, diagnose or prescribe.

The information contained herein is in no way to be considered as a substitute for a consultation with a duly licensed Health Care Professional.

DEDICATED TO

Samuel Hahnemann, M.D.,
my Admirable Teacher...

...also to

the Faculty and Staff of the Post-Graduate School of the
Asociación Médica Homeopática Argentina.
I am forever grateful for the quality of your Teaching,
for all your kindness, patience and
understanding...

...and to my family, my friends and my patients,
they are my source of joy in the good times,
they give sense and meaning to my life,
and they are my bulwark and guide when things become difficult...

Athenian "Do you agree that there are [these] two kinds of Physicians? ...Have you observed that, as there are slaves as well as freemen among the patients, there are also Physicians for slaves and Physicians for freemen?

Slaves...are treated by slave Physicians, who pay their slave patients a hurried visit... Slave Physicians scarcely give their patients time to express their complaints. They will then give their slave patients some...potion with airs of great knowledge and the demeanor of despots, and then rush away to see other slaves...

A free Physician who attend free men, on the other hand, treats his patients' diseases by going into them thoroughly in a methodical manner, and he takes his patients and families into his confidence. Thus, a free Physician learns from his patients, and at the same time instructs them to the best of his ability. A Physician for freemen will not prescribe before completely winning his patients' trust and, after gaining their trust, he will steadily aim at bringing about a complete restoration of health by persuading his patients to comply with his treatments.

Now, which of the two do you consider to be a better Physician?"

From Book IV of *The Laws of Plato.*

TABLE OF CONTENTS

"There are more things in Heaven and Earth,
Horatio, than are dreamt of in your philosophy"
Hamlet, Act 1, Scene 5.

PROLOGUE

Allopathy, or Mainstream, or Scientific Medicine cures *disease-syndromes*.

Homeopathy cures *Whole disease-bearing patients*.

They often complement each other nicely when it comes to decide how to treat someone who is ill.

Homeopathy is based on the principle of *like cures like.*

It uses mainly natural products.

How it works is still a mystery.

In order to be Homeopathically active, a natural product must be diluted, triturated and/or shaken. The more diluted, triturated and shaken, the more active that Homeopathic remedy becomes. Evidence is starting to emerge that, when diluted and shaken, there are changes in the *physical* characteristics of water[1]. Similar or related physical changes could be responsible for the Homeopathic activity found when a substance is diluted and shaken.

Many remedies are prepared starting from natural products that, in their original state, have no usefulness whatsoever, or else may be poisonous. How these substances develop a curative capacity, once sufficiently diluted and triturated or shaken, is an enigma.

Yet, Homeopathy works; and its existence, mode of action and therapeutic capacity have become a thorn on the side of Allopathy ever since its inception.

Homeopathy has been pilloried and called Voodoo Medicine and all kinds of other uncomplimentary names—some very imaginative—by the

---

[1] Lo, S-Y., Lo, A., Chong, L.W., Tiazhang, L., Hua, L.H., Geng, X. *"Physical properties of water with I_E structures"*. Mod. Phys. L. 10 (19) 921-930, 1996; and Lo, S-Y. *"Anomalous state of ice"*. Mod. Phys. L. 10 (19) 909-919, 1996. The authors subjected water to stirring, heating, succussing and freezing, and found changes (or *enhancement?*) in its physical characteristics.

Allopathic establishment. It has been roundly despised and laid to rest a number of times. Its practitioners have been called quacks or worse.

Its patients have been labeled as gullible fools, despite of the fact that people like Mark Twain, Disraeli, the Mahatma Ghandi, Goethe, Manet, Dickens, Marie Curie, Rockerfeller, generations of the British royal family and a host of others have chosen Homeopathy as their preferred form of treatment.

The responsible for all this commotion is Dr. Samuel Hahnemann, a German Physician who rebelled against the Medicine *en vogue* some 200 years ago.

Homeopathy is his brainchild.

Dr. Hahnemann was born in 1755 in Meissen, Saxony, at a time when the practice of Medicine was limited to bleeding, purging, blistering and creating accumulations of pus to then drain it. The purpose behind these therapeutic abominations was "to purify the organism" in order to make it healthy.

Dr. Hahnemann's given names were Christian Friedrich Samuel. He was called Samuel to avoid confusion, because his father's first name was also Christian.

Young Samuel was a frail child. He loved to study. He graduated as a Medical Doctor in 1779, at age 24. By that time, Dr. Hahnemann was also an accomplished chemist and fluent in several languages.

He quitted the practice of Medicine shortly after graduating. He couldn't bring himself to needlessly mortify his patients. Ever since, and until he created Homeopathy, Dr. Hahnemann earned his keep as a translator.

Dr. Hahnemann was endowed with incorruptible moral and professional principles and many other talents and virtues. Unfortunately, professional tact was not his forte. With his colleagues, he was as diplomatic as a grizzly bear recently roused from hibernation. His acerbic and biting criticisms of the atrocious Medicine practiced in his time—and of its practitioners and followers—never failed to stir up the wrath of his peers, who expelled him from town after town.

In one of those many towns he was allowed to stay long enough to meet and fall in love with Henriette Küchler, the 17 year old daughter of a local pharmacist. Henriette became Dr. Hahnemann's wife and staunch companion in the very difficult years ahead, and bore him several children.

Dr. Hahnemann's family life was sad, difficult and trying. He was haunted by poverty as he constantly roamed from town to town. He had to work all hours to make ends meet. His eldest son lost his mind, his second daughter died in a coach accident as a baby, and 2 other daughters were killed. His wife Henriette died when Dr. Hahnemann was 75 years old.

Dr. Hahnemann was a prolific writer, as well as a keen self-made Medical Researcher. Above all, he was a compassionate Physician. Since his graduation until 1835, the year when he semi-retired, Dr. Hahnemann's literary production can only be described as colossal. After repudiating Allopathic Medicine, Dr. Hahnemann created and started the practice of Homeopathy and also wrote many books and essays, among them his Organon, his Materia Medica, and his Treatise of Chronic Diseases.

Dr. Hahnemann had planned to spend the rest of his life with his two spinster daughters after the death of his wife and his semi-retirement, seeing a small number of patients and writing to friends and disciples. Fate, however, had other plans. Mélanie D'Havilly, a Parisian noblewoman, went to see him as a patient. Instead of creating a Doctor-patient relationship, they both fell head over heels in love with each other. He was 80 years old at the time, she 30. Dr. Hahnemann's two spinster daughters were shocked and horrified at this unusual relationship. Mélanie and Dr. Hahnemann nevertheless married in 1835.

Mélanie took her husband to Paris after the wedding. Her dynamism and connections opened every door. Soon Dr. Hahnemann's practice was famous. Mélanie also became her husband's assistant and, in time quite an accomplished Homeopath. After Dr. Hahnemann's death, Mélanie continued practicing Homeopathy, mostly as a hobby since she was quite rich. Her fortune, however, vanished after she financed some harebrained inventor's idea. Mélanie then started to do Homeopathy in earnest, but the French Government accused her of practicing without a license, and ordered her to cease and desist. Mélanie fell into hard times. Many years later the French Government finally yielded and granted her a license as a Homeopathic Physician.

Dr. Hahnemann died in Paris in 1842, at age 90.

Even after his death was Dr. Hahnemann to remain a wanderer. He was originally buried in the Parisian Graveyard of Montmartre. In 1898, however, his remains were exhumed and re-interred, with great pomp and circumstance, in Père Lachaise, the most *chic* of Parisian cemeteries.

Dr. Hahnemann created a form of Medicine based on the uniqueness of each Human Being, and on the fact that each Human Being is an indivisible Whole.

The Wholeness of each Human Being is nurtured, maintained and healed by the Vital Force; that is, by the immaterial principle that keeps each one of us alive and functioning.

The Vital Force is fully in control when an individual is in balance, but may loose its grip in some organs and tissues when a patient looses his or her balance. Under conditions of imbalance, some organs and tissues become devitalized and vulnerable, may become ill and even be invaded by Nature in the form of bacteria and the like. Areas bereft of Vital Force scream for help. Those cries are interpreted as suffering and distress by the patient, and as a disease by the Physician.

Whenever an individual Human Being is sick, then, the first priority should be to assist him or her regain balance.

Once in balance, the patient will be in harmony with him or herself and also with Nature. The Vital Force will gain access to the areas that were diseased. Its healing power will make distress and suffering disappear. Ill organs and tissues will heal. And Nature's invasion, if present, will be checked and reversed.

Allopathy has gone a long way since the purging, blistering and bleeding prevalent in Dr. Hahnemann's days.

Its basic tenets, however, remain unaltered.

Allopathy considers itself to be a science, which is a fallacy; and postulates that all other forms of Medicine are quackery, which is even worse.

It still believes that contrary cures contrary.

It assumes that we Humans are hostages of Nature (which is true, but only when we are ill).

It affirms that there are a limited number of diseases, and that those diseases attack every Human Being with equal gusto and ferocity. And that diseases is what make people ill.

It decrees that diseases are entities, and that the only way a patient may ever regain health is by means of destroying diseases as they appear. It believes that destroying diseases is what cures and brings about health.

It claims that Pharmaceutical drugs, Surgery, and/or radiations are the only means of curing people. And that only vaccines, plus environmental devastation, can prevent diseases from happening.

Above all, Allopathy considers that our only fate as Humans is to suffer and to die an untimely death unless we follow the Allopathic dicta to the letter—another inconsistency.

Much in this line of thought is misleading.

To start with, Medicine has never been, is not, and will never be a science. Medicine is an *art,* because it is not based on knowledge, but on *care taking.*

Medicine was *not* born when someone started to study diseases and their treatments; but rather when someone was ill or hurt, and somebody else was moved enough to assist that sufferer. Along eons of Prehistory and History, and all the way until the present time, caring has been the *raison d'être* of Medicine. Care is in the essence of our Hippocratic Oath, that thread of Ariadne that unites one generation of Physicians to the next. This need to care for others is what makes a Physician a Physician, and not his or her scientific proclivities. Scientific knowledge helps, granted; but it's only the icing in this particular cake.

Science is the rage nowadays. Which is understandable, considering how successful a scientific approach to Medicine has been in many instances. Problem is, many Physicians take it for granted that they are scientists!

Like so many fads that have preceded Allopathy, this one will eventually vanish into the limbo of History, leaving behind only what has proven to be useful—while *caring* will remain, and continue to be the foundation, of whatever Medical fashions that may follow.

Everything deceptive and misleading in Scientific Medicine stems from its meretricious identification with science.

For starters, Allopathy considers each Human Being as a more or less organized association of molecules that interact through electromagnetic and biochemical forces instead of an individual Whole, where that individual Wholeness is infinitely greater than the sum total of its parts.

Then, it considers that every part and syndromes of each Human Being can be interchanged by those of another Human Being, immunity permitting; when, in actual reality, each Human Being is a unique individual Whole. Mr. Smith's liver is not identical to that of Ms. Jones, nor are their respective sinusitis or indigestions.

Allopathy considers that diseases are real entities when, in actual fact, the only existing entities are the patients who suffer those diseases.

Scientific Medicine also believes that there is a limited number of diseases and a limited number of treatments, one or several for each disease. Allopathy appears to be incapable of understanding that there are as many diseases as there are diseased Human Beings—and also perhaps as many treatments.

I recall a man I once saw one evening. In a spot that, in Tokyo, is the equivalent of Times Square in New York. He was standing there, attired in a kimono and wooden sandals as cars and buses rushed by. Perfectly happy and at ease in the midst of all the stridence and bustle. Immense luminous ads, scrolling down the walls of skyscrapers all around, inundated him and his kimono and his sandals with a constant and ever changing cascade of multicolored lights. It was such a contrast, this man in his ancient garment amidst such a display of modern technology! On second thought, though, I realized that what happened was that this man was first and foremost Japanese; although he also approved of technology, its uses and its benefits.

Ever since, I have often wished that Allopathic Doctors would emulate this Japanese man; perfectly happy and at ease with the advances of Science but always aware that, prior to anything else, they are not scientists but Physicians—and therefore *caregivers.*

Allopathic treatments have been designed with the purpose of destroying diseases.

These treatments have no action whatsoever on the patient's Vital Force—nor on the evolution of the patient's imbalance. Everything progresses in Nature. Imbalance is no exception.

Allopathy can control a patient's disease, while at the same time the patient's imbalance progresses unchecked—meaning that it worsens.

Ultimately, then, Allopathy produces the therapeutic paradox of improving or curing a disease while the Whole patient continues to worsen. This, aside from the fact that Allopathy often swaps one disease (the one the patient is bearing) by another (that caused by the side effects and toxicities of the Allopathic treatments used to combat the original patient's disease). Allopathy's inability of controlling imbalance, plus the disease/s it produces through its side effects and toxicity, contributes in no small measure to increasing Human misery and untimely death.

Basically, Homeopathic remedies act like firefighters.

It is not the firefighter who snuffs the fire, but rather the water that gushes off the nozzle of the hose the firefighter is aiming at the source of the fire.

In a similar fashion, Homeopathic remedies do not cure. They direct the Vital Force towards the fulcrum of the Whole chronic patient's imbalance; or else towards the fulcrum of the Whole patient's acute disease.

And then the patient's Vital Force, by means of regaining a full grip of every organ and tissue, makes imbalance vanish. It thus effectively restores health in the Whole patient.

This is so because the only thing that can bring about balance and harmony, and heal a patient—that is, the only element that can ultimately *cure*—is the patient's own Vital Force.

Homeopathic remedies are obtained mostly from natural products that are triturated, diluted, and shaken. The more triturated, diluted and shaken, the more Homeopathically powerful a remedy becomes.

To study the range of efficacy a new remedy is administered, every day, to a group of healthy male and female Human volunteers. When administered in this fashion, the remedy provokes changes in the volunteers. Volunteers carefully record the changes they experiment in themselves. The sum total of changes found in this form of Homeopathic Clinical Research is known as the *profile* of that Homeopathic remedy.

Then the remedy is prescribed to patients whose profile resembles that of the remedy, following the principle that *like cures like.*

So far, over 3,000 natural substances—and also others manufactured by mankind—have been prepared and studied in this fashion.

Homeopathic remedies lack side effects and toxicity. The do not elicit allergic reactions. And they don't alter in any way the development of healthy Human embryos and fetuses.

Remedies are inexpensive and have no expiration date. Their therapeutic capacity will last forever if they are keep in a dry place, and away from strongly scented substances and direct sunlight.

Homeopathy has been used for generations, all over the world, for the past 200 years or so.

It is particularly important in France, Great Britain, India and Latin America.

In France, Homeopathy made its début long before Dr. Hahnemann settled there. It is estimated that one fourth of the French population is currently treated with Homeopathy, and that approximately 10 % of Physicians practice Homeopathy.

Homeopathy was imported in Great Britain in the 1830's, when the British royal family adopted Homeopathy as their preferred form of treatment; an attitude they have unswervingly maintained to this day.

After a period of stonewalling, most Continental Medical establishments finally surrendered to the efficacy of Homeopathy. The only exceptions were communist Russia, Hitler's Germany and Franco's Spain.

Homeopathy reached India in the 1820's, and has been wholeheartedly accepted by most of its population and many of its leaders. Currently, India has around 100,000 Homeopathic Practitioners, approximately one fourth of who are Medical Doctors.

In Latin America, Homeopathy has been seriously considered in Mexico, Brazil and Argentina for a long time. I have personally seen the Homeopathic kit that General José de San Martín carried at the time he crossed the Andes to emancipate Chile and Perú, in the 1810's. It is likely that he obtained the kit in Spain, where he lived for many years. Throughout Latin

America there are many excellent Homeopathic Post-Graduate Medical Schools, and an ever-increasing number of Latin American Physicians are becoming interested in Homeopathy.

Homeopathy was imported in America early in the 1800's.
It grew luxuriantly here.
By the turn of the Century there were over 14,000 Homeopathic Physicians that had graduated from 22 Homeopathic Medical Schools. There were also 112 Homeopathic Hospitals and 143 Homeopathic Medical Societies.
Then came a tremendous decline.
Only 2 Homeopathic Medical Schools remained in 1932, that either closed or became Allopathic shortly thereafter. Currently, there are no Homeopathic Medical Schools in America.
Homeopathy is taught as part of the Curriculum in Naturopathic Schools. At an Allopathic level it is one component of a Wholistic Residency in Tucson, Arizona.
The practice of Homeopathy is licensed and Board regulated only in Connecticut, Arizona and Nevada. In Connecticut, the Board of Homeopathic Medical Examiners is over 100 years old. Boards in Arizona and in Nevada are much more recent.

The decline of Homeopathy in America came about mainly because of three reasons, namely, squabbles between diverse homeopathic schools of thought, the Flexner Report and the promises of Allopathic Medicine early in the 20th Century.

Homeopathic Physicians became divided into two schools of thought during the second half of the 19th Century. One school stated that only low potencies should be used, whereas the other school favored higher ones. Soon this academic discussion became acrimonious, and eventually degenerated into a battle.
The only victim of this absurd conflict was the practice of Homeopathy—and the homeopathic patients[2].

---

[2] Apropos of this absurd struggle, let me quote a stanza from *Martín Fierro*, a poem written by Argentine poet José Hernández,

Los hermanos sean unidos,

sea esa la ley primera,

tengan unión verdadera

en cualquier tiempo que sea,

Footnotes continue in next page

During the 19th Century, Medical training in America could only be described as chaotic. Anybody could open a Medical School and teach. Medical Schools would open and close all the time, termination usually due to scarcity or lack of students and/or of funds. The quality of Medical Schools, both Allopathic and Homeopathic, ranged from excellent to poor to unspeakable—and so ranged also the quality of their graduates.

At the dawn of the 20th Century, the Council of Medical Education decided to correct matters. It asked the Carnegie Endowment Council for the Advancement of Teaching to evaluate Medical Schools. The Carnegie Endowment Council commissioned Drs. Abraham Flexner and Nathan Colwell to carry out the evaluation.

The result of their evaluation became known as the Flexner Report[3]. This report was heavily biased against non-Allopathic Medical Schools. Funds soon started to dry out for Schools that had been left out in the cold.

The Flexner report sounded the death knell for Homeopathic Medical Schools.

Allopathy trumpeted, since early in the 20th Century, the existence of "magic drugs". Like William Tell's arrow, these miraculous chemicals were supposed to hit the disease and spare the patient. Surgery made astonishing strides, too. Scientific Medicine also promised that, with its vaccines, nobody would ever fall ill again.

Allopathy assured sufferers that all they had to do was to throw themselves into the arms of any Allopathic Doctor or Hospital, receive drug treatments and/or vaccines, be operated upon and/or receive radiations and bingo! They would become cured and healthy, and become immune to every disease. And also almost immortal—without any change in lifestyle, to boot.

Millions upon millions were enticed by this Allopathic siren song. The promise was too good to let it pass—but it was also too good to be true, alas!

---

porque si entre ellos pelean

los devoran los de ajuera.

Freely translated, it would read something like this: May siblings remain united/let that be the first law/let them have a true union/at all times/because if they fight amongst them/they are devoured by outsiders. And devoured was Homeopathy by the same Establishment they had resisted so successfully until then.

[3] Flexner A. *"Medical Education in the United States and Canada"*. Carnegie Endowment for the Advancement of Teaching, Bulletin # 4, New York, 1910.

A Century has passed since those promises were first proclaimed. Results turned out to be considerably more modest than originally asserted. Most successful Allopathic treatments have proven to be of limited value. Aside from being fraught with side effects and toxicities that can be serious and very unpleasant.

Not only that. Useful as it is, Allopathy has left many problems unsolved.

Take for instance antibiotics, one of its greatest glories. An increasing number of bacterial strains are becoming resistant to all of them.

Or consider viral diseases. They still remain virtually incurable by Allopathy.

Vaccination has proven to be a Pandora's box. Vaccines are indeed useful to prevent diseases. But many of them have serious consequences that range from mild episodes of fever to brain damage and death.

And mortality by cancer has been steadily increasing since 1950; despite of the trillions of dollars spent and the swarms of workers, scientists and Medical Doctors dedicated to its research[4].

The possibilities and limitations of Allopathy and of Homeopathy—and of all other modalities of Wholistic Medicine too, for that matter—have created a collective awareness regarding the urgent need of *integrating* all forms of diagnosis and treatment in the benefit of the patients.

This collective awareness has stimulated the creation of *Integrative Medicine.*

The purpose of this new Medical approach is to proffer each individual patient the form of treatment most useful for his or her needs; whether that treatment may be Allopathic, Homeopathic, based on any other form of Wholistic Medicine or on any combination or combinations of the above.

---

[4] Bailar J.C. III, Gronick H.L. *"Cancer undefeated"*. New Eng. J. Med 336 (22):1569-1574, 1997.

One single Unity, one single Harmony.
Hippocrates.

Chapter 1

WHOLENESS

Allopathy is interested in diseases. It is also interested in what conse-quences diseases may have in the immune system and other suchlike organs and structures. It doesn't go any farther than that.

Homeopathy, instead, is interested in the *Whole* disease-bearing patient[5]. That is why it is so important to understand what Wholeness actually is.

Pharmacological treatments consist in an interaction between a well known molecular structure (the *drug*) and a subcellular molecule (the *recep-tor*). Receptors are located either in the cell wall or in its interior.

The receptor is either stimulated or inhibited by the drug. Pharmacol-ogical success, as well as side effects and toxicity, are all consequences on this interaction between molecules.

Allopathic drugs, then, act on the patient's cells; but have no effect whatsoever on the patient's Wholeness.

In Homeopathy, on the other hand, the healing power of the Vital Force is the only element that *cures*. The Homeopathic remedy only *directs* or *ori-ents* the patient's Vital Force.

In the instance of an *acute disease,* the Homeopathic remedy directs the patient's Vital Force towards the acutely ill organ and/or tissue. It will ulti-mately be the Vital Force, and not the Homeopathic remedy, what will cure the acute disease-syndrome, and therefore the Whole patient.

In chronic disease-bearing patients, the Homeopathic remedy directs the Vital Force towards the fulcrum of the Whole patient's chronic imbal-ance. Then the healing power of the Vital Force corrects the imbalance. The chronic disease-syndrome often vanishes once the patient regains balance.

---

[5] A patient's Wholeness means the disease the patient is bearing + the disease bear-ing patient + the disease bearing patient's circumstance (Tomás Paschero, M.D., Homeopathic Physician).

Jose Miguel Mullen, M.D.

Unlike the drug-receptor interaction of Allopathy, Homeopathic treatments act on the patient's Vital Force. The healing power of the Vital Force is the only element that cures the Whole patient.

I shall briefly consider now *Matter, Energy, Living Beings* and *Vital Force*, as well as how they interact with each other.

The purpose of this description is to attempt to clarify what is the Vital Force, and how it creates the Whole when interacting with the physical aspects of living beings.

Matter consists of all the simple elements that form our planet; such as water, carbon, oxygen, nitrogen, hydrogen, metals and the like.

Matter is composed by atoms that, in turn, are constituted by a nucleus and one or several orbiting electrons. When the nucleus of an atom splits, or degrades, or decays, or disintegrates, the atomic structure disappears. Only *energy* remains.

Ultimately, though, matter is composed by the stuff that makes the stars. Matter is what makes our physical beings. As far as matter is concerned, then, we are made of *stardust.*

Energy exists within and around the atoms. The atomic aspect of energy is liberated as atoms decay. Conversely, when free energy is *condensed*, atoms are created or formed.

Energy is constantly being condensed into atoms, and atoms are constantly disintegrating into energy.

The material aspect of an atom, together with its invisible energy, constitutes de *Wholeness* of that atom. An atom's material aspect consists of particles; some located in its nucleus while others orbit around that nucleus. When the atom's *Wholeness* ceases there is only energy; the atomic particles disintegrate.

Matter + condensing energy = one Whole atom

Living beings consist of an association of incredibly structured, orderly and complex accumulation of matter. This structure is held together and functioning by the *Vital Force.*

When Vital Force *condenses*, atoms become simple molecules, and simple molecules combine to create complex molecules. This is how Whole living beings are formed, become structured and function.

2

Conversely, when a living being degrades, or decays, or disintegrates, that is, when it *dies*, its Wholeness disappears, the Vital Force is liberated and the physical structure disintegrates into its simplest elements.

The material aspect of a living being, together with its invisible Vital Force, constitute that living being's *Wholeness*. The physical structure is composed of an unbelievably structured, complex and orderly aggregate of atoms and molecules.

When the *Wholeness* of a Living Being ceases, all that remains is free Vital Force and a physical structure that now, without the Vital Force to organize and maintain it, will decompose and disintegrate from its complexity into its simplest elements.

Matter + Vital Force = one Whole live being

Every Human culture has been aware of the existence of the Vital Force since the dawn of Time.

Greeks of old called it *Pneuma*[6] or *Physis*[7], Vedas *Atma*, ancient Egyptians *kah* and the Chinese *Chhi*.

When the nucleus of an atom splits, or decays, or is destroyed, it liberates energy according to Einstein's famous equation $E = mc^2$.

This equation means that the energy (E) liberated by an atom that has disintegrated equals its mass (m) multiplied by the square of the speed of light (c^2).

An equation such as VF = M?, in turn, would mean that the Vital Force (VF) liberated by a disintegrating—that is, a dead—being would equal the matter (M) of that being, multiplied by a factor we still know nothing about(?).

The Vital Force is all pervading. It is also very powerful.

If any area in Nature is razed by fire, or scorched by lava or by any other suchlike catastrophic event, it doesn't take long to find a hint of life budding here, then a furtive movement there, till soon Life burst forth again in all its splendor.

---

[6] If considered as the breath of life, as in *Genesis* **2**:7.

[7] If considered as the element in Nature that allows living beings to thrive, procreate and become.

3

All around us, we can witness the existence of many forms or manifestations of life (that is, of matter + Vital Force). All the way from sub-cellular to unicellular to multicellular living beings.

In multicellular living beings, some structures specialize for specific functions. They start to move, to feel, to communicate and to love in a most marvelous fashion.

Complexity progresses until it reaches the Wholeness of Human Beings.

Energy is to be found everywhere.
So is Vital Force.

Energy exists in what is called call the *Energy Field*.
Vital Force exists in what we call *Biosphere*, if it has to do with Life; and *Ecosystem*, if with the relationship of living beings among themselves, or between living beings and simple elements.

Energy and Vital Force coexist throughout Nature.
It could perfectly well be that both Energy and Vital Force are only aspects or manifestations of the same immaterial and ubiquitous element. An element or phenomenon we call "energy" when dealing with matter and "Vital Force" when considering living beings.

Wholeness, for matter, consists on the integration of Energy and atomic particles. In turn, each atom coexists and interacts with other atoms within the energy field.

For living beings, *Wholeness* is the complex and orderly interaction of matter with the Vital Force it harbors. Each living being's Wholeness also interacts with the Wholeness of other living beings in the Biosphere.

There is a constant struggle between the Vital Force and Nature.
Nature likes simple things. Like atoms and simple molecules that interact through energy forces such as electromagnetism and the like, structures that constantly disappear and re-constitute.

The Vital Force, on the other hand, needs extremely complex molecules in order to thrive. Consequently, the existence of each Whole living being is a tug-of-war between Nature and the Vital Force. Nature always triumphs at the end. Death marks the point where complex molecules gradually become atoms and simple molecules, that are too elementary to allow the Vital Force to nestle and flourish.

Health exists when the Vital Force holds adequately to complex matter, and when both Vital Force and matter interact *harmoniously*.

If there is harmony, the Vital Force can reach every nook and cranny of each Whole living being, and each Whole living being thrives and develops in a balanced fashion.

If there is disharmony, on the other hand, Wholeness is threatened. It becomes limited. If the disharmony is severe enough, the patient's Wholeness suffers and will eventually disintegrate.

Disharmony happens when the Vital Force is forced to detach itself from any or all of the structures it maintains. When this happens, the Vital Force develops a healing capacity or mode in order to reconnect. If allowed to work successfully, the healing capacity allows the re-attachment the Vital Force. Re-attachment makes disharmony disappear.

Each Whole living being is an *individual*.
Each individual is *unique*.

No two things that are identical in Nature.
There are no two clouds, two sunsets, two rivers, two hills, two stars, two creatures that are exactly alike.

In a similar fashion, Whole Human Beings, or rather, *each* Whole individual Human Being is preciously unique and unlike any other individual Whole Human Being that has ever existed, exists, or will ever exist.

This awareness of each patient's individualized and unique Wholeness is one of the linchpins of Homeopathy. It is also the only coherent starting point of any correct Homeopathic evaluation, diagnosis and treatment.

Chapter 2

HEALTH, DISEASE AND DEATH.

According to Homeopathy, the Wholeness of each individual is composed by the *totality* of that individual.

In the healthy individual, his or her Vital Force is in permanent and harmonious contact with every cell, organ and structure.

A healthy Human Being is balanced, and lives in harmony with him or herself, and also with his or her circumstance—meaning those who surround him or her, Nature and ultimately the Universe.

The Wholeness of an ill individual is composed by the patient + the disease the patient is bearing + the patient's circumstance. In this totality, the Vital Force has a precarious hold of certain cells, organs or tissues that, thus deprived, cry for help. Such cries are interpreted as pain and distress by the patient, and as a disease-syndrome by the Doctor.

The ill individual is out of balance, and lives in disharmony with him or herself and consequently also with his or her circumstance.

According to the most basic tenets of Allopathy, we Humans spend our lives as dysfunctional individuals in an irrational world.

Illness is our normal way of living and Health is the exception. We are hostages, and spend our lives governed by the whims of an unpredictable and generally hostile Nature, in an environment full of perils—perils that start within our own bodies.

Allopathic Medicine assumes that our bodies are walking time bombs constantly ready to unpredictably explode with a heart attack, diabetes, a malignant tumor or something similarly horrendous; all of which is supposed to strike us out of the blue, without warning of any kind and without any rhyme or reason.

Allopathy also assumes that Nature constantly imperils our lives with bacteria and the like—and that the only possibility of survival in this nightmarish valley of tears consists in throwing ourselves at the mercy of Allopathic Doctors and their ministrations.

This outlook entails that

- harmony and balance are a pipe dream,
- disease is inevitable,

- all Human Beings are equally susceptible to *any* disease,
- health is only a lull between bouts of disease,
- disease is always the *cause* of the patient's imbalance,
- the only way to cure is to destroy diseases, and that
- The only way to avoid disease is to protect ourselves, either by means of overstimulating our immune systems with vaccines, or else by subjugating Nature.

The policy of eliminating one disease-syndrome after another leaves a patient in a rather disconcerting situation.

If victim of an acute disease, a successful Allopathic treatment may cure the disease, but not the Whole patient. This is so because Allopathic treatments have no effect on the patient's overall balance.

If the patient is chronic, a successful Allopathic treatment may cure the disease, while his or her imbalance continues to worsen.

The degree of health achieved in this fashion is bound to be feeble and short-lived. After suffering a stressful situation, or a shock or an accident of some kind, or at the next change in the weather, the Allopathically cured chronic disease—if not a new one—will strike and shatter that chronic patient's precarious well being.

The new disease or the reappearance of an old and supposedly cured one, and the corresponding worsening of the patient's chronic imbalance, will again be treated by drugs and/or by Surgery. Or by radiations or whatever. And hopefully also eliminated.

These cures—only reprieves, actually—leave the patient more imbalanced and in an even more deceptive state of health, that will collapse with the onset of a new bout of illness.

Paradoxically, then, each new Allopathic "cure" becomes another step into new unnecessary suffering, a still more severe imbalance and, eventually, an untimely and painful death.

The ways and means Allopathy has of preventing diseases are not salutary, either.

They basically consist of immunizations and of taming Nature.

Immunizations overstimulate and consequently alter the immune system, and therefore the Whole patient's balance.

Allopathy's other means of preventing diseases consists on radically altering the balance present in Nature by means of subjugating it, pretty much as a rodeo cowboy breaks in a bronco.

Homeopathy, on the other hand, considers that health is the consequence of living in a state of balance. Or Wholesomeness. Or Harmony. Within oneself and consequently with others and also with Nature—ultimately with the Whole Universe.

Homeopathy also believes that disease is the consequence—not the cause—of imbalance. Consequently, Homeopathic treatments consist in returning the patient to balance. The newly acquired balance often makes the disease vanish.

And there is no need to prevent anything, either—one doesn't need to protect oneself from something one lives in harmony with.

From a Homeopathic standpoint health, harmony and balance are interchangeable concepts. In fact, health stems from balance, and is the consequence of living in a state or condition of *balanced Wholeness*. Health allows a person to thrive and to interact beneficially within him or herself, those who surround him or her, and Nature.

Disease, on the other hand, is the consequence of a loss or disruption of balance. Once balance is lost, health and harmony disappear and the imbalanced Whole Human Being becomes a hostage of Nature, prey of elements and circumstances that make the patient suffer unto untimely death.

When a Human Being is out of balance, the Vital Force becomes incapable of reaching, nurturing and harmonizing the Whole.

Conversely, when an individual is balanced, the Vital Force becomes free to roam at its pleasure; and can perform its task in an organism that puts no barriers to its action.

Imagine the Vital Force as a paymaster.

A paymaster that distributes daily a certain amount of vitality to each and every one of the different entities and structures within the Whole Human Being. From the most insignificant and distal cell in the tip of a finger to the most recondite thought and feeling.

The Vital Force is truly munificent. It distributes its goods in considerably larger quantities than needed for the performance of daily tasks.

The Vital Force is also autonomous, i.e., not conditioned to the individual, and/or to the relationship that individual may have with the environment (Hahnemann S. *Organon*, 6th Ed., § 9).

Being autonomous, it cannot be deformed, altered or harmed in any way by any situation of disease or imbalance, no matter how severe. At most, the Vital Force may become *untuned* or *disturbed*, but nothing more serious than that (Hahnemann S. *Organon*. 6th. Ed. § 7, 11 and 12. In § 7, Dr.

Hahnemann refers to the Vital Force of an imbalanced Human Being as being *disturbed*. In § 11 and 12, as being *untuned).*

Each well-balanced individual Human Being interprets the harmonious interaction between the Vital Force and his or her physical and emotional structures—and, through them, with the environment—as health and well being. Which, more often than not, are taken for granted.

In a poorly balanced individual, on the other hand, the Vital Force does not have good hold on all of the patient's organs and structures.

This disconnection will be more marked in some cells and tissues.

Those organs will scream for help. Patients interpret those screams as pain and distress and Physicians as disease-syndromes.

The constant toil of a living organism is called *metabolism.*

Metabolism produces refuse or garbage.

In a situation of balance, garbage is disposed of without any problems and in a timely manner, mainly through the kidneys and bowels.

In a situation of imbalance, and due to the fact that the Vital Force cannot fully reach the patient's organs and structures, the organism becomes devitalized and sluggish.

Consequently, garbage tends to accumulate, producing variable degrees of intoxication in each and every cell, structure and tissue. This accumulation, and the subsequent constant and increasing intoxication, will intensify the already present imbalance—a vicious circle.

When we are healthy, we interact with the environment that surrounds us in a constant, fluid, to-and-fro, harmonious interplay.

The boundaries between us and the environment are well kept, though. If perchance there is a breakage in the border and the environment invades—usually as bacteria, or as viruses, or as pollen, or as whatever other organism or element—then the boundary is promptly mended. The invading element is brought under control, neutralized, and either destroyed or expelled. All while the well-balanced Human Being becomes barely aware of this mini-drama as some transient and quite bearable discomfort of one kind or another.

When ill—particularly when *chronically* ill—our individual Wholeness is out of balance. The Vital Force gradually recedes from organs, including those that are our boundaries with Nature.

Organs and tissues thus deprived scream for help.

Boundaries weaken, and subsequent invasions by Nature become frequent and severe. Even though invaders may be expelled, the damage brought about by intruders is likely not to heal properly, and to worsen after each successive invasion.

The resulting damage worsens the already present disharmony and imbalance.

Progressive individual imbalance, in turn, also disrupts harmony with others and with Nature.

Health is not a static thing.
Nothing is static in Nature.
And nothing progresses in time along a straight line.

There are days and nights, winters and summers, high tides and low tides, breathing in and breathing out, and so forth.

Progress, in Nature, follows the model of a sinusoid curve. With occasional disturbances. Each high is followed by its corresponding low. The only straight line here is the imaginary one of that sinusoid's *trend* or *mean.*

In this sense, each healthy person is a bit like a ship, soundly built and ballasted, as it sails through the seas.

If that ship could feel, it would become uncomfortable when it reaches extreme, say, starboard; to then feel better and better as it sways towards center. To feel again more and more stressed as it sways toward the prow or the stern or wherever—all the more when the seas grow rough.

We all go through periods when we feel fine, followed by others when we don't feel so well; moments that, in turn, are again followed by others of increasing well being.

The important thing here is not the highs and the lows, but the trend or the mean of the sinusoid curve. A trend that is even in health, descending in disease and ascending during convalescence into health—health, disease, and/or convalescence that become manifest, in *each* individual Human Being, in his or her own *uniquely individual* way.

As it will be shown in the following Chapter, an *acute disease* is like a strong gust of wind that hits a well-ballasted ship. The ship will list, but will straighten up as soon as the wind abates.

In a similar fashion, an acute disease-bearing patient will loose balance and fall ill when assaulted by an acute disease; but will return to balance and harmony as soon as the disturbance is over.

A *chronic disease*-bearing patient, on the other hand, is like a poorly ballasted ship; that is, one careening and out of balance to start with. Every disturbance in the sea or the ship will worsen the pitch. The list will eventually become so marked that anything, even the slightest breeze or the smallest wave, will make that unfortunate ship capsize and sink.

As mentioned before, nothing is static in Nature. The imbalance of a chronic disease-bearing patient does not remain static, either.

Any problem brought about by stress, an illness, and even a change of season or in the weather may worsen that chronic patient's imbalance. Unless, of course, that patient's underlying chronic imbalance is adequately treated and corrected[8].

Regarding *death*.

Vedantic thought often compares living beings to the waves on the sea.

A wave forms when wind makes the sea surface surge. Each wave, then, derives its individualization from an interaction of sea and wind. In a similar fashion, each living being is formed by an interaction of Vital Force and Nature.

Waves are unstable because of their very nature. As soon as the wind weakens or abates, the force of gravity attracts the water that shaped the wave. The wave looses its identity and becomes part of the sea again.

In living beings, very complex molecules assemble to form cells. Orderly accumulation of cells becomes tissues and systems. The association of tissues and systems become structures. Finally, structures give shape to what, when interacting with the Vital Force, becomes a living being.

The combination Vital Force-matter is as complex as it is unstable.

Nature is composed by simple elements, and is forced to make them complex because of the demands of the Vital Force.

But these complex molecules are only a lease of Nature, that will constantly claim back its own. The pull exerted by Nature becomes evident

---

[8] As far as I know, Homeopathy and Acupuncture are the only forms of treatment capable of correcting imbalance in Whole living Beings.

when the grasp exerted by the Vital Force weakens, as it happens with advancing age.

At that time, the structure of each cell is gradually lost, and complex molecules revert to their simpler elements.

The Vital Force, unable to dwell in simple molecules, detaches itself; and what we call death ensues as the inevitable consequence of this detachment.

There is an exception to this trend toward cellular death and simplification. It happens in unicellular living beings. These simple individuals, being independent of each other, can maintain their complex molecular structure constantly in existence. They reproduce when reaching a certain size—or, what is the same thing, a certain volume to surface ratio.

When cells associate with each other beyond the level of a syncytium[9], however, they cannot keep their independence any longer. They become *interdependent*. In each tissue or system, every cell or group of cells specializes in a certain function.

One of the consequences of specialization is that cellular function and reproduction are conditioned, not to the cell's individual needs as in unicellular beings, but rather to the needs of the whole structure.

All of which, in turn, makes multicellular organisms much more unstable that unicellular ones.

Multicellular living Beings go through several periods that, when added up, conform a cycle.

This cycle can be depicted as a vertical parabola that starts at birth, ascends during youth, finds its plateau in adulthood and declines into old age into death.

The first or ascending aspect of the parabola corresponds to the period of *youth*. It is characterized by *growth*.

The Vital Force exerts a very powerful grasp in this stage.

The stability of that complex living organism—save for the early moments of mutual adaptation between Vital Force and matter—is at its peak.

---

[9] *Syn–*, from Greek *together*; *–cytos–*, from Greek *cell*. A syncytium is a group of cells that associate, but that do not become complex or interdependent enough to form a structured living being.

Then comes the dome of *maturity*, that is the time when the Vital Force and matter reach a situation of balanced interaction.

The dome of maturity is followed by the downward slope of the parabola. What we designate as *old age.*

Here the pull of Nature becomes more and more intense, and the grasp exerted by the Vital Force correspondingly weaker. This period ends when Nature and the Vital Force separate.

This separation is called *death.* During the downward slope of the parabola, the vessels that carry nutrients and garbage narrow, making transport difficult and hazardous. Elastic tissue is gradually replaced by hardened fibers. Finally, the communication and interrelation afforded by the nervous tissue become sluggish; as the grip of the Vital Force on the diverse structures becomes progressively weaker.

It is interesting to notice how, throughout the whole parabola, a living being loses water as it becomes more burdened with solid matter.

At conception, the fecundated ovum is close to 100 % water. The total body water at age 80 is between 45 and 55 %. The remaining corresponds to solid matter[10].

Within this context, each disease can be considered as a tug of Nature, as it reclaims its own. These tugs tend to weaken the bond that exists between matter and Vital Force.

The Vital Force is not attached to all organs and tissues with equal force.

Organs to which the Vital Force is more weakly attached are the first to feel the pull brought about by imbalance and detachment, and are the first to cry for help. This cry is interpreted as pain and/or distress by the patient, and as a disease-syndrome by the Physician.

In youth, during the ascending slope of the parabola described above, these tugs of Nature may throw a young Human Being out of balance for a time. But the grasp of the Vital Force is so powerful that it will reattach itself to matter with ease.

Consequently in youth, after each disease, the Human Being tends to rapidly return to balance.

---

[10] Johnson J.F. "Considerations on prescribing for the older patient". *Clinical Pharmacy Review* 8 (1). In http://www.druglist.com/vol8no1.html.

Something similar happens during the period of maturity, provided that the mature Human Being completely restores his or her balance after each bout of disease.

Thing become different during the downward slope of the parabola, that corresponds to old age.

Here the grasp of the Vital Force becomes progressively weaker, and the tugs of Nature correspondingly stronger and more frequent.

If the aging Human Being is in balance, the re-attachment of the Vital Force will be complete after each bout, although slower than in youth or adulthood.

During the latter years of a well-balanced individual, the Vital Force detaches itself slowly and uniformly from diverse organs and tissues until separation is complete, and the person dies.

If, on the other hand, the aging Human Being is out of balance, Nature's tugs will be usually ferocious and sudden, and the Vital Force will not be able to re-attach itself properly to diseased organs or tissues after each bout.

Successive tugs of Nature will be experienced as severe suffering, and will lead to an untimely and painful death.

Between July 1958, and June 1959 I spent one year as a Pathology Resident in the George Washington University Hospital, Washington, DC. It was part of my training as an Oncologist. During that year, I became interested in the pathology of the Human placenta and its microscopic changes. The placentas I studied were sent to Pathology from the Operating and Delivery Rooms of the Hospital.

I noticed that, as pregnancy progresses, the placenta shows changes that correspond to aging.

At the time of birth, the placenta shows modifications that are similar to those observed in old age: the blood vessels show sclerosis and narrowing, there is a considerable increase in fibrous tissue, and so on.

In other words, for the embryo and later the fetus to grow, the placenta has to age; and for the baby to be born, that placenta must *die of old age, or become too old to continue living.*

Death marks the end of the interaction between the Vital Force and the complex molecules lent by Nature.

14

Interaction ceases; and the complex molecules that structure living beings revert to their simpler components—so dear to Nature—as the Vital Force departs.

In a well balanced, healthy Human Being, death happens when the journey is over, and fulfilled.

It is felt as a delightful weariness. Like tiredness at the end of a day well spent, when one wishes nothing better than to lie down and give in to sleep, that becomes irresistible.

The only difference between the moment of falling asleep and that of death is that, when about to fall asleep, a well balanced Human Being is conscious of the fact that the following day he or she will wake up. When in the verge of death, though, he or she is aware that there will be no such form of awakening.

There is some impatience at the time of death. Like a pleading for one more day, for one more moment. To enjoy, for at least one more time, all those beautiful things that, in our senseless haste to achieve, we impatiently tossed aside, and had no time or inclination to enjoy when they happened. Another sunset, please; another starry night like those we never noticed before because we were so busy doing things that now we realize were, o! so worthless. Another moment to listen to the sound of the laughter of children as they play in some park, or to the crash of the surf on the rocks when the tide is rising; another moment to feel the texture of a newborn leaf, or to find ourselves reflected on the eyes of our dearest ones, or to smell a rose as it opens in a fresh morn in spring.

All, as we are being gently lured, willy-nilly, into that infinitely pleasant drowsiness. Like a child who doesn't want to go to sleep, who wants to remain awake just a little bit longer. And who finally gives in, sighing and closing his or her eyes, while a smile plays on his lips.

The death of a well-balanced Human Being fulfills that old adage that says

"When you were born, you were crying while all those around you smiled. Live in such a fashion that, when you die, you may be smiling, while all those around you cry".

Jose Miguel Mullen, M.D.

There are as many diseases as there are patients.
Hippocrates.

Chapter 3
NATURAL AND INDUCED DISEASES.

According to Homeopathy, health presupposes that the Whole patient is in balance; that is, that the Vital Force has a good grip on every organ and structure. Conversely, *all* disease-syndromes[11] (such as acute otitis or tonsillitis, bronchitis, congestive heart failure, abnormal menstrual periods, peptic ulcers, infectious diseases, tumors, arthritis, etc.) are associated with, or are the direct consequence of, a situation of *devitalization* and *imbalance.*

Diseases can be divided into natural and induced.
Natural diseases can be divided into acute and chronic.
Being the disease-syndrome and the imbalanced patient who bears it part of the same Whole, "acute disease" and "acute patient", and also "chronic disease" and "chronic patient" are interchangeable terms in Homeopathy.
Induced diseases are produced or triggered by manufactures.
Manufactures can produce acute and chronic diseases in Human Beings, and also in animals.

The grip of the Vital Force on organs and tissues varies from individual to individual.
This grip is stronger on some organs and structures and weaker in others—a fact of little importance as long as an individual remains in balance.
Once imbalance sets in, however, the Vital Force first loosens its grip on a particular organ or structure—that is, on the organ or system where its grasp is weakest to start with.

Nothing is static in Nature. Everything progresses.

---

[11] Two Greek roots, syn- and -drome compose the word "syndrome". *Syn-* means "together" or "together with", while *-drome* means "to run"; that is, a group of symptoms that not only appear together in a particular disease; but that also *run* or *progress* together. In turn, *disease-syndrome* means all the symptoms that characterize a particular disease.

In untreated patients, progress is manifested as a constant worsening of imbalance.

As imbalance worsens, the Vital Force will loosen its grip on other organs and structures, and finally on the Whole patient.

Untimely death ensues when the Vital Force lets go of the Whole patient.

Each particular organ will respond to the loosening of the Vital Force in a particular and predictable fashion.

If, for instance the slackening of the Vital Force happens first in the appendix, at the beginning of the large intestine, the manifestations of this slackening will be pain in the right lower abdomen, stiffness of the abdominal wall, constipation, vomiting, etc. If in the ear, the patient will experience pain, redness and bulging of the eardrum, fever, etc. If in the heart, the manifestations will be a feeling of pain or oppression in the chest often radiated to the left shoulder and arm, and the patient will feel that he or she is dying. And so on and so forth.

Loosening of the Vital Force's grip is perceived as pain and distress by the patient, and recognized as a disease-syndrome by the Doctor.

Loosening of the Vital Force is manifested at first as a discomfort that is readily perceived by the patient, although no lesion is yet apparent. In this instance, we will say that the patient is suffering from a *functional* disease. If the grip continues to loosen, however, a lesion of some kind will soon become evident, and we will say that an organic disease is afflicting the patient.

Let me consider a patient's stomach as the Vital Force starts to loosen its grip. At first, the patient will feel heartburn, indigestion, etc. while the stomach wall remains intact. Afterwards, and as the detachment of the Vital Force progresses, tissues will die and an ulcer will appear. Here the heartburn, indigestion, etc., are manifestations of a *functional* disease, and the ulcer of an *organic* disease.

"It is more important to know what kind of person has a disease than what kind of disease a person has".

Sir William Osler (1849-1919)

NATURAL DISEASES

Natural diseases are the consequence of *devitalization* and *imbalance.*

Natural diseases—or natural disease bearing patients—can be divided into *acute* and *chronic*.

Acute disease bearing patients

They are the consequence of a *temporary* and/or *reversible* localized devitalization and loss of balance—or of the sudden worsening of an already existent state of overall imbalance.

In acute patients, the Vital Force loosens its grip on diverse organs and tissues. This loosening triggers a form of imbalance that is sudden and acute—and generally easy to reverse with adequate Homeopathic treatment.

The cause of this loosening of the Vital Force's grip → acute imbalance is to be found within the patient or in the Nature that surrounds him or her. The cause of acute diseases is usually easy to determine.

In Nature, the cause can be a bacterial invasion, a brusque atmospheric change, etc.

Within the patient, emotional shocks, personal losses, etc can trigger acute diseases.

These blows must be powerful enough—and/or the patient sensitive enough—to bring about a *temporary* and *reversible* loss of balance.

Acute diseases can affect patients who are either balanced or imbalanced to start with.

In patients who are well balanced to start with—that is, in *acute patients*—the imbalance caused by an acute disease will fully disappear once the reason for the imbalance is brought under control and the Vital Force re-attaches itself to the affected area.

If the stimulus that triggered an acute disease is too powerful and/or the treatment insufficient, a healthy and well balanced patient may die, or else his or her Vital Force will not re-attach itself adequately to the affected area. In this instance, an acute and potentially reversible imbalance may become chronic.

Otherwise, patients start to recover as soon as they are treated and the force of the disruptive stimulus weakens. In many acute childhood diseases, for instance, Nature's impact makes an otherwise healthy child become so sick that parents despair. Then the child recovers as the problem is often pushed toward the skin in the form of a rash. Soon thereafter the child starts a rapid recovery with an enormous burst of energy, a leonine hunger and a growth spurt—as parents learn the hard way where gray hairs come from.

There are acute diseases that occur, not in acute patients, but rather in patients who are *chronic,* that is, out of balance to start with.

In these patients, adequate treatment *of only the acute disease* may indeed eliminate that acute disease, but accelerating their underlying chronic—and progressive—imbalance.

Acute diseases in chronic patients can be *intercurrent,* or else *acute exacerbations.*

Examples of an intercurrent disease in a chronic patients are an infection, an emotional shock, a traumatism, etc.; and of an acute exacerbation a hypertensive peak in a hypertensive patient, a diabetic coma in a patient with insulin dependent diabetes, etc.

After the acute problem is over, the chronic patient's progressive imbalance usually becomes more pronounced—unless, of course, the Whole patient's imbalance is treated together with the acute problem.

Acute diseases can be *sporadic*, when they affect only a few individuals; *epidemic*, when they affect many, and *contagious* when the disease passes from person to person.

In addition, there are diseases that Dr. Hahnemann called *fixed*, like smallpox, measles, etc. They appear once in a lifetime and have fairly constant clinical manifestations, as opposed to others acute diseases that happen with some frequency along the lifetime of the patient, and that may have varied clinical manifestations (Hahnemann S. *Organon*, 6th Ed., § 73).

Both Allopathy and Homeopathy are useful in the treatment of acute diseases.

Homeopathy is to be preferred whenever possible, though, because it allows the re-attachment of the Vital Force to the affected area. It also lacks side effects and toxicity, doesn't trigger allergic reactions and brings about no ill effects on embryos and tissues and is very inexpensive.

Allopathy may also make an acute disease disappear. However, it cannot re-attach the Vital Force to afflicted organs and tissues. The detachment of the Vital Force becomes more and more pronounced with time, despite of the meretricious "cure" obtained with the Allopathic treatment. This progressive detachment often becomes the starting point of chronicity in many otherwise curable patients.

It is convenient, therefore, to associate Allopathy with Homeopathy if Allopathic treatment becomes indispensable in any particular patient. This association will bring about a firm re-attachment of the Vital Force to the acute patient's organs and tissues.

To sum up:

A healthy, well-balanced individual becomes an acute patient when afflicted by an acute disease. Acute diseases demolish the Whole individual's balance.

Acute diseases usually have a clearly discernible cause. This cause can be external (bacteria, a stroke of heat, etc.), or internal (sudden grief, being fired from one's job, etc.).

An acute disease is manifested by an array of symptoms. These symptoms vary according to the organ afflicted by the acute disease. Characteristically, the Vital Force is not firmly attached to organs that may eventually suffer acute diseases.

Acute diseases can be treated Allopathically, Homeopathically or by an association of both forms of treatment.

Homeopathic treatment allows the patient's Vital Force to re-attach itself to the organs afflicted by an acute disease. By doing so, it re-establishes balance in the Whole individual and frequently makes the acute disease vanish. Re-attachment of the Vital Force returns the patient to balance and harmony, and makes the Whole individual fully hale again.

Allopathic treatments can eliminate acute diseases, but cannot re-attach the Vital Force to the affected organs and tissues. The detachment of the Vital Force becomes progressive with time, and so the imbalance of the patient, acute and temporary to start with, becomes chronic.

Chronic disease-bearing patients.

Here the Whole patient is out of balance to start with. If untreated, the chronic patient's imbalance inexorably progresses toward a difficult and untimely death.

In *acute* patients, acute disease results when the Vital Force loosens its grip on one organ or another, usually as the consequence of some aggression.

In *chronic* patients, progressive imbalance comes first. Increasing imbalance loosens the grip the patient's Vital Force has on some organ or system, and then on another and still another. The prognosis of untreated chronic patients—or of chronic patients exclusively treated Allopathically— is hopeless in the long run.

Chronic imbalance makes patients prone to many disease-syndromes, as the Vital Force loosens its grip on one organ after another.

Some diseases develop from this loosening of the Vital Force's grip, such as neuroses, inability to get pregnant, bronchial asthma, ulcerative colitis, malignant tumors, autoimmune diseases, etc. Others come from outside in the shape of infections, triggers of allergic reaction and the like. Chronic patients, as the consequence of their imbalance, tend to be particularly receptive, and to respond poorly, to many negative outside influences—more and more so as imbalance worsens.

Chronic diseases, no matter where they come from, if left untreated, are as *permanent* and as *progressive* as the chronic imbalance from which they directly or indirectly stem.

This worsening of chronic imbalance can only be corrected by Homeopathy[12]. Allopathy can do nothing to correct imbalance. It only treats disease-syndromes, consequence of the chronic imbalance and, furthermore, it adds the load of its side effects and toxicity to the patient's imbalance.

Chronic diseases can be psoric, sycosic or syphilitic according to the miasma from which they arise. Only chronic *psoric* patients—or psoric disease-bearing patients, which is the same thing—will be discussed here within the context of natural diseases. Diseases originating in the sycosic and syphilitic miasmas will be discussed in Chapter 22 *"Treatment of gonorrhea, genital warts and syphilis"*.

A psoric disease may be either *latent* or *manifest*—or, same thing, a chronic psoric patient may be latent or manifest. When one is young, and/or living a healthy life, a chronic disease may remain dormant—or *latent*—for years. However, it will become *manifest* in full force later on in life when triggered by adversity, or sorrow, or worry; or when the Vital Force has been abused by weakening appetites, as pointedly put by Dr. Hahnemann in his *Organon,* 6th Ed., § 78.

Progressive imbalance brought about by Psora is at first a threat of decay that, if left unchecked, may well end up in actual decay. Decay starts when the Vital Force loosens its grip on one organ or another of a particular psoric patient, and that loosening is not properly corrected. Any organ or system sufficiently *de*vitalized—i.e., lacking in Vital Force—will first cry for help. If left unattended, that organ or system will eventually become visibly damaged or decayed.

Loosening of the patient's Vital Force in an organ or system is first manifested as a so-called *functional disease*. Patients afflicted by a func-

---

[12] And probably by Acupuncture, too.

tional disease will complaint of pain and/or distress in the affected organ or system, but there will be no evidence of damage to be found.

An organ or system becomes functionally ill when forsaken by the Vital Force. That organ or system will scream for help. The patient perceives this desperate call as pain and distress, and goes to the Doctor. If the Doctor is an Allopath, he or she will interpret what the patient describes as a disease-syndrome and prescribe a treatment. And, if the Doctor is a Homeopath, he or she will diagnose a manifestation of the patient's chronic imbalance, and will dispense a remedy to correct the chronic imbalance the brought about that disease. A functional disease, then, is the first cry for help of an organ or system that feels deprived of Vital Force.

An *organic disease*, or actual decay, is the physical evidence of a more advanced degree of devitalization. A lesion can be detected in the sick organ and/or system, either clinically or with the aid of some ancillary diagnostic procedure or other, such as X Rays, lab work, etc.

This progression from functional to organic is very likely to happen in psoric patients because imbalance, like everything else in Nature, is not static, but tends to progress.

Often, Allopathic Physicians dismiss a functional disease bearing patient with a shrug and a "it's all in your head" statement, while organic diseases are always given careful consideration. There is often little awareness among Allopathic Physicians that, if functional diseases are left untreated, they may well end up as organic disease-syndromes; much more difficult and expensive to treat.

Homeopathic Physicians, on the other hand, take functional diseases very seriously. We are aware that, if ignored, functional diseases may eventually end up in actual detectable physical damage.

Allopathy has no idea regarding Wholeness, balance or imbalance.

It considers that, to make a chronic or psoric patient hale, each cry for help of organs or systems must be stifled—or, expressed differently, that each of those disease-syndromes must be *individually* treated and brought under control.

Chronic imbalance is all pervading and constantly progressing if left unchecked. Elimination of a disease-syndrome in a psoric patient (i.e., the Allopathic "cure" of each clinical disease, accomplished without modifying the underlying imbalance from which that disease stemmed) *affords the chronically ill patient a fallacious and short-lived sense of health and well being. Not long after such a "cure", the progressive worsening of that patient's chronic imbalance will devitalize another organ or system. That organ will cry for help, in the form of another disease-syndrome. This domino effect will then extend to other organs and structures.*

Allopathic treatments are quite able to aid, drug, mend, burn away, remove and/or replace structures and organs piecemeal as they cry for help, but they do nothing to correct in the least the underlying imbalance. In time, the patient's chronic imbalance inevitably reaches a point incompatible with life. Despite of all the Allopathic toil and expense. No matter how scientific, sophisticated and expensive a care the chronic patient may receive while his or her imbalance progresses unhindered—or rather becomes accelerated by the side effects of toxicity of Allopathic treatments. The bottom line here is that Allopathy inexorably leads psoric patients toward an early grave.

In other words Allopathy, if used alone, has very limited usefulness in psoric patients. This is so because, even if useful to combat diseases, it either has no action whatsoever on, or else hastens, the appearance and/or progression of chronic imbalance.

Homeopathy, on the other hand, can cure psoric patients. This is so because Homeopathic treatments proffer the psoric patient's Vital Force the possibility of

- reaching the fulcrum of a psoric patient's imbalance,
- making that imbalance disappear and, consequently
- allow the re-attachment of the Vital Force to the ill organs and structures.

When so re-attached, the healing power of the Vital Force will cure the disease-syndrome/s afflicting that patient. Exceptions being traumatisms and bone fractures, surgical syndromes, early malignant solid tumors, gangrene, and insulin dependent diabetes and the like—although, even here, Homeopathy can be of very considerable help.

Take the instance of a peptic ulcer-bearing patient. Unlike their Allopathic colleagues, Homeopathic Physicians won't bother to ponder if the stomach is producing too much acid that, in turn, is burning a hole into the stomach lining. Perhaps stimulated by abnormal nerve impulses and the recently discovered *Helycobacter pilorii* bacteria.

A Homeopathic Physician will consider, instead, that the psoric patient's stomach is crying for help because his or her chronic imbalance has weakened the grip of the Vital Force on the stomach to the point that part of its wall has disappeared. And so, instead of treating the ulcer, the acidity, the abnormal nerve impulses, and/or the *Helycobacter* infection, what a Homeopathic Physician will do is to attempt to bring the Whole patient into balance. The Vital Force will then regain a good hold on that patient's stomach, the ulcer will vanish, the stomach will heal and the patient will be cured.

Nor will a Homeopathic Physician say that a bacterium, or a parasite, or a virus is the *actual* or *single* cause of an infectious disease in a chronic patient; and consequently *the only thing that needs to be eliminated in order to make the patient well.*

What we will say is that the cause of the chronic patient's infection or infestation is the imbalance brought about by the detachment of the patient's Vital Force from a particular organ or tissue. And that the organ to which the Vital Force is partially detached is located in the patient's boundary with Nature—of which Nature bacteria, parasites or viruses are a part. Such a flaw in the boundary allows bacteria, or parasites, or viruses to find a portal of entry into the patient. Once inside, microorganisms cause disease-syndromes according to each species' or strains' particular style (i.e. *pneumococci* will produce pneumonia, *staphylococci* abscesses, *mycobacteria* tuberculosis, etc.).

Again, bacteria and the like are far from being the bad guys. Their problem is that they are very small and don't have enough space inside them for a digestive tract. They cannot take a bite, chew and swallow it as we do. Instead, they have to spread their digestive juices around, and then absorb their food already digested. Nothing untoward happens to us when they do that in Nature. When we are their meal, however, those digestive juices become the *toxins* that make us ill. So, in reality, bacteria and the like are not the bad guys, but instead just freeloaders, small uninvited critters that are having a meal in the wrong fashion and in the wrong place.

Allopathic treatment will kill bacteria and the like again and again, but will always leave the boundary' s weakness unaltered—or rather weaker, due to the progressive worsening of the patient's chronic imbalance.

On the other hand, Homeopathy will ultimately bring that patient into balance, and thus allow the Vital Force to get a firm grip on that patient's boundaries. This firm grip will close the gap that admitted those bacteria, or parasites, or viruses, into the patient in the first place. Treatment can be aided with antibiotics if necessary, of course. Several strains of bacteria, parasites and fungi can be still successfully fought off with antibiotics and the like.

Viruses are still beyond the usefulness of antibiotic treatment. Homeopathy and other forms of Wholistic Medicine should therefore be very seriously considered in the treatment of viral infestations—as well as in the treatment of infections by bacteria and molds that have become antibiotic-resistant. But treatment can*not* be considered successful only if and when bacteria and the like are killed by an antibiotic but rather only if and when the patient regains balance and the rent in the boundary is closed. When this happens, it is unlikely that new incursions by microorganisms may take place. As a rule, Nature doesn't attack a well-balanced organism, in harmony with itself and its surroundings.

Examples abound. One among many, that of psoric children with repeated upper respiratory or ear infections. On a steady diet of antibiotics, and still stumbling downhill. You know the type: weak, pale, abnormally thin, enlarged lymph nodes, circles under the eyes, no appetite to speak of, low energy level, poor sleepers, looking sick and anxious and unable to ward off any disease by themselves. Their infections will usually vanish under successful antibiotic treatments, only to recur within a short time, leaving the child worse off than before. After a successful Homeopathic treatment, though, the newly balanced child will usually remain well as friends and classmates continue to fall ill and to load themselves with antibiotics again and again[13].

Untreated and/or inadequately treated chronic diseases may eventually lead to the untimely death of a psoric patient—a form of death vastly different from that described at the end of Chapter 2 *"Health, disease and death"*.

This form of death is a very tragic occurrence indeed. Those unfortunate Human Beings have not reached the fullness of their lives, and therefore are not yet ready to die. The problem is, when a patient reaches a certain degree of imbalance, the Vital Force cannot remain associated with matter any more.

I have witnessed many such untimely deaths in my years caring for terminal patients, both as a Mainstream Physician and as a Clinical Cancer Researcher. I have always felt horror at these untimely deaths, as well as impotence at being unable to do anything to assist those poor people in their agony—aside from administering narcotics and the like to somehow ease their suffering.

The death of one patient—one among so many, alas! —still haunts my memory after all these years.

---

[13] "Bacteria are directly implicated in certain diseases, but they are only one of their causes. The indispensable cause of any disease is always a weak—or weakened—organism". Dr. L. Rosembach quoted in the Chapter of Pulmonary Tuberculosis by E. B. Nash, M.D., in his book *"Leaders in Respiratory Organs"*.

She had been a charming lady in her mid-40's, well traveled, witty and wonderful to be with. She was dying of advanced breast cancer. She was ravaged by her disease. She wasn't ready to die—but then, who would at her age? She ceaselessly tossed and turned from side to side in her bed, despite restraints and narcotics, for three endless days and nights; as she alternatively grunted and moaned and mumbled and screamed that she didn't want to die. Finally, totally exhausted, she gave up and passed away. Her expression, even after death, was one of excruciating pain, fear and anxiety.

Unknown to me at that time, Homeopathy would have been of immense help for her and so many other chronic terminal patients. There are Homeopathic remedies that can considerably ease these patients' last moments on Earth, and that can assist them to pass away in peace.

But then, I did Allopathy in those days, and was prejudiced and totally refractory towards every form of Wholistic Medicine—particularly Homeopathy.

To sum up:

Chronic diseases are the consequence of a chronic and progressive situation of imbalance.

The original cause of chronic imbalance is frequently difficult to determine. Its consequence is a progressive worsening of the patient onto untimely and miserable death.

INDUCED DISEASES

They are caused by diverse manufactures.

The damage caused by alcohol and street drugs is well known.

Less known is the harm caused by the side effects and toxicity of Pharmaceutical drugs. These chemicals give rise to the so-called *iatrogenic*[14] diseases.

Iatrogenic diseases range from mild to very severe and even lethal, and their incidence and severity are increasing by leaps and bounds. This increase is due in part to the abuse of Pharmaceutical drugs, and in part to the

---

[14] This word, coined in the 1920's, came as the consequence of associating two Greek roots, *iatros,* meaning healer or Physician, and *genesis,* that means origin or cause. Iatrogenic diseases, then, are diseases caused by Physicians.

manufacture of drugs and vaccines that carry an increased load of side effects and toxicity.

Let me now describe and give you an example of iatrogenic diseases.

Allopathic remedies act by means of interacting with sub-cellular structures, called *receptors.*

Let me bring up the β-blockers to illustrate this point. β-blockers are frequently used in the treatment of high blood pressure and other diseases.

Researchers discovered that there are some cellular receptors, related to regulation of blood pressure, that they called β-receptors. They determined how a β-receptor looks like as a 3-dimensional structure. And then they created a molecule that fits onto the structure of the β-receptors, pretty much like a plug fits in an electrical outlet or like a key fits into a lock. Since the fitting is so perfect onto the β-receptor—in effect, blocking it—they called these manufactured molecules β-blockers.

Then Researchers started to test this new molecule and found that β-blockers can indeed decrease blood pressure; but that they also slow down the heart rate, narrow the diameter of the bronchi (or tubes that take air to the lungs), contract small blood vessels and disturb sexual function and sleep, among other effects unrelated to their original function of decreasing an elevated blood pressure.

Every pharmaceutical drug has this combination of wanted and unwanted effects.

β-blockers decrease elevated blood pressure *(therapeutic action),* but can also have a host of unwanted effects on other organs and tissues *(side effects).* If given in large enough quantities, these β-blockers, as virtually every other drug, can make a patient ill and may even kill him or her *(toxicity).* There are also many drugs that can deform or kill embryos and fetuses *(teratogenic effects).* And many drugs can make patients allergic to it and others chemically related to it *(induction of allergic reactions).*

Most drugs have both therapeutic actions *and* side effects because the receptors they interact with exist in cells of many organs and tissues. Let us go back to the β-blockers again. β-receptors exist, not only in structures related to blood pressure *(target organ),* but also in the heart, bronchi, small blood vessels, sexual organs and central nervous system among other organs and tissues *(organs other than the target organ).* When β-blockers work they do so in *all* β-receptors, wherever those receptors may be; either in the target organ *(therapeutic effect)* or in organs other than the target organ *(side effects, etc.).*

A hypertensive male receiving a β-blocker, for instance, may find to his delight that his blood pressure returns to normal—and also, to his horror, that he has become impotent and that he can't sleep.

All of which means that most drugs are *not* specific. They may indeed work on the sick organ, but they will also act in many other perfectly healthy organs and tissues. They do indeed have the therapeutic effect they are prescribed for, but the patient will have to put up with a host of unwanted and sometimes dangerous consequences.

Not only are drugs non-specific. They can often have a two-way action; that is, they can improve a particular problem to then worsen it. Let me briefly describe two examples among many.

Take a patient with a plugged nose who uses a spray to shrink swollen tissues. The nose clears up at first, but soon it will plug up again—more so than before. Or take a constipated patient who takes a laxative. At first the laxative will work nicely, but afterwards constipation almost invariably returns with a vengeance.

The side effects, toxicity and teratogenic effects of many drugs and the two-way effect of decongestants and laxatives are so many examples of *iatrogenic diseases.*

The ill effects of Surgery and of blood transfusions and the antibiotic-resistant infections patients pick up in Hospitals are also iatrogenic diseases.

As far as other manufactures, some have been devised with the purpose of killing microorganisms or insects, or of harvesting more plentiful grains or produce, or of hastening the development of poultry and cattle, or of increasing the production of milk, etc.

Still other stuffs were manufactured to improve communications or transportation, or to make workplaces and homes more comfortable.

Chemicals designed to fertilize the soil, or to destroy pests, often find their way into drinking water or foodstuffs and intoxicate, thus creating induced diseases. Some of those chemicals, banned in America because of their toxicity, are freely used in other countries with looser legislations and and a healthy appetite for bribes. Those chemicals are then imported in America, into the produce grown in those countries, to intoxicate our children and us.

Or take the case of indestructible molecules, such as that of the insecticide *di-chloro-di-phenyl-tri-chloro-ethane,* or DDT. Though banned decades ago throughout the world, this product was used with such largesse that it will keep on contaminating our environment and our foodstuffs probably for Centuries to come.

Adhesives and chemicals used to manufacture things, or that we use in our buildings, designed to increase our comfort, may also make us ill.

Finally, there are manufactures that have been devised with the express purpose of destroying fellow Human Beings.

Materials prepared with the single purpose of hurting, maiming, suffocating or killing Human Beings, conveniently labeled as "enemies", are an entirely different and vastly more sinister proposition than that of the manufactures briefly described above. Human folly has indeed gone a long way since the days when dynamite was considered to be so dangerous that nobody would dare to start another war!

The problem here is that what goes around comes around. In our shrinking world, all these infernal contrivances manage to find their way back to those who originally used them, one way or another. Often because the whole World becomes so contaminated that it is almost impossible not to become exposed to them.

Take all-pervading radioactivity as an example.

During a Fellowship granted by the West German Government, years ago, I was invited to visit a state-of-the-art Center of Nuclear Medicine located in the city of Heidelberg. Among other things, this Center featured a whole body radiation detection chamber[15] made of steel. It looked like an immense elongated safe box. In order to obtain the radiation-free steel needed to construct it, engineers had to re-float a ship that had been sunk during the First World War. Nothing out in the open since 1945 would do. Every scrap of metal, after that date, has enough radioactivity as to make it useless for purposes of building radiation-free chambers.

All these formidable weapons—nuclear, bacteriological, chemical; indeed, even psychological! —have opened the lid of an appalling Pandora's box.

It is impossible to know to what an extent radioactivity, and/or chemicals, and/or bacteria, parasites or viruses designed to destroy Humans by the millions are affecting friends and foes alike. There is no way to evaluate the full impact of these destructive monstrosities on our offspring and us. Nor is there any way to know which weapon of mass destruction may be spawning any of these new horrible diseases that are currently devastating our Human-

---

[15] An enclosure where the whole patient is confined, during a certain period of time, in order to detect the amount of radiation he or she emits; either without having received any radioactive substance, or else after having received it for purposes of diagnosis or treatment.

ity—or up to what an extent these weapons are responsible for the increased incidence of certain forms of cancers, fetal deformities and the like.

Induced diseases can be acute and chronic.

If exposure is mild and limited, well-balanced patients will return to health soon after exposure—here again, if the treatment is Homeopathic or associated with Homeopathy.

Imbalanced or chronic patients, on the other hand, will likely worsen; no matter how limited their exposure may be.

If exposure is too prolonged and/or intense, manufactures may bring about a chronic situation of imbalance to all persons exposed to it, whether well balanced before exposure or not.

And, if sufficiently long and severe, exposure may even kill.

In Nature nothing is static. Everything tends to progress.

In Natural and Induced diseases, the patient *progresses towards imbalance*. This progress can be *reversible* in acute diseases adequately treated, but is *progressive* in chronic patients—unless the Whole chronic patient is treated, and not just the disease afflicting the Whole chronic patient.

To sum up:

In **acute diseases,** imbalance is usually triggered by a blow originating in Nature, or by an emotional shock of some kind.

Acute diseases can affect individuals who are otherwise healthy—or balanced—and also patients who are imbalanced at the time when those acute diseases happen.

If an acute disease attacks an individual who is otherwise healthy, balance will be lost for the duration of the acute disease. Balance will re-appear when the patient's balance is restored with a treatment consisting of, or associated with, Homeopathy.

Acute patients who do not recover their balance will almost inevitably become *chronic.*

In patients out of balance to start with—that is, in **chronic** patients—acute diseases will usually end up worsening the patient's imbalance; even if the acute disease appears to be completely cured by Allopathic or Homeopathic means. In these patients nothing will do, except for the Homeopathic treatment of their overall imbalance, associated or not with the treatment of their acute disease.

Chronic psoric diseases tend to start very gradually, and then progressively undermine the patient's organism while the Vital Force—untuned to start with—can do little or nothing to assist the patient, or to stop the free fall into constantly worsening imbalance.

Eventually, the psoric patient's imbalance becomes so severe as to be incompatible with life (Hahnemann S., *Organon*, 6th. Edition. § 72).

In **induced diseases** the imbalance is produced by manufactures.

The imbalance induced by manufactures can be acute or psoric.

Chapter 4
THE SUPPRESSIONS

Each individual Human Being constitutes a Whole.

When a patient is chronic, his or her Wholeness is out of balance. This imbalance, as everything else in Nature, does not remain still, but constantly progresses—in this particular instance, toward worsening of suffering and untimely death. The tempo of progression is accelerated by many factors, such as negative thoughts and feelings, unresolved stress, a disorderly life, food additives, the side effects and toxicity of Pharmaceutical drugs, the bad effects of X Rays and Surgery and many others.

The Vital Force attempts to slow down the destructive effects of progressive imbalance by means of deliberately concentrating itself into the most important organs and tissues of the patient, thus leaving a weaker hold in peripheral and less significant structures (Hahnemann S., *Organon*, 6th. Edition. § 201).

This stratagem of the Vital Force may decrease the momentum of chronic imbalance, but the devitalized superficial organs or tissues inevitably start to scream for help—meaning that they develop some form of pathology that rapidly worsens.

A suppression occurs when that localized scream manifested as pathology is treated *locally,* as if it were an entity in itself. It doesn't matter what it is treated with, whether with Allopathy or Homeopathy or whatever. A successful local treatment forces the patient's Vital Force, in the midst of a progressive and worsening imbalance, to strengthen its grip on the "cured" superficial organ or tissue—thus inevitably loosening its grip on deeper and more important structures. Consequently, deeper and more important structures rapidly evince a more severe devitalization as the local pathology improves, and the Whole patient rapidly worsens.

This is one the scenarios I would like to discuss in this Chapter.

Another scenario is the one that unfolds when a chronic patient's progress towards health is thwarted, again by some imprudent localized form of treatment.

The metabolism of a chronic patient becomes progressively more and more sluggish. The organism consequently accumulates increasing quantities of muck. Some of this muck comes from by-products of metabolism, while others are products of degradation of diverse foreign substances. The later are usually residues of Pharmaceutical drugs, food additives and other waste of diverse origin.

Allow me to remind here that the elimination of these substances is *exponential.* An exponential equation never reaches zero. By the same token, the excretion of Pharmaceutical drugs and other chemicals is never complete.

Our metabolism is geared in such a fashion that it normally uses the kidneys, bowels, skin, genitals, lungs, nasal cavities, etc. to excrete what it doesn't want or need—again, in an orderly fashion when the person is healthy. A chronic patient's metabolism activates as he or she is returning to balance. Activation brings about the need to get rid of muck accumulated through years of imbalance. The patient's Vital Force deals with this problem by *accelerating* the normal processes of excretion through diarrhea, increased bronchial and sinus secretions, vaginal discharges, skin manifestations of various kinds, etc. These exaggerated patterns of excretion can mimic to perfection diverse pathological conditions.

A suppression frequently develops when these seemingly pathological conditions are successfully treated locally unto disappearance.

None of the above is applicable to acute patients, with the exception of the paragraph dedicated to metabolism and excretion of drugs.

Acute diseases happen when, for one reason or another, the Vital Force finds itself compelled to loosen its grip on a particular organ or structure.

Acute patients are well balanced to start with. Here, the disease is what precedes and precipitates an acute situation of imbalance and not vice versa, as it happens in chronic patients.

Consequently, imbalance rapidly disappears once the *local* disease is cured. The Vital Force promptly regains its grip as the acute patient returns to his habitual state of balance and harmony—an event that happens if and when the acute patient is treated Homeopathically.

Such an excellent result may, but may also not happen in Allopathically treated patients. Allopathy may eliminate diseases, though it's totally unable to reconnect the Vital Force to injured organs or tissues. After a successful Allopathic treatment, then, the Vital Force may or may not reattach itself to the sick organ in acute patients. If it reattaches itself, these lucky patients will regain balance and harmony—though only up to a point. Otherwise, they will inevitably start to slide into chronicity.

We must also keep in mind that Allopathic treatments have side effects and toxicity. Consequently, however well an Allopathic treatment may manage to strengthen the Vital Force's grip in an ill organ, its side effects and toxicity will weaken its grip in many other organs and tissues.

Take, for instance, several children suffering their first bout of acute otitis media, treated with antibiotics and painkillers. Some may regain balance and will never suffer from otitis media again, and their tremendous vitality will in time overcome the treatment's side effects and toxicity. Most, however, will suffer one bout of acute otitis media after another, and will end up with tubes in their ears—with worse to come decades later as their now chronic imbalance increases. However, if the first bout of acute otitis media is treated Homeopathically, it is quite likely that these patients will never suffer acute otitis media again.

There are times when Allopathy indeed becomes necessary. If used *alone,* however, it can push many acute patients into chronicity. The only way of preventing such a disservice is to associate Homeopathic treatment to Allopathy in patients in whom Allopathy is indicated.

> *A suppression, then, is a dramatic plunge towards death that happens in chronic patients only. It is characterized by*
> i) *The localized treatment and cure of a disease-syndrome afflicting a superficial and non-essential organ, and*
> ii) *The appearance, after a variable period of time, of a serious disease-syndrome in more profound and vital organ or tissue. This new and more severe disease-syndrome is known as a morbid metastasis.*

FIRST SCENARIO. SUPPRESSIONS WHILE THE PATIENT'S IMBALANCE IS PROGRESSING ONTO DEATH.

Chronic patients' progression toward self-destruction rarely proceeds smoothly. It usually does so by fits and starts. A period of apparent wellness ends as a disease-syndrome, apparently out of the blue, overcomes the patient. If Allopathically treated, the patient may get well, although without ever fully recovering his or her former degree of well being. This succession of wellness → disease → less wellness continues till the patient dies. This sequence tends to be mild in childhood, adolescence and adulthood; but it becomes much more brutal as the patient grows older.

The reason for this sequence is that the Vital Force, as imbalance progresses, loosens its grip on one superficial organ after another, in order to concentrate on structures important for the patient's survival. And so, organ after organ becomes ill and never fully recovers as organ after organ, because of devitalization, becomes prey of disease.

This is why, along the years, chronic patients experience their increasing overall imbalance as first perhaps a disease in the skin, that will be cured Allopathically; then as some joint inflammation, that will be treated with anti-inflamatories; then as digestive problems, also treated Allopathically. Then maybe the liver, or the lungs, or the kidneys will become imbalanced. Till finally a heart attack, a malignant tumor or some other suchlike calamity brings about the patient's death.

This sad and bumpy progression may start and proceed more or less gradually. The patient may notice that he or she suffers one disease after another, in organs that are more and more important for the patient's well being.

But progression can also be sudden and dramatic, and go from a "cured" very superficial organ to the flare-up of an illness in a considerably more important one.

I have seen many suppressions along my Medical career.
Here are a few.

The first I saw while still practicing Oncology.

The man was 62, although he didn't look a day older than 45. His hair was jet black, wavy, and impeccably combed. He was made up, though so skillfully that I had to make a double take to realize it. His fingernails were manicured. His attire was immaculate; he held himself ramrod straight, walked with grace and had a disarming smile.

His arrival was preceded by a delicate whiff of expensive perfume. A beautiful young lady who was perfectly made up and gorgeously—though discreetly—dressed escorted him. She walked by the patient until he was seated in front of me. Then she smiled, bowed and departed. "I am a cosmetologist" the patient said seriously as the lady was leaving, but with a spark of mischief in his eyes "and the young lady is my assistant".

He had brought a set of X-Rays and a biopsy report, together with his referral slip that said the patient had inoperable oat cell carcinoma of the right lung. A diagnosis that I rapidly ratified when seeing his X-Rays, obtained a bit over one month previously. The patient was totally asymptomatic. His breathing sounds were normal. I requested new X-Rays and lab work, and asked him to return in one week. Lab work came back almost normal and his new X-Rays showed no changes when compared with the one he had brought with him. So I refused to start treatment and asked him to return in 15 days with a set of new chest X-Rays. I refused to treat him because his tumor was obviously quiescent, and I saw no point in pulverizing his immune system with something as brutal as Chemotherapy; all the more because such a treatment was not going to cure him anyway. And I didn't think he needed Radiotherapy and its side effects at that time, either. Later on, when his tumor would start growing again I would consider treatment, but not before. And, until then, I was planning to keep him under very close observation and supervision.

Again the scent, and his assistant with the patient on tow 15 days later. X Rays showed no changes. To make a long story short, I followed him in the same fashion for the next 5 months or so. The patient remained well, with lab work and X-Rays showing no changes. Every once in a while he would bring me, as a present, some of the cosmetics he manufactured. He would urge me to try them. I would politely decline. Then I had to go abroad for a Congress. I was going to be away a bit over one month. I referred the patient to an Oncologist who worked in another Hospital and whom I respected—until then, at any rate. I told this Oncologist about the patient, and insisted about the facts that he was under observation only, that his tumor was dormant, that his was in excellent physical condition and to please not to start treatment unless the tumor started to grow again.

The first time I saw him, after my return, the patient looked at least 30 years older. His hands were shaking. He was dragging his feet and stooping as he walked. His gaze was vacant and downcast. He was gasping for breath. The assistant, consternation all over her features, was holding him as he shuffled toward my desk. He was deathly pale and his lips and fingernails were bluish. His shirt collar was at least one size too large. There were no breathing sounds in his right lung. He wasn't a shadow of the man I had last seen, a bit over a month before. I asked what had happened. He told me that my colleague had started Chemotherapy as soon as he saw him. I became furious and went to the telephone.

"Why the hell did you started him on Chemotherapy?" I demanded.

"Well," he replied after a moment hesitation. He had been taken aback by my outburst "He has cancer, doesn't he? Inoperable. So I started him on Chemotherapy. I was to complement his treatment with Radiotherapy shortly before you returned because he didn't fare well with Chemotherapy alone. Standard procedure".

"You bet he didn't do well! Didn't you see that he was asymptomatic and that his tumor was in remission?"

"Of course I did notice that he was asymptomatic and that the tumor was in remission. So what? How long would it remain like that? He still had inoperable cancer and positive histology. The tumor could become active at any time, and start throwing metastases all over the place. He needed treatment, didn't he?"

I wanted to admit the patient into the Hospital and somehow attempt to contain this disaster. He declined. It was the last time I saw of him alive. He died shortly thereafter. His cadaver wasn't autopsied.

Heaven knows in how many places had his Vital Force attempted to lodge before I saw him. At that point in time, even his lungs had lost its grip; subsequently, an oat cell carcinoma had developed in his right lung.

Obviously, the inopportune Chemotherapy he received destroyed the last holds of his Vital Force. Consequently, imbalance progressed unchecked, directly into his death.

The second example corresponds to a 43-year-old woman, a chronic sinusitis sufferer. Drug treatment, however prolonged and intense, had done nothing to alleviate her condition. Finally, she underwent sinus surgery. Shortly after Surgery, the patient started to develop excruciating premenstrual pains, as well as progressively severe shortness of breath. The latter eventually required the use of oxygen and inhalers. Chest X Rays showed a marked thickening of her bronchial network.

The Gynecologist referred the patient to a Pneumonologist, who diagnosed the patient as having a rare condition called lymphangioleiomyomatosis[16]. The diagnosis was clinical. No biopsy was performed to confirm it. He suggested a lung transplant.

The patient came to see me at that point. She didn't want even to contemplate the possibility of such surgery, and wanted to know if there was any alternative treatment. She could hardly breathe, let alone speak, even with the aid of oxygen and inhalers.

After several weeks of Homeopathic treatment her premenstrual pains became very mild and tolerable. Her breathing condition improved only slightly. The patient remained adamant in her rejection of Surgery.

I was finally able to talk about the possibility of a transplant. I suggested requesting a second opinion. If the diagnosis was not lymphangioleiomyomatosis, then perhaps something less risky could be considered. I referred her to a second Pneumonologist, who agreed that a biopsy was necessary due to the rarity of the original diagnosis, the seriousness of the clinical picture and the risk implicit in a lung transplant operation.

---

[16] *Lymph* means related to the lymphatic system, *-angio-* related to blood and lymphatic vessels, *leio* smooth, *myo* muscle, *mat* benign tumor, *osis* generalized. A syndrome whereby lymph vessels thicken and lymph nodes enlarge in the chest, while the bronchi (or tubes that take the air to the lungs) muscles thicken and progressively narrow the diameter. The disease impairs breathing and generally ends up in respiratory failure. Allopathic treatment is useless. The cause is unknown, but Allopathic Doctors consider it to be hormone-related, because it tends to appear in premenopausal women.

I didn't see nor hear of this patient again for the next two years or so. At that time I learnt that she had died.

The third patient is a traveling salesman, 30 years old at the time of his suppression.

He had been suffering from excessive watery nasal discharge for years. So much so that he would hold a kidney basin between his legs while driving his car. The discharge was most embarrassing and annoying for this man, particularly during his many business interviews. Nothing had worked for his problem. In desperation, he decided to go see a Homeopathic Physician.

The Doctor prescribed a Homeopathic remedy useful *for the patient's increased nasal secretion,* but not for the patient's chronic imbalance.

The discharge disappeared very rapidly afterwards. The patient was exhilarated. Several days later he complained of a very severe sudden headache. The patient rapidly became unconscious and developed a fever of 110°3 F (43°5 C). The diagnosis was encephalitis. He was immediately admitted into a Hospital.

His recovery was nothing short of a miracle, for he got well after all Allopathic treatments had failed. Recovery was slow but complete.

His nasal discharge reappeared some 10 days afterwards, as intense and as severe as before.

The fourth patient had hemorrhoids, and went to see a Homeopathic Doctor in an emergency visit.

He was still weeping and moaning as he walked into the office, leaning on his wife's arm. His rectal pain was tormenting. A few hours before he had a bowel movement. He dreaded them, because of the excruciatingly sharp, stitching, hours-long pain that always followed each defecation. Only local cold applications would bring about some measure of relief.

On examination, the hemorrhoids were very large. mottled and purplish-red. The patient was going to have them removed the following day. He had gone to see this Homeopathic Doctor as a last ditch thing, a last minute attempt to avoid an operation. Surgery terrified him.

The Doctor, seeing the patient in such agony, decided to alleviate him rapidly by means of *Homeopathically treating the hemorrhoids* but not the patient's chronic imbalance, probably with the idea of treating his imbalance later. He prescribed a Homeopathic remedy for the hemorrhoids. Pain relief was almost immediate and, after a few days, his hemorrhoids had all but disappeared.

The patient did not immediately return to the Doctor's office, now that he was feeling well. Three weeks afterwards he developed an extremely severe and acute case of Graves' disease[17], though he had never had any problems with his thyroid gland before. He started to loose weight at a fast clip, to tremble and to become extremely nervous and agitated. His eyes began to bulge grotesquely.

The patient didn't dare to try any more Homeopathic remedies after this fiasco, so he went to an Endocrinologist, who promptly administered a therapeutic dose of ^{131}Iodine by mouth. The γ radiation of the radioactive Iodine made his Graves' disease disappear, together with most of his thyroid function.

The patient has been symptom free since the radioactive treatment, but has needed to take replacement thyroid hormone treatment ever since.

The fifth example corresponds to a 42-year-old male who developed severe diarrhea while touring the Middle East. The diarrhea was cured with some local prescription. The patient started to develop malaise a few days later. He saw many Doctors after his return, both Allopathic and Wholistic as his malaise progressively worsened. He was admitted to Hospitals, underwent all kinds of studies and tests and received all forms of treatment. Nothing helped. He died some time afterwards.

SECOND SCENARIO: SUPPRESSION AS THE PATIENT IS RECOVERING BALANCE.

There are some disease-syndromes that appear in chronic patients when their imbalance is being correctly treated with Homeopathic remedies.

These disease-syndromes appear as the chronic patient is successfully returning to balance.

In each office visit, the Doctor sees the chronic patient *as is*. In other words, all the Physician perceives is a *snapshot of the patient's evolution at the time of his or her visit.*

This snapshot belongs to a reel or to a story that had been, is, and will continue unwinding over the lifetime of the patient.

The snapshot the Doctor sees, at the time of the visit, is part of the patient's progress towards balance and health, or else towards imbalance and untimely death.

---

[17] The thyroid gland overworks in *Graves' disease*. The thyroid gland is to the body what bellows are to a forge.

As abundantly mentioned so far, nothing is static in Nature. Progress toward balance and health, or towards imbalance and death, is a constantly developing process.

It is often very difficult to determine what way a patient is progressing in only one visit.

Successive Clinical and Homeopathic Histories, Physical Exams and ancillary studies in the same patient frequently help to clarify if that patient is progressing towards untimely death or else towards health—equally as often, though, these studies don't make this elucidation any easier.

The weight loss, anxiety, weakness and pain of an advanced cancer patient clearly configure a progression towards death.

On the other hand, the apparent skin pathology of pimples and scabs that cover a chicken pox-bearing child, afebrile and feeling better, are clearly clinical manifestations of a progression towards health.

These two are easy, distinct, black-and-white, extreme examples.

But what happens when one approaches the gray zone in between?

How to evaluate, say, an eczema in an otherwise healthy baby? Is that eczema, at the time that baby is taken to the Doctor, a snapshot of progress toward that infant's imbalance and untimely death? Or, by the contrary, is it a manifestation of the infant's striving to push something out, to get rid of muck and consequently to regain balance and progress towards health? More pointedly, should that eczema be treated *locally* onto disappearance, or should the patient's chronic imbalance be treated first?

As mentioned above, chronic patients tend to have a sluggish metabolism. Their processes of excretion are also sluggish. Refuse tends to accumulate under these circumstances.

Metabolism becomes more active as patients improve and start their sojourn toward health. Metabolic activation promotes rapid elimination of all accumulated muck.

Most of the rubbish is eliminated through the bowels, kidneys and lungs that are likely to be overwhelmed during early recovery. So the patient may put to work other organs and structures for purposes of elimination. Such as the skin, that may develop a rash. Or the nose, vagina, urethra, bronchi or sinuses, that may produce a secretions of some kind. Or the anus, through hemorrhoids.

Changes that appear in a certain organ or tissue may be the manifestation of an acute disease, or be the evidence of a chronic patient's progression towards health or towards death.

What to do with that change? First to decide whether it is normal or pathological. And, if pathological, whether to treat it locally through Homeopathy or with a combination of both Allopathy or Homeopathy. Or whether to treat the Whole patient's imbalance while ignoring the localized disease-syndrome. Or, whether that change is normal or pathological, to treat or to leave that particular disease-syndrome and/or that patient alone.

The Doctor's criterion becomes irreplaceable here.

Ultimately, in chronic patients progressing towards health, many abnormalities that look like manifestation of pathology are but attempts of getting rid of muck.

A successful treatment of these disease-mimicking processes of elimination may indeed make that process disappear—together with the patient's only possibility of eliminating muck and thus of ever recovering balance and health.

This ominous form of localized "cure", that aborts the progress of patients towards health, is another form of *suppression.*

> *The suppression as the patient is recovering balance, then, is a meretricious form or cure, generally brought about by the inopportune and successful treatment and subsequent disappearance of disease-mimicking changes.*
>
> *These changes are usually characterized by an abnormal secretion, a skin rash or whatever else, if and when such a disease-mimicking change is a mode, however weird, that the patient's organism has chosen to disburden itself of toxic metabolic and pharmacological by-products in order to reach balance and consequently health.*

I would like now to briefly describe one example in which imprudent treatment of a disease-mimicking process of excretion brought about a suppression.

The patient was a frail 10 years old male at the time of his first visit. A severe asthmatic. His asthma had started at age 3, when his parents divorced. He had been using all kinds of inhalers ever since—including Prednisone-based—and also allergy shots. All with minimal or no beneficial effect.

Both the patient and his mother were weary of the forthcoming cold weather. Previous winters had been a dismal sequence of asthma attacks, respiratory infections with fever and Hospital admissions. He had constantly needed to use inhalers; and had to undergo one antibiotic treatment after another. To boot, he had to remain indoors throughout the whole season—at home or in a Hospital.

On Physical Examination the boy was pale and in respiratory distress. His fatigue was noticeable and his lung fields were full of wheezes.

The patient received his Homeopathic remedy (in Homeopathy we give one single remedy for the Whole disease-bearing patient at a time) and left. Shortly thereafter he started to feel better and better, and eventually well. He gradually discontinued the allergy shots and the inhalers.

Winter was exceptionally cold, damp and snowy. Despite of the weather, and for the first time, this boy was able to play outdoors with his peers. The patient did so well that he didn't catch a cold throughout the whole cold season, even though most of his friends and schoolmates fell sick with all sorts of respiratory and ear infections at one time or another.

Then, in March, the boy developed a rash. His mother promptly took him to the Pediatrician without calling me beforehand. The Pediatrician pre-scribed Atarax, an *antihistaminic that made the rash disappear* (the mother later told me that the patient had, as a baby, a similar kind of rash. It had been *cured* at that time with a Doctor-prescribed cortisone-based ointment).

It is interesting, in this context, to recall what Dr. Hahnemann had to say about the skin in the Chapter devoted to *Psora*, in his *"Treatise of Chronic Diseases"*. He stated that the skin is not something by itself, but a part of the living Whole. Therefore, nothing pathological can happen to the skin unless the Whole organism is ill. Consequently, to treat a skin problem locally, without first studying what is wrong with the Whole patient is wrong and can be dangerous. To treat the *Whole disease-bearing patient* yields more successful and enduring results than the use of any form of local therapy. Here again, the treatment of a *Whole* patient presupposes the use of Home-opathy, or else Acupuncture; instead of the ointments, lotions, cauteriza-tions, pills, shots and the like routinely used by Allopathic Physicians.

The patient never stopped his Homeopathic treatment. However, his asthma returned, though less severe than before, shortly after the rash had been forced to vanish. The boy had a succession of asthma attacks through-out the following spring, summer, autumn and winter. His asthma would improve when a mild rash appeared in elbows and knees; to promptly return as soon as the rash cleared spontaneously (I had warned the mother never again to treat any rash without consulting me). I increased the potency of his Homeopathic remedy, until he was receiving a hefty dynamization. His asthma vanished and returned, on and off, and throughout the following summer, fall and winter.

The rash returned the next spring, after a short spell of no asthma at-tacks. It covered his face, and subsequently part of his trunk and legs. It was not treated at all despite of the fact that the patient felt disfigured, as well as self-conscious in front of his friends and classmates. The patient's mother reported only very mild sporadic asthma attacks during the rash. Eventually the rash disappeared, and whatever remained of his asthma went away with it. I followed up the boy for an uneventful year afterwards.

Then he moved with his mother to Florida. I haven't heard of him since.

I am acquainted with five of the suppressed patients briefly described in this Chapter. I learnt about the sixth through hearsay.

Of the five, three developed suppression after being treated with Pharmaceutical drugs, two with Homeopathic remedies and one with Surgery.

Four of the patients I treated for some time. Other Doctors saw the other two.

In all instances, their localized diseases or manifestation of excretion vanished to move into deeper, more vital structures. From lung to death in the first patient, from sinuses to genitalia and chest in the second, from nasal cavities to brain in the third, from anus to thyroid in the fourth, from the bowels to Heaven knows where in the fifth and from skin to the bronchial tree in the sixth[18].

All of these patients, as the consequence of their *suppressions*, developed *morbid metastases.*

In other words, all six patients were *suppressed.*

Suppression does not seem to be related to the treating agent; whether a Pharmaceutical drug or a Homeopathic remedy, Surgery, or whatever.

Instead, a suppression—or a cure, for that matter—appears to be related to how, when and in what fashion a pathological entity is treated.

Any localized treatment for a disease-syndrome afflicting a chronic patient may accelerate his or her progress towards death. And *any* treatment that may "cure" a disease-mimicking form of excretion in a chronic patient who is evolving toward health may reverse that trend and again plunge him or her into the path towards death.

Sometimes subtly and gradually, sometimes dramatically through a suppression.

---

[18] In Dr. Hahnemann's *"The Chronic Diseases"*, in the Chapter devoted to *"Nature of Chronic Diseases"*, there are 15 pages devoted exclusively to case after case of well-documented suppressions.

One of the nicest things of Homeopathy is that, when used properly (i.e., to reach, and then treat, the *fulcrum* of a *Whole* chronic patient's imbalance), it becomes suppression-proof.

If used in a chronic patient who is advancing towards balance and health, a Homeopathic treatment of the Whole patient will enhance and accelerate recovery, by means of helping straighten up the fulcrum of imbalance more rapidly and completely. And, if the chronic patient is aiming towards imbalance and untimely death, then the Homeopathic remedy will cure by means of reversing the patient's trend towards death and making imbalance disappear.

Either way, a win-win proposition.

Another nice thing in Homeopathy is that, as we shall see in greater detail later on, most localized diseases disappear whenever a chronic patient reaches balance. And it makes sense.

Due to imbalance, the Vital Force loosens its grip on superficial organs or tissues in order to concentrate in more profound and essential ones. Consequently, superficial structures become vulnerable and develop pathology.

As Homeopathic treatment corrects the patient's chronic imbalance, the Vital Force doesn't need to concentrate exclusively in important organs or tissues. The Homeopathic treatment has "liberated" the Vital Force. Again it will be able to roam all over, and to strengthen its grip in superficial organs where, and due to the prevailing former imbalance, its grip had weakened. Thus, vulnerable organs become strong again, and whatever pathology they may have developed during weakness simply vanishes.

The catch here is that superficial organs will become strong again according to how fast the now liberated Vital Force reaches them. This is so because the speed of action of the Vital Force, like everything else, varies from person to person.

So what has to be done when, for one reason or another, a local disease kicks up or becomes worse as the patient's overall imbalance is being successfully treated?

The first thing is to discern to what scenario that local illness corresponds.

Let us take the first scenario.

Take someone tumbling toward death and has sinusitis. Someone not unlike the patient described above in this Chapter and who ended up with respiratory failure.

The patient is likely to go to the Doctor and demand a solution for this problem. It is very uncomfortable, brings about a secretion that is yacky, makes him or her swallow constantly post-nasal drip, and causes pain and headache. Please do something, Doctor. Do ti now.

Antibiotic follows antibiotic and corticoid follows corticoid. Finally comes Surgery.

And with Surgery, as likely as not, a suppression; because the Vital Force has to quit whatever is holding to in order to heal the patient's sinuses. And, when the Vital Force quits a deep and important organ, however partially, that organ will get sick.

As to the second scenario, that is, in patients who are progressing towards health, the Doctor has to be absolutely certain of what he or she is about to treat.

If what the patient is suffering from is a more or less covert form of excretion, my advice is to leave it alone, not to touch it, not even with a 10-foot pole. The Doctor must make absolutely sure that this particular sore throat, or uretheral secretion, or diarrhea, or hemorrhoids, or cough, or whatever is or is not a process of excretion before starting to tamper with it.

And, just in case, even if the Doctor is sure to be dealing with *bona fide* pathology, my advice in this scenario is to treat it in the mildest and most limited manner possible.

I would like to describe two patients to clarify what I mean in the context of the second scenario. I treated the first. The second was seen and treated by an outstanding Homeopathic Physician.

The first is a 32-year-old female who came to my office complaining of severe dysmenorrhea, or menstrual pain. I disregarded her complaint. I dispensed a remedy to straighten her overall imbalance. Her pain soon started to subside.

As her pain was completely disappearing, this patient developed a fairly large area of weeping eczema in the back of her right leg. It looked very ugly and itched a lot. To make matters worse, this inopportune skin problem appeared when she was in charge of a summer camp, where she had to wear shorts all the time.

She begged me to give her something to make this vexing thing disappear, it was so embarrassing and such a nuisance. I implored her to leave it alone, that it would disappear all by itself; that if we did anything local her dysmenorrhea could return with a vengeance.

Fortunately, I was able to convince her. After two weeks the rash gradually went away, all by itself.

I didn't hear any more of this patient until some 7 months or so after the eczema had disappeared. She phoned to ask me if it would be all right to take another dose of the remedy, for she was starting to have some mild discomfort at the time of he period. Of course, I said OK.

Haven't heard of her since.

The second is a 53-year-old male who went to see an excellent Homeopathic Physician complaining of fatigue and a peptic ulcer, among other problems. All symptoms disappeared under treatment.

But the patient developed eczema in both lower legs and feet as he was getting well. Weeping eczema, like two boots reaching all the way up to mid-calf. And very itchy. The discharge was so copious that the patient had to change socks several times a day. The cuffs of his trousers were always soaked, no matter how often he would don new ones, or how well he would bandage his legs and feet.

Somehow, both his will power and the pleadings of the Doctor prevailed. No local treatment was used.

By and by, the patient's mother told him that, when little, he had had something similar in his legs, though much milder; and that the Pediatrician had treated it with some kind of an ointment.

The eczema started to improve, all by itself, some four months after its appearance—or perhaps I should say *re-appearance*—to eventually vanish.

In the patient's—and his eczema's—own good time.

He has been well ever since. Or at least until I left Argentina. I have no reason to doubt that he is still doing well. I would have certainly heard of any change in his condition, for this particular patient is very well known there, and widely respected.

To sum up,

A suppression can only happen in chronic patients. It can happen in two scenarios—perhaps more.

In the first scenario, imbalance is so pronounced that, in order to continue life, the Vital Force loosens its grip on superficial organs to concentrate its usefulness in deeper and more important ones. Suppression here happens when an imprudent local treatment, aimed at curing a devitalized superficial organ or tissue, coerces the Vital Force to loosen its grip on a deeper and more important organ or tissue in order to re-vitalize a superficial organ less important for the patient's overall survival. The paradoxical result is an improvement or disappearance of the pathology of the superficial organ or tissue followed by a marked worsening of the Whole patient.

The second scenario happens as a chronic patient is improving and balance is being restored. The patient's metabolism becomes more active. A more active metabolism stimulates the excretion of muck accumulated during the period of imbalance. Some forms of this exaggerated excretion can mimic certain pathological conditions, such as diarrhea, discharges, eczemas, etc. If these forms of excretion are considered to be pathology, and treated as such, excretion stops, progress toward balance is arrested and the patient is again plunged into imbalance.

APPENDIX

Can Homeopathy be suppressive?
It can certainly be.

If a Physician provides *local* treatment for a localized pathology in a superficial organ in a worsening chronic patient, or if a discharge or the like is aborted in a chronic patient returning to balance, then a suppression is likely to occur.

Can Pharmaceutical drugs be suppressive?
Only if and when they re-vitalize superficial organs or tissues or if they stop processes of excretion in chronic patients. Each Pharmaceutical drug should be studied individually to determine its capacity to suppress. However, let me share with you some drugs as a guide.

Antibiotics, for instance, are not suppressive. They only kill bacteria. They do little to attract the patient's Vital Force toward the infected—and therefore devitalized—organ under bacterial siege.

Anticancer drugs can be suppressive. They are generally used in advanced cancer patients, that is, in patients with severe and worsening imbalance. These drugs often work by means of altering the structure of chromosomes. If these alterations persist, as they frequently do, then the Vital Force will become engaged in a prolonged attempt to untangle the mess.

Antidiarrheic, antiallergic, anti-discharge and suchlike drugs can be, and often are, suppressive. If the discharge, skin manifestation or whatever in a chronic patient is pathological, then by all means it needs to be treated. But if the abnormality is a manifestation of discharge in a chronic patient coming into balance, then it should be left alone.

Attending Physicians should be knowledgeable both in Homeopathy and Allopathy, and so acquire the criterion necessary to discern when a treatment can be suppressive.

Can Surgery be suppressive?

Here too it depends. Let me describe a few instances.

If we are talking, say, of an acute appendix or a localized malignant tumor, then we are dealing with a problem the chronic patient's Vital Force cannot deal with, and that exhausts it. Surgical removal here means that the Vital Force will be relieved. It will be engaged for a few days afterwards in the process of healing the wound, venting away the ill-effects of anesthetics and the like, but afterwards it will be free to continue sustaining and assisting its bearer.

I don't believe curettage of the uterine lining in a premenopausal woman is suppressive either. Here the uterine lining will normally reconstitute during the following menstrual cycle.

It is a different story with sinus surgery, for instance. Sinuses are devitalized in patients with chronic sinusitis. This form of Surgery generally consists in either curetting or else burning with laser rays and the like the lining of the sinuses. It is usually attempted after more conservative forms of Allopathic treatment have failed. After Surgery, the re-constitution of the sinus lining is never normal, as it happens with the lining of the uterus after a curettage. Here the Vital Force will have to struggle with a lining that will consistently be abnormal after surgery because of the chronic devitalization of the structure that sustains it—a devitalization that Allopathic Medicine can do nothing to correct. Sinus surgery and the like, then, can be and often are suppressive.

Here again, the knowledge and criterion of the treating Surgeon can avert a suppression.

Can radiations be suppressive?

Radiations, needless to say, are usually administered to chronic patients with progressively worsening imbalance.

Radiations can be of two kinds, those delivered from outside the patient, through the use of some kind of an X Ray machine, and those that are injected into the patient, in the form of radioactive isotopes.

If radiations are strong enough the kill tissues, then the organism removes the debris and whatever is healthy remains. There is no possibility of suppression in removed dead tissue. The Vital Force and dead tissues are incompatible with each other.

Things are different in structures that have received less radiation. These structures usually surround areas where radiation has been strong enough to kill. These surrounding areas remain alive, but devitalized for a long time to come. The Vital Force will attempt to reverse this devitalization, often present in organs that are important for the patient's survival.

Radiations, then, can be suppressive in areas surrounding those where the radiations have been powerful enough to destroy living tissue.

Chapter 5

THE CHRONIC MIASMAS

One of the basic tenets of Homeopathy is that, with the exception of acute diseases, *the Whole Human Being must be chronically imbalanced in order to fall ill.*

The chronic miasmas are the different *weaknesses* or *faults*, or *abnormal leanings*, or *cracks in the foundations* that underlie and eventually activate chronic imbalance.

The three Classic Chronic Miasmas, then, are the mother lode of chronic imbalance and consequently of all disease-syndromes and sundry problems chronic imbalance brings in its wake.

The three Classic Chronic Miasmas, as originally described by Dr. Hahnemann, can also be considered as three steps leading to self-annihilation.

Psora, the first step away from health, makes the patient aware of his or her vulnerability.

In the second step, *Sycosis*, the patient covers up his or her psoric vulnerability with a mantle of spurious grandeur, invulnerability and excellence. With Psora so disguised, the patient entices him or herself into believing that he or she is great and important—and invulnerable, too.

In the third and last step toward self-annihilation, *Syphilis*, the patient's Psora and its glittering cover are blown away, leaving only a hideous ulcer. This ulcer grows and gnaws, and does not stop until it devours the whole patient.

Latter Homeopathic Physicians studied and described others chronic miasmas like *Tuberculinism, Cancerinism,* etc.

The term *miasma* can be defined as a harmful emanation from rotting matter, or as a deadly influence or ambiance.

Up to the present time in China it is considered that emanations from swamps and the like can indeed cause disease. It is interesting as well as intriguing to know that, for the past two or three millennia, the Chinese have considered that disease happens when *evil air* obstructs the flow of *chhi*, or Vital Force. The Chinese concept of evil air is quite close to that of Dr. Hahnemann's miasma.

The term *miasma* was brought into Homeopathy by Dr. Hahnemann.

It is quite likely that, regarding the definition of miasmas; Dr. Hahnemann had more in mind than just evil emanations and the like. The whole of Europe was on the grip of a cholera epidemic in the winter 1831-32. Dr. Hahnemann wrote 4 essays regarding its origin and treatment. In one of the essays, Dr. Hahnemann commented that the miasma responsible for cholera could be composed by many invisible living organisms. Here, like in so many other aspects of his Medical thoughts, Dr. Hahnemann was well ahead of his time.

Chronic miasmas are very powerful. Neither the most robust constitution, nor the most orderly way of living, nor the strongest Vital Force can eradicate them. Only a successful Homeopathic treatment can eliminate chronic miasmas (Hahnemann S., *Organon*, 6th Edition, § 78).

The understanding of chronic miasmas is indispensable to comprehend both the thought of Dr. Hahnemann and the real nature of chronic diseases.

Knowledge of chronic miasmas is also important to reach a *miasmatic diagnosis* after examining each patient.

The miasmatic diagnosis helps attaining the correct perspective to interpret the patient's symptoms. It also helps to determine what *Nosode*, or miasmatic remedy, that particular patient may need as part of his or her overall Homeopathic treatment.

I shall first briefly describe the three Classic Miasmas, studied and described by Dr. Hahnemann; and then Tuberculinism and Cancerinism.

I consider that both Tuberculinism and Cancerinism are not the result of clinical observation, but rather of Clinical Research (or Provings) done with the nosodes *Tuberculinum* and *Carcinosin*. These two are the only non-classic miasmas I am going to describe here.

PSORA

Psoric patients have becomes hostages of Nature. Consequently, the keyword here is *vulnerability*—perhaps more accurately, *awareness* of vulnerability.

Psoric patients feel vulnerable because they have relinquished balance and harmony.

The majestic harmony of the Universe is maintained through order and balance.

All creatures are part of the Universe.

When in balance, Whole Human Beings partake of Universal harmony and thrive and develop within it. Balanced Human Beings are aware that they, as well as every other creature, participate of that Harmony and are thus part of the Whole. There is a sense of joy and fulfillment in identifying with the Universe and its magnificent Harmony. The strength of the Universe vitalizes and strengthens balanced Whole Human Beings and that strength allows them to love, grow and identify with the Universe and all of its manifestations.

Not only that. Participation allows Whole Human Beings to radiate this Cosmic harmony into Nature's chaos. Consequently, Nature becomes more harmonious. Nature does not attack—*cannot* attack—well balanced Whole Human Beings. Harmony and aggression are antonyms. They simply cannot coexist with each other. Consequently, harmony breeds health and health breeds harmony. Until, once our part in this *magnus opus* has been concluded, we surrender back to Nature the body that she granted us to bring her a bit closer to Cosmic harmony.

Loss of overall balance is the main characteristic of Psora. Psoric patients become so many discordant notes in the Symphony of the Universe due to their imbalance. Psorics isolate themselves from the Whole.

And, by doing so, become hostages of Nature.

All that Nature has to proffer is its chaos. One of the characteristics of Nature's chaos is the survival of the strongest; that is, of the most successful predators. Psorics have no way of protecting themselves against the combined ravages of Nature's chaos and its predators.

Psorics feel extremely fearful and vulnerable, and desperately search for some form of protection, no matter the cost. Even if protection means the destruction of whole ecosystems—even if it means the destruction of other Human Beings.

Psorics consider this dog-eat-dog way of living as normal, and endeavor to find some sense or meaning in order to control and successfully survive. Most Philosophical Schools, as well as the Whole body of Allopathic Medicine and militarism, have stemmed from this Psoric awareness of vulnerability.

There is very little psorics can safely trust in this Earth. Their very bodies become time bombs.

Awareness of vulnerability strengthens enslavement to chaos and begets suffering. This subjugation, in turn, makes psorics still more acutely aware of how vulnerable they are.

A vicious cycle.

Vulnerability + submission ↔ rebellion.

Psorics know that they have no choice but to abide by Nature's whims. At the same time, they are profoundly aware that there is something very wrong in this scenario.

Deep inside, psorics feel they deserve at least some modicum of peace and fulfillment, that they shouldn't be hostages, and that Nature should not really be a cruel master to be feared.

The happiness they seek in their chaos is elusive, yet it frequently appears to be so close at hand—even attainable sometimes. As when one feels great, or falls in love, or has a child, or succeeds in one's career, or becomes one with a beautiful spring sunset. But then, for psorics, happiness is what a mirage is for travelers dying of thirst in the desert. It soon vanishes. Suffering strikes soon after those brief moments of bliss, usually out of the blue.

Again psorics feel crushed by the weight of their yoke as they realize still again how vulnerable and defenseless they really are, how little control they have over themselves and their fate, and how much they are at the mercy of Nature, its chaos and its whims.

It is then that they let out their cry of rebellion.

A cry that eventually becomes mired in impotent anger and frustration, as psorics feel that fulfillment has eluded them again; that they are nothing but shadows that stagger in a valley of tears where meaninglessness suffering, disease, heartbreak and untimely death are rampant and out of control— while constantly knowing, deep inside, that they deserve a different and vastly better fate.

This profound yearning for what psorics deserve as Human Beings is found at the root of many beliefs, fables and legends that are as old as Humanity. All the way from the belief of a Heaven after death to that of the existence of a pot of gold at the end of the rainbow, all the way from the awareness of Paradise lost to the moral in the fable of the ugly duckling.

There is constant joy out there, somewhere; there is peace and happiness that rightfully belong to everybody. Yet, and aside from a few fleeting moments, joy is always beyond the psorics' reach, alas! —at least during their lifetimes.

The emotional and physical costs of Psora are appalling.

Emotionally, this cost is manifested by confusion, double guessing and self-doubt, as well as an overwhelming and all-consuming feeling of anxiety, distrust and frustration. Distrust, in turn, breeds isolation, because it makes it very difficult for psorics to reach out to other Human Beings. The psorics' inner chaos and turmoil are but the mirror image of the chaos and turmoil that surround them.

Physically, the imbalance brought about by Psora gives rise to most disease-syndromes, that are acute when they are the consequence of an acute imbalance brought about by Nature or by the patient's own chaotic emotions and feelings. In chronic patients, disease-syndromes arise mainly from their chronic and progressive imbalance; and only occasionally by blows dealt by Nature.

Constant suffering and uncertainty, together with yearning for happiness and inability to grasp it, makes psorics imagine that they are probably being punished for some wrong deed. Such is the only conceivable explanation for the lifetime of misery and hopelessness they are forced to endure.

Perhaps they, or else some of their forebears, may have committed some unspeakable crime that justifies their suffering. Whatever that transgression may have been, all psorics feel that they have to atone for it. Sometimes I wonder if this is where the myth of the Original Sin sprung from, for it is encountered in the myths and legends of many peoples, from the most primitive to the most evolved.

Guilt, in psorics, is the consequence of feeling as if they must have committed some crime they know they have not committed, but that nevertheless they have to atone for.

The imbalance of psoric patients, like everything else in Nature, is always *progressive*.

It is this quality of progressiveness what makes psorics more and more vulnerable to every conceivable disease, whether acute or chronic, as they inexorably progress toward an untimely death.

Also due to their progressive imbalance, psoric patients are not able to successfully terminate any disease. Each illness leaves them weaker, more intoxicated and more imbalanced—and also better prepared to welcome the next, and usually more severe, disease-syndrome.

Dr. Hahnemann called Psora "the Hydra of the thousand heads, that grows one thousand heads per each that has been chopped off." Each head corresponds to an individual chronic disease-syndrome, and each decapitation to an Allopathic cure.

The meaning of Dr. Hahnemann's metaphor is that myriad new chronic disease-syndromes will appear every time a chronic disease-syndrome has been successfully "cured" in a psoric patient by Allopathic means.

This is so because each successful Allopathic "cure" does nothing to correct the patients' subjacent chronic and progressive imbalance. To boot, it usually replaces the patient's disease by the one produced by the side effects and toxicity of the treatment. Both factors make the patient more vulnerable to Nature's next onslaught.

In his *Treatise of Chronic Diseases*, Dr. Hahnemann divides Psora into *Latent*—or dormant—and *Manifest.*

Patients can harbor latent Psora for many years. At this stage, psorics are asymptomatic and rarely or never afflicted by chronic disease-syndromes.

Patients suffering from Manifest Psora, on the other hand, sustain every form of acute and chronic disease-syndrome known and still to be known by Humanity, with the exception of illnesses arising from the chronic miasmas Sycosis and Syphilis (please see *Sycosis* and *Syphilis,* below).

In the Chapter concerning *Nature of Chronic Diseases*, under the heading *Symptoms of Latent Psora*, Dr. Hahnemann describes a long list of its manifestations.

And, in the Chapter devoted to *Psora*, he mentions the factors that can transform Latent Psora into Manifest. Those factors are usually the consequences of improper treatments and of severe emotional and/or physical stress.

Dr. Hahnemann affirms that, in many people, Latent Psora is slumbering within, ready to become Manifest. He illustrates this assertion with many examples.

In every instance, Latent Psora becomes Manifest in the form of some serious chronic disease or another—that, if insufficiently treated, will inevitably give rise to another serious chronic disease, and then to still another and another, all the way unto untimely death.

Elimination of Psora will bring the patient back to health.

Its worsening will make the psoric patient slide into Sycosis. This can happen very easily. All the psoric has to do is to throw a mantle of arrogance over his or her Psora.

SYCOSIS.

The keyword of Psora is *vulnerability.* That of Sycosis is *aggrandizement.*

Sycosics believes that they are truly great, that they have bona fide, authentic greatness and that they are invulnerable.

This feeling of self-aggrandizement, brought about by arrogance and accepted by the patient as real, brings about a very heady sensation of power and strength.

Sycosics will attempt to control the environment, as well as those who surround them. This is as close as they can get to their meretricious grandeur.

There is no vulnerability and no anxiety in sycosics. There may be some mistrust, but it generally doesn't bother them. They feel in control of it all.

Sycosics feels quite smug and secure—and powerful.

The irony here is that sycosics don't know that the stuffing of their illusory greatness and power is actually their Psora.

Sycosics don't recognize this fact because they have carefully concealed their Psora underneath a glittering mantle of haughtiness and self-importance. All sycosics see, therefore, is how big, wonderful and powerful they are— while conveniently ignoring the stuff that meretricious greatness is really made of.

Sycosics are organized. They like to have everything planned and on the go. People and events must become predictable. A very important source of uncertainty and ultimately of insecurity is thus eliminated.

Predictability increases the sycosics' smugness.

Sycosics tend to be found at meetings, around an Executive Board table. Impeccable, poised and alert, receiving tough problems and delivering their answers with gusto, ease, aplomb and *éclat*. They have an aura of self-confidence. They like to lead and to command.

They also tend to be very competitive and ambitious.

And they are not particularly scrupulous when it comes to choose the means to use in order to reach the top of the heap.

Sycosics tend to be contradictory.

They are wonderfully clear-minded and organized in matters that are set outside and around them. Yet, they appear to be totally incapable of grasping whatever may be going on inside themselves.

For instance, their families are usually well provided for, but the sycosics' capacity to relate to family members is generally superficial and limited, lest care and solictiousness may make them aware of their vulnerability and thus also of their Psora.

Their bodies (and let us not forget that our bodies are our most obedient servants) will also react in a sycosic fashion, that is, abnormally increasing or enlarging.

Benign growths, such as warts and the like, will start to appear. Blood cholesterol may also start to go up—with their blood pressure often in tandem.

Their lively mantle of arrogance is frazzled here and there after life roughens sycosics up a bit.

This is when they start to catch glimpses of the Psora that is writhing underneath. And they don't like it a bit. These glimpses bring about the first chills of insecurity and vulnerability, as they see where their power and strength actually stem from.

Sycosics usually become workaholics at this stage—anything in order to run away from the terrifying awareness that they can indeed be as vulnerable as every *[psoric]* body else.

They will tend to live at a frantic pace, as they run away from themselves and their self-awareness.

Soon they start needing stimulants that they will consume in larger and larger quantities.

At this stage, stress begins to increase by leaps and bounds, as well as the sycosics' inability to deal with it.

Stress must be ignored at all costs, though. It is a manifestation of weakness, and therefore of Psora.

Sycosics will disregard their bodies' calls of distress, as they overlook anything that may be construed as weakness. Eventually, those calls of distress will evolve into a coronary attack or something similar.

And then, in the anonymous twilight of the cardiac unit of some Hospital, lying lonely and melancholy amongst tubes and beeping fluorescent screens, as white- or green-clad shadows silently speed about, sycosics finally have no choice but to face themselves and surrender and accept, and make peace with their Psora.

From Sycosis, patients may progress toward health through Psora, or else descend into

SYPHILIS.

The keyword here is *ulcer*; that is, the festering sore that remains after the sycosic's mantle of arrogance is blown away, together with the Psora that fills it.

A second keyword for the syphilitic miasma would be *destruction*—ultimately, *nothingness*[19].

This chronic miasma ends up destroying the Whole patient, if left untreated. The first thing that vanishes, or is sucked into nothingness if you wish, is the fine system of checks and balances that allows us to live and interact with others and with Nature.

We all make blunders.

But in a syphilitic, the progressive derangement brought about by the extinction of checks and balances will cause more frequent and serious blunders as time goes by. Some of those blunders will be clearly asocial and/or harmful, yet the syphilitic is bound to experience genuine surprise at how society's reacts at his behavior.

Al Capone, when brought into trial, is reported to have said "But all I did was to make people happy!..."[20].

Another thing that soon disappears is the dam that separates our unconscious and conscious minds.

As the result, the powerful and jumbled currents of the unconscious flush into the syphilitic's conscious mind. These currents subvert, disorganize, overthrow and wash away any semblance of coherent ideas and feelings[21].

Consequently, the syphilitic feels desperately frightened and confused.
Particularly at night.

The dark, quiet hours when folk rest peacefully are the ones that make the syphilitic suffer the most. There will be no slumber for him or her, no peace at night.

No distraction will suffice to lure the syphilitic's mind away from the roaring chaos alternatively skulking and howling inside. The syphilitic will

---

[19] The French Existentialist philosopher Jean Paul Sartre, in his monumental essay *"L'être et le néant"* (in English, approximately *Being and Nothingness*), defines nothingness as what sucks the Human Being into the ultimate vacuum of non-being, and so gives rise to the most extreme form of Existential anxiety.

[20] At the time of that trial, Al Capone was reportedly suffering from clinical syphilis.

[21] The uncontrollable confusion of the syphilitic mind can be clearly perceived in the latter paintings of Francisco de Goya and of Vincent Van Gogh. In Goya, in all its naked, crushing, deformed and demented fury. In Van Gogh, through his bold strokes, sharp colors, swirls and mandalas.

go out and look for noise and entertainment, and so attempt to run away from his or her inner horror. Nightclubs, cabarets and drug alleys are full of syphilitics wanting to drown their inner turmoil and bewilderment. There are syphilitics, though, who will seek refuge in work or in a similar constructive activity. Some syphilitics say their best time to work is at night. They feel fine at night and can think more clearly—but only as long as they are busy. Their capacity to work is at its peak during the night hours. These patients are unable to rest at night. They choose work instead of noise or drugs to run away from night's stillness. Doctors should suspect the syphilitic miasma when a patient states that his or her best time to work is at night. By the same token, patients who feel worse at night—or infants who cry and cry all night long—may also be victims of this miasma.

Syphilitics will drug themselves.

Sycosics and psorics also do. But psorics drug themselves to anesthetize their anxiety and vulnerability. Sycosics, on the other hand, will drug themselves to develop a sharper mind, and so deal more successfully with their problems—or else in search of a spurious buttress for their flagging self-aggrandizement.

Syphilitics, in turn, will abuse drugs in order to gain access to some kind of ephemeral paradise, away from their constant inner swirls of horror—and also as a means to slowly continue destroying themselves.

The syphilitic's self-esteem, like everything else, is in a constant and frantic roller coaster, that is a gross exaggeration of the ups and downs experienced by psorics and sycosics.

Syphilitics will go from feeling omnipotent one moment to imagine they are the scum of the Earth the next.

Eventually, as self-destruction advances, syphilitics may become fixed in one of the two extremes.

Some syphilitics will delude themselves into believing that they are Napoleon Bonaparte or some other suchlike exalted historical figure, while others may congeal their minds in an extreme self-debasement and -recrimination—and eventually end up committing suicide.

Frustration, that occasional and inevitable side effect of interacting with others and with Nature, becomes unbearable for syphilitics.

They have as much control of their frustrations as 3-year-olds, perhaps less. This absence of control can lead to fury, and fury to a violence impossible to control, due to the syphilitic's lack of checks and balances.

There is an impulsive desire/fear of violence that can be triggered by many factors and circumstances. There is a need of hurting themselves and/or others when things don't go the syphilitics' way, or else when whatever they may want does not materialize immediately.

The consequences of uncontrolled fury and violence that can be devastating. Once fury subsides it may bring about a guilt so crushing, and a self-recrimination so brutal, that the patient may well end up killing him or herself on impulse.

With this crushing guilt comes awareness of vulnerability. This awareness is infinitely more severe and devastating than that experienced by psorics.

In psorics, vulnerability is related to themselves and else to their surroundings; that is, towards elements readily perceivable. In syphilitics', instead, vulnerability is the consequence of confronting what they perceive as nothingness[22].

Humans are totally incapable of even contemplating Nothingness, let alone dealing with it.

Syphilitics will run away from Nothingness, and attempt to project their vulnerability onto surroundings that have substance and existence. They will consequently become extremely frightened and suspicious of everything and everybody, for they will consider their surroundings as a real threat to their existence—like the Nothingness they are incapable to face but that nevertheless surrounds and imbeds them.

Suspiciousness and distrust will urge syphilitics to destroy whatever they consider as threatening for their survival.

The destruction their suspiciousness bring about unleashes yet another wave of self-destructive nausea, recrimination and guilt—and also an even greater awareness of their vulnerability as syphilitics see how easy it is to destroy someone, and therefore how easy it also is to be destroyed themselves.

As the syphilitic miasma progresses, memory starts to wane; and with it, the awareness of the syphilitic personal identity.

---

[22] Vulnerability and anxiety, as well as related subjects, are beautifully described and explained in *"The Courage to Be"*, an excellent essay by the famous late Protestant Theologian Paul Johannes Tillich (1886-1965).

The physical organism also shows this self-destructive process, that seems to have a perverse predilection for the most important and vital organs of the patient.

The heart, brain and/or main arteries slowly erode until despoliation becomes incompatible with mental sanity or with life.

At this stage the syphilitic may well die suddenly, or may end up in a mental institution.

Or in a Hospital for chronic incurable diseases, or in prison, a death chamber, or an early grave.

PSEUDO-PSORA.

This miasma appears when disease-syndromes, derived from the chronic miasmas Sycosis and Syphilis, are improperly dealt with—usually because of *local* treatments.

Patients suffering from these chronic miasmas become suppressed because of a *local* and *improper* treatment.

The chronic miasmas Sycosis and Syphilis will become Pseudo-Psora as the consequence of *local* and *improper* treatments of the disease syndromes gonorrhea, genital warts and syphilis—and probably of all other sexually transmitted diseases.

TUBERCULINISM

Keywords here are *restlessness* and *changeability*. As well as their logical consequence, *irritability*.

Tuberculinics are whimsical because, even though they are aware of what they don't want, they have no idea about what they actually want and need.

Nevertheless, tuberculinics are constantly in search of that elusive something they don't know what it is, but that they know will make them happy. Thus their restlessness, dissatisfaction, capriciousness, changeable moods, constant desire to move and to change everything and everybody around them. Also their episodes of irritability politely concealed in adults but explosive in children.

Tuberculinic children may have long and terrible temper tantrums, as the child lets him or herself fall down on the floor and bang his or her head against it, howling like a banshee and driving everybody up the walls.

These temper tantrums, and the chronic irritability that underlay them, bring about a poor appraisal of reality that continues throughout the tuberculinics' lives.

In children, and aside from the tantrums, irritability often leads to restlessness. A short attention span may also be present, since these children will often loose interest as soon as they realize that the happiness they seek is not in what they are studying or doing.

All of which leads, in turn, to a slowing down of the process of maturation.

Irritability and changeability bring about confusion. Which helps explain the tuberculinic's poor mood after awakening and having to face the day that lies ahead.

Irritability and changeability could also be the reason for their pale and haunted features, early in the morning.

Music—orderly, harmonious and rhythmical—has a markedly soothing effect in tuberculinic patients.

This could be due to the fact that music constitutes an interval of relaxation in their irritable, incessant and constantly thwarted search of happiness.

Adult tuberculinics feel compelled to travel. They try to live in different places. Perhaps somewhere, somehow, they will find the contentment that constantly eludes them.

If they can't travel, then they will change, arrange and re-arrange their clothes and the furniture of their abode—anything to alter what they have, anything to make things appear novel and different.

The tuberculinic patient has a weak chest, that typically attracts diseases like a magnet—and that, also like a magnet, finds it hard to let them go.

These disease-syndromes frequently start in the upper respiratory tract (throat, ears, nose, etc.), generally more than one per winter; and may frequently end up in pneumonia, pneumonitis or bronchitis, that the tuberculinic may drag for weeks or months, and that may end up becoming chronic.

Tuberculinic patients have also a tendency to suffer intermittent fevers, and to feel weak and tired all the time.

They may sweat excessively, particularly at night in bed.

Jose Miguel Mullen, M.D.

They often have a delicate constitution and an aura of helplessness, which elicits in others a desire to protect, particularly if the tuberculinics are children.

The complexion may be pale or waxy in Caucasian tuberculinics. They may have fair hair, circles under their eyes, long lashes and little hair on the tail of their eyebrows. Children tend to have lanugo or fine hair on their backs.

Tuberculinics can be very passionate, mercurial and romantic, and are particularly susceptible to catch tuberculosis.

The tuberculinic miasma and its offspring, the disease-syndrome tuberculosis, had their heyday in late 19th Century, during the so-called *belle époque.*

At that time to be weak, pale and anemic was stylish in European social, cultural and artistic circles. Women would daily consume large quantities of vinegar with the purpose of destroying their blood cells and thus appear weak, sickly and anemic.

One cut above being pale and anemic was to actually become a tubercular patient. It was considered a most chic and romantic thing. Those unfortunate enough to be healthy would stain their handkerchiefs with red ink. When in public, they would discreetly cough and politely bring the handkerchiefs to their mouths—making certain that the red ink stains were clearly visible.

Frederick Chopin, the famous 19th Century pianist and composer, is the archetypal tuberculinic.

CANCERINISM

I shall discuss here the conclusions of my observations on the cancer patients I assisted during decades as a Clinical Cancer Researcher.

The keyword of this miasma is *clinging.*

As we grow up, we displace our center of gravity from parents and suchlike figures into ourselves.

Cancerinics are powerless to bring about such a shift. This inability causes them to cling to someone or something throughout their lives.

Cancerinics desperately cling to their job or their spouses or children. Or to their parents. Or to pets, money, status or position. Or to jewels or valuables. Or to a house, a ranch or some other kind or property. Or to power.

Take Neville Chamberlain, for instance. He became Prime Minister of Great Britain in 1937. He was deceived by Hitler, in their 1938 Munich meeting, into believing that there would be "peace in our time". After Hitler unleashed WW II, Chamberlain was forced to resign in May 1940. He died of cancer six months later, in November 9, 1940. And Chamberlain was not, by far, the only politician or statesman to develop a malignant solid tumor after power was ripped off his or her grasp[23].

These are the main elements, all of them beyond the cancerinics' selves, capable of providing something to identify themselves with, and thus provide sense and meaning to their lives.

The centers of gravity and identity of cancerinics, then, never quite shift to themselves as they grow up into adulthood; rather, they remain on their parents or else are transferred to the things and/or people cancerinics cling to.

For cancerinics, then, *outside things and/or people, precious to them, have more value than the cancerinics themselves. Those things and/or people are the only elements that give a sense of identity and meaning to cancerinics' lives*—in absolute terms. It is either that or nothing.

Cancerinics love others *more* than they love themselves, but only insofar as those others—or those objects or situations—provide identity sense and meaning to their lives.

Cancerinics will go to any extreme in order to maintain a *status quo* of clinging and dependency. Nothing will be allowed to threaten the bond of dependency lest that bond may be strained, damaged and even perhaps—Goodness forbid! —destroyed.

This attitude may make the cancerinic very rigid and averse to change.

Cancerinics will go to any extreme, even to that of stunting their own self-development, in order to retain and/or appease the object of their dependency. Which is the reason why cancerinics tend to be so meek, to never complain and to swallow their anger and their sadness.

And all cancerinics will ask in return for this abject devotion is the certainty that their subjugation will last forever.

This extreme self-debasement sours cancerinics, and make them feel ensnared. Such a situation of progressive and suffocating entrapment creates a

---

[23] Data obtained from several bibliographical sources. Among them, William Manchester's *"The last lion, 1932-1940"*. Little, Brown and Co., Ed. Boston, 1988. Page 513.

dilemma between remaining dependent and breaking free. Which leads to fear of forsakenness and its twin byproducts, sadness and resentment.

The very hint of forsakenness, in turn, leads to panic and again into dependence.

The vicious circle dependency/clinging → entrapment → desire for freedom → forsakenness → panic → dependency/clinging again, fosters guilt and confusion. Plus the need to atone, through physical suffering and/or punishment, for the terrible sin of wishing to break free.

This concatenation of feelings, added to envy towards those who don't need to cling, provoke still more conflict. It makes the cancerinic impatient and angry.

In turn, impatience and anger seriously interfere with the *niceness indispensable to be accepted into dependency* ("What will the person I so desperately cling say if he or she learns that I'm angry?", or "Will the object or situation I so desperately need to cling to be taken away/fall from my grasp if I'm angry?", followed by the terrifying "What if he or she rejects or forsakes me?", or "What if the object or situation I so desperately need is not mine any more?").

It is small wonder that cancerinics negate any vestige of anger and irritability, and bury those feelings in some dark recess, deep inside.

No matter how deeply buried and supposedly forgotten, however, these negative emotions will bear heavily, and quietly grow in their secret abode.

Every once in a while, those hidden feelings will hurl a devastating hint of their existence, which the cancerinic will rapidly repress.

In time, anger and its *ad lateres* will seep into, and poison, the entire cancerinic's life.

Cancerinics will carefully avoid every opportunity to enjoy themselves.

There is always the lingering possibility that mirth may distract cancerinics from their immediate and constantly reinforced submissiveness to that person or object dear to them, so necessary to identify themselves with and cling to.

There is also the possibility that joy may vex fate or bring about bad luck.

Again here, the main thing is not to rock the boat.

And so cancerinics will go through life dutybound, displaying with pride a stoic smile and a stiff upper lip; finding in their exquisite secret suffering one of their very few satisfactions.

Consider, within this context, a 42 years old extremely rigid cancerinic male suffering from gastric leiomyosarcoma[24] I saw only twice.

Among other things, he told me he loved to ski, but that he had given it up several years ago, when he married. He was still in good enough shape to re-start skiing if he wanted. Ever since his marriage, though, he had devoted himself, with ferocious single-mindedness, to the sole purpose of providing for his family by means of overworking.

I asked him if anybody in his family objected to his skiing. Nobody did.

I encouraged him to continue his Allopathic treatment, referred him to a counselor and started Homeopathy and imaging.

Both the counselor and myself encouraged him to start skiing again. Both of us failed.

Our permissiveness, plus the absence of suffering of the Homeopathic/psychological treatment, so confused this man that he quitted after the second visit. He went back into continuing Chemotherapy treatment alone. I never saw nor heard about this patient again.

When Fate decrees that the cancerinics' patiently braided bond of submission/dependence is to be severed, or when there is even a hint that such a thing may happen, cancerinics become overwhelmed by a sudden uncontrollable surge of shock and panic.

The terrible feelings of anger, resentment, sadness, envy and guilt so carefully repressed that by now are almost totally forgotten and ignored, burst forth in all their formidable ripeness. The subsequent stress is unendurable.

Some 6 months to 2 years afterwards the cancerinic is likely to develop a clinically detectable solid malignant tumor somewhere.

Allopathic Doctors believe that malignant solid tumors cause the imbalance suffered by cancer patients.

Holistic Physicians consider that the malignant tumor appears as the consequence of activation of the patients' chronic cancerinic miasma—or, to put it differently, that a malignant tumor appears at the time when the cancerinic patient's *latent* cancerinism becomes *manifest*.

Another feature I have invariably found in cancerinics is their inability to adequately react to bacterial infections and the like.

---

[24] *Leios,* smooth, *myo,* muscle, *sarcos,* flesh, and *oma,* tumor. A malignant tumor of non-epithelial tissues; in this instance, a very malignant solid tumor of the stomach muscle wall, quite resistant to every form of treatment.

How often have I heard, from the surviving spouse of a cancer patient "You know, Doctor, my husband/wife was always so healthy! This horrible thing came as such a shock to everybody. He or she was never sick, not even one day in his/her life, before being stricken with cancer!"

This inability to react when bacteria, fungi or viruses trespass into the patient makes doleful sense within the context of the cancerinic miasma.

Cancerinics will nip in the bud any form of rejection towards other persons, objects or circumstances—even bacteria and viruses—no matter how dangerous. Their immune system, like everything else in the cancerinic's Wholeness, needs to be nice to the outside and to please, in order to be accepted and be able to cling.

And so cancerinics will accept viruses, bacteria, etc., with their characteristic submissiveness ↔ gratitude ↔ resentment. Consequently, cancerinics will never feel sick because to feel sick is the reaction of a patient's immune system to any foreign form of invasion. The cancerinic's immune system is forbidden to recognize pathogenic microorganisms as dangerous, and to fight against them. Like everything else in a cancerinic's life, bacteria and the like need to be pleased. Therefore, when pathogenic microorganism intrude there will be no fever, pain, malaise or inflammation of any kind.

It is generally accepted that some cells may eventually mutate and become malignant in all of us at some time or another. These cells are recognized as abnormal, and quietly destroyed and disposed of. The cancerinic's stifled immune system won't recognize malignant cells as perilous, either.

Those cells will therefore have carte blanche to grow at will, and eventually to metastasize and kill the patient.

As mentioned above, Psora is the mother lode of all forms of diseases not originating in the chronic miasmas Sycosis and Syphilis.

Sycosis, in turn, causes many *aggrandizing* inflammatory and/or draining diseases, whether sexually transmitted or not.

Sycosic disease-syndromes can be either acute or chronic.

Gonorrhea brings about a severe inflammation[25] of the genital area and a secretion that may be excessive, foul and/or purulent[26].

Genital warts produce aggrandizement in the form of benign tumors.

---

[25] Inflammation is ultimately a form of aggrandizement.

[26] The secretion of Psora is characteristically clear.

Similar aggrandizement/swelling/inflammation/secretion can also be found in rheumatoid arthritis, as well as in some forms of sinusitis and bronchial asthma, among other sycosic disease-syndromes.

Dr. Hahnemann, in his *Treatise of Chronic Diseases*, considers that the miasma Sycosis is brought about by the contagion of gonorrhea or genital warts in susceptible individuals.

If treated *locally*, Sycosic disease-syndromes will become internalized as Pseudo-psora.

The destructive chronic miasma Syphilis is related to the disease-syndrome syphilis; and also probably to other destructive diseases, all the way from varicose ulcers to dementia to perhaps even AIDS.

Localized treatment of the syphilitic chancre, popular before antibiotics entered the Allopathic arena, was also an important cause of Pseudo-psora.

Tuberculinism, said to be a combination of Psora and Syphilis is, of course, related to tuberculosis; and Cancerinism, supposedly a combination of Psora, Sycosis and Syphilis, to the development of malignant solid tumors.

Psora is considered to be the underlying cause of all diseases not derived from Sycosis or Syphilis.

Consequently, those who do not suffer from Psora, or *a-Psorics*, are likely never to get sick, except for some transient, mild acute illness. Dr. Hahnemann is said to have been an example of this exceptional and enviable state of health and balance.

A non-tuberculinic person is extremely unlike to develop the disease-syndrome tuberculosis, even after repeated exposure to *mycobacteria*.

It is similarly difficult to develop a malignant solid tumor in a non-cancerinic; no matter how severe the stress or loss that person may have been subjected or exposed to, or how much they may smoke or engage in any other suchlike risky behavior.

By the same token, the possibility of becoming sick of all the way from gonorrhea to rheumatoid arthritis in a non-sycosic is very remote.

As it is that of contracting clinical syphilis, despite of unprotected exposure; or of developing dementia or any other degenerative or destructive syndrome in non-syphilitics.

Let me illustrate this difficulty of falling ill, if the miasma is not present, with two examples.

I once had the dubious privilege of sharing my workplace with an elderly lecher—a very repellent individual, actually. He was employed in the Central Supply of one of the institutions where I did Cancer Research, so I had no choice but to see him with some frequency.

He was fond of boasting about his feats in the red light district during his youth. He would go regularly there with his best friend. Their idea of a good time was to have unprotected sexual intercourse with the same prostitute, one immediately after the other.

"And you know, Doctor" he would lisp with a puzzled grin that exposed part of his inflamed gums and a few rotting teeth "my friend would catch the crabs, and I would get the clap!".

From a Homeopathic standpoint, this uncouth comment means that this man was sycosic, and his friend psoric.

One of my excellent Professors—can't remember whom—in the Post Graduate School of the Asociación Médica Homeopática Argentina, had once been the Director of the Department of Urology in a Public Hospital located in Vicente López, a suburb of the city of Buenos Aires, Argentina.

All services were free of charge in the Hospital at that time. Drugs were also dispensed *gratis et amore.*

The suburb was rapidly growing. Lots of high rises were going up. Construction workers would come from a shantytown located in the wrong side of the tracks in the same suburb.

The inhabitants of the shantytown, all very poor, would go to the Public Hospital for assistance—they couldn't afford anything else, and other Hospitals were too far away for their very limited budgets.

The noon break used to be quite a ceremony in Argentina in those days. One of the workers would spend the whole morning caring for the *asado,* a barbecue that had to be grilled to perfection by noontime. Lunch consisted of barbecued beef, wine and then a siesta. This noon break would last a couple of hours or so, all counted. Then work would start again until sunset.

This idyllic noon break was used by a local prostitute to make business. All workers would have unprotected sexual intercourse with her.

What puzzled my Professor was the fact that, of all the workers who had had sex with that same woman, some would not go to the Hospital at all—presumably because they had gone through the ordeal without catching anything. Some would visit the Hospital with pediculosis, others with gonorrhea, and others with syphilis. And still others with a combination of two and even all three diseases.

My Professor could not figure out any reasonable explanation for this selectivity.

If all men had been equally exposed to the same infections when having sexual intercourse with the same partner, why was it that not all had caught *all* three diseases? Particularly since Humans are not naturally resistant to pediculosis, gonorrhea or syphilis. The quest for an answer to this conundrum eventually led him to Homeopathy. The Homeopathic concept of Chronic Miasmas gave my Professor the answer he was seeking.

He quitted his prosperous practice of Urology, and in time became an outstanding Homeopathic Physician and teacher instead.

Sometimes, the patient's Past Medical History and Family History are useful to detect the possibility of a chronic miasma.

In everyday Medical practice, one finds patients who manifest either having, or else having had certain diseases that frequently point toward a particular Miasma.

Equally as often, though, one finds patients who deny having had gonorrhea, or genital warts, or syphilis—or tuberculosis or cancer, for that matter—but who have clinical manifestations of being affected by the corresponding miasmas.

Those patients may be affected by a *hereditary* form of those chronic miasmas.

Hereditary miasmas are usually found in the Family History.

For instance, a Family History of asthma and/or arthritis may well point toward hereditary Sycosis.

Patients with insulin-dependent diabetes, pernicious anemia and/or malignant tumors may have hereditary Cancerinism.

And those with clinical tuberculosis hereditary Tuberculinism.

In turn, a Family History with a lot of destruction, like violence, substance dependence, suicide, mental and/or sexually transmitted diseases and the like may strongly point towards Syphilis.

Sexually transmitted diseases used to be called "shameful diseases". They still are, according to the data I daily obtain in my office.

Of all the patients I have seen, only one or two so far have confessed that an ancestor had suffered of the disease-syndromes gonorrhea, genital warts and/or syphilis. Either the families of most of my patients have been paragons of virtue and temperance, or else to mention these diseases at home was strictly taboo—very much to the chagrin of Homeopathic Physicians.

If I were to compare a chronically diseased patient with a house, I would say that chronic diseases attack *the house*, while Chronic Miasmas *erode its foundations*.

Psora would be a *generally faulty foundation*. Pseudo-psora, in turn could correspond to a powerful petard placed by Allopathic Medicine, and made to explode, in the patient's core.

Sycosis, Syphilis, Tuberculinism and Cancerinism would be specific areas of erosion, or cracks *in the patient's foundation*, perhaps already weakened by Psora.
These areas of weakness could be due to heredity, individual susceptibility, inappropriate treatments or poor life habits.

The entire house is in danger with the faulty foundation of Psora.
That building will have decreased resistance to stress, and will run the risk of collapsing.

If Chronic Miasmas other than Psora are present, then the house will *lean* in a certain fashion.
Then that house tends to collapse in a manner that is characteristic of the weakness brought about by each of those Chronic Miasmas.

The damage brought about by the Chronic Miasmas, with Psora as drum major, is incalculable.
So far I have only briefly discussed the consequences of the chronic miasmas in individuals. I would like to comment now their effects in societies—and in Allopathic Medicine.
But let me start with Allopathy.

Psora has made Physicians feel insecure along Millennia, threatened and at the mercy of Nature, bacterial diseases and the like.

Something good and useful came from this miasma, however. Psora frightened Allopathic Physicians and Scientists alike into the discovery of vaccines, antibiotics and radiations, and also into the startling advances of Surgery.

Allopathy started to feel sycotically big and powerful with these new therapeutic tools in their hands, after Centuries of being psorically intimidated by Nature. With characteristic sycosic and then syphilitic misjudgment, it fantasized that antibiotics would rid the world of disease-producing bacteria and viruses. And that anything that could not be cured in this fashion could be removed by Surgery or else burnt away with X Ray treatments.

So they went after microorganisms and sick organs with a syphilitic vengeance.

Had Allopathic Doctors been a-psoric to start with, they would have realized that the thought of destroying bacteria and the like was a patent absurdity. Microorganisms have thrived in this Earth for eons before Humans arrived, constitute 9/10ths of our Earth's biomass and have learnt to survive and to adapt to every challenging situation. Allopathic Physicians would have also clearly realized that the search of bacterial killers in mold extracts—for antibiotics are either mold extracts, or else chemical modifications of those extracts—was ludicrous because bacteria have learnt how to live with molds and their extracts throughout Millennia.

Had Allopathic Doctors been a-psoric, they would have realized that the only thing that can be done with bacteria and viruses is to learn how to live harmoniously with them. Instead of ways and means on how to destroy them, Allopathic Physicians would have developed methods that would have lead toward harmony and integration.

Instead, the prevalence of a succession of these miasmatic outlooks led Allopathic Physicians to the unilateral declaration of all-out war of Humanity against microorganisms. Bacteria met the Allopathic threat as they met all the ones that preceded it. Zillions of bacteria perished because of antibiotic treatments, granted; but a few survived because they learnt how to resist the action of drugs. Survivors shared their resistance with as many other bacteria as possible, and also with their offspring—a tried and true method of bacterial survival through the ages.

The mad race between antibiotics and bacteria has almost reached the finish line. Bacteria appear to be the winners. As these lines are written, there is a strain of *mycobacterium*, associated with human tuberculosis, and another one of the dreaded *staphylococcus* that have become resistant to *every* known antibiotic. Other bacteria are likely to follow suit[27]. Viruses, in turn, have proved to be uniformly insensitive to antibiotic treatment.

Sycosic/syphilitic Allopathy is also creating vaccines, seemingly useful to immunize against everything under the sun. All the way from tetanus to the common cold. The long-term effect of all this excessive stimulation of the immune system is still in need of being thoroughly evaluated.

Surgery, on the other hand, appears to have completed, in many instances, the cycle Psora → Sycosis → Syphilis and then back to Psora again.

Consider, within this context, the evolution of the surgical treatment of cancer of the cervix of the uterus during the past 60 years or so.

First, Surgeons would remove the ovaries, tubes, uterus and the upper part of the vagina in these unfortunate patients. Then the uterus, most of the vagina plus tubes and ovaries were taken away. Then all of the above plus the urinary bladder and the rectum and anus, aside from every lymph node all the way up to the pit of the stomach. Then, Surgeons would cut their poor victims in half at the level of the waist, keeping the upper part and discarding the lower. This operation was aptly called "hemicorporectomy", or cutting the body in half (*hemi,* half; *corpo,* body; *ectomy,* removal)[28]. Now Surgeons have quietly gone back to much more conservative Surgery.

Surgery of localized breast cancer has gone through a similar evolution. First, Surgeons removed the tumor-bearing breast and the lymph nodes of the axilla of the same side. Then the breast + the lymph nodes of the axilla of the same side + the lymph nodes located above the collarbone. The next step consisted in the removal of all of the above + a chain of lymph nodes located immediately underneath the ribs. Then came the removal of *both* breasts plus all of the above. Currently, the standard procedure is a lumpectomy, or removal of only the tumor and surrounding tissues, followed up by radiation or chemotherapy or both.

It would appear that when a procedure of any kind is *partially* successful, or when it has exhausted its usefulness, Allopathic thought seldom looks for an alternative approach. Instead, the tendency is to intensify the treat-

---

[27] Dr. Ernst F. Sauerbruch (1875-1951), the famous German Surgeon and father of Thoracic Surgery, once said that "perhaps the purely bacteriological and serological conception of disease may have led Medical Science into a blind alley". (Prof. Mario M. Brea, M.D., Personal communication. Dr. Brea trained in Thoracic Surgery with Dr. Sauerbruch in the 1930's).

[28] The term "basket case" was coined after the upper part of these hapless women, who had to be kept in some kind of a basket. The mortality of this form of Surgery was as terrible as was its consequences in the few women who survived it.

ment until such and intensification unequivocally proves to be dangerous to the patients' life and physical integrity. Take as examples atrocities like the extravagant blood letting and sundry other treatments of yesteryear, more recently the excesses of cancer surgery and currently the so-called stem cell transplant.

When it comes to History, Psora makes entire peoples and nations feel insecure, and thus at the mercy of other peoples.

Those supposedly threatened nations need to feel strong and big to face such a constant danger. This need brings into power someone capable of transforming a timid psoric population into an arrogant and belligerent sycosic one.

From sycosis to syphilis there is only a tiny leap. It takes very little for a sycosic population to become emboldened and to start attacking and destroying its neighbors.

Syphilis exhausts itself into wholesale destruction. There is a point where too few people remain alive and in one piece—particularly when a crushing war debt has been accumulated as the consequence of such a murderous folly.

Warfare peters out and a peace is signed—a peace that is likely to last until survivors, or the generation that follows those survivors, starts to feel insecure, threatened and at the mercy of other peoples. At that time, the cycle Psora $\rightarrow$ Sycosis $\rightarrow$ Syphilis $\rightarrow$ back to Psora inexorably starts all over again.

Consider, within this context, the evolution of Europe from the days of Cardinal le Duc de Richelieu (1585-1642) and his *éminence grise* till mid-20th Century or thereabouts, to understand the tragic repetition of these miasmatic cycles in diverse countries and cultures. Cycles that were disconnected from each other at first but that, as time went by, became more and more synchronized until they debauched in the blood baths of the Great War first, and then of WW2. Perhaps peoples have now learnt and grown beyond these cycles. But then again, perhaps we are in the midst of the Psoric aspect of the next one.

Chapter 6

ORIGIN OF THE HOMEOPATHIC REMEDIES

Most Homeopathic remedies are prepared with natural substances, as they exist in Nature.

Some substances are man-made; or else admixtures and preparations of natural substances, such as in the instance of *Causticum* and *Hepar Sulphur*; both of which, by the way, were first prepared by Dr. Hahnemann himself.

Please note that most Homeopathic remedies have Latin names.

This, I suppose, is to help Homeopathic Physicians of different languages understand one another.

Many Homeopathic remedies are minerals, such as gold *(Aurum metallicum),* sand *(Silicea),* or volcanic lava *(Heckla Lava).*

Most are obtained from plants.

Some originate in the animal kingdom and in Humans.

Others are prepared by mixing substances used singly as Homeopathic remedies, as in the case of *Hepar Sulfur* and *Causticum,* mentioned above.

And there are some, like gunpowder *(gunpowder)* and nitroglycerin *(Glonoinum),* which are prepared starting from manufactures originally unrelated to Homeopathy.

Chapter 7

PREPARATION AND DISPENSATION OF HOMEO-PATHIC REMEDIES.

PREPARATION OF HOMEOPATHIC REMEDIES.

There are three methods to prepare a Homeopathic remedy: Centesimal, Decimal and Fifty-millesimal.

For the sake of clarity, I shall describe in some detail the preparation of *Centesimals*, most commonly used in America[29]; and then take the Centesimals as reference when describing the preparation of *Decimals* and *Fifty-millesimals*.

There is nothing quite as easy, or quite as mysterious, as to prepare a Homeopathic remedy.

First the easy part. One must obtain a substance or product—or, less frequently, a manufactured one. Then one must filter, dilute and shake it, if the product is soluble in water and/or in ethanol/water; or else triturate it, if it is not soluble in ethanol/water. That's all. Nothing could be easier.

The mysterious part is the therapeutic action that emerges after that substance has been subjected to trituration, and/or to dilution and shaking; a therapeutic action usually absent in the original natural substance.

In order to simplify, and to avoid introducing new words before they are explained, I shall use the totally inadequate term *dilution* in the first part of this Chapter.

---

[29] Dr. James T. Kent has undoubtedly been the most influential of all Homeopathic Physicians in America. He had no knowledge of the Fifty-millesimals because he died in 1916, and the 6th. Edition of Dr. Hahnemann's *Organon*, where the Fifty-millesimals are first described in § 270, was not published until 1921. So Dr. Kent did most of his work with Centesimal dynamizations. Consequently, most American Homeopathic Physicians prefer the Centesimal or the Decimal dynamizations to work with.

Correct terms, such as *trituration, dynamization, succussion* and *potency* will be gradually introduced later on.

As mentioned above, there is nothing quite as simple as the preparation of a Homeopathic remedy.

For Decimals and Centesimals, the solvent is either water, or else a mixture of ethanol and water. The spirits *should preferably* be obtained from wine.

For substances insoluble in water and/or ethanol, the solvent—or rather, the dispersing agent—used is lactose powder.

For Fifty-millesimals, as we shall see later on, the ethanol used *must* always be obtained from wine.

When the original substance is soluble in *water,* the first three steps are performed by means of diluting the substance in increasing amounts of ethanol in water.

When the original substance is soluble in *water and ethanol,* *all* steps are done using 87% or 95% dilution of ethanol in water.

Lactose powder is used for the first three steps when the original substance is *insoluble both in ethanol and in ethanol/water.*

From there on, all the following steps must be done using ethanol 87% or 95% in water.

PREPARATION OF CENTESIMALS.-

When the original substance is soluble in ethanol/water…

Macerate the original substance in 60 % ethanol in water.

After maceration, solids are usually filtered away.

The remaining ethanol-water solution, after filtration and elimination of solids, is called **Mother Tincture**, and symbolized "Θ".

Take one part of Θ, and dilute it 1/100 (or $1/10^2$ or 10^{-2}) in 87% or 95% of ethanol in water. Shake vigorously several times.

This *dynamization* (i.e., dilution + vigorous shaking), is called **First Centesimal Hahnemann**, or 1 **CH** [30] (1).

Take one part of (1), and dilute 1/100 in 87% or 95% ethanol in water. Shake vigorously several times. This *dynamization* (i.e., dilution + vigorous shaking), is called **Second Centesimal Hahnemann**, or 2 CH (2).

The 2 CH is the 1/10,000 of Θ, because 1/100 of (1) × 1/100 of (2) = 1/10,000 (Or $1/10^4$ or 10^{-4}).

Take one part of (2), and dilute 1/100 in 87% or 95% ethanol-water solution. Shake vigorously several times. This is the **Third Centesimal Hahnemann**, or 3 CH (3).

It corresponds to a *dynamization* (i.e., dilution + vigorous shaking), of 1/1,000,000 of Θ (1/100 × 1/100 × 1/100 = 1/1,000,000; or $1/10^6$ or 10^{-6}).

Take one part of (3), dilute in 1/100 of 87% or 95% ethanol-water solution. Shake vigorously several times. This is the **Fourth Centesimal Hahnemann**, or 4 CH.

It correspond to a *dynamization* (i.e., dilution + vigorous shaking), of 1/100,000,000 of Θ (1/100 × 1/100 × 1/100 × 1/100 = 1/100,000,000; or 10^{-8}).

And so on, diluting and shaking in the same fashion, if one wishes to obtain higher *dynamizations* (i.e., dilution + vigorous shaking), such as 5 CH, 6 CH, etc.

Thus, for instance, a 10 CH is 1/1 followed by 20 zeroes; or 10^{-20}.

And these are considered to be *low dynamizations.* Two hundred CH (or 10^{-400}), 1,000 CH (or $10^{-2,000}$) and even higher dynamizations are not uncommonly prescribed.

When the original substance is soluble only in water...

...the procedure is slightly different than that followed when the original substance is both water- and ethanol-soluble.

For the Homeopathic preparation of water-soluble substances such as sodium chloride—that is, table salt—one proceeds like in (1) to (3) above,

---

[30] In "CH", "C" is for Centesimal and "H" is for Hahnemann. Some Pharmacies design Centesimal dynamizations (i.e., dilutions + vigorous shaking) simply by a "C" or a "c".

Jose Miguel Mullen, M.D.

but *using 30 % ethanol in water for the first dynamization, 60 % ethanol in water for the second and 70 % ethanol in water for the third.*

Starting on 4 CH onwards, though, all *dynamizations* are done using as solvent 87% or 95% ethanol-water solution.

When the original substance in insoluble both in water and in water/ethanol...

As it happens with platinum, sand, gold, etc.

Here the procedure is done with mortar and pestle for the first three dynamizations. It is called *Trituration.*

In this instance, the first three steps are,

Take one part of the substance and place it in a scrupulously clean unglazed porcelain mortar[31].

Add 100 parts of pure lactose powder.

Triturate the insoluble substance and lactose powder together in the mortar for one hour, with the aid of a pestle. Stop every so often to scrape the walls of mortar and the sides of the pestle with a scrupulously clean spatula.

This trituration will produce the **First Centesimal Hahnemann**, or 1/100, or $1/10^2$ or 10^{-2} or 1 CH (4).

Take one part of (4), and place it in another scrupulously clean and unglazed porcelain mortar.

Add 100 parts of lactose powder.

Triturate in mortar for one hour, stopping every so often to scrape walls of mortar, and sides of pestle, with a scrupulously clean spatula.

This will produce the **Second Centesimal Hahnemann** trituration, or 1/10,000 or $1/10^4$ or 10^{-4} or 2 CH (5).

Take one part of (5), and place it in a third scrupulously clean and unglazed porcelain mortar.

Add 100 parts of lactose powder.

Triturate in mortar for one hour, stopping every so often to scrape walls of mortar, and sides of pestle, with a scrupulously clean spatula.

This will produce the **Third Centesimal Hahnemann** trituration, or 1/1,000,000 or $1/10^6$ or 10^{-6} or 3 CH (6).

---

[31] The mortar's interior should be *unglazed,* prior to being used, with the aid of its pestle and very fine, pure, wet sand.

After the 3 CH, all substances become soluble in 87% or 95% ethanol-water solutions. From here onwards, all successive *dynamizations* are done in 1/100 dilutions, using only 87% or 96% ethanol in water.

The vigorous shaking of each *dilution* is called *SUCCUSSION*.

Dr. Hahnemann recommended to succuss by hand, by means of getting the hermetically closed tube or flask into one's fist; and then pounding the fist onto something firm and elastic, such as the cover of a leather-bound book, several consecutive times.

Each of the successive *succussions* and *triturations* produce *DYNAMI-ZATIONS*.

Each dynamization creates a *POTENCY*.

Thus, in order to obtain 3 CH *potency*, for instance, one has to carry out three *dynamizations* (i.e., three consecutive 1/100 *succussions)* if the original substance is soluble in ethanol-water, or in water.

Or else three *triturations* (i.e., three successive one-hour 1/100 *mixings*, using three scrupulously clean and unglazed mortars and pestles) will be needed to reach a *potency* of 3 CH if the original substance is insoluble in water, or in water-ethanol.

There are workers who prefer the terms *dilution* and/or *attenuation* when referring to both dynamization and potency.

Dr. Hahnemann, in note *d.* to § 269 of his *Organon*, complaints about those who use the term *dilutions* when referring to Homeopathic remedies. As he correctly points out, if one is to dilute table salt more and more, there is only going to be only water after a while.

If, instead, one dilutes *and* shakes—that is, if one *succusses*—then the therapeutic potential, present but hitherto hidden in that product, will become evident.

As to *attenuations*, the term is used in Bacteriology to describe ways of making bacteria less dangerous; and in Physics, to define a decrease of energy in a wave or a flow of particles. The word *attenuation*, therefore, conveys a sense of weakening; which is totally contrary to what succussion brings out of a substance. That is why I shall stick to the terms *dynamization* and *potency*, and will disregard *dilution* and/or *attenuation* throughout the text of this book.

According to the **number of Avogadro**, none of the matter present in the original substance remains in dynamizations above 12 CH (i.e., 10^{-24}, or one trillionth-trillionth)[32].

Which means that, above that dynamization, *only the diluent, i.e., the 87% or 95% ethanol/water solution, is present in a Homeopathic remedy.*

How can potencies above 12 CH (i.e., 13 CH, 14 CH. 15 CH, 16 CH, etc.) be therapeutically active, even though none of the original substance is present, has not been clarified yet.

Preparation of high dynamizations by hand can become a very cumbersome procedure.

The *Korsakoff Dynamizer* has been devised for the purpose of preparing dynamizations higher of 30 CH or 200 CH, depending of the Pharmacy.

Korsakoff dynamizations are often called "CK".

The inventor of this Dynamizer was General Andrei von Korsakoff, a Russian soldier and Homeopathic aficionado. He invented the artifact early in the 19th Century.

In most Homeopathic Pharmacies, the first dynamizations, up to the 30 CH or the 200 CH, are done by hand. They are usually prepared with the aid of the Korsakoff Dynamizer from then on.

Thus, a 400 CK is a dynamization that, up to the 30 C or 200 C was done by hand and afterwards with the aid of the Korsakoff Dynamizer.

---

[32] Count Amadeus Avogadro (1776-1856) was a French Physicist who discovered the constant 6.02×10^{23}, called the *number of Avogadro*. It represents the number of atoms in a gram atom, or else the number of molecules in a gram molecule (a *gram atom* is the quantity of element whose weight in grams is numerically equal to the atomic weight of the element; and *gram molecule*, the quantity of a substance whose weight in grams is numerically equal to the molecular weight of the substance).

This constant can also be expressed by saying that there is nothing left of the original substance at dilutions of 6.02×10^{-23} and beyond. If we recall that 12 CH is 10^{-24}, it can be concluded that there is nothing but ethanol 87 % or 96 % in water at dynamizations of 12 CH and higher (i.e., 13 CH, 14 CH, 15 CH, etc.).

PREPARATION OF DECIMALS.-

Decimal dynamizations are prepared in a fashion similar to that used to prepare Centesimals. The only difference is that dynamizations are prepared *in 1/10's* increases, instead of 1/100.

A Centesimal potency is symbolized by a **CH**, and a Decimal potency is symbolized by an "**x**" or an "**X**".

A 1 x dynamization is the original product, that has been dynamized one in ten (or 1/10, or $1/10^1$, or 10^{-1}); either by succussion or by trituration.

A 2 x dynamization is the original product, that has been succussed or triturated *twice*, one in ten each time (or $1/10 \times 1/10 = 1/100$, or $1/10^2$, or 10^{-2}).

And so on, in such a fashion that a potency of 30 x means that the original product has been dynamized 30 consecutive times by the Decimal method; that is, it has been ultimately succussed to $1/10^{30}$, or to the 10^{-30}.

Dr. Hahnemann used Decimal potencies at first. He afterwards let them aside, because he found Centesimals more gentle and useful.

The preparation of a Homeopathic remedy in Centesimal and Decimal dynamizations is not difficult, although it is indeed laborious.

Fiftymillesimal are a bit more complicated to prepare, as we shall presently see.

I have a very amusing anecdote regarding how simple it is to prepare a Homeopathic remedy. This story was protagonized by a delightful patient of mine, well into his 90's the last time I saw him.

It happened over half a Century ago.

My patient, an inveterate hiker, was overcome by a seizure while hiking in some very remote location in Florida, well beyond any vestiges of civilization. His son, who was with him at the time, became understandably alarmed. He rushed to the nearest telephone and called his father's Homeopathic Physician.

The Doctor asked several questions, after having carefully listened to the patient's symptoms. Then he said "Do you have any remedies with you?". The answer to this question was no. "Do you have whisky or something similar in your kit?". The answer again was no. "Do you have vinegar in you hiking kit?", was the third question. The son said yes. "Do you have any pennies?". The son agreed again, a bit mystified. "Good," went on the

Doctor "this is what I want you to do. Pour vinegar into a glass. Drop a penny into the vinegar and stir vigorously for a few minutes. Then discard both the penny and the vinegar. Then fill the glass with vinegar again, and stir vigorously. Throw that vinegar away, and put new vinegar into the glass. Stir vigorously, and then give your father a couple of spoonfuls of that vinegar".

My patient never had seizures again.

This is, of course, stretching Homeopathy a bit too far, albeit genially.

Vinegar is sour wine, in which ethanol has become acetic acid. In vinegar, acetic acid is at a concentration of about 12%. The penny was made of copper[33], and when copper and acetic acid are put together one obtains copper acetate.

Its dynamization—if in 12 % acetic acid in water, instead of 87% or 96% ethanol in water— was achieved by stirring instead of shaking. And this was neither a Decimal or Centesimal dynamization.

But, anyway, it all happened in an emergency in the middle of nowhere.

The two following replenishing of vinegar and vigorous stirrings were the equivalent of two further dynamizations. Therefore, what the patient eventually received was the third (? Decimal, ? Centesimal, ? whatever) dynamization of copper acetate, or *Cuprum Aceticum*—a Homeopathic remedy that works very well in some forms of seizures!

PREPARATION OF FIFTY MILLESIMALS.-

Dr. Hahnemann created this particular dynamization toward the end of his life. He minutely describes its preparation in § 270, in the 6th. Edition of his *Organon*.

Fifty millesimals are also known as Q (or *quinquagintamillesimals)* and also as LM's.

The substance to be prepared is triturated, as in a manner similar to that described in steps (4) to (6) above (7).

Take 50 milligrams of (7), and dissolve in 500 drops of ethanol 22.5 % in water (this ethanol, as well as that used in the following steps, should *always* have been obtained from *wine*).

---

[33] Remember that this happened in the days when quarters and dimes were made of silver, nickels of nickel and pennies of copper throughout.

One single drop is to be placed in a vial (8).

Add 100 drops of 95 % ethanol in water to (8), and give 100 strong succussions by hand (9).

This potency has been obtained by means of using 500 drops of 22.5 % ethanol in water, followed by 100 drops of 95 % ethanol in water.

$500 \times 100 = 50,000$; thus the denomination *Fifty-millesimal*.

When tiny lactose pellets are wetted with (9), and then dried, we will have the **First Fifty-millesimal potency**, or 1 LM (10).

When one pellet of (10) is dissolved in one drop of water, and then placed into another vial containing 100 drops of 95 % ethanol in water, and given 100 strong succussions by hand, the **Second Fifty-millesimal potency**, or 2 LM, is obtained.

A similar procedure is used to prepare each of the higher LM potencies.

DISPENSATION AND STORAGE OF HOMEOPATHIC REMEDIES

Lower dynamizations of Centesimal and Decimals, if water and/or water-ethanol insoluble, are usually dispensed in little envelopes, mixed with lactose powder.

The contents of each envelope are to be taken only once, by means of placing all the powder into the patient's mouth.

All dynamizations, soluble either in water or in water-ethanol, may be dispensed dissolved in water, in a multi-dose flask.

These preparations are not all that popular.

To start with, they may inactivate rapidly, after a certain amount of time and of opening and closing the flask.

The flask containing the remedy must be stored in a refrigerated place. It must be removed from the refrigerator, and opened and closed, each time the patient needs to take a dose of the remedy. All this opening and closing facilitates contamination of its contents.

Water-ethanol dynamizations are frequently dispensed embedded in lactose pellets (not so water soluble dynamizations, because water dissolves the lactose pellets).

This form of dispensation is preferred because pellets are easier to carry and to store, even indefinitely, at room temperature—if away from dampness, sunlight and strongly scented substances. There is very little danger of contamination, even if the container is frequently opened and closed, because pellets are dry.

LM's can be dispensed in the form of pellets. Also in a water solution, in a container sturdy enough to withstand repeated succussions.

When dispensed dissolved in water, these dynamizations are usually called *LM Plus*.

They can be taken daily, and have to be succussed vigorously ten times before each take; so that the patient takes each individual potency only once (succussion changes the potency of the contents of the flask).

The flask can be refilled with water as it is emptying, and so continue its administration for as long as it is effective, always succussing before each administration—that is, increasing its potency each time.

Like everything dissolved in water, and subjected to frequent opening and closing, these solutions run a considerable risk of becoming contaminated with the microorganisms present in the environment.

Containers for pellets are usually made of transparent amber-colored glass or opaque plastic.

Flasks manufactured with colorless glass should probably be discarded, because sunlight—with the exception of ultraviolet radiation, that is stopped by glass—can freely pass through a clear glass container, and may inactivate the Homeopathic remedy inside.

Flasks made of amber-colored glass are to be preferred.

Water solutions are to be kept refrigerated at all times, in tightly covered flasks, when not in use.

Pellets, on the other hand, can be kept at room temperature, with their containers tightly closed.

Homeopathic remedies are to be kept away from dampness, strongly smelling or perfumed stuffs, and also sunlight.

I recommend keeping them at the back of the white clothes drawer; which is usually dry, has no strongly scented stuffs, and is dark.

Homeopathic remedies should *never* be kept in the medicine cabinet of the bathroom; there is no damper place in the house, nor any other so full of strongly scented substances.

I don't believe remedies should be kept in purses.

Purses can carry make-up and other strongly scented materials. Perfume, particularly when concentrated inside a purse or similarly enclosure, may inactivate Homeopathic remedies.

Another thing I like to recommend in never to touch Homeopathically prepared pellets with one's fingers. The sweat, fatty acids and dirt present in the hands may inactivate a remedy.

Camphor can rapidly inactivate Homeopathic remedies. This warning may be obsolete in some instances, though.

In the old days, camphor was kept at home, in the form of large crystals. People, particularly children and adolescents, would carry these large crystals hanging from a string around their neck, for purposes such as warding off diseases and diminishing libido.

Nowadays, one can find only traces of camphor in stuffs like shaving cream.

And I don't believe that whatever insignificant amount of camphor may volatilize from the container, or from the skin once applied, may pose any risk to the stability and efficacy of Homeopathic remedies.

The Homeopathic preparation of substances of diverse origin may release interesting and hitherto hidden properties.

Some, that did not originally have any therapeutic effect whatsoever in their natural state, such as table salt *(Natrum Muriaticum)*, the windflower *(Pulsatilla Nigricans)*, or cuttlefish ink *(Sepia)* among many others, become wonderful remedies.

Extremely powerful and beneficial remedies are obtained by Homeopathically preparing substances that are formidable poisons in their natural state, such as white arsenic *(Arsenicum Album)*, the deadly nightshade *(Belladona)*, the toad stool mushroom *(Agaricus Muscaricus)* or the poison of the Brazilian snake surucucú *(Lachesis Muta)*, among many others.

Also, an interesting reversal of effect may happen when some products are Homeopathically prepared.

For instance raw coffee *(Coffea Cruda)*, in its natural state, tends to keep people awake, happy and excited. When prepared Homeopathically, it helps happy and excited patients—particularly children—go to sleep.

Digitalis, used Allopathically to slow down failing hearts, and thus help them pump more effectively, accelerates heartbeats when Homeopathically prepared.

Ipeca, or *Ipecacuanha*, a South American plant, is used in its natural state as a powerful emetic, or substance used to induce vomiting. When prepared Homeopathically it eases, or makes disappear altogether the necessity to vomit; if the profile of the patient corresponds to that of the remedy.

Homeopathy also proffers the Homeopathic Physician a salutary lesson: there is nothing to fear in Nature.

And also that everything is good and helpful if one learns how to correctly prepare and use it.

In order to be Homeopathic, a remedy must

be prepared Homeopathically, that is, according to the guidelines described in this Chapter;

be administered usually *by mouth*;

be administered *one remedy at a time* (even if minutes apart, as in the instance of an acute disease);

and, if the patients bears a chronic disease, the remedy must be administered to the *totality of the disease-bearing patient;* that is, the remedy must be prescribed according to the results obtained in Provings and the toxicological changes found when material doses of the natural substance is used; which, in turn, means that the remedy should be chosen according to the principle of "like cures like"; i.e., the Physician should match the remedy with the *totality* of the Whole disease-bearing patient, in the case of chronic patients; in such a fashion that the symptoms of the patient correspond with, correlate to, and/or overlap, the symptoms found in the Proving of the Homeopathic remedy administered or in the toxicological effects. And that in the case of acute disease-bearing patients, the principle of "like cures like" is applied by matching the profile of the acute disease with that of the Homeopathic remedies.

Any remedy that does not fulfill *all* points above is *not* Homeopathic; or, at least, it is not being administered in a Homeopathic fashion.

All cats are animals.

From which it doesn't necessarily follow that all animals are cats—even if those other animals may show one, or some, or several, or even many of the characteristics found in cats.

In the same fashion, there are many preparations out there that may have originated in a natural substance, and that may have been succussed prior to being dispensed.

But they will not be Homeopathic unless they fulfill every one of the requisites described above.

Chapter 8

THE PROVINGS, AND THE HOMEOPATHIC REME-DIES' MODE OF ACTION.

THE PROVINGS

Pharmacological trials study Pharmaceutical drugs. Drugs are designed with the single purpose of destroying disease-syndromes through the principle of *contrary cures contrary*—and also to determine if the drugs under study are safe enough to administer to Human Beings.

The latter is necessary because most drugs act, no only on the disease-syndrome they have been created to eliminate, but also on every normal organ, including those of embryos and fetuses. Furthermore, most drugs are also *toxic* meaning that, beyond a certain dose, they can kill patients. Consequently, Pharmacological trials must study the efficacy, toxicity, side effects, teratogenesis (or ill effects in embryos and fetuses) and dosage levels of the drugs being tested.

Provings, on the other hand are concerned with the study of Homeopathically prepared products, whether those products are natural or manufactured.

These studies are done with the purpose of finding the usefulness of Homeopathically prepared products, according to the principle of *like cures like.* There is no need to study the safety of Homeopathically prepared substances because Homeopathic remedies have no side effects, no toxicity and no allergy-inducing capacity.

Provings are performed exclusively in *Whole healthy male and female human volunteers.*

The purpose of Provings is to imbalance healthy volunteers through the constant daily administration of a Homeopathically prepared substance. The imbalance induced in volunteers is manifested by changes that can be normal or pathological. The sum total of those changes—or *symptoms*—constitute the *profile* of the Homeopathically prepared substance under study.

Provings can also be done on *ill* volunteers, instead of on healthy ones. Here, however, as Dr. Hahnemann points out in § 142 of the 6t. Edition of his *Organon*, it would take a "master observer" to be able to discern between the symptoms elicited by the new remedy under study, and those caused by the active disease the ill volunteer is bearing. Which is the reason why Provings using ill volunteers have been left aside.

The changes or symptoms brought about in Provings are legion.

They range from cravings for sweets to a slump between 4 PM and 6 PM, to fear of thunderstorms. Or else nervousness, a feeling of oppression in the chest, acute and sharp abdominal pains, etc.; that is, the whole gamut of both *normal* and *abnormal* or *pathological* phenomena, as perceived by the prover.

Symptoms, then, can be defined as *anything different or unusual,* whether normal or pathological, that the healthy volunteer may experience during the Proving of any substance Homeopathically prepared. Symptoms elicited in Provings are carefully recorded, and configure the *profile* of the new Homeopathic remedy.

The remedy is ready to be used in patients once its profile is elucidated.

There are more than 3,000 substances that have been prepared Homeo-pathically and tested or proven in this fashion.

The remedy chosen to treat a patient bearing an *acute disease-syndrome* will be the one that, in Provings, has shown a profile similar to that found in the the organ or system that bears the acute disease-syndrome afflicting that patient. The remedy so chosen will direct the acute patient's Vital Force to-wards the organ or system that bears the acute disease-syndrome. Through its healing power, the Vital Force will regain a good grip on that organ or system and the disease-syndrome will usually vanish.

In the instance of *chronic patients,* the remedy chosen will be the one that, in its Proving, produced in healthy volunteers manifestations of overall imbalance similar to those found in the Whole chronic disease-bearing pa-tient. The Homeopathic remedy will act by means of directing the Vital Force towards the fulcrum, or axis, or hinge of the Whole chronic patient's imbalance. The healing power of the Vital Force will then bring the Whole chronic patient into balance. When balance is restored, the patient's Vital Force takes a firm hold on whatever organs were affected by the disease-syndrome/s afflicting the patient. The disease-syndrome/s ailing the chronic patient will often vanish as the consequence of this sequence of events.

In either case, and in order to successfully treat a patient, the profile of an acute disease-syndrome in acute patients, and that of a Whole chronic pa-tient, must match the profile of the Homeopathic remedy, as found in its Proving.

Sometimes, symptoms found in acute and chronic intoxications are also useful to select a remedy for acute diseases and for chronic patients.

Dr, Hahnemann carried out the first systematic set of Provings before the end of the 18th Century. He published the results in 1796, in his *Essay on a New Principle.*
Provings have been continued to this day on diverse substances, always following the method originally designed and utilized by Dr. Hahnemann.

In *Provings,* the Homeopathically prepared substance or product is generally used in Centesimal potencies.
In a Proving, the Homeopathically prepared product to be tested is administered *daily,*

- *by mouth,*
- at the *same potency,*
- to *healthy male and female human volunteers,*
- *until symptoms* (or changes) *appear in the volunteers who participate in the experiment.*

The Proving has to be discontinued immediately as soon as provers experiences changes or symptoms.

Symptoms will rapidly vanish if the Proving is stopped at that time. But if the Proving is continued beyond the appearance of symptoms, those symptoms may become permanent in the prover. This phenomenon is known as *engrafting.*
I remember in this context a very good friend of mine, one of the best Homeopathic Pharmacists I have ever met. He was one of the provers of *Histaminum,* or Homeopathically prepared histamine. A symptom of this particular remedy is heartburn. My friend did not stop the Proving when starting to notice heartburn. The heartburn has persisted ever since; and no treatment, Allopathic or Homeopathic, has been able to make it disappear.
Allow me to remind that this doesn't happen when the remedy is administered in *LM Plus* because LM Plus solutions are succussed prior to each daily take. Here, potency increases each time the remedy is succused. Therefore, no two consecutively succussed doses have the same potency. There can be no Proving if different potencies are used in successive days. Symptoms attributable to Provings cannot appear unless all daily doses have the same potency.

As an example, I would like now to briefly describe the Proving of *Lycopodium clavatum*, or the Homeopathic preparation of the spores of the club moss.

In their natural state, these spores have no effect whatsoever. In point of fact, extracts or preparations of the club moss are so inert that they are routinely used as excipients in Pharmaceutical preparations. An *excepient* is an inert substances used to bind active principles together, or to make pills, syrups and the like more palatable, or to add bulk, or to provide a particular color. An excipient have no therapeutic capacity whatsoever.

When the club moss is dynamized it becomes the remedy *Lycopodium clavatum.*

If administered every day at the same potency, volunteers will gradually start to feel inadequate, vulnerable and in need of protection; although they will tend to ignore these facts. Both vulnerability and need/denial of protection are at the very core of *Lycopodium's* profile.

Lycopodium provers will lock themselves into an armor to protect their vulnerability. There is nothing wrong with living inside plate armor, of course, provided that one knows when to use it and when to hang it in the closet. The problem with *Lycopodium* provers or patients is that they *identify themselves* with their plate armor and can never let it go.

Volunteers will do everything within their power to identify themselves with that shield. Everything inside their armor will be disregarded— including feelings. With feelings so carefully tucked away, volunteers will communicate with others through their cuirass. And so volunteers will appear to others as being articulate and intelligent, but also stiff, cold and distant.

The everyday maintenance of the shield consumes a lot of Vital Force. The Vital Force needed for these purposes will perforce have to be diverted from the maintenance of healthy organs and tissues. Those organs and tissues will become devitalized. This devitalization results in much of *Lycopodium's* pathology.

Stiffness will alienate volunteers, and enhance their feelings of inadequacy. Which in turn will erode their self-esteem and -confidence still further and increase their fear of failure. Inability to unbend and to communicate freely, low self-esteem and fear of failure will trigger anxiety, distrust and the need to control others.

In the workplace, volunteers will notice that they cannot tolerate contradiction and that they must control others and tell them exactly what to do. Trust in co-workers will vanish. Lack of self-confidence will stifle creativity and originality. Provers will become scheming and very competitive. They will become subservient with their superiors and despotic with their subordinates.

Provers will need to please in order to fit. They will become conformists and attempt to live up to the Joneses. Volunteers will find it increasingly difficult to commit themselves[34]—and it is impossible to have a satisfactory sexual life without commitment. Both males and female volunteers will experience problems in this sphere, ranging all the way from episodes of dryness and impotence to anorgasmia. Women provers may also suffer all kinds of menstrual troubles.

They will become very shy when having to face or to talk with others, or when discussing ideas or plans. Every public presentation will be preceded by a lot of suffering, stress, abdominal symptoms and not infrequently diarrhea.

And they will be very embarrassed when they find themselves weeping uncontrollably whenever they are thanked.

Provers may become constipated. They will also crave sweets and hot drinks and foodstuffs. They will bloat easily and have flatulence in the least convenient moments. Their right side will be affected more often than the left. They will experience a slump from 4 to 8 in the evening and may develop pain in their kidneys, especially in the right one. They may find a reddish deposit when they urinate. These among many, many other changes are brought about when the club moss is diluted and shaken and administered, every day, to healthy volunteers.

Dr. Hahnemann considered *Lycopodium* responsible for over 1,000 symptoms. In Dr. Kent's Repertory, *Lycopodium* is found opposite 463 symptoms, many pathological.

Let us suppose that a psoric patient goes to see a Homeopathic Physician, and that the *profile* of that particular patient is similar to that described above, in the Proving of *Lycopodium Clavatum*.

If this is the case, the Doctor will prescribe *Lycopodium,* and the result of the treatment will likely be a resounding success.

Homeopathic remedies are to be found in the *Materia Medica Homeopathica* where the remedies, followed by a description of their profiles, are listed alphabetically.

---

[34] Characteristically, one has to twist *Lycopodium*'s arm until it hurts to obtain a very reluctant "perhaps".

To sum up,

Through *Provings,* Homeopathic Physicians learn about the range of usefulness of each of the remedies. Provings are done only in Humans, never in animals or unicellular organisms.

To do a Proving, healthy male and female Human volunteers take a Homeopathically prepared product or substance by mouth, every day, until they notice the appearance of changes, normal or pathological. These changes, known as *"symptoms",* are carefully recorded.

The s*ymptoms* will configure the *profile* of the Homeopathically prepared substance being proven or tested in those healthy Human volunteers.

Then, the remedy so tested will be administered to patients whose profile corresponds to that of the remedy, according to the principle of *like cures like.*

The methodology used in Provings is minutely described in § 121-148 of the 6th. Edition of Dr. Hahnemann's *Organon.*

THE HOMEOPATHIC REMEDIES' MODE OF ACTION

Homeopathic remedies act according to the principle of *like cures like.*
Allopathic drugs act according to the principle those contrary cures *contrary.*

Drugs are molecules.
Allopathy explains the mode of action of drugs through the lock and key theory.
According to it, the tri-dimensional structure of a drug's molecule must fit exactly that of a sub-cellular live molecule (the *receptor)* like a key fits into a lock. When coupling happens, the drug either stimulates or inhibits the subcellular molecule with which it interacts.
Drug receptors are located in practically all cells. Results of drug-receptor interaction vary according to where the receptor is located. If located in the organ or structure in need to be treated, the stimulation or inhibition of the receptor will bring about in be the desired therapeutic effect; but results will be unpleasant or downright dangerous when receptors are located in organs and tissues other than those in need of treatment. We call unfavorable effects *toxicity* and *side effects,* and *teratogenesis* when

favorable effects *toxicity* and *side effects,* and *teratogenesis* when receptors are in cells of embryos and fetuses.

This lock-and-key theory has been repeatedly verified although, as far as I know, it has never been ascertained at a molecular level.

Provings uncover the profile of a new Homeopathic remedy.

We have a very clear profile of the remedy if the Proving has been thorough. Remedies thoroughly proven are called *Polychrests.* If, on the other hand, the remedy has not been thoroughly proven, we only have partial knowledge regarding its profile. We call these remedies *small remedies.*

Provings are not the only source of knowledge regarding Homeopathic remedies. One can learn about the remedy's profile by studying intoxications with material doses of the substance the remedy is made of, and also by clinical observations.

For instance, there are some clinical pictures that imitate almost to perfection the acute intoxication of white arsenic. The therapeutic results are usually excellent when those patients receive *Arsenicum album,* that is, dynamized white arsenic. Also, results of the Proving of *Chlorum* are remarkably similar to changes found in chlorine workers chronically intoxicated with this gas[35].

Clinical observations describe some characteristics often observed in patients who responded to a Homeopathic remedy. For instance, it has been frequently noticed that patients who have responded to *Pulsatilla nigricans* tend to be blonde women who weep easily, that patient who have responded to *Arsenicum album* tend to show alternations of symptoms, that patients who have had a favorable response to *Lycopodium clavatum tend* to be thin and dark and to a wrinkled forehead, etc. None of these symptoms can be brought about in Provings. No dark haired male prover of *Pulsatilla nigricans,* for instance, has become female and blonde during a Proving.

There is still another source of knowledge. It is based on certain characteristics of the remedy, not found on Provings, acute intoxications or clinical observations. For instance, it has been found that the sap of *Chelidonium majus* is as yellow and as bitter as gall. Consequently, *Chelidonium* has been used since antiquity for the treatment of liver problems. *Sepia* (the ink of the cuttlefish) patients tend to hide their true feelings in the same fashion that the cuttlefish hides behind its ink. *Lac felinum* patients are said to be catty in

---

[35] Chirila M., Badulici S., Freilich A., Bica N. *Occupational pathogenesis of chlorine.* Brit. J. Hom. 83: 142-147, 1994.

their demeanor, etc. In the case of *Chelidonium,* the analogy between its sap and bile is valid as far as therapeutic results. *Chelidonium* is an excellent hepatic remedy, both in material doses and when Homeopathically prepared. In some other remedies, though, this form of analogy is valid only for mne-motechnical purposes. And, in most others, it has no usefulness at all.

As far as I am concerned, I place the greatest confidence in the profile of a remedy as provided by Provings. In a second place, I trust results provided by the study of intoxications with material doses and last—and also very, very least—on conclusions of clinical observations.

I find it very difficult to assign credibility to the conclusion provided by comparing certain characteristics of the remedy with therapeutic applica-tions, with the exception of *Chelidonium.*

After doing a thorough Homeopathic History—or after a good *case tak-ing,* as some workers are fond of calling the same thing—the Doctor will have a fairly clear idea of what the profile of the patient is.

Then, the Doctor will match the profile of the patient with that of Ho-meopathic remedies, till he or she finds a remedy that covers all, or at least a part, of the patient's profile.

If the remedy covers all of the patient's profile, then we will call that remedy the patient's *simillimum.* Its therapeutic results tend to be rapid and spectacular.

If the remedy covers only part of the patient's profile, what we will have is a *similar* remedy. Its therapeutic results will be partial and variable. Some of the patient's symptoms are bound to remain after treatment with a similar. So the Doctor has to find another remedy—that is, another similar—for the symptoms that remain, and then another and another, until finally all or most of the patient's pathological symptoms have disappeared.

As mentioned and described above, in Homeopathy patients can be di-vided into *acute* and *chronic.*

For the purposes of the paragraph that follows, let me divide diseases into *natural* and *artificial,* instead of into acute and chronic.

Within this context, *natural diseases* are those that appear in patients as the consequence of some acute cause in acute patients, or else as the conse-quence of chronic imbalance in chronic patients.

Within this context also, *artificial diseases* are caused by a successful Homeopathic treatment.

Regarding how Homeopathy works, Dr. Hahnemann considered that a natural disease (that is, the disease afflicting the patient) can be eliminated. He states that this end can be achieved through the induction of a *stronger artificial disease caused by a Homeopathic remedy,* if and when that remedy, in Provings, *produces symptoms similar to those of the natural disease* that afflicts the patient.

The artificial disease, being more powerful than the natural one, *displaces* the natural disease ailing the patient. Once displaced, the natural disease disappears because it has yielded its hold on the patient to that of the stronger artificial disease brought about by the Homeopathic remedy. Then, the artificial disease is eliminated by the simple expedient of discontinuing the Homeopathic treatment (Hahnemann S., *Organon*, 6th. Edition. § 26, 34 and others).

In acute patients, the acute natural disease would be first displaced by the stronger and similar disease caused by the administration of the Homeopathic remedy (the therapeutic disease mentioned here happens only after the administration of the patient's *simillimum* or after the administration of a succession of *similars).* The stronger disease elicited by the remedy is then eliminated when the Homeopathic treatment is suspended.

The disappearance of both diseases allows the patient's Vital Force to regain its hold in the formerly diseased area.

A chronic patient's natural disease is the consequence or manifestation of his or her overall imbalance. In chronic patients, then, the stronger artificial disease elicited or induced by a Homeopathic remedy (either the patient's *simillimum* or a succession of the patient's *similars)* displaces the patient's weaker chronic disease or, what is the same thing, the patient's overall imbalance. Then, the artificial imbalance or chronic disease caused by the Homeopathic remedy is eliminated by simply discontinuing its administration. The elimination of the artificial disease induced by the *simillimum* or the succession of *similars* allows the Vital Force to gain a firm hold in the Whole former chronic patient. This new and wonderful hold allows him or her to gain balance and to blossom into health. And, through health, into harmony with him or herself and everything and everybody that surrounds the now healthy person.

Chapter 9

THE REPERTORIES

The only purpose of the Repertories, their only reason to be, *is to assist Homeopathic Physicians in their search of the correct remedy with which to treat each individual patient.*

Repertories are books, and more recently computer software, designed with the purpose of assisting Homeopathic Practitioners to find the correct Homeopathic remedy/ies for their patients.

In Materia Medicæ, as we will see in Chapter 11, *remedies* are listed first.

In Repertories, instead, symptoms are listed first. Opposite each Repertory symptom are all the remedies known to elicit that symptom in Provings, or when taken in large enough material doses to cause intoxications, or else when a remedy is found associated with that particular symptom in certain clinical settings or circumstances.

Repertories are as old as Homeopathy. They exist because no Human mind can remember *all* the symptoms brought about by every remedy—nor, for that matter, all the remedies that produce or modify each individual symptom.

In everyday Homeopathic practice, the Homeopathic Practitioner first harvests each patient's symptoms through the obtention of the Homeopathic History. Then, the Practitioner will go to the Repertory and look there for the remedies that correspond to the chronic patient's symptoms—or, in acute patients, to the symptoms of the disease-syndrome that patient is bearing.

Afterwards, the Doctor will go the Materia Medica, and study there each of the remedies that, according to the Repertory, correspond to the patient's symptoms. The purpose here is to find *the single remedy* that corresponds more closely to the symptoms found in the Homeopathic History.

Finally, the Practitioner will prescribe or dispense the remedy that, according to the Materia Medica, has a profile that corresponds most closely to the profile of the Whole chronic patient, or to the acute patient's disease-syndrome.

There are many Repertories.

Among those written in English, the most widely used is undoubtedly that designed and written by Dr. John T. Kent.

Jose Miguel Mullen, M.D.

I shall first describe Dr. Kent's Repertory in some detail, and then I briefly others, written in English, that I consider of importance.

KENT'S REPERTORY.-

It is very complete.
Symptoms can be found with little difficulty.
It has gone through several editions, that have been printed by several editorial houses in many languages.

In most editions, the *first part* has a Preface, which contains valuable hints regarding its use. Afterwards there is a list of remedies' abbreviations arranged alphabetically. Opposite each abbreviation is the full name of the remedy it corresponds to.

Some Editions have a Postface with sections covering affinities, remedies that affect diverse parts of the body and relationships between remedies, plus a word index of symptoms and the page where they can be found.
Throughout the Repertory, only the abbreviated name of each remedy will be shown opposite each symptom.

The *second part* of the Repertory consists of *sections*.
The sections are

- **Mind**   page 1,
- **Vertigo**   page 96,
- **Head**   page 107,
- **Eye**   page 235,
- **Vision**   page 271,
- **Ear**   page 285,
- **Hearing**   page 321,
- **Nose**   page 324,
- **Face**   page 355,
- **Mouth**   page 397,
- **Teeth**   page 430,
- **Throat**   page 448,
- **External Throat** page 471,
- **Stomach**   page 476,
- **Abdomen**   page 541,
- **Rectum**   page 606,

Each *section* encompasses the symptoms that correspond to that particular organ or system. For instance, the section of Sleep, in page 1234, contains the symptoms anxious, bad, during chill, comatose, during convulsions, etc.

After each symptom there is a long list of factors that can *modify*—or rather *modalize*— it.

Modalities are characteristics or peculiarities that transform vague and general symptoms into an individual patient's own live and personal symptoms.

Vague and general symptoms such as "headache", "otitis", "constipation", etc. suffice for Allopathic prescribing. This is so because Allopathy deals with disease-syndromes, that is, with what afflicts *all* patients. Individual characteristics have only nuisance value in Scientific Medicine, for the most part.

In Homeopathy, instead, we deal with one Whole disease-bearing patient at a time. We are interested in knowing how each individual patient lives his or her symptoms, how those symptoms interact with the patient's

Wholeness—more precisely, how those symptoms *modify* or *alter* each patient's individual Wholeness.

Each modalized symptom is an essential piece in the jigsaw puzzle that shows, when completed, the individual profile of the unique disease-bearing Human Being we are assisting.

In Homeopathy, then, what we take into consideration and treat is either the totality of an acute disease in a well-balanced patient, or else the totality of a chronic patient. The best way to reach these totalities is via a thorough modalization of the patient's symptoms, and then through a careful consideration of those modalized symptoms.

A non-modalized symptom, no matter how dazzling or worrisome, is too impersonal, too general. It can apply to thousands of patients. It has no way of fitting into the unique, Whole live jig-saw puzzle we are trying to understand, and eventually treat Homeopathically.

These indispensable modalities are in the Repertory, immediately after each one of the symptoms, in the following order,

- The first modality listed is that of *time;* that is, when does that symptom happen. This modality is listed in chronological order.
- The second modality deals with what causes the symptom or triggers it. Modalities here are listed in alphabetical order.
- The third modality is what the symptom is associated with, also in alphabetical order; and whether that modality worsens or ameliorates the symptom.
- The fourth modality deals with where the symptom does extend or radiates to.
- The fifth modality deals with where the symptom is located. Each location is followed by the above mentioned four modalities. Sometimes here the first modality is one of laterality, whether right or left.
- In very extensive symptoms such as in Section head, symptom pain (that ranges from pages 132 to 221), the distribution is somewhat different. There are sub-sections with the characteristics of the symptom, such as boring pain, burning pain, bursting pain etc., also in alphabetical order. Each of these sub-sections then scrolls along the modalities bulleted above.
- In the section devoted to **Generalities** (pages 1341 to 1423), much of what is listed are modalities that affect the Whole Human Being.

Most symptoms and modalities are written in a language patients would use to describe them, rather than in Medical jargon. Which doesn't necessarily mean that Medical terms are totally excluded. In Kent's Repertory one can find words like nevi, epistaxis, etc.

Archaisms can also be found here and there (sordes, mania-a-potu, etc.)

As mentioned above, remedies are listed in alphabetical order opposite the symptom they produce or act upon.

Remedies are printed in three different typesetting, according to their relative importance. Plain style, also called grade 1; *Italic* style, also called *grade 2;* and **Boldface** style, also called **grade 3.**

PLAIN STYLE. - Also called grade 1. It includes

Remedies that have OCCASIONALLY and INFREQUENTLY produced, in *Provings*, the symptoms they are opposite to in the Repertory.

Toxic effects found, OCCASIONALLY and INFREQUENTLY, in persons who took large material doses of the natural product from which the Homeopathic remedy was prepared.

In *clinical settings*, changes or characteristics found in PATIENTS WHO HAVE THE PROFILE OF THE REMEDY; and who have shown, OCCASIONALLY and INFREQUENTLY, characteristics and/or changes not observed in the Provings or intoxicated patients. These remedies have been found to OCCASIONALLY and UNFREQUENTLY cure the symptom they are opposite to in the Repertory, in patients WHOSE PROFILE MATCHES THE PROFILE OF THAT PARTICULAR REMEDY.

Because of all of the above, remedies with grade 1, of printed in plain style, have to be contemplated with caution, even hesitation, when considering their potential usefulness in a particular patient.

ITALIC STYLE.- Also called *grade 2*, and it includes

Remedies that have FREQUENTLY produced, in the *Provings*, the symptom they are opposite to in the Repertory.

Toxic effects that have FREQUENTLY been found in persons who took large enough material doses of the natural product from which the Homeopathic remedy was prepared.

101

Jose Miguel Mullen, M.D.

In *clinical settings*, changes found in PATIENTS WHO HAVE THE PROFILE OF THE REMEDY; and whom have FREQUENTLY shown characteristics and/or changes not observed in Provings or intoxications.

These remedies have been found to FREQUENTLY cure the symptom they are opposite to in the Repertory, in patients WHOSE PROFILE MATCHES THE PROFILE OF THAT PARTICULAR REMEDY.

BOLDFACE STYLE.- Also called **grade 3**. It includes

Remedies that have ALWAYS, or ALMOST ALWAYS produced, in the *Provings*, the symptom they are opposite to in the Repertory.

Toxic effects found ALWAYS or ALMOST ALWAYS in persons who took large enough material doses of the natural product from which the Homeopathic remedy was prepared.

In *clinical settings*, changes found ALWAYS or ALMOST ALWAYS in PATIENTS WHO HAVE THE PROFILE OF THE REMEDY; and who have shown ALWAYS OR ALMOST ALWAYS characteristics and/or changes not observed in the Provings or intoxications.

These remedies have been found to ALWAYS or ALMOST ALWAYS cure the symptom they are opposite to in the Repertory, in patients WHOSE PROFILE MATCHES THE PROFILE OF THAT PARTICULAR REMEDY.

This capacity to cure requires some elaboration.
Not all symptoms listed in the Repertory are necessarily pathological, and consequently in need of being cured.
Opposite "Sympathetic" (page 86), for instance, **Phosphorus** appears with **3**. What the **3**, or **boldface**, means here is that Phosphorus, in the Provings, ALWAYS, or ALMOST ALWAYS, made the prover feel sympathetic.
Phosphoric acid and **Veratrum album** appear with **3** opposite craving for fruits (page 485). This means that provers of Phosphoric Acid or Veratrum Album developed ALWAYS, or ALMOST ALWAYS, a craving for fruits during Provings.

In no way this is supposed to mean that treatment with Phosphorus will make sympathy disappear in the treated patients, or that Phosphoric Acid or

102

Veratrum Album will eliminate the desire for fruits in patients whose profiles they match.

Pathological symptoms will indeed be frequently cured by remedies with **2** or **3** opposite them in the Repertory, BUT *ONLY IF AND WHEN* THE PROFILE OF THE WHOLE CHRONIC PATIENT, or OF THE WHOLE ACUTE DISEASE, MATCHES THAT OF THE REMEDY WITH **2** or **3**.

Take for instance Abdomen, Distention, eating, after (One SYMPTOM "Distention", two MODALITIES "eating" and "after"), in page 545.

This modalized symptom has six remedies with grade **3**, or in **boldface**, facing it in the Repertory: **Carbo Vegetabilis**, **China**, **Kali Carbonicum**, **Lycopodium**, **Nux Vomica** and **Sulfur**.

Say that a patient has a profile that matches that of Lycopodium. This will mean that, of the six remedies listed with **3** opposite Abdomen, distention, eating, after, *only Lycopodium will cure his or her distention after eating* (in all likelihood, as well as most if not all other symptoms— provided that those symptoms are not the consequence of hormonal insufficiency, or are produced a malignant tumor or by a surgical disease). None of the other five remedies will help this Lycopodium patient, even if all have grade **3**, and have consequently demonstrated capacity of curing the symptom Abdomen, distention, eating, after.

This is so *because none of the other five remedies exhibit a profile that can match that of our patient.* Only Lycopodium does match, and therefore can cure here—even if distention after eating appears in all, or in almost all of the provers of Carbo Vegetabilis, China, Kali Carbonicum, Nux Vomica and Sulfur.

For all intents and purposes, the same applies to remedies with *grade 2*, as far as their capacity to produce, and/or cure, any particular pathological symptom.

In other words, the main thing here, as everywhere else in Homeopathy, is how well the profile of a remedy and that of a chronic patient match, or how good is the match between the profile of a patient's acute disease and that of the corresponding remedy.

Adequate matching is what ultimately brings therapeutic success. To find a particular remedy opposite a symptom—or two, or three, or more—is indeed important. The grade of the remedy is important, too. *But the essential thing here is how closely the profile of the remedy matches that of the chronic patient or of the acute disease.*

BOERICKE'S REPERTORY.-

It is a jewel of a Repertory, at the end of a volume that is small and easy to carry.

This Repertory, that is the appendix of the Materia Medica, has sections that are not found in Kent's, such as Circulatory and Nervous Systems, and disease-syndromes.

According to their relative importance, in regards to their effect on the symptom they are opposite to in the Repertory, remedies are printed in plain or *italic* typesetting.

BENNINGHAUSEN'S REPERTORY.-

One of the oldest. Important to consult. It is mainly concerned with modalities.

According to their relative importance, remedies are printed in plain, *italics*, **bold** and CAPITAL typesetting.

KNERR'S REPERTORY.-

It clearly indicates which symptoms come from Provings and which from other sources. No other Repertory has this kind of information, to my knowledge.

Sections are not easy to find. The volume has no thumb index.

Remedies opposite symptoms are classified as follows, according to their relative importance: |, those in which usefulness has been only occasionally confirmed; | |, those in which usefulness has been more frequently confirmed; |, those in which usefulness has been frequently verified; and | |, those in which usefulness has been repeatedly verified.

In this Repertory, "θ" stands for remedies found effective in pathological conditions; a vertical "..." for remedies found useful by practitioners of the "Old School", as early Homeopathic Physicians would all their Allopathic colleagues; "π" for remedies found to be effective in the sick only; and ☞, for cross-reference to related symptoms.

Here, symptoms coming from Provings are mainly the result of the observations, experience and experimentation of Dr. Constantine Hering, the Father of American Homeopathy. Dr. Hering was Dr. Knerr's father-in-law.

This Repertory has sections on Pregnancy, Parturition, Lactation, Tissues, Stages of Life and Constitution; absent in Kent's.

One of its most useful features is that it gives a short description regarding how each remedy acts on to the symptom is opposed to; instead of only mentioning the remedy. It is the only Repertory to do this, as far as I know.

MIXED OR COMBINED REPERTORIES.-

Where symptoms and remedies, as observed *by different authors*, are placed together in the same Repertory.

Barthel's, the Synthetic Repertory and computer software Repertories are good examples of mixed Repertories.

BARTHEL'S REPERTORY.—

It has 3 volumes, the third written by Dr. Klunker.

This Repertory is incomplete, because the first two volumes deal with Mental Symptoms and Generalities, and the third with Sleep, Dreams and Sexuality.

According to their relative importance, remedies are printed in plain, **bold** and **CAPITAL BOLD** typesetting.

I feel that this Repertory is important because, here again, some of its symptoms and their modalities do not appear in Kent's.

The **SYNTHETIC** Repertory is very complete.

It incorporates information obtained by many Homeopaths.

From now on, I am going to refer exclusively to **KENT'S REPERTORY**, unless specifically stated otherwise.

Most of the information present in Repertories has been obtained from the *Provings* of diverse remedies.

Toxicology is another important source of information, both in its acute and chronic form.

Take for example the anxiety, fear of death, burning in the abdomen, and terrible vomiting and diarrhea characteristic of the acute intoxication with white arsenic. Or the extreme restlessness, anxiety, high fever, redness of features and mucosas, dilatation of the pupils and dryness of the mouth found in the acute intoxication with Belladona or deadly nightshade.

Toxic substances that produce intoxications are found in Repertories opposite the symptoms they produce—but with their Homeopathic name. White arsenic will appear as Arsenicum album opposite the symptoms anxiety, fear of death, burning in abdomen, etc.; the deadly nightshade will appear as Belladona opposite the symptoms extreme restlessness and anxiety, high fever, etc.

In chronically intoxicated people, the changes found are often strikingly similar, if not actually identical to, symptoms found in the Provings.

This overlapping is probably the reason why Repertories have so few symptoms brought about by chronic intoxications.

A third source of information is clinical manifestations that cannot be brought about in the studies described above, but that can be observed in patients who have responded to treatment. Take for instance Pulsatilla nigricans, that appears to be very effective in blonde females.

A fourth source is the so-called *cured symptoms*—of which more below.

Regarding *Keynotes.*

A keynote is a symptom opposite either one, or up to only a very few remedies.

By the same token, a *keynote remedy* is either the only remedy, or one of very few remedies opposite a particular symptom. Take for instance the horsey odor of the urine of patients whose profile matches that of Nitricum acidum, the worsening by movement of Bryonia alba, or the improvement by bending backwards of Dioscorea villosa.

There are those who believe that the horse-like odor of the urine points unequivocally to Nitric acid, worsening by movement to Bryonia and improvement by bending backwards to Dioscorea; meaning that a patient whose urine smells like that of a horse is for certain Nitric acid, and that another one who is worse by movement Bryonia, and so on and so forth.

The keynote remedy only indicates that the remedy of a particular patient is *likely* to be Nitric acid, or Bryonia, or whatever. This fact, however, cannot be validated unless the *profile of the whole patient*, or of the *whole acute disease*, points *unequivocally* towards that of Nitric acid, or Bryonia, or whatever other Homeopathic remedy.

Treatments based on keynotes may not always be of help. They may even backfire on occasion.

Take for instance the following sequence of symptoms: pain at rest → increase of pain as the patient starts moving → easing of the pain as movement persists. This sequence is the keynote of the remedy Rhus Toxicodendrum or poison ivy—Rhus tox for short.

Yet, there are many patients who have this sequence of symptoms but *do not* respond to Rhus Tox. Simply because Rhus Tox does not coincide with the profile of the acute disease or of the Whole patient—even if the patient displays this particular sequence of symptoms.

Furthermore keynotes are often *local* symptoms.

Injudiciously used, keynotes may cure a local symptom, but without bringing a Whole psoric patient into balance.

Worse yet, they may well produce a suppression. The local symptom may vanish under keynote treatment. And, after some time, a new symptom or disease-syndrome may appear in a deeper, more vital organ or structure.

The injudicious administration of a local remedy under these circumstances, then, may well revert the progress towards health, and turn it into a plunge toward destruction.

Keynotes are very important. They are invaluable when the Doctor is undecided between a few remedies and only one is a keynote.

But, whenever possible, they should not be used as the sole basis of a Homeopathic diagnosis or treatment—what is known as *keynote prescribing.*

Suppression may well follow.

This said, I must also add that, on occasion, a Homeopathic Physician has no choice but to do keynote prescribing. This form of prescribing becomes particularly unavoidable when contemplating the administration of a small (or poorly studied) remedy that, by definition, has very few symptoms, most of which tend to be keynotes.

Take a 25 year old male patient I once saw, with severe hives. The keynote here was that he repeatedly dreamt of being bitten by snakes. The only remedy opposite to this very unusual dream in Kent's Repertory is *Bovista* (Sleep, dreams, snakes, of being bitten by). I prescribed it and the patient responded beautifully.

Or take that 48-year-old lady, suffering from serious allergies and elevated cholesterol levels, who had responded only partially to the administration of several consecutive Polychrests (that is, well known and thoroughly studied remedies). One of her symptoms was that her menstrual flow would stop when taking a bath. This keynote I found in the first volume of Prof. Dr. Bernardo Vijnovsky's "Tratado de Materia Médica Homeopática", under the remedy *Ætusa cynapium.* This patient responded very well to treatment.

Allow me to mention again that there are three sources to evaluate Homeopathic remedies: Provings, acute intoxications, and clinical observations.

Allow me also to remark that Provings and acute intoxications are the only genuine sources of information. Clinical observations are not quite as reliable because, among other things, they may produce erroneous interpretations—as the so-called *cured symptoms* generally do.

I shall now describe *cured symptoms* in some detail—and explain why I find them so misleading.

Homeopathic Physicians use Repertories to find remedies capable of curing an array of symptoms that, as disease-syndromes, afflict their patients. These remedies are able to produce those symptoms, either in Provings or in acute intoxications.

But also in Repertories there are remedies that have *not* been found neither in Provings nor in acute intoxications, and that consequently are unable to cure those symptoms. The unholy alliance between these remedies and the symptoms they don't cure is called *cured symptoms.*

As mentioned in the beginning of this Chapter, Repertories are tools that exist for the single purpose of assisting Doctors in their search for the correct remedy/ies for their patients.

First the Doctor obtains the patient's symptoms through the Homeopathic History. Then he or she modalizes the symptoms obtained, to finally reach the profile of the acute disease or that of the patient. The Doctor will afterwards compare the profile so obtained with that of Homeopathic remedies by means of using the Repertory.

Finally, the Doctor will choose a remedy that has a profile that matches the profile of the patient, or of the patient's acute disease. The end result is to find the remedy that may be able either to cure the patient's acute disease, or else to bring about balance in a Whole chronic patient.

For the purpose of understanding the so-called *cured symptoms*, let me consider as an example the modalized symptom—or *rubric*—Cough, dry, night, lying aggravates, found in page 787 of Kent's Repertory. By that modalized symptom one finds the following remedies: *Conium, Hyosciamus,* Kali bromatum, Laurocerasus, Oleum jecoris aselli, *Phytolacca, Pulsatilla,* **Sulphur** and Zincum.

Sepia is not here. Sepia, or cuttlefish ink, is not toxic, so there are no toxicity symptoms of Sepia in Repertories nor in Materia Medicæ. Sepia has not produced this symptom in Provings, either. Sepia, therefore, cannot cure the modalized symptom cough, dry night, lying aggravates.

Let me show now how Sepia can slither into this rubric as a cured symptom, and mislead Doctors into prescribing it.

Say that a psoric patient, an adult male, goes to see Doctor # 1 with a variety of symptoms. Among those symptoms, he complaints of a dry cough that worsens at night when the patient lies down.

Sepia happens to be this patient's *simillimum*. It will therefore straighten the fulcrum of the Whole patient's imbalance and attune his or her Vital Force. Then the healing power of the patient's Vital Force will cure *all* of the patient's symptoms, including his dry cough worse when lying down at night—even if this modality of cough has never been found in the Provings of Sepia.

Let us now suppose that another psoric patient, this time a woman, visits Doctor # 1. She is suffering from many symptoms, among them dry cough that worsens when lying down at night.

Sepia is also her *simillimum*.

All her symptoms disappear with Sepia, including her cough.

Let us now suppose that several other patients, in all of whom Sepia is their *simillimum*, all with dry cough that becomes worse at night when lying down, go to see Doctor # 1. All patients are cured of all their symptoms with Sepia, including the cough.

Doctor # 1, impressed with these results, notices that Sepia is nowhere to be found opposite the rubric Cough, dry, night, lying aggravates, in page 787 of Dr. Kent's Repertory. Doctor # 1 is stupefied at this glaring omission. Hasn't he or she seen how patients with dry cough, worse when lying down at night, were cured with Sepia again and again?

Unbeknownst to Doctor # 1—whose knowledge and understanding of Homeopathy is undoubtedly a bit sketchy—Sepia has *never* produced dry cough that worsens when lying down at night in Provings, which is the reason why Sepia is not in the Repertory opposite the symptom. Doctor # 1's psoric patients were cured because Sepia, being the patients' *simillimum*, brought about balance or attunement of their respective Vital Forces, and consequently disappearance of *all of the patients' symptoms;* whether brought up by Sepia or not in Provings.

Doctor # 1, backed by his brilliant therapeutic results, adds Sepia, with grade 1 (or perhaps, Goodness forbid! **2** or even **3**), to the remedies opposite Cough, dry, night, lying aggravates.

From now on there is going to be a new *cured symptom* in the Repertory. Sepia will be found after the symptom "Cough, dry, night, lying aggravates", and therefore will be considered as capable of curing this modality of cough.

And so, if Sepia is there, not only Doctor # 1, but also all Homeopathic Physicians will be deceived into believing that Sepia is capable of curing dry cough, night, lying aggravates.

Enter Doctor # 2.

Doctor # 2 sees an acute patient who complaints of cough that is dry and worse at night, when the patient lies down. Doctor # 2 goes to the Repertory and sees Sepia opposite to this modalized symptom.

He prescribes Sepia to his patient and, of course, nothing happens.

Enter Doctor # 3.

He studies a psoric male patient. This particular patient is complaining of dry cough that becomes worse at night when lying down, among other symptoms.

Doctor # 3 is undecided as to what remedy to use. The patient's profile is, in principle, compatible with several remedies, among them perhaps Sepia, with many question marks.

So Doctor # 3 goes to the Repertory and sees Sepia there, opposite to Cough, dry, lying aggravates, hopefully only with grade 1. This information tilts the scales, and Doctor # 3 prescribes Sepia to the patient—a*nd nothing happens!*

The patient continues complaining of all his symptoms, including his dry cough, worse at night when lying down. Treatment with Sepia has been a failure.

These treatments failed because the profile of the acute disease, and that of the chronic patient did not correspond to that of Sepia.

Consequently, both in the acute disease and in the psoric patient, Sepia couldn't bring about balance, nor could it attune the Vital Force with the Wholeness of the patient. Nor make pathological symptoms—among them this annoying cough—disappear.

Doctors # 2 and # 3 were misled into treating their patients with Sepia because they found the remedy in the Repertory *vis-à-vis* the modalized cough symptom and considered that, if it was there, it was because it could cause this symptom in Provings, and therefore cure it.

The bottom line is that Doctors # 2 and # 3 were misled into prescribing a useless remedy due to the totally needless addition to the Repertory of a *cured symptom;* an addition that was the consequence of an injudicious interpretation of a clinical observation.

Most remedies that produce cured symptoms are dumped in Repertories with grade 1—which is a good reason to be weary of remedies that appear with grade 1 in the Repertories.

The use of the Repertory is absolutely essential for the work of a Homeopathic Physician.

Consequently, every Homeopathic Physician should become thoroughly familiar with his or her Repertory. It takes time, though.

It is strongly recommended to read at least one page of the Repertory every day.

Very often, a bit of leafing back and forth, at the end of the patient's visit is all that is needed to find the correct remedy.

This happens when the Doctor has some idea of what remedies may be useful for the patient—or his or her acute disease—and all that is needed is to narrow the choice to a few remedies, or to a single one.

There are instances, however, when the Doctor has to rely exclusively on the Repertory to reach the diagnosis.

To reach a Homeopathic diagnosis in this fashion is called *repertorization.*

A good History and Physical Examination are the first indispensable steps for a successful Repertorization.

During the patient's visit, the Homeopathic Physician finds him or herself jotting down a lot of symptoms as the patients speaks. Then, through questioning, knowledge and intuition, the Doctor will *modalize* those symptoms, i.e., will *individualize* those symptoms into the patient as much as possible.

Only then, after symptoms are modalized, will the patient's data be ready for repertorization.

Repertorization is different in acute diseases and in chronic patients.

In acute diseases, *all* modalized symptoms are useful to reach a diagnosis/treatment.

In psoric patients, the Doctor selects the symptoms that are most important and significant for each particular patient.

This process is called *Hierarchization of the symptoms.*

As a general rule, the most important symptoms are those the patient proffers spontaneously, without being prodded or questioned. Equally as important are the *strange, rare and peculiar* symptoms, i.e., those unique, or almost unique to our patient (Hahnemann S., *Organon*, 6th. Edition. § 153).

These symptoms are followed, in order of importance, by the *Mentals* (listed under "Mind" in Kent's Repertory, pages 1 to 95).

Then come the *General* symptoms (i.e., sleep, reaction to temperature and weather, menses, transpiration, movement, etc.) that can be found throughout the Repertory and also in Generalities (pages 1341 to 1423).

General symptoms are followed by the symptoms of the *patient's disease-syndrome.*

Local symptoms, no matter how well modalized, lag far behind.

Vague and general symptoms, also called *common symptoms*, such as diarrhea, headache, etc., have to either be exhaustively modalized, or else disregarded altogether.

After a correct Repertorization, the Doctor will end up with a few remedies to consider seriously.

A trip to the Materia Medica Homeopathica will then help him or her find the remedy that best fits the profile of the particular acute disease or of a particular chronic patient.

Computerized Repertories have considerably simplified the hard and monotonous work of repertorizing.

But let us recall that the accuracy of a diagnosis, and therefore the efficacy of a treatment, still rests on the ability and criterion of the Homeopathic Physician and on the knowledge he or she may have of the Materia Medica Homeopathica.

Repertories are only a guide to the right remedy for a particular acute disease or chronic patient.

A golden thread of Ariadne, if you wish. But nothing more than that.

The successive steps that must be followed, between seeing a patient and the administration of the correct Homeopathic remedy, then, are:

Obtention of the Whole disease-bearing patient's Homeopathic History → hierarchization and modalization of symptoms → rough estimate of possible remedies by means of consulting the Repertory → final selection of the correct remedy in the Materia Medica Homeopathica → administration of the remedy that covers all or most of the profile of the Whole acute disease, or of the Whole chronic disease-bearing patient.

One Parthian shot before closing this Chapter—or rather two. They deal with diseases and Repertorization.

Dr. Tomás Paschero judiciously mentioned that the totality of the patient consists of the patient + the patient's disease + the patient's circumstance. Here the patient, his or her disease and his or her circumstance become the three legs of a tripod. Each leg is equally important for the integrity of the whole. In Homeopathy, as mentioned above in this Chapter, we shred off each individual symptom described or found in the patient, to then modalize it according to disease, patient and circumstance.

We need to evaluate each symptom individually in order to determine its hierarchical importance (particularly in chronic patients) and also in order to modalize each symptom. Modalization is essential because it is the only way of transforming each symptom into the *Whole patient's* symptom. This is as true for the patient and his or her circumstance as it is for the disease he or she bears.

Each disease, then, must also be shredded into each individual pathological symptom, and each pathological symptom must then be hierarchized and modalized. Ditto for the non-pathological characteristics of the patient and for the patient's circumstance. This clarification becomes paramount if we are to practice good quality Homeopathy and Integrative Medicine.

This clarification is important for the practice of quality Homeopathy because it is impossible to adequately shred a disease-syndrome, symptom by symptom, if the attending Physician does not have a sound knowledge of diseases in the first place. And sound knowledge of diseases is only imparted in Medical and Osteopathic Schools. Without this knowledge, the Practitioner can only repertorize adequately the patient's mental, general and local symptoms, as well as those pertaining to the patient's environment; but not those related to the disease the patient is bearing. Under these circumstances the evaluation of each individual patient becomes, per force, incomplete.

By the same token, this clarification is also important for the practice of Integrative Medicine, because here we must decide what treatment or combination of treatments to proffer to each Whole disease-bearing patient; that is, what therapy proffers that patient the greatest possibility of cure coupled with the lowest possible risk. Such a decision is impossible without having a clear idea regarding what disease-syndrome is afflicting the patient. In turn, it is impossible to have such a clear idea without having had a sound Allopathic Medical training.

The second Parthian shot has to do with the presence, in Repertories, of diseases mentioned by name. These diseases pose an apparent paradox, since Repertories deal with individual symptoms, and not with diseases.

Among acute diseases, there are some that have the peculiarity of being capable of recurring frequently, or else of being contracted only once in a lifetime. Such as measles, mumps, diphtheria, cholera and others. These disease-syndromes are included as such in the Repertory.

The reason for these in appearance paradoxical inclusions is to be found in § 73 of the 6th. Edition of Dr. Hahnemann's Organon. There, Dr. Hahnemann describes what he defines as the *acute miasmas* that may be contracted once in a lifetime, or else that may recur frequently; such as measles, mumps, diphtheria, cholera and others.

Symptoms are fairly similar in all patients bearing these particular acute diseases. There is very little symptomatic dispersion to be found here when comparing modalized symptoms of diverse patients suffering from these particular disease-syndromes. Consequently, one usually doesn't find the scattering of modalized symptoms seen in other acute disease-bearing patients. The uniformity of symptoms, in these *acute* problems, make most patients who suffer them amenable to treatment with the same few remedies.

Which is the reason why these disease-syndromes are the only ones that appear by name in the Repertories.

Chapter 10

THE MATERIA MEDICA HOMEOPATHICA

Materia Medica is the description of Homeopathic remedies.
Each Chapter starts with the name of a remedy.
Remedies are listed in alphabetical order.

The name of each remedy is followed by a description of the changes it elicits in several settings; meaning that the name of each remedy is followed by the description of the symptoms that configure the *profile* of each particular remedy.

In some Materia Medicæ, symptoms are written down one after another. In others, symptoms are commented upon, or else put together in a fashion that makes the description of the remedy easier to understand and to remember.

Homeopathic Physicians consult Materia Medicæ with the purpose of either to learn about the profile of remedies, or else to determine how well the profile of a particular remedy matches that of a particular patient.

Symptoms listed under the heading of each remedy are obtained from the following sources

- Acute intoxications
- Provings
- Some clinical observations
- Cured symptoms.

Of these four groups, only the first two, namely, Acute intoxications and Provings, provide truly useful data.

Changes brought about by acute poisoning, whether accidental or voluntary, are carefully studied and described in the Materia Medicæ. They are extraordinarily useful to help find a remedy for many *acute diseases.*
In turn, results found in Provings are very useful to find the remedy that matches the profile of *chronic patients.*

Let me clarify regarding the relative usefulness of acute intoxications and Provings. I will use as an example *Arsenicum album,* the Homeopathic preparation of white arsenic.

Arsenicum album is a remedy useful in the treatment of both acute diseases and chronic patients.

White arsenic is an extremely poisonous mineral; so much so that it is also known as the "inheritance powders". It is so nicknamed because of its success as a dispatcher to the hereafter of rich elderly relatives. Napoleon Bonaparte was one of its victims. He was slowly poisoned to death in Santa Elena, apparently not by his British captors, but by infiltrated French royalists who dreaded his return to power.

As it happens with many poisons, white arsenic becomes a wonderful remedy when Homeopathically prepared.

In victims of acute poisoning, white arsenic produces extreme anxiety that is worse in the middle of the night, restlessness, prostration, fear of death, severe burning pains, vomiting, colics and diarrhea that calm with very hot drinks; as well as other less important symptoms.

Take now an acute, very anxious and restless patient worse in the middle of the night. This patient is vomiting, has diarrhea and complaints of burning pains that are relieved by very hot drinks, among other symptoms. Since in Homeopathy *like cures like,* this patient will need Homeopathically prepared white arsenic, or *Arsenicum album.* No matter what has caused that patient's acute clinical picture. The only important things here are the patient's symptoms and the profile of the remedy that matches those symptoms.

Symptoms of acute intoxication with white arsenic are in the Materia Medica, under the remedy *Arsenicum album.*

In Provings of *Arsenicum album,* volunteers experience the anxiety, burning pains, fear of death, restlessness, etc. found in acute arsenic intoxications although in a milder, more persistent form. But provers also display other symptoms. They become extremely orderly, driving and fastidious, start dressing with a lot of care and become stingy with their money. They also develop a grave and somber countenance and an passion to collect things of value. Changes found in Provings are remarkably similar to those observed in individuals who are being chronically intoxicated by white arsenic.

When a Homeopathic Physician sees a chronic patient with anxiety, restlessness and fear of death, burning pains, worsening after midnight, desire for scalding hot drinks and baths; and who is somber, well dressed and miserly, that Doctor will seriously consider prescribing *Arsenicum album.*

Therefore, it is important to include in the Materia Medica the symptoms found both in acute intoxications and in the Provings of *Arsenicum Album.*

Higher up it was mentioned that, aside from symptoms found in acute intoxications and in Provings, one also finds *some clinical observations* and *cured symptoms* in the Materia Medica.

I also mentioned than only acute intoxications and Provings provide important data.

Some clinical observations are characteristics observed in patients who have responded well when treated with a particular Homeopathic remedy.

Take, for instance, the *Pulsatilla* patients who are blonde and blue-eyed, a *cliché* one finds in many a Materia Medica.

Problem here is that, even though *some* blonde and blue-eyed women have responded to *Pulsatilla,* there are legions of dark-eyed women—and of men, for that matter—who also respond to this remedy. And there are also crowds of blue-eyed blonde women who respond to remedies other than *Pulsatilla.* The guide provided by this blue-eyed blonde symptom is therefore of very limited value, and often deceiving.

Other clinical observations that are as deceiving as they are ensnaring, and that one finds in many a Materia Medica are, the philosopher in rags *Sulphur,* the man with the golden cane *Arsenicum album,* the broad shouldered and narrow hipped female *Sepia,* the dying and cold as marble *Carbo vegetabilis,* whose breath is as cold as if coming from a cellar, etc.

These descriptions appeal to our desire to simplify. They also give rise to vivid images in our minds. They ensnare us because we tend to think of *Sulphur* only when we see a philosopher in rags, *Sepia* when we see a broad-shouldered and narrow-hipped female, etc.

My own fixation with the archetype of the dying and cold *Carbo vegetabilis* led me to miss the Homeopathic diagnosis in a very much alive, though ill, *Carbo vegetabilis* patient for several months.

Cured symptoms, another frequent source of deception, have already been discussed in some length.

The first Materia Medica Homeopathica was written by Dr. Hahnemann. It was his *"Materia Medica Pura".* The first part was published in 1811, the second in 1815, and the third in 1816. All three parts were then published together for the first time in 1817.

Several followed, authored by famous Homeopathic Physicians.
Nowadays, the most widely used in America are those written by Drs.
John T. Kent and William Boericke.

Dr. Kent's is very didactic, and conveys the *feeling* of the remedies.
It is also full of very pointed comments, differential diagnoses, and
pearls of knowledge.
Its shortcoming is that it describes relatively few remedies.

Dr. Boericke's, called *"Pocket Manual of Homeopathic Materia Medica"* because of its size, describes many more remedies, but their description
is greatly summarized.
Its conciseness makes it difficult to get a clear enough picture of the
profile of a remedy if the Doctor has had no previous Homeopathic training
and knowledge. The book, however, is an invaluable *aide-mémoire* for Practitioners with knowledge of Homeopathy.
It also includes an excellent, if summarized, Repertory after the Materia
Medica.

There is a relationship between the Materia Medica and the *Repertories*.

Materia Medicæ list remedies in alphabetical order, with symptoms
written down afterwards, underneath or after the heading of each remedy.
Therefore, in Materia Medicæ we will first find the name of the remedy, and
then the symptoms that constitute that particular remedy's profile.
Conversely, in the Repertories, we will find first a list of symptoms.
Immediately after those symptoms are written the remedy/es that have elicited those symptoms in Provings, in toxicological studies or in clinical observations.

The systematic and serious study of the Materia Medica is essential for
the understanding and practice of Homeopathy. And also to be able to prescribe the correct remedy for each of our patients.

"Homo sum, et humani nihil a me alienum puto"[36].

Chapter 11
HISTORY TAKING AND DIAGNOSES

A good quality History is still the only way of obtaining reliable data regarding a patient.

In other words, everything begins with the obtention of the patient's History.

The drawing of a quality History is a delicate art. It requires knowledge and much practice.

ALLOPATHIC HISTORY

In Allopathy, a sound History and Physical Examination are necessary to reach a Medical diagnosis; that is, the diagnosis of *the disease a patient is bearing.* It is also essential for Homeopathic Physicians, who need to obtain pathological symptoms that, once modalized, will allow the Doctor to adequately repertorize the disease the patient is bearing.

If the History and Physical Exam do not suffice, the Allopathic Doctor can request lab work, X Rays and/or a variety of other ancillary diagnostic procedures to complement or supplement data obtained in the patient's History.

As far as *learning* the art of how to obtain good Allopathic Histories.

Probably the best choice is to do at least one year of Residence in Internal Medicine or Family Practice in any Hospital approved for that purpose. During that time, the new Resident writes supervised Histories on all kinds of patients. Those Histories are then discussed with Senior Residents and members of the Hospital Staff.

In an Allopathic Medical History, a *"symptom"* is anything *abnormal* or *pathological* that is subjective; that is, anything the Doctor can*not* verify

---

[36] I am human, nothing human is alien to me. Terencius (180-159 BC), *Hænton Timorumenos*, Act 1.

through his or her senses (i.e., headache, nausea, abdominal pain, etc.). Symptoms may or may not be modalized. Modalization is not all that important here.

What the Allopathic Doctor can see, hear, smell or feel in the Physical Examination is considered to be *objective* data, or *"signs"* (i.e., blood pressure, temperature, unequal pupils, a heart murmur, the characteristic breath of a patient in diabetic coma, the board-like hardness of the abdominal wall in peritonitis, etc.). Here again, modalization is definitely not of the essence.

Information provided by X Rays and laboratory results, or through the use of any other ancillary diagnostic procedure, is called *"findings"*.

The *subjective* part of the History—or the recording of *symptoms*—starts with the Chief Complaint/s; that is, the problem/s that brings the patient to the Doctor. The Chief Complaint is followed by the History of the Present Illness, that is the chronology of the patient's complaint/s and treatment/s. Both the Chief Complaint and the History of Present Illness are only concerned with whatever may be *abnormal* and/or *pathological.*

Then comes the Past Medical, Family and Social History; the latter usually of little importance in an Allopathic History.

The History is followed by the Review of Systems, or Systemic Review; which is a questionnaire regarding *[abnormal]* symptoms organ by organ and system by system. In everyday practice, this review is either obviated or greatly summarized. Most of the relevant pathological information, if not all, has already been obtained through the Chief Complaint and the History of Present Illness.

During the *objective* aspect of the History, that is, the complete Physical Examination, the Allopathic Physician searches the patient's body for *signs.* The Physician first assesses whether the patient is in any kind of distress, and if he or she is alert and oriented or not. Then the Doctor estimates the patient's mental status. The Physical Examination continues with the obtention of the vital signs (body temperature, blood pressure, pulse and respiratory rate). It is completed with the visual, auditory, olfactory, tactile and percussive examination of the patient and, often, with an exploration of the patient's natural cavities.

Laboratory, X Ray and other studies are frequently required to round up the patient's History, and consequently to help reach a correct Allopathic Diagnosis.

In actual day-to-day practice the patient's Chief Complaint, History of Present Illness, Family, Past Medical and Social History, as well as the Systemic Review and the Vital Signs, may be obtained by an assistant.

Then the Doctor, after perusing the data so obtained, may ask some pointed questions, perform the Physical Examination, order the necessary lab work, X Rays, etc., prescribe the treatment and leave.

Sometimes the diagnosis can be reached at a glance, as in patients suffering from advanced Parkinson's[37] or Graves'[38] disease, for instance.

This procedure may vary from patient to patient, from Doctor to Doctor and from specialty to specialty.

Visits to the Dermatologist are characteristically short: a few verbal exchanges, a rapid visual and tactile examination—followed sometimes a microscopic scrutiny of skin scrapings—and a prescription.

Psychiatrists may obtain the History themselves, and defer the complete Physical Examination.

And so on and so forth.

HOMEOPATHIC HISTORY

The Homeopathic History is fundamentally interested in evaluating the Whole disease-bearing patient, including the disease-syndrome the patient may be bearing. It is therefore considerably more complex and complete that the standard Allopathic History.

Ancillary studies (X Rays, lab work, etc.), crucial as they are for Allopathic and Integrative Diagnoses, are of little use here. The data they provide is limited to certain aspects of the disease the patient may be bearing. Lab and X Ray findings can neither be modalized nor hierarchized. They may help a bit in the modalization and hierarchization of the symptoms of the disease-syndrome the patient bears, but that's about all.

Ancillary studies can't help in the least to evaluate a chronic patient's circumstance, or to find the fulcrum of his or her imbalance.

---

[37] A degenerative disease of the central nervous system. When sufficiently advanced, the patient's body leans forward as he or she walks. Steps are short and hurried, as if in a constant attempt to prevent a fall. The hands tremble, and the index and thumb rub together in both hands. The patient's features tend to be totally expressionless.

[38] A malfunction of the thyroid gland of the neck, characterized by extreme nervousness and restlessness, enlargement of the thyroid gland, weight loss, bulging eyes and very fine trembling of the hands.

Jose Miguel Mullen, M.D.

X Rays have been aptly defined as "shadows of the truth". A radiologist can only describe what he or she sees in an X Ray or MRI or whatever, and even go as far as to suggest one or several Allopathic diagnostic possibilities as the interpretation of those shadows. But the radiologist can go no further.

And if we send, say, a tear to the laboratory to be analyzed, the report will accurately inform regarding its contents and other characteristics, and will also state if findings are within normal limits or not. But results so obtained will be totally incapable of clarifying whether that tear was shed because a foreign body recently entered the patient's eye, or because the patient was in the Delivery Room when his baby was born, or when he or she was at the wake of his or her best friend. Or if that tear was shed while listening to the Pilgrims' Choir of *Tannhäuser*.

All the data obtained in the Homeopathic History must be *modalized*. In this fashion, the Homeopathic Physician can integrate the data so obtained into the patient's Wholeness.

The Homeopathic Physician must always start by *listening* sedately and with sympathy, with the mind blank and senses at a maximum level of alert, and leave the patient talk. It is better to take notes as the patient talks for, if written later, they may be modified by the Doctor's biases. The Homeopathic Physician must encourage the patient to go on talking, even when the patient feels there is nothing more to say. Open questions such as *"and what else?..."* are very useful for this purpose. The Doctor should refrain, whenever possible, from asking direct questions and, even more so, from asking leading questions that can only be answered by a "Yes" or a "no". These direct and leading questions elicit responses that can't be modalized and that are usually misleading.

It is advisable *not to interrupt* the patient. Interruption may make him or her forget what he or she was saying (Hahnemann S., *Organon*, 6th. Edition. § 84). This is particularly important, because often the patient may be describing thoughts, feelings, circumstances and the like he or she had never entertained, let alone verbalized before. When, in effect, there is nothing more to say, the Doctor may ask questions to clarify the patient's statements—and also to start modalizing them.

The first thing a Doctor must determine is whether the patient is acute or chronic, something that can only be achieved through the obtention of a Homeopathic History.

In acute patients, imbalance is brought about by the disease-syndrome they are bearing.

The Homeopathic History here should concentrate on what brought that imbalance about, and what are the characteristics of the modifications that imbalance produced in the affected areas and in the Whole patient. This study is also valid for those chronic patients who, at one time or another of their chronic treatment, may suffer some acute problem.

After obtaining all the data, each of the symptoms will have to be considered individually, and then progressively modalized, through the Doctor's questions, into the *patient's* disease-syndrome. Until finally, when the modalization is completed, that impersonal disease-syndrome becomes, in the Doctor's mind, *that particular patient's disease-syndrome.*

It is an entirely different story when it comes to obtaining the *Homeopathic History of chronic patients.* Here we have to take into consideration the patient + the patient's disease + the patient's circumstance.

As in every form of Homeopathic History, one will start by observing the patient and listening without interrupting. The Doctor may ask open questions when the patient appears to run out of steam, and then remain silent for a while awaiting the chronic patient answers. Until eventually the patient has nothing more to say, and has ran out of answers for the open questions.

Perhaps some reticent silences may remain here and there. Such silences, that the Doctor will perceive only through experience and instinct, can be crucially important. They may help to understand why the patient has become imbalanced in the first place. Here the Homeopathic Physician will have to trod, with utmost care and tact, until he or she is able to pry those silences open—or at least try.

By now, the Doctor will have a certain amount of information about the patient, the patient's disease-syndrome and the patient's circumstance; all incomplete, all in disarray. Now comes the time to peel symptom by symptom from that hodgepodge. And to start the job of modalizing each of the symptoms. Some semblance of order can be established here. The Doctor may first modalize the patient's symptoms, then the symptoms of the patient's disease, and finally those corresponding to the patient's circumstance.

Modalization of the symptoms corresponding to the chronic patient.- After listening to, and observing the patient, the Doctor may start by asking how are the patient's days and nights. Does the patient awakens rested? Is it safe to get close to him or her before breakfast? Is there anything he or she must do in a hurry upon awakening? Does the patient have a slump and, if so, when? At what time he or she goes to bed? What does he or she need at that time (window open or closed, to be covered or uncovered, lights on or off, etc.) Whether or not he or she awakens in the middle of the night, if there are dreams that repeat themselves, whether he or she thrashes, etc.

Then perhaps the Doctor may ask about menstrual characteristics, pregnancies, deliveries, breast feeding, menopause. Sexuality and sexual life, including orientation, satisfaction or lack thereof, faithfulness or promiscuity, jealousy, etc. How was the patient's pregnancy, delivery, childhood, adolescence, adulthood, marriage, divorce, widowhood. Whether the patient has received enough love or not, and how has this fact influenced his or her life. Attitude toward music, dancing. Is the patient orderly? Is he or she a pack rat or a thrower away? Is there any guilt? Is he or she spender or saver? What are his or her fears? How does he or she feels in regards to him or herself? Demeanor. How does he or she deals with his or anger, sadness, etc.? Can he or she cry or not, and what about? Is he or she relieved after weeping? Accepts consolation? Does he or she explodes when angry, or does he or she swallows his feelings? In either case, how does he or she feels afterwards? Whether or not there is resentment or indignation and, if so, directed toward what or whom, why, and for how long. How fast or how slowly does the patient forgives those who have offended him or her? Does the patient dwell on negative thoughts? Reactions to aging. Is he or she thirsty or thirstless? Hot or cold drinks? Attitude regarding alcoholic drinks and drugs. What taste does he or she prefers? Is he or she hungry and, if so, when? Conversely, is there a time when there is repulsion towards food and, if so, when? What dishes does the patient loves or hates? Which don't agree with the patient? How are the patient's bowels, urination, perspiring? Does he or she like to bathe? How hot the water? How he or she feels after getting out of the water and drying up? Level of exercise. Whether he or she is patient or impatient. Reaction towards horrible things, blood, pointed objects. Is the patient religious? Superstitious? etc. *Always modalizing each symptom; always modalizing, modalizing.* The key here is to modalize, and then to modalize again. As a matter of fact, it is better to have only a few symptoms very well modalized than a bunch of them with a poor modalization.

Modalization of the symptoms corresponding to the chronic patient's disease-syndrome.- Before modalizing these symptoms one has to obtain them. Symptoms vary from disease to disease. The capacity to obtain symptoms of disease is directly proportional to the knowledge the Doctor has of pathology and his or her ability to obtain sound Allopathic Clinical Histories. The subject is very complex. So much so that I will be able to cover this section only with very broad brush strokes, and that for descriptive purposes only. If the patient is psoric, sycosic or syphilitic, then the disease-syndrome ailing him or her can be an intercurrent disease[39], an acute exacerbation of the patient's chronic disease or a *flare-up,* or else *a verifiable evi-*

---

[39] A disease that appears when another one is progressing.

dence of aggravation of the imbalance already present in the Whole chronic disease-bearing patient. After obtaining the History, the Doctor may start by asking what the patient thinks brought about the disease he or she is bearing. If there is pain, what kind of pain he or she feels (sharp or dull, piercing, burning, stinging, etc.), where he or she feels it, whether it is fixed or if it goes from one place to another and, if so, from where to where; what makes that pain worse, better, or disappear. When do symptoms occur, hour of the day, season of the year. Whether they are periodic or not. How they are affected by the diverse factors. Whether or not symptoms change with changes of position, or when coughing, sleeping, or awakening, or menstruating, or when the patient thinks about them. If they radiate and if so, where to. What treatment, Allopathic or otherwise, is the patient receiving? How is he or she reacting to those treatments? What other *concomitant* (or accompanying) problems may appear together with the symptoms of the disease, or before, or after. If there are chills and/or fever, and when. How the patient was before being stricken with the disease, and how he or she is now. How the patient lives his or her disease; if impatiently, with anger, patiently, etc. And modalize, modalize, and modalize still some more; as the patient responds to the questions and also afterwards—until the Doctor can link, as seamlessly as possible, the disease the patient is suffering with the patient who bears that disease.

Modalization of symptoms corresponding to the chronic patient's circumstance.- What are the patient's feelings towards others, occupation, passage of time, money. What he or she find intolerable in others and him or herself. How is or was his or her relationship with parents, teachers, fellow students, siblings, friends, spouse, children, co-workers, bosses. Reactions to personal loses. Significant people and events in the patient's life, and how they affect him or her. Drugs and addictions. Reactions to seasons and weather. How does the patient feel in the seaside and mountains, and what does he or she prefers. How is he or she affected by the weather and by seasons of the year. Care he or she takes of others, pets, objects. Whether the patient is sociable or prefers small groups or being alone. Hobbies and occupations. Whether or not he or she likes or dislikes the job, and why. Attitude toward superiors, subalterns, equals. Whether the patient is competitive or not. Or stubborn. Or capable or not of delegating responsibilities, etc. Here again, every symptom and each one of the patient's answers must be modalized, modalized, modalized; until the patient's circumstance fits, in the Homeopathic Physician's mind, with the patient and his or her disease.

In the Past Medical History we will search for situations, treatments and operations. And, of course diseases, particularly those that point toward a chronic miasma. And we shall also attempt to gauge what kind of an impact those situations, treatments, surgeries and diseases may have had on the patient. For instance, whether or not some feelings remain toward an abortion several years back and what are those feelings, or towards a road accident, etc.

In the Family History, we will be looking for trends that may evince a miasma.

In the Social History we will like to learn more about the patient's circumstance.

Finally, in the *complete* Physical Examination (it *always* has to be performed, even if the patient only came to see us just for a sore throat or something equally innocuous), we shall attempt to find his or her physical characteristics and also any abnormalities that may be present.

Through a correct modalization and hierarchization of the patient's symptoms and signs, the Doctor will often have the necessary data to draw the patient's profile and that of his or her chronic miasma. Such information will enormously facilitate the task of finding a Homeopathic remedy the profile of which best matches that of the chronic patient—or of the patient's acute disease, in the instance of an acute patient.

The Homeopathic Physician must rivet all of his or her attention on the patient since arrival till departure. This way, the Doctor will be able to verify the patient's attitude while in the waiting room, the quality of handshake and voice; how he or she looks, straight in the eye, averted glances, askance, etc. How the patient walks and enters the office or examining room; how he or she dresses, gesticulates, walks and talks. Hesitations, grimaces, frowns, smiles, pouts, crying, laughter, etc. How the patient sits in the office; if comfortably, on the edge of the chair or leaning on the desk, as if wanting to get closer to the Doctor. Or perhaps leaning backwards defensively, with arms crossed over the chest, etc.

The Homeopathic Physician *must remain with the patient throughout the whole visit.* That is why Homeopathic Physicians can see only one patient at a time, and also why a no show, or a cancellation within 24 hours, can create such a serious disruption; economic and otherwise.

Nothing and no one should interrupt the Doctor's concentration during the patient's visit. Sometimes a comment, often in passing, may be all that is needed to make the whole picture fall into focus. And it can be easily missed if the Doctor is not paying close attention, or has been distracted.

This concentration on the patient cannot be sufficiently emphasized.

Take the patient who, at the end of the visit, and as an afterthought, told me that his hoarseness was worse in the morning. Until then, and with all the modalized symptoms, his physical appearance and examination, I had been contemplating *Kali Carbonicum* and *Causticum.* I couldn't decide which. And if I hadn't been attentive I would have missed the keynote about his voice that pointed toward *Causticum*. A few more questions confirmed that this patient was indeed *Causticum*. His treatment was a success.

Or take that other patient with headaches. She had done well with *Sepia* until, and despite of increasing potencies, many of her symptoms returned, if less severely. During re-evaluation she mentioned, as in passing, that her headaches were different. Now they started in her scalp. I thought of *Agaricus Muscaricus*. The rest of the re-evaluation confirmed that impression. Perhaps I would have missed this comment had I had interrupted or been inattentive. I prescribed *Agaricus*, instead of a still higher potency of *Sepia*. The patient was doing well when I left Argentina three years afterwards.

Most patients are used only to Allopathy. They usually go to the Homeopathic Physician's office with no previous exposure to Homeopathy—and often not knowing what to expect, to boot.

Patient may start talking about what they have found is important for Allopathic Doctors, only to find that what they say is being ignored—while they watch, stupefied, how the Homeopathic Physician writes down, in minute detail, facts such as whether or not they pop their feet out of bed at night, or whether or not they salt their food before tasting it.

Sometimes, Homeopathically important symptoms may not be mentioned because the patient has no way of knowing that they are relevant. Patients have been conditioned to consider important only whatever is abnormal or pathological, instead of what is most important in Homeopathy; that is, whatever is *unusual*, *unique* and *peculiar* to the patient (Hahnemann S., *Organon*, 6th. Ed., § 153). The patient may also believe that what he or she feels is not important because of the tragic circumstance that disease has become second nature to him or her, after years and years of suffering (Hahnemann S., *Organon*, 6th. Ed., § 95).

INTEGRATIVE HOMEOPATHIC-ALLOPATHIC HISTORY

The integrative History fuses the Allopathic and Homeopathic Histories into one single History.

The result is a Medical History valid to reach both an Allopathic and a Homeopathic diagnoses.

In turn, both diagnoses permit the Integrative Doctor to proffer a treatment that can be Allopathic, Homeopathic or a combination of both, according to the patient's needs.

It is also useful to learn what form of Complementary Medicine, aside from Homeopathy, can be beneficial for each patient.

To sum up some of the similarities and differences between Allopathic, Homeopathic and Integrative Clinical Histories,

Scientific Medicine deals with disease-syndromes. It is based on knowledge.

In order to Allopathically assist a patient, the only communication needed is that between the knowledge in the Doctor's mind and the patient's disease. Rapport is not necessary.

Homeopathic and Integrative Medicine deal both with disease-bearing Human Beings.

The Doctor ↔ patient relationship here also requires knowledge, of course. It is not based on knowledge, however, but on caring. It can only happen between a Human Being in need of assistance and another Human Being willing and able to help.

There is no way a Human mind can achieve intellectual knowledge of a Whole Human Being, no matter how powerful and well trained that mind may be. The span between two Human Beings can only be bridged through understanding.

Understanding, within a Homeopathic or Integrative context, leads to *compassion,* which in turn generates a *rapport,* absolutely indispensable in any Doctor ↔ patient relationship.

THE RAPPORT

It is important to know the patient and the patient's problem. But it is indispensable to *understand* if one is to reach the patient's core, to become aware of what makes him or her sick. And, in chronic patients, understanding means to grasp the real reason for—and the fulcrum of—their imbalance.

The relationship Human ↔ Human is essential here. This mutually enriching relationship can only be reached by means of developing a solid rapport between the Doctor and his or her patient.

Rapport allows the patient to feel comfortable revealing him or herself. The Doctor is allowed, through this sacred trust, to see beyond appearances and to listen beyond spoken words.

The compassionate Physician will be able to understand both the patient and that patient's suffering. And will thus become capable of reaching the fulcrum of what ails that patient. Which, in turn will lead to a successful Homeopathic and Integrative treatment.

THE ALLOPATHIC DIAGNOSIS

The coherent interpretation of the data obtained through a Clinical History and Physical Examination, plus other procedures (lab work, X Rays, etc.), results in an impersonal diagnosis such as pneumonitis, fibrosarcoma, nephrosis, eczema, sinusitis, etc.

Once a disease-syndrome has been diagnosed, the Allopathic Doctor will choose the drug/s and/or other Allopathic procedure/s best suited to neutralize that disease-syndrome (i.e., Penicillin, Prednisone, hydrochlorothiazide, Surgery, radiation, etc.)

THE HOMEOPATHIC DIAGNOSIS

Diagnosis of the remedy.-

In Homeopathy, *like cures like.*

Homeopathic remedies are like living entities. Like living bits of experience. This fact confuses many Physicians—until they carry on a Proving in themselves. Pharmaceutical drugs have to be *studied* in textbooks of Pharmacology. They have to be *learnt;* that is, transported from the textbooks into the students' minds as *knowledge.* In a Proving, instead, the self-administration of a remedy brings about several changes within the prover, all at approximately the same time. These changes are *experienced* but not *learnt,* as it happens with the student. And, like everything experienced, these changes—that are the actual profile of the remedy—become as alive, and as intuitively *understandable* by the prover, as any other element born of the prover's experience.

Reaching a correct Homeopathic diagnosis/treatment, therefore, is like superimposing two live images. Being one the images the profile of the remedy and the other the profile of a Whole chronic patient or of an acute disease. This is similar to what happens when one superimposes both images in the range finder of a photographic camera. The closer the superimposition, the more successful the outcome of the treatment is likely to be.

In Homeopathy, the profile of the Whole acute disease in acute patients, and that of the Whole chronic patient, constitute the *Homeopathic diagnosis.*

Since *Homeopathic diagnosis* and *Homeopathic treatment* correspond to the same profile, Homeopathic diagnosis and treatment are considered to be the same thing, and are known by the same name. One hears Homeopathic Physicians refer to a sore throat as "this throat is *Belladona* ", or to a chronic patient as "this patient is *Lachesis* " or whatever other remedy. What this means is that the Homeopatic Physician actually alludes to the *diagnosis of the acute disease-syndrome,* or to the profile of the *Whole chronic patient's, as corresponding to the profile of* the remedy *Lachesis,* or *Belladona,* or whatever other remedy.

The Homeopathic Diagnosis is a coherent interpretation of symptoms, viewed from the standpoint of the *Whole* disease or the *Whole* patient.

In *acute* disease-bearing patients, the modalized symptoms of the acute disease are matched against the symptoms produced by Homeopathic remedies. The remedy chosen will have a profile similar to that of the acute disease ailing the patient.

In *chronic*—or *psoric*—patients, the modalization of symptoms will yield *two* diagnoses, namely

- Homeopathic, and
- Miasmatic.

In *psoric patients,* the Homeopathic Physician first modalizes, and then hierarchizes the data obtained from the patient (that is, the Doctor arranges the symptoms according to their relative importance). Afterwards, the Doctor selects the most important modalized symptoms and then the remedy that best matches those modalized symptoms.

There are three ways of reaching a Homeopathic diagnosis in psoric patients: rapport, scarce use of the Repertory and repertorization.

Rapport allows the Doctor to reach the root of the psoric patient's suffering; that is, the fulcrum of the patient's imbalance.

I would like to give an example.

One dreary winter evening, a few years ago, my wife, who is also the office manager, told me there was a man in the waiting room. He wanted to see me. It was most unusual, since appointments are made in advance, usually over the telephone.

The man was standing, swaying slightly. He was drooling and drying his mouth with his sleeve every so often. He had an expression of extreme suffering in his features. He could hardly speak.

He told me he had very painful sores in his mouth. He had gone to many Doctors and Hospitals. No one could help him. Some Doctors made him suffer needlessly. He said he had come to see me at the behest of his wife. He had not wanted to come. He was weary of Doctors. He didn't want to see any more Doctors. He was resigned to live with his sores for the rest of his life.

These extremely painful sores—ulcers, actually—had been mortifying this patient along the past three years. He also suffered from rectal bleeding. Those were his main complaints.

I learnt through the History that his ailment had started shortly after his mother, whom he dearly loved, had passed away three years before. He was still mourning her like the day she had died.

This prolonged mourning was at the root of his pathology, at the fulcrum of his imbalance. I had figured out the connection between symptoms and mourning through the *rapport* I had been able to establish with the patient. It hadn't been easy to establish such a rapport, due in part to his hopelessness, and in part to the excruciating pain he felt every time he talked.

His mouth was a mess of ulcers and inflamed tissues. He could hardly open it. I found no other abnormalities in his Physical Examination.

I prescribed *Ignatia amara,* the main remedy for protracted mourning and its consequences.

His mourning gradually became a very dear, resigned, warm memory of his mother. The ulcers in his mouth rapidly closed. His rectal bleeding and other symptoms also disappeared—all after receiving only one dose of the remedy.

His rectal bleeding returned after a few weeks. I couldn't figure out why because, when a Homeopathic treatment is successful, all pathological manifestations are supposed to vanish. Furthermore, he was feeling fine and doing wonderfully in every other respect. So I questioned him very closely. Among other things, I asked him if he had been eating anything unusual. "Oh, yes!" he replied promptly "Tons and tons of pepperoni. I haven't been able to eat them for years because of my mouth, and I like pepperoni so much…". I requested him to quit eating hot and spicy things. His rectal bleeding disappeared

The second way of reaching a Homeopathic diagnosis in psoric patients is through the *sparse* use of the Repertory. It happens when the Physician has a fairly clear idea about the patient, but is not sure what remedy best matches the patient's profile.

Some leafing back and forth in the Repertory—and also perhaps a trip or two to the Materia Medica Homeopathica—will help find the right remedy.

The third way of reaching a Homeopathic diagnosis in psoric patients is through the *exclusive* use of the Repertory. This procedure is known as *repertorization.*

The Doctor must repertorize when he or she has no idea regarding what remedy matches the patient's profile, or when no rapport has been established.

Beginners should *abstain from repertorizing all symptoms* of chronic patients—always a heady temptation, particularly when having access to computer software. If all symptoms are repertorized—particularly if they are poorly modalized beforehand—chances are that the remedy chosen will be either *Sulfur, Lycopodium clavatum* or *Calcarea carbonica.* This is so because the Provings of these remedies has yielded an extraordinarily large number of symptoms. Consequently, these three remedies are found opposite most symptoms in the Repertory. A treatment based on such a megaRepertorization will necessarily result in therapeutic failure.

When repertorizing a psoric patient, modalized symptoms should be hierarchized in order of importance, and so create what Dr. Tomás Paschero used to call *"the minimal syndrome of maximal importance or significance".*

For a correct hierarchization, the Doctor should choose first the symptoms more *forcefully* and *spontaneously* told by the patient, without prodding of any kind; and also those symptoms that are as *strange, rare* and *peculiar* as possible, i.e., as unique as possible for that particular patient (Hahnemann S., *Organon,* 6th. Ed., § 153). In order of importance, those symptoms should be followed by Mental and General symptoms, as well as by the symptoms of the patient's disease-syndrome and those corresponding to the patient's circumstance—here again, as modalized as possible. Local symptoms not related to the disease-syndrome should always lag far behind, no matter how well modalized.

To repertorize properly, in the absence of a computer, the *minimal syndrome of maximal significance* is plotted on a sheet of paper.

Symptoms are written horizontally, above; and remedies vertically, in the left hand side of the sheet of paper, as in the example below—which is not hypothetical, by the way. It belongs to a patient I couldn't figure out and who did well with *Phosphorus.* The repertorization below is done with the first 3 remedies of a much larger repertorization.

For this patient's first symptom, *Phosphorus* appears in the Repertory with **3**, *Natrum muriaticum* with **2**, and *Cactus grandiflorus* with 1. Consequently, those digits are to be written underneath Symptom #1, where symptom # 1 coincides with *Phosphorus, Natrum Muriaticum* and *Cactus Grandiflorus,* respectively.

For Symptom #2, *Phosphorus* appears with *2, Natrum muriaticum* with 1, and *Cactus grandiflorus* does not appear. A *2* should be written where Symptom # 2 and *Phosphorus* coincide; 1 where Symptom # 2 and *Natrum muriaticum* coincide, and 0 (or Zero) where Symptom # 2 and *Cactus grandifolia* coincide.

In symptom # 3, *Phosphorus* appears with **3**, but not *Natrum muriaticum* or *Cactus grandifolia,* then **3** should be written on top, and then 0 and 0 where Symptom # 3 and the other two remedies coincide.

In order to calculate the figures under TOTAL, we have to make a fraction. The numerator is the result of the addition of all the values; and the denominator, the addition of how often they appear.

Thus, for *Phosphorus,* we have a value of **3**, another one of *2* and another one of **3** in the numerators. So we place **3** + *2* + **3** = 8 in the numerator of TOTAL. All three spaces are occupied, so the denominator will be 3; thus, in TOTAL under *Phosphorus,* we will write 8/3.

For *Natrum muriaticum,* we will find a *2*, a 1 and a Zero. *2* + 1 + 0 = 3; and, since values appear only twice (because Zero does not count), it will be 3/2.

As for *Cactus grandiflora,* there is only 1, that appears only once; and will thus be, under TOTAL 1/1.

	Symptom # 1	Symptom # 2	Symptom # 3	TOTAL
Phosphorus	**3**	*2*	**3**	8/3
Natrum muriaticum	*2*	1	0	3/2
Cactus grandifolia	1	0	0---	1/0

After repertorizing, I chose *Phosphorus* for this particular patient, because *Phosphorus* was the remedy that scored highest in the Repertorization (underlined underneath "TOTAL", above).

It is a good idea, though, to administer the remedy that best matches the patient's profile, whether or not it ranks first in the Repertorization. The only way to do achieve this goal is by going to the Homeopathic Materia Medica, and studying and comparing there the remedies that scored highest in the repertorization.

I still like to start my repertorizing with Knerr's Repertory first, because here most of the symptoms present have been obtained in Provings and other studies performed by Dr. Hering. I consistently find better results when I start with his Repertory, and then compare results with those found in other Repertories, but *using always one Repertory at a time.* Conversely, I have found that I err more frequently when I choose the remedies from a mixed Repertory.

I feel this happens because of *biases,* or the outlook, or framework, or perspective, or jaundiced eye if you wish, from which each one of us sees— and interprets—any bit of evidence. Bias will find its way in, no matter how objectively any author may write down his or her Repertory. This is so because of the author's subjective way of perceiving and evaluating things. Each person's—and consequently each author's—bias is as individual and as unique as his or her own personality, experience, and the way how he or she responds to things, persons, circumstances, etc.

Dr. Kent's Repertory, for instance, is not only the outcome of Dr. Kent's gigantic knowledge and experience, but also of *his* biases. Still, though, only *his* biases are present in his Repertory. And his biases are more than neutralized by the wealth of information present there. The same can be said of the Repertories of Drs. Knerr, Boericke, etc. Each of them has a lot of extremely valuable information, but each is tinged by the individual bias of each author. Here too, the subjectivity of biases corresponds to, and is more than neutralized by, each author's knowledge and experience.

What we end up having, therefore, is *one bias per Repertory.*

In a mixed Repertory, on the other hand, remedies from several authors are pooled together opposite each symptom, with the inevitable addition of many biases—*many biases per symptom, instead of one bias per Repertory.* We have the biases *of several authors,* not just one. Add the inevitable biases of the Editor of the mixed Repertory (his or her personal biases, how he or she interpreted some of the very subtle terms used to define some symptoms, how the Editor used that interpretation when making a cross index of synonyms, how he or she distributed the remedies per symptom, etc.).

Another bit of bad news is that, unless done by master Homeopaths, however, repertorization is a very tricky business; a poor man's way of reaching a Homeopathic diagnosis. And it can often be misleading.

The bottom line here is, I believe, that only a good *understanding* of the Homeopathic patient and of the remedies is of real help in reaching a diagnosis.

I would like to narrate two anecdotes to illustrate this point.

The first I heard about in a discussion. It had to do with a patient whose symptoms could have corresponded either to *Arnica* or to *Pulsatilla.*

The Homeopathic Physician, after repertorizing this patient, reached the diagnosis with the aid of the keynote "Well, says he or she is, when very sick" (Kent's Repertory, page 95) where, and among other remedies, *Arnica* appears with grade **3** and *Pulsatilla* with 1. The Doctor chose *Arnica* because it appears with grade **3** in the Repertory. The treatment didn't work.

This particular patient was quiet, tactful to a fault and withdrawn, would accept consolation, felt forsaken and would go to any extremes to pacify. Had this colleague understood the profiles of *Arnica* and of *Pulsatilla*, he would have known that the "Well, says he or she is ..." of *Arnica* is grunted by a loner who never admits being sick, who doesn't want to be disturbed and whose anger flares up easily, particularly when touched; and who will readily jump out of bed, grab the Doctor, drag him or her to the door, throw him or her out and then slam the door; whereas the "Well, says he or she is ..." of *Pulsatilla* is hesitant, whispered by someone afraid of complaining, lest people may get angry and then forsake him or her still again, tired of his or her whimpering—even if, opposite the symptom, *Pulsatilla* appears with only 1, and Arnica with **3**.

The second example deals with a 35-year-old woman, whose Chief Complaints were extremely severe sinusitis for several years, fatigue and frequent respiratory infections. Allopathic Physicians had recommended Surgery after the failure of several treatments with antibiotics, corticoids and decongestants. The patient went to a Practitioner in an attempt to avoid Surgery. The Practitioner repertorized the patient and prescribed *Natrum muriaticum*, that didn't help. After this failure she came to see me.

I prescribed *Hepar sulfur.* She took it one night and awoke next morning free of symptoms. In her first follow-up visit, the patient told me with a smile that her husband had told her at breakfast, stupefied "Are you so-and-so? Are you the woman I married? Are you the same person I went to bed with last night?"

Both *Natrum muriaticum* and *Hepar sulfur* share many symptoms, among them glowing anger, and sadness. In both remedies, these feelings tend to be silent and carefully hidden. And in both anger and sadness lead to resentment and inability to forgive and forget. But in *Natrum muriaticum* the hue is more of sadness, whereas in *Hepar sulfur* is more of anger. And in *Natrum muriaticum* the silent sadness/anger leads frequently to quiet resentment, whereas in *Hepar sulfur* the smoldering anger/sadness, transformed into hatred, may become explosive and dangerous; to the point that *Hepar sulfur* patients, when anger erupts, may start fires and do things of the same ilk.

There were other symptoms, of course, that also helped; such as this patient's extreme sensitivity to cold, another key characteristic of *Hepar sul-*

fur. But it was this awareness of the patient's profile what lead me to pre-scribe *Hepar sulfur*. Had I repertorized this patient, *Natrum muriaticum* would have been way ahead, because it is far richer in symptoms than *He-par sulfur*.

By the way, Allopathic Doctors had treated the second patient with anti-biotics first and then suggested Surgery. They had no inkling regarding how useful Homeopathy can be in sinusitis-bearing patients.

I always strenuously recommend to consult a knowledgeable Homeo-pathic or Integrative Physician for a second opinion whenever a patient is requested to undergo some serious Allopathic procedure—at least until enough Allopathic Physicians become familiar with Homeopathy and other forms of Complementary Medicine.

This book—and collective experience also, alas!—is strewn with exam-ples of patients who underwent unnecessary suffering because they didn't follow this advice. Let me briefly add another one here.

That of a 35-year-old woman diagnosed as having interstitial cystitis, which is a very severe and protracted form of inflammation of the urinary bladder. This patient had been having this problem for years. It would burn every time she urinated, sexual intercourse with her husband was very pain-ful and her menstruations were miserable. She had gone to one Urologist af-ter another. Finally an Urologist had suggested instilling cortisone deriva-tives into her urinary bladder. Here the patient said enough and started searching for other forms of therapy. She came to see me. Her Constitu-tional remedy is *Scutelaria*. Her symptoms started to vanish shortly after starting treatment. She has been free of symptoms ever since, except for very tolerable discomfort during her periods.

As mentioned above, the Repertory only *narrows* the selection of the remedies to only a few. The Doctor should then go to the Materia Medica Homeopathica to see which of the remedies rated at the top of the repertori-zation match the patient's profile. If remedies don't match, and the Doctor is reasonable certain that he or she has modalized and hierarchizised the symp-toms properly, then another hierarchization of symptoms and a further reper-torization are in order.

One of the most delicate aspect of reaching a diagnosis is to become ob-jective enough to first detect, and then determine, the real importance of the patients' symptoms; while, at the same time, remaining sufficiently subjec-tive as to be able of establishing a good rapport.

A sound Homeopathic History, in a chronic patient, must take into consideration the patient, the patient's disease and the patient's circumstance. There are no exceptions to this rule.

However, sometimes a Homeopathic Physician can use shortcuts to reach the fulcrum of imbalance. These shortcuts are particularly useful when the Doctor finds it hard to obtain useful symptoms from his or her patient for some reason or another.

Sometimes, the Doctor may successfully attempt to reach the fulcrum of imbalance starting from the disease-syndrome the patient is bearing, from the patient's standpoint or from the patient's circumstance.

Let me offer examples.

I once saw a 22-year-old male who was finding great difficulty in abandoning his drug and alcohol addictions. He was accident prone and depressed, lacked self-esteem and felt forsaken. There was also guilt and self-recrimination. This patient would set unreachable goals and then berate himself when unable to achieve them.

His addictions, his hidden desire to do away with himself, depression, guilt and self-recrimination led me directly to the fulcrum of his imbalance.

The patient did well after receiving *Aurum*.

A 15-year-old male, in turn, is a good example of reaching the fulcrum of imbalance starting from the patient and ignoring the symptom complex.

This patient had been suffering terrible migraines for several years. They would start suddenly, incapacitate him, and make him vomit until he was exhausted. The Pharmaceutical drugs he was taking weren't helping him at all. If stricken at School, he would go to the Clinic, see the Nurse, and then lie down till somebody would come and take him home, he would become so limp. This adolescent was very authoritarian, competitive and intelligent, had a very low self-esteem and a great fear of failing. He also had a sweet tooth, always wanted his drinks hot, and had a daily slump between 4 and 8 PM.

I ignored the headaches and concentrated instead on the patient's personal characteristics.

I gave him *Lycopodium clavatum*, but also sent the patient to a Neurologist, to rule out the possibility of a problem in the brain, or its blood vessels. The Neurologist report came back negative.

He did well, to everybody's surprise at how these terrible headaches had vanished.

As to the patient's *circumstance*. One can start seeking the fulcrum of the patient's imbalance from the patient's circumstance whenever there is clear evidence of some important negative outside influence.

Sometimes the negative influence that started the patient's chronic imbalance is acute, such as it happens with a child never well since a vaccination, or in a patient who started his or her asthma after the injudicious treatment of a skin rash, or after the loss of a dear one, or after an accident or some other suchlike kind of incident.

Other times, the negative influence is insidious, such as it happens in a bad marriage, or after many a long night of caring for a sick dear one, or after years of a job the patient hates, etc.

The only way to perceive subtle differences such as the ones described above is by means of establishing a sound rapport with patients.

Miasmatic diagnosis.-

This diagnosis is extremely important because of three reasons.

- It will give the Doctor an idea of how to approach the diagnosis/treatment of the patient. The therapeutic approach of a psoric patient is different from that of a sycosic or a syphilitic one.
- It may help the Doctor understand what modifies the patient's clinical picture.
- It may help give the Homeopathic Physician an idea of the *Nosode* that may have to be administered at some point during treatment.

There are many instances, in everyday practice, when the Homeopathic Physician is perplexed. Oftentimes, this perplexity stems from unawareness of the patient's miasma. Most Doctors find it not too arduous to diagnose, say, a tuberculinic *Pulsatilla,* a syphilitic *Aurum* or a sycosic *Nux vomica.* But when the patient happens to be a psoric *Pulsatilla* or a syphilitic *Nux Vomica,* for instance, diagnosis becomes harder. Unless, of course, the Homeopathic Physician have some idea regarding the patient's chronic miasma, and how it can modify the way a patient presents his or her profile.

Awareness of the patient's miasma, of its characteristics, and of how that miasma can *color* or *alter* the essence and the profile of a particular patient, are therefore of the utmost importance.

The Mexican School has placed a great deal of emphasis on chronic miasmas, an emphasis I consider to be amply justified—although too frequently disregarded, alas!

INTEGRATIVE DIAGNOSIS.-

The Integrative Diagnosis is composed by the

- Allopathic,
- Homeopathic,
- Miasmatic and
- Wholistic diagnoses.

A correct Integrative Diagnosis provides the necessary data to consider the best treatment for a particular patient, be it Allopathic, Homeopathic, Wholistic or any combination of the above—that is, the form of treatment that, for each particular patient, carries maximum benefit and minimum risk.

Integrative Physicians should be well versed in Allopathic and at least in one of the major forms of Wholistic Medicine. However, Integrative Physicians should also have a working knowledge of all major forms of Wholistic Medicine. Only then will Integrative Physicians know what treatments or treatments to proffer to each individual patient and for what, what treatments they can deliver themselves and to what Practitioner they must refer their patients for other forms of treatment; and how to coordinate the whole therapeutic team.

There is a growing awareness of the need for Integrative Medicine.

As an example, Bristol BBC got in touch with the Department of Complementary Medicine at Exeter University's Post-graduate Medical School, in England. The School was asked to interview local General Practitioners regarding adverse effects of different forms of Complementary Medicine.

When it came to Homeopathy, Allopathic Doctors said that the main problems they had found were delayed diagnosis of cancer, imprudent withdrawal of Pharmaceutical drugs that brought about relapses of diseases and even death, and the inappropriate use of Homeopathy when Allopathy should have been indicated—all consequences of a poor knowledge of Allopathic Medicine.

Results of these interviews were then broadcasted[40].

---

[40] Scott-Moncrieff C. *"The 'dangers' of Homeopathy"*. Simile (suppl. of Br. Hom. J.) Vol. 7, Oct. 1997, page 1.

Conversely, ignorance of Wholistic Medicine on the part of Allopathic Practitioners has been directly responsible for unnecessary mutilations; extremely painful, unnecessary and expensive procedures; the proliferation of potentially dangerous vaccines for the prevention of childhood diseases that are curable with Homeopathy; the rapid increase of antibiotic-resistant strains of bacteria, etc.

Integrative Medicine is necessary because all forms of Medicine have limitations—and that, of course, includes Homeopathy (Hahnemann S., *Organon*, 6th. Ed., § 153). The limitations of a form of Medicine are often compensated by the possibilities of others.

The knowledge an Integrative Physician has of both Allopathic and Wholistic Medicine allows him or her to combine, whenever necessary, diverse forms of treatment for the benefit of the patient.

Many patients require an Integrative approach. Let me illustrate with examples.

Take for instance a 30 year old female who suffered from rectal bleeding, among other problems. *Pulsatilla* cleared up her whole Clinical picture, with the exception of her rectal bleeding.

I referred the patient to a Proctologist, who found polyps in the large intestine. Colonic polyps usually are benign structures—at least to start with—that grow, from a stalk, into the lumen of the large intestine If left untreated, they may eventually degenerate and become malignant.

Homeopathy could not make those polyps disappear, for they were still present after an otherwise successful treatment. So I asked the patient to have them removed by colonoscopy[41]. This treatment brought about the disappearance of both the polyps and her rectal bleeding.

Or that other patient, a 60 year old male, also had polyps, but in his urinary bladder. He came to my office in search of a treatment other than Surgery. The Urologist had proposed Surgery as the only therapeutic possibility.

I called this Urologist and asked him to please put off Surgery for a time, unless it became an emergency; to which he agreed, if a bit miffed. I made my request because polyps in the urinary bladder, even if originally benign, often become malignant if tampered with; till finally the whole bladder becomes invaded with malignant tissue and has to be removed, irra-

---

[41] That is, through a tube inserted into the anus and then into large intestine.

diated or treated with anticancer drugs. After bladder removal, patients have to urinate through two orifices on his abdominal wall, one corresponding to each ureter and kidney, each of them emptying in an individual little bag. Either that, or else undergo the construction of an artificial urinary bladder. In this latter instance, the patient must press his lower abdomen hard every time he or she has to void. The artificial bladder never empties satisfactorily, a situation brings in its wake all kinds of problems, infections and the like.

This patient did well, and the polyps disappeared with the Homeopathic remedy alone—*Calcarea carbonica*, if I remember correctly.

Let me described still another instance of the usefulness of an integrated approach.

A male in his 40's went to see a Homeopathic Practitioner with little Medical training. The patient was complaining of oppression in his chest. The Practitioner gave him a Homeopathic remedy, then another and still another to no avail. The oppression in the patient's chest became slowly but progressively worse. The patient quitted after one year of fruitless Homeopathic treatment. He went to an Allopathic Physician who, after examining him, asked X Rays and lab work. The chest X Ray showed the presence of an intrathoracic goiter[42]. The Doctor sent the patient to Surgery. The goiter was removed and all symptoms disappeared. It would have been almost impossible to make that thyroid gland shrink to its normal size with Homeopathic treatment alone.

I shudder every time I think about what could have happened if, instead of a benign intrathoracic goiter, this patient would have had a malignant tumor. That one year delay could have well meant the difference between life and death.

Another example. A woman in her 20's, after having had her baby at home, developed malaise, severe pelvic pain, high fever and foul vaginal discharge.

The Health Provider in charge wanted to give her *Pyrogen*[43], while keeping the patient at home under observation. It would have been danger-

---

[42] A goiter is a benign enlargement of the thyroid gland of the neck that usually grows forward and sideways. Exceptionally, it may grow downward into the chest cavity. It is then called *intrathoracic goiter*. Being the chest cavity enclosed by the ribs, the spine and the sternum, anything growing inside compresses the structures that normally lodge there, and cause symptoms of increased intrathoracic pressure.

[43] A Homeopathic remedy often used when there is a severe infection. Its keynote is a high fever and a slow pulse, or vice versa.

ous to await results of *Pyrogen* treatment at home. Homeopathic remedies may put the Vital Force to work immediately in some patients, but it may also take months for the Vital Force to work in others.

If *Pyrogen* wouldn't have acted immediately her reproductive capacity, and indeed her life, would have been placed in jeopardy. What this patient had was a life-threatening acute post-partum pelvic infection that was quite advanced, to the point that her pulse and temperature were totally divorced form each other.

Following my advice, the patient was rushed to the Hospital. She did indeed receive *Pyrogen*, but together with intravenous antibiotics while being evaluated for Surgery. I lost track of her, so I don't know how she evolved under the combined Homeopathy + antibiotic treatment.

Or take that sad girl, whom I first saw when she was 10 years old. She suffered from advanced juvenile rheumatoid arthritis. Many of her joints were inflamed and deformed, with important limitation of movement. Her left elbow, for instance, could only go as far as some three-fourths of full extension—and that at the cost of severe pain.

She was also complaining of episodes of low grade fever of unknown origin and of severe, intermittent pain in her left lower abdomen.

This girl was taking powerful anti-inflammatory drugs, including Prednisone. Her mother brought her to my office because drugs were at best only slowing down the progress of the disease; and also because she was concerned about the drugs' side effects and toxicity on her pre-adolescent daughter.

The girl's Constitutional remedy was *Causticum.* The remedy brought about a rapid improvement, and eventual disappearance of the pain, inflammation, fever, abdominal suffering and all her other problems. Here again, drugs were tapered down slowly, but only after the patient had began to respond to *Causticum.*

Stiffness remained after inflammation of her joints had subsided. This residual stiffness was largely overcome with Chiropractice and Osteopathic Physical Therapy.

She quitted all her Pharmaceutical drugs after some time. When I last saw her she was blooming into adolescence.

The Integrative approach should also take into account the Pharmaceutical drug/s the patient may be taking, as well as every other form of Allopathic treatment.

Some drugs can be discontinued before starting an Integrative treatment. Others may be tapered down and eventually suspended. And the patient may have to continue taking others.

It all depends on the disease-syndrome the patient may be bearing and how that disease is evolving; and also how important it is, or isn't for the patient, to continue taking those drugs and/or other forms of Allopathic treatments.

Let me insist still again, within this context, that Wholistic Medicine is indeed a valid aspect or approach to diagnosis and treatment, as valid as Internal Medicine or Surgery are currently considered to be.

There will be instances when Homeopathy, or any other forms of Wholistic Medicine, will suffice to successfully take care of a patient's problem.

With other patients, though, there may be a need to work in a team with either Internal Medicine, and/or Surgery, including their specialties. Or with Radiotherapy, or with some other form of Wholistic Medicine, etc.

A Homeopathic and a Miasmatic diagnoses is all that is needed if Homeopathy suffices to control a patient's problem.

An Allopathic diagnosis is *de rigueur* if a patient requires immediate treatment for any life-threatening condition[44], and also for other problems that are beyond the scope of Wholistic Medicine.

In turn, an Integrative diagnosis is essential if one wants to proffer each individual Whole patient a treatment that has a maximum of benefit and a minimum of risk; that is, a treatment or combination thereof capable of assisting both the Whole patient and Whole patient's pathological condition.

To sum up the similarities and differences between Allopathic, Homeopathic and Integrative diagnoses,

In Allopathy, the only diagnosis that counts is the *Clinical Diagnosis;* that is, that related to the disease-syndrome afflicting the patient.

---

[44] This is so because, in an emergency, what is usually available are ambulances and Emergency Rooms—not the places where one is likely to find Homeopathic remedies. Another reason is because often Allopathic drugs may work in a more predictable and consistent fashion than Homeopathic remedies.

Jose Miguel Mullen, M.D.

The diagnosis of the disease-syndrome affecting the patient is one thing, and the treatment that follows is quite another.

Treatment is only aimed at eliminating the disease afflicting the patient.

In Homeopathy, the only diagnosis that counts, in *acute diseases,* is that of the Whole disease-syndrome afflicting the patient.

In a *psoric patient,* instead, the diagnosis is that of the Whole psoric patient. The diagnosis, and the treatment that follows, is one and the same thing.

Treatment of an acute disease is aimed at revitalizing the diseased area, and treatment of a Whole psoric patient is directed toward bringing the Whole patient into balance.

In Integrative Medicine, both the Allopathic and the Homeopathic diagnoses are taken into account.

Treatment here will be Homeopathic, Allopathic, or a combination of both, according to the needs of each individual patient.

Allopathic diagnosis lead to Allopathic treatments that, useful as they are, are riddled with complications, side effects and toxicity.

It would be wonderful if Homeopathy—or any other form of Wholistic treatment, for that matter—were a Panacea. After all, Wholistic treatments usually proffer all benefit and no risk.

Unfortunately, Wholistic treatments are no Panacea. They have enormous possibilities, but also real limitations. Many of those limitations can be adequately covered by the usefulness of Allopathic treatments.

Different diagnoses, reached by different Health Care Providers, lead toward diverse therapeutic approaches.

A correct Allopathic diagnosis leads toward an adequate Allopathic treatment.

An accurate Homeopathic diagnosis is followed by a successful Homeopathic treatment.

A correct Integrative Medical diagnosis allows the Doctor to assess whether the patient will benefit from Homeopathic treatment alone, from a combined Homeopathic-Allopathic treatment, or else from Allopathy or Homeopathy associated with other form/s of Wholistic Medicine.

144

Which is the reason why it is so convenient to consider the patient's Integrative diagnosis when planning his or her treatment—and also why all serious and valid forms of Medical diagnosis and treatment should integrate.

Chapter 12

CHOOSING A PATIENT'S TREATMENT

Integrative History and Physical Examination

↓

Obtention of an Integrative diagnosis

↓

Selection of treatment

Allopathic   ↓   Wholistic

Integrative
(Allopathic + Wholistic)

There are several ways of treating a patient.

Treatments can be basically divided into *Allopathic, Wholistic* or Complementary, and *Integrative.*

Allopathic Medicine teaches how to reach a Clinical diagnosis, and also how to use Pharmaceutical drugs, Surgery, Radiation Therapy, etc. Allopathic Medicine is only taught in Medical and Osteopathic Schools, and also in Post-graduate Medical training. Here, the teaching of subjects related to Allopathic Medicine occupies all, or almost all, of the Curriculum.

In Wholistic Schools, instead, subjects related to Allopathic Medicine is taught only as a part of the Curriculum. Furthermore, graduates have no access to Post graduate training in Allopathic Medicine.

Graduates of Allopathic Medical Schools, then, have a considerable greater knowledge of Clinical Medicine than graduates of Schools devoted to diverse forms of Wholistic Medicine.

In turn, Wholistic Medicine is completely disregarded in most Medical Schools, although it comprises most of the Wholistic Medical Schools' curricula. Meaning that most Medical Doctors graduate being completely ignorant of subjects related to Wholistic Medicine.

Wholistic Medicine includes therapeutic procedures such as Homeopathy, manipulations of various kinds, Acupuncture, Ayurveda, Antroposophy, Anti-ageing Medicine, herbal treatments, etc.

Graduates of Wholistic Schools, then, have a considerably greater knowledge of Wholistic Medicine than Medical Doctors.

The paradigm of Allopathy, as well as that of the diverse forms of Wholistic Medicine, has limits to its usefulness.

Integrative Medicine, by means of coalescing Allopathy and Wholism, creates a paradigm that also has limits; but that encloses a much larger area of usefulness within its limits.

There are patients who benefit from one or several forms of Wholistic Medicine alone. Others need an association of Complementary and Allopathic Medicine.

There is a very powerful movement nowadays towards integrating all forms of Medicine into one.

Patients are demanding more than just Pharmaceutical drugs, Surgery, herbs, applications of needles and the like. They are demanding to be treated according to their needs, and not to the extent of knowledge—or of prejudice—of their respective Health Care Providers.

Take for instance cardiovascular diseases, for a long time one of the main strongholds of Allopathic Medicine.

Currently, an array of Wholistic treatments, all the way from Nutrition to Counseling to Homeopathy are being used in these patients with remarkable success, either alone or else associated with Allopathic treatments. Dr. Stephen Sinatra, a Manchester, CT, Cardiologist, is one of the pioneers in this field.

I would like to illustrate the importance of integrating Medicine with two patients I saw in my office—too late in both instances.

147

These patients had been seen by Health Care Providers whose knowledge was limited to only Allopathic or Wholism.

These patients—and these Health Care Providers, too—are by no means unique. I have seen many in my practice.

One of the patients to be described immediately below had cancer of the stomach. The other started her odyssey with a problem as simple as recurring sinusitis.

Cancer of the stomach must be diagnosed in time and operated upon as soon as possible. Early surgical removal proffers the only possibility of cure or, at the very least, of long-lasting symptom-free survival. The disease usually starts insidiously, with very few symptoms.

The earliest symptoms in this particular patient, a 49 year old male, had been minimal discomfort in the pit of the stomach and some heartburn for 6 months, plus some weight loss and weakness. The patient treated himself with this and that and, in general, paid little attention to his symptoms. Then he had one tarry stool[45]. Two days afterwards he consulted a Health Care Provider with very little knowledge of Allopathy.

The patient's symptoms—including the tarry stool—failed to alert this Provider. His poor knowledge of Allopathy didn't permit him to make a differential diagnosis of the patient's pathological symptoms, and thus consider the possibility of stomach cancer.

He modalized the patient's symptoms and prescribed one Homeopathic remedy. The patient slowly worsened. He continued loosing weight. His weakness increased.

The Provider gave the patient another Homeopathic remedy, and then another, according to the progressive worsening he was finding in the patient. The patient's general condition continued to deteriorate. He started to vomit coffee ground stuff[46], and the discomfort in the pit of the stomach gradually became severe pain. This was some 18 months after his first visit to this Health Care Provider.

The patient decided to come to my office. I immediately referred him to a Gastroenterologist.

It was too late. The tumor was inoperable. He was started in Chemotherapy, that is pretty useless for this kind of problem. Chemotherapy only succeeded in increasing his misery. The patient died a few short months afterwards.

---

[45] That is, with the general consistency and color of tar. It is usually the manifestation of important blood loss high up in the digestive system.

[46] It appears when there is blood loss into the stomach.

Then there is a very personable 42-year-old woman. She had suffered for many years from congestion, stuffiness and pain in the head. Her Family Physician had prescribed course after course of antibiotics and decongestants. She had also received allergy shots.

She was referred to Surgery. Both her Family Physician and her Surgeon were totally ignorant of the usefulness of Wholistic Medicine in the treatment of sinusitis-bearing patients. The patient found, upon awakening from the anesthetic, that she had lost all smell and taste. The Surgeon had inadvertently cut both olfactory nerves, a not uncommon accident during sinus surgery. Olfactory nerves run close to a set of sinuses located in the dome of both nasal cavities. If the brain cannot receive reports from the olfactory nerve there is no smelling; and, since smelling controls most of the taste sensations, there is no taste either.

Symptoms of sinusitis re-appeared a few months after her operation.

Some two years after Surgery she came to see me. She responded quite well to Homeopathic treatment. Most of her symptoms vanished. She has remained well except during the season of high pollen count, when she experiences minimal sinus discomfort—but she was still unable to taste or to smell the last time I saw her.

In the first patient, the diagnosis was missed because his Health Care Provider did not know enough Allopathic Medicine to think of cancer of the stomach. Consequently, the patient missed Surgery that, if done in time, could have saved him.

In turn, ignorance of the usefulness of Wholistic Medicine forced the second patient through course after course of decongestants, antibiotics, Surgery and her loss of smell and taste.

None of these mishaps would have happened if the respective Health Care Providers would have had adequate training in Integrative Medicine.

If Homeopathy is chosen as the most adequate form of treatment for a particular patient, and that patient is found to be chronic, then the *Whole patient* has to be treated. Not just the problem or lesion that may be the single manifestation of the chronic imbalance.

In paragraph 201 of his *Organon,* Dr. Hahnemann states that the Vital Force, in an attempt to preserve the harmony of the Whole, may localize a chronic patient's imbalance into some organ or structure, thus creating a localized disease-syndrome. The organ so chosen is thus sacrificed to preserve some semblance of harmony in the Whole patient. Put in another way, when imbalance reaches a certain point, the Vital Force may be forced to loosen its grip in a superficial organ or tissue in order to concentrate all its power in deeper organs, more important for the patient's survival. The loosening of the grip produces devitalization of the superficial organ. Devitalization makes that organ cry for help. This cry for help is recognized as distress by the patient, and a disease-syndrome by a Doctor.

Local treatments of disease-syndromes arising from this loosening of the Vital Force's grip, however successful, will do nothing at all to correct the imbalance of the Whole chronic patient.

What's worse, such a successful local treatment will coerce the Vital Force to re-enforce its grip in a superficial organ or tissue, thus loosening up its grip in others more important for the patient's survival. The consequence is the creation of a suppression—while the untreated chronic imbalance continues to inexorably worsen unto increasing unnecessary suffering an untimely death.

This doesn't mean that local disease-syndromes should not be treated in a chronic patient, or that the patient should wait until balanced is sufficiently restored for his or her local disease to vanish.

If the patient is found to suffer from an acute disease-syndrome in some organ or tissue, then that patient should start receiving the correct Allopathic treatment without delay if indicated. While, at the same time, using Homeopathy bring the patient into balance and thus prevent the possibility of a suppression.

To sum up,

Homeopathic Medicine has usefulness and limitations, but no risk.

Allopathic treatments have usefulness and limitations, and also risks that can be very important (side effects, toxicity, damage to embryos and fetuses, surgical mutilations, etc.).

Patients don't go to a Doctor to specifically receive a particular form of treatment, but rather to get rid of whatever may be ailing them through the fastest, safest, cheapest and least harmful and limiting means available.

There are patients who are best treated by Homeopathy. Others benefit from non-Homeopathic forms of Wholistic Medicine. Still others are helped by Allopathic treatments, whether Pharmacological, Surgical or radiation. Or by diverse combinations of the above.

What is important here is to find the best, less injurious, fastest and most economical way of making patients well; be it through Homeopathic, Allopathic or whatever other form of treatment, or combination of treatments thereof. That is, the form or forms of treatment that, in each individual instance, can produce a maximum of benefit and a minimum of risk.

Health Care Providers should be able to determine what disease-syndrome is ailing the Whole patient—that is, they should learn how to reach both a *Clinical* and a *Wholistic diagnosis*. They should also have sufficient information regarding diverse *forms of treatment,* both Allopathic and Complementary.

Only then will each patient receive the form of treatment best suited for his or her Wholeness; that is, the *Integrative* therapeutic approach that offers the highest possible benefit to risk ratio.

*"The ultimate goal of any treatment is to re-establish
health as rapidly, gently and permanently as possible;
to eliminate diseases in the shortest, surest and least
harmful way; and to accomplish all these goals following
clear and understandable principles".*
Hahnemann S. *Organon*, 6th Edition, § 2.

Chapter 13

ALLOPATHIC AND HOMEOPATHIC TREATMENT OF ACUTE AND OF CHRONIC PATIENTS

Homeopathic remedies have never cured any disease-syndrome.

*In a car, the starter primes the engine. Then the engine starts,
and moves the car.*

*In a similar fashion, Homeopathic remedies are only primers of
the patient's Vital Force. Then the healing power of the Vital Force
starts to work, gains a good hold on every organ and structure, and
brings about balance and harmony into the Whole patient.*

*It is the patient's Vital Force, then, and not the Homeopathic
remedy, what will ultimately cure the patient in a very gentle, yet
steady and powerful fashion.*

*No Pharmaceutical drug can compare with a patient's own Vi-
tal Force in curative power.*

*Perhaps that is the reason why, when patients are cured
Homeopathically, they become so reluctant to return Allopathic
Medicine.*

I was firmly convinced that Homeopathy was only an artful lie during
my many years of practicing Allopathy. I also thought that only fools could
be mystified by it.

Let me share with you what convinced me, beyond the shadow of a
doubt, that Homeopathy can indeed be extraordinarily useful. It happened
when I first witnessed my first Homeopathic cure—or rather, something that
could have well become an astounding cure, had the patient taken proper
care of himself.

It happened during my second month as a student in the Post-Graduate School of the Asociación Médica Homeopática Argentina; that is, after my having been in contact with Homeopathy for only two months. I still had 4 years of study and training ahead of me. I wasn't sure I would go all the way. I thought that Homeopathy was a hoax, and all I wanted at that time was to unmask it.

I had enrolled in the School because, after 27 years of practicing Allopathy and 23 of doing Cancer Research, I had realized that malignant tumors are the *consequence,* and not the *cause,* of the disease-syndrome cancer. Such a realization is tantamount to Medical heresy and blasphemy. It was contrary to everything I had been taught and believed in. It left me very confused. It blew away all my outlooks, expectations and perspectives. I had nowhere to look for clarification in Allopathic Medicine. So I found myself compelled to search for answers in diverse forms of Complementary Medicine.

In my search I had snooped into, and in some instances studied in depth, diverse forms of Wholistic Medicine. All the way from Massage to Folk Medicine to Acupuncture to Anthroposophy. None fully satisfied me. In none of them I found the answer I was seeking.

At the end, I had no choice but to see what this Homeopathy thing was all about. It was the last stone that still remained unturned. I had left it aside because I had been brainwashed into believing that Homeopathy was pure charlatanism, or worse.

I finally enrolled in the Post-Graduate School of the Asociación Médica Homeopática Argentina, in Buenos Aires.

Classes at the Post-graduate School are either lectures or else workshops with patients. During lectures, a Professor explains a Homeopathic remedy, or else some aspect of Homeopathy or Homeopathic Philosophy. Workshops with patients are held in a relatively large classroom-office. A Professor first obtains a patient's Homeopathic History, and afterwards calls for questions and comments. Subsequently, one of the students ushers the patient into an adjacent examining room to complete the Clinical History and perform the Physical Examination. Then the patient's remedy is considered, discussed and dispensed. As a rule, several patients are seen in this fashion every day.

I was very skeptical and critical of what I was seeing and learning. I witnessed many cures. Some I could attribute to a placebo effect. Others were real, bona fide cures. The latter puzzled me, and were thawing my obstinate scorn and skepticism toward Homeopathy.

I wasn't prepared for what I was about to witness, though.

153

The incredible result I am about to describe happened during a busy workday like any other. The patient was the second or third that day.

He was 42 years old and in extremely poor physical shape. He had a History of chronic severe alcoholism, advanced clinical syphilis and Chagas' disease[47]. He was also a heavy smoker. Advanced syphilis had weakened the walls of his big arteries, and Chagas' disease had severely damaged the heart.

He was literally dragged into the office-classroom by two sturdy relatives or friends, gasping for breath. His legs wobbled and would have buckled under him if he hadn't been so firmly held. His complexion was dusky. He was in severe distress.

The patient was receiving many Pharmaceutical drugs to aid his faltering heart. Also diuretics, or water pills, to force the kidneys to eliminate salt and water and thus relieve the heart's load. None of these drugs were working—but then, on what were they going to work, if part of the heart pump had been destroyed by Chagas' disease? Besides, his main arteries were grossly and irregularly dilated, damaged beyond repair by advanced clinical syphilis.

Needless to say, he was also receiving many other drugs that weren't helping him in the least, either.

He had been unable to sleep for many nights, even when sitting up, due to his extreme fatigue. He was exhausted and deathly anxious.

I completed the History and performed the Physical Examination, after the Professor obtained this Homeopathic History. His lips and fingernails were purplish-blue, his blood pressure was very high and his pulse was racing. The jugular veins in his neck were bulging. The liver and spleen were enormous, due to the pooling of blood into them. They were also tender to palpation because of how distended and tense they were. There was a great deal of clinically detectable fluid in his severely distended abdomen. His

---

[47] Brought about by the parasite *Tripanosoma cruzi*. Its vector is the coleopteron *Triatoma Infestans*, a.k.a. *vinchuca*. It is endemic in warm areas of Latin America. The disease is unknown in North America. *Ranchos*, the *gauchos'* miserable dwellings, are walled with adobe and roofed with straw. *Vinchucas* slumber in crevices during daytime. At night they crawl out. The gut of infested *Vinchucas* is full of *trypanosomes*, sucked together with the blood of patients ill with Chagas' disease. Vinchucas defecate as they suck. *Trypanosomes* are left on the skin surface with their feces. The *vinchuca's* bite is itchy. The victim scratches the area during sleep, sufficiently injuring the skin as to allow *Trypanosomes* to enter. *Tripanosoma cruzi* is a very dangerous parasite. Among other things, it slowly and gradually destroys the heart muscle.

legs were massively swollen, almost as high up as the knees. There was fluid in his chest, and the lungs above the fluid level made weak crackling noises—what we call *crepitant râles*. Both lung fields were very congested. He had very little lung tissue available to breath with at the time of examination.

He was prescribed *Arsenicum album* (can't recall the potency) and asked to return in a week. He was carried away by his friends, gasping pitifully and completely exhausted. I didn't expect to see this poor man ever again.

I couldn't believe my eyes when I saw him return, one week later! He walked in, alone and with a firm step. And smiling. He stated that the very first night he took the remedy he fell asleep lying down, because his breathing had become normal.

He was feeling fine and had no complaints. The color of his skin, lips and fingernails was normal. His breathing were regular. His jugular veins could neither be seen nor palpated. Breathing sounds were normal. There was no clinically detectable fluid in his chest nor in his abdominal cavity and his breathing sound were normal. Blood pressure was almost normal, as was his pulse. The liver and spleen were only slightly enlarged, and not tender to palpation. The swelling in his legs had vanished, together with his anxiety. To boot, he had quitted taking all the drugs prescribed by his Allopathic Doctor. As he explained "Because I don't need them any more".

Nothing I had learnt in Medical School and afterwards, nothing in my store of experience and knowledge had prepared me for what I was witnessing. What I had in front of my eyes did not make any sense at all. All the clinical evidence of this patient's advanced syphilis and Chagas' had disappeared from one day to the next—literally! There was no way of brushing this evidence aside as a placebo effect. Something had happened here. Whatever heart tissue this man still had, and that no drug treatment had been able to assist, seemed to be working adequately.

To my utter surprise, none of my Professors shared my astonishment. For them, what had happened to this man was a most natural thing, another commonplace occurrence in their daily schedules.

This patient's saga ended on a sad if predictable note.

His self-destructive leanings, consequence of his syphilitic miasma, resurfaced as soon as he felt well. He resumed his heavy drinking and smoking. He also began pursuing anew other forms of suchlike self-injurious and -destructive behavior.

Even so, the effect of that single dose of his Homeopathic remedy lasted for approximately one year. He deteriorated rapidly afterwards, despite further Homeopathic treatment. I heard that he died a few months later.

What would have happened if this man had taken care of himself? Of course, it is impossible to tell. My belief, though, is that he might have been able to live well, and symptom free, for at least several more years.

A disease-syndrome becomes apparent when, due to the patient's imbalance, the Vital Force loosens its grip on a particular organ or structure. The affected area screams for help. The cry is interpreted as suffering and distress by the patient, and as a disease-syndrome by the Physician.

This loosening of the grip happens to the organ or structure where the Vital Force is less strongly attached. The affected organ or structure varies from person to person.

The cause, in acute patients, is characteristically some external or internal insult that loosens the grip of the Vital Force on some organ. This insult, and the subsequent loosening of the Vital Force, brings about the imbalance manifested of acute diseases. Here the insult comes first, and the imbalance follows.

In most instances, balance is restored when the the patient's Vital Force is re-attached to the bereft organ.

In chronic patients things don't happen this way. Here the loss of the patient's overall balance comes first. Imbalance is always progressive in chronic patients because nothing is static in Nature, but constantly progresses.

In chronic patients, the Vital Force loosens its grip in one organ after another, usually starting in the most superficial and less essential for subsistence and then progressing toward structures that are deeper and crucial for the patient's survival.

Loosening may happen without insult or injury, or else may be brought about, or hastened, by some external or internal injury or disease. Either way, the final result is an increase of the chronic imbalance already present—unless imbalance is checked and reversed.

It follows that what has to be done to cure an acute patient is to re-attach the Vital Force to the organ or tissue that is screaming for help. This procedure re-establishes balance in the Whole patient.

In psoric patients, on the other hand, Homeopathic treatment must re-establish the Whole patient's balance as an indispensable first step. Any attempt to re-attach the Vital Force to individual organs and tissues must come later. To reverse this order is like attempting to placing the roof of a building before building its walls.

Treatment can be Allopathic or Wholistic, or else a combination of both. I will concentrate my discussion mainly on Homeopathy and drug treatment. I may tangentially mention Allopathy and other forms of Wholistic treatments.

Allopathy can be used—indeed, sometimes it *must* be used—in acute and in chronic patients, but never alone. It should always be used *combined with* Homeopathy and/or Acupuncture if overall balance is to be reestablished.

This is so because Allopathy carries implicit the paradox of curing diseases, while at the same time allowing imbalance to worsen, and sometimes even hastening its progress. This is due to its incapacity of working on the patient's balance and also because of the inevitable side effects and toxicity of its treatments. In turn, this inevitably happens because Allopathic treatments have been designed with the aim of fighting and destroying diseases, not of correcting Whole patients' imbalances.

Balance and imbalance, as well as the notion of Wholeness, are beyond the reach of Allopathy.

Take for instance an acute infection of any kind, say a tonsillitis, a pneumonitis or whatever. Antibiotics will kill bacteria and therefore make the disease disappear. Drug action, however, will not go any further.

Or take the action of antiinflamatory agents in diseases of the joints. These drugs will indeed improve pain and even lessen inflammation, but will do nothing to slow down—far less to stop—the overall imbalance that brought about that inflammation in the first place.

As mentioned above, *all* drugs stimulate imbalance through their side effects and toxicity. Even antibiotics, that are supposed to be the safest of drugs.

Antibiotics are said to be specific because bacteria have receptors that are not present in Human cells. Antibiotics, then, act by interacting only with receptors present in bacteria. Meaning that supposedly they should not have any ill effects on patients. Like every other drug, however, antibiotics must be metabolized and excreted by the patient. They also devastate the patient's bacterial flora.

Our normal bacterial flora is composed by hundreds of strains of bacteria that live and thrive in an *entente cordiale* with us and with other strains on our skin and inside our cavities. Some of those microorganisms—as well as newcomers—proliferate and attack when there is imbalance. The consequence is an infection. Antibiotics will only destroy bacteria that are sensitive—whether or not those sensitive bacteria are the ones that bring about the infection or are members of our normal flora. Spaces left vacant by annihilated strains become occupied by strains that are resistant to the antibiotic. And this seizure is not friendly. It can be compared to what happens when several inner city gangs fight with each other to occupy a turf left vacant by another gang that has disappeared. This final result of this antibiotic-induced struggle between bacterial strains is usually manifested by diarrhea, mouth sores, yeast infestations, malaise, and a host of other problems that tend to increase the imbalance already present in the patient. Some strains of bacteria can and do become resistant to antibiotics, and thus survive treatment. Resistant bacteria share parts of themselves, called *plasmides,* with others. Those other bacterial strains then become antibiotic-resistant through the use of plasmides. Resistant bacteria, in turn, transmit those plasmids to their descendants. There are currently several bacterial strains that are resistant to every known antibiotic—and counting.

I don't believe that antibiotic resistance is the consequence of prescribing too many antibiotics. Bacteria have successfully survived for millennia under many adverse circumstances. They are bound to survive our puny onslaughts as they have survived everything else—all the more because antibiotics are obtained from molds, with which bacteria have shared space and nutrients for eons. If antibiotics would have been prescribed with less largesse, perhaps it would have taken *longer* for bacteria to become resistant to antibiotics—but resistant they would have become, either way.

Molds produce allergic reactions. Antibiotics are produced by molds. Therefore, Human Beings can become allergic to antibiotics. Some allergic reactions may be mild, a rash or something of the kind. Others can be severe. Penicillin, famous as the safest of antibiotics, can produce a form of allergic reaction that can fatal if not treated immediately—a sudden swelling of the throat, followed by an immediate closure of the larynx or voice box.

Allergies also worsen the imbalance already present in the patient.

The worse part is that, quite often, these indiscriminate antibiotic-induced bacterial massacres fall short of a complete cure. Take the typical 9 or 10 year old who gets the first bout of pneumonitis—or inflammation/infection of the lungs—in November. The child is treated with antibiotics and supposedly cured. Then the child has another bout in January, and is cured again; to have still another infection in March. Or take a little patient with otitis or infection of the ears, considered as cured when tubes are stuck into his or her middle ear through the eardrums—after the failure, or rather the partial success, of successive courses of treatment with many antibiotics.

Not only do antibiotics—and every other form of Allopathic treatment, for that matter—fall short of a definitive cure. They may also transform acute patients into psorics.

The first bout of an acute infection, in a well balanced patient, loosens the grip of the Vital Force on an infected organ. The balance of the patient, although affected, can still be restored. The infection is treated with an antibiotic. This treatment, even though it may kill bacteria, does nothing to re-attach the Vital Force to the affected organ or structure. The treated organ remains devitalized after the Pharmaceutical "cure", and thus prone to another infection. The patient becomes more imbalanced. The second infection loosens the Vital Force still more, even if antibiotics again cure the patient. By that time, the imbalance of the originally acute patient is well on its way of becoming chronic.

This is how drug treatments, even when using substances as "harmless" as antibiotics, can progressively transform an acute patient into a psoric one.

Most Pharmaceutical drugs are not as safe as antibiotics, by far.

Some can reverse normal physiologic processes; even to the extreme of inducing suppressions.

A nose spray, for instance, shrinks swollen tissues inside the nose. But this swelling is necessary to accumulate fluid into the nasal tissues—and, dissolved in that fluid, organic garbage in need to be eliminated. The liquid and garbage are there to be discharged afterwards, when the Vital Force orders the swollen nasal tissues to shrink so that liquid and garbage is discharged into the nasal cavity and thus eliminated.

A nose spray will shrink the swollen tissues of the nose before enough liquid accumulates. Worse yet, it may dry up the nasal passages. Fluid and garbage will be forced to remain in the organism.

Finally, and in the long run, many a drug treatment may rebound and trigger the opposite effect. Dr. Hahnemann described this sequence of action → reaction in his *Organon,* 6th Ed. § 63.

Take for instance the administration of laxatives to chronically constipated patients. Most laxatives work by means of irritating the intestinal wall, thus forcing the cells lining the wall to react by means of shedding water into the intestine—pretty much as the eye combats irritation caused by a foreign body by means of shedding an abundance of tears. The *action* of a laxative, then, is to irritate the intestinal wall and, as the consequence, to increase the amount of water inside the intestine. This larger amount of water increases the volume of intestinal contents. Expansion of intestinal contents by this excess liquid, plus irritation to the intestinal wall, increases both the motility of the intestine and the amount of feces. The result is a large and often loose stool a few hours after ingesting the laxative. The *reaction,* secondary action or counteraction of the laxative is also the consequence of irritation of the intestinal wall. After some time, the discharge will dry up, and the intestinal wall will become chronically inflamed. The bottom line is that the patient will end up more constipated, and feeling worse, than before starting to use the laxative.

There are times, however, when Pharmaceutical drugs need to be used. The reason being that their action is often more reliable than that of Homeopathic remedies.

An antibiotic, for instance, is quite likely to start working in less than one hour. It may also exterminate most sensitive bacteria in close to 100 % of the patients treated. And the Doctor, as a rule, doesn't need to be a super-specialist in order to prescribe the right one. A Homeopathic remedy, on the other hand, may start acting anytime from instantly to up to several months, depending on the patient. And the percentage of patients helped will depend largely on the acumen of the Homeopathic Physician and his or her ability of finding the correct remedy.

Allopathic treatments, then, are *more* reliable; both regarding how fast they act, and also on how many patients. This reliability weighs very heavily in acute and in life-threatening situations, both in acute and in psoric patients; in the latter because many acute exacerbations, as well as many acute intercurrent diseases, must be treated immediately and with whatever means at hand.

In acute diseases, Allopathy eliminates the invading agent and/or makes the symptom disappear, or else lessens pain and inflammation, etc.; but does nothing to allow the Vital Force to regain full hold of the affected organ or structure. What's more, the patient has to deal with the side effects and toxicity of the drugs used during the treatment.

Homeopathy allows the Vital Force to regain a full hold on the affected organ or tissue. By doing so, it activates the healing power of the Vital Force that cures the acute disease-bearing patient. The con here is that Homeopathy is not quite as reliable as Allopathy, a factor that becomes important when a prompt successful therapeutic effect is required.

Acute diseases, then, should be treated either with Homeopathy alone, or else Allopathy + Homeopathy, according to the needs of each individual acute patient.

Psoric patients, on the other hand, are beyond the reach of Allopathic Medicine—although here, too, Allopathic treatments may have to be used now and then.

In a psoric patient, for instance, an antibiotic may indeed kill the bacteria that are causing an infection, but will be totally impotent to correct the overall and progressive imbalance that brings about the localized weakness and that consequently allows the infection to start.

By the same token, surgical removal of the large intestine may make an ulcerative colitis patient symptom-free. But will do nothing to cure the imbalance that, in that patient, is manifested by ulcerative colitis—and that, in all likelihood, will bring about another and more serious disease-syndrome after the colon is removed.

Since nothing is static in Nature, Allopathic treatments are unable, not only of bringing patients into balance, but also of preventing the constant and progressive *aggravation* of psoric patients' imbalance.

As Dr. Hahnemann pointed out, the psoric hydra will sprout a thousand heads or disease-syndromes—call them infections, degenerations, tumors or whatever—from the stump left behind after any *successful* Allopathic treatment.

Allopathically treated psoric patients, no matter how successfully, are likely to fall ill again and again. They will continue living on a daydream of unfulfilled hopes as imbalance slowly progresses and erodes the meretricious well being afforded by pill popping, shots, Surgeries and the like.

For Homeopathy, healing is the consequence of controlling acute diseases, and also of bringing *Whole* psoric patients into balance. When an acute disease is controlled, or when a Whole psoric patient is brought into balance, the Vital Force and the patient become one harmonious Whole. Harmony is then radiated into the patient's circumstance.

This said, allow me to iterate that, in the same fashion that Allopathy cannot cure psoric patients, Homeopathic remedies can't cure them, either.

This is so because *only the patient's Vital Force*—and the Vital Force's *healing power*—can

- restore the grip of the Vital Force on organs or tissues affected by acute diseases,
- restore the Whole psoric patient's balance,
- once the patient is in balance, comfortably reach that patient's every nook and cranny and, by doing so,
- firmly attach itself to every organ and structure of that patient and thus,

161

- bring about harmony into the patient's Wholeness.

Imbalance in cells and subcellular fractions will also be corrected *as part* of the Vital Force's healing process, by means vastly more perfect and comprehensive that those achieved by any drug-receptor Allopathic interaction, means of which we still know nothing about.

The added bonus here is that the Vital Force will never bring about any adverse effect to its bearer.

The participation of a Homeopathic remedy in any therapeutic plan or, same thing, the Homeopathic remedy's mode of action, is that of directing the patient's Vital Force, and its healing capacity wherever it is needed.

Let us consider a firefighter in this context.

No firefighter has ever put out a fire.

All a firefighter does is to direct the nozzle of the hose toward the fire. The water pouring from the nozzle, and not the firefighter, is what extinguishes the fire.

In a similar fashion, a Homeopathic remedy directs the healing power of the Vital Force toward ill organs and tissues in acute patients.

In psorics, the remedy directs the Vital Force towards the source of the Whole psoric patient's imbalance. Then the Vital Force interacts with the fulcrum of the psoric patient's imbalance → brings the patient into balance → attunes the patient and the patient's Vital Force → cures any disease-syndrome through the Vital Force's attunement with the patient.

This form of cure permits the psoric patient to span, for the first time in his or her life, the space that stretches between just not being sick (that is, what is considered as being *healthy* or *cured* by Allopathy), and being effectively hale.

Therapeutic success, in a psoric patient, is largely conditioned to *how much Vital Force each patient has for healing purposes;* that is, how much Vital Force remains after the everyday business of keeping the patient alive and functioning.

If too little Vital Force is available, as it happens in very feeble patients, then a Homeopathic treatment may well bring about worsening instead of a cure.

Prompted by the Homeopathic remedy, the scant Vital Force remaining free in a weak patient will attempt to continue performing the patient's day to day maintenance and also heal, all at the same time. The little Vital Force that remains free for healing purposes will not suffice to satisfactorily perform the job.

As the result, the patient's maintenance will suffer while the disease-syndrome progresses unchecked. All of which is manifested by a considerable worsening of the clinical condition.

In some patients, both acute and psoric, the Homeopathic cure is immediate.

I have seen ill patients walk out of the office virtually symptom-free, after having taken one single dose of their Homeopathic remedy.

Others may take the remedy at night and awake well in the morning.

In most psoric patients, though, the cure can take from days to weeks to become evident; and even months in some instances.

Any number of factors may be involved in this delay.

Severe chronic imbalance may be one factor. Or the patient may be slow to respond to treatment.

It may also be that the patient is chronically intoxicated, after years and years of taking drugs laden with side effects and toxicity. Chronic intoxication may considerably slow down the effect of an otherwise successful Homeopathic treatment.

Or it can also be that the Homeopathic Physician may find it difficult to find the correct remedy.

Let me illustrate with two clinical examples how long it may take for a patient to feel well. Both examples are extreme. The first corresponds to a patient who felt well immediately. The second needed over one year to feel well.

The first example has to do with a single working mother in her early 30's. Her menstrual pains were so excruciating as to turn her into an invalid during her periods. She had to take morphine-like painkillers to ease her agony during menses.

Her Pap smear was borderline cancer, so her Gynecologist was following her very closely.

The clinical diagnosis was endometriosis. Sometimes, as the female embryo is being formed, part of the uterine lining remains *outside* the womb, in the abdominal cavity. When the girl starts to menstruate, those nests undergo the same changes as the lining of the uterus during the menstrual cycle, but without an outlet at the time of menstruation. Blood and tissues accumulate inside those little bags, that become fuller and fuller, more and more tense, and correspondingly more and more painful as blood accumulates month after month. Understandably, the pain reaches its peak during menstruation, the time when new blood joins the old in the little sacs, increasing the tension and pain to an unbearable extreme. This is called *endometriosis.*

This patient had undergone several laparoscopies, or introduction of a tube into the abdominal cavity, through which her Gynecologist visualized and destroyed many areas of endometriosis. There were so many that others invariably remained. Adhesions appeared after each laparoscopy as part of the healing process. Adhesions trapped loops of intestine, bringing about even more pain and distress.

Finally, the Gynecologist recommended a hysterectomy, or surgical removal of her womb, as the only remaining solution. All the more because of her risky Pap smear. The patient refused. She wanted to have more children.

She decided to search for another answer in complementary Medicine, and asked for an appointment.

After studying the patient, I gave her the remedy I considered matched her profile.

The remedy helped her, but did nothing to alleviate the menstrual pains. So I prescribed another remedy, and then still another.

I was obtaining only minimal results, a far cry from what I am used to expect from a satisfactory Homeopathic treatment.

I was puzzled at my failure. Also bewildered.

Five months afterwards I had reached the end of my rope. I simply didn't know what else to prescribe.

Her next visit coincided with her menstruation. The patient chose to keep her appointment despite of terrible pains. Somehow she made it. Once in the office, with the patient bent double and grimacing in agonizing pain, I asked her to describe what she was feeling. The patient, gasping, described it accurately. She also told me that she was vomiting all the time and that she had nausea even after vomiting at the time of her menses. This constant nausea was unbearable and made her deathly sick. She compared her lower abdominal pain to a knife cutting her entrails. Her tongue was clean.

It was essential information she had never given me before. Maybe because she would forget it between her periods. Or perhaps as the consequence of an unconscious attempt to put suffering aside until it became inevitable. Whatever the reason, the patient gave me all the facts I needed. Right then and there I gave her one dose of *Ipeca* 200 C. *Ipeca* matched her profile quite nicely.

The effect was dramatic. Her pain started to subside almost immediately, and she walked out of the office virtually symptom-free minutes later.

The patient told me in an ulterior visit that the Pap smear had become completely normal, much to the astonishment of her Gynecologist, who didn't understand what had happened, how, or why.

I continued seeing this patient, though less and less frequently.

More than one year after the onset of her wellness, in one of her sporadic follow-up visits, I asked why she had continued to come to my office, despite of my repeated failures.

"My plan was to give you six months" she replied, smiling "I would have quitted if I wouldn't have seen any results after that time".

She was happy and working the last time I heard of her, some years ago. Her menstrual periods were usually painless. Occasionally she would only feel a quite tolerable level of discomfort that would promptly disappear with one dose of *Ipeca*. Her Pap smear remained normal.

The second patient was a 32-year-old female who didn't show improvement in her chief complaint of severe back pain for years after an accident—and then one day she was well.

She had been under the care of a very competent Physical Therapist, for many months, at the time of her first visit. Physical Therapy continued throughout her Homeopathic follow-up and treatment.

I prescribed *Natrum muriaticum,* that I considered matched her profile. She received the treatment in several increasing Centesimal potencies.

She improved everywhere but in her back.

I increased the potency, without any effect whatsoever on her back.

She phoned me one afternoon, after months of incredible perseverance. She was crying. She told me her pain was such that she was totally discouraged and didn't know what to do. I consoled her the best I could.

Here too, I was at the end of my tether. I continued her Homeopathic treatment, nevertheless.

One day, more than one year after her first visit, she came to the office for a routine follow-up visit. She was radiant and smiling. The pain had disappeared.

Nothing had basically changed in her treatment, except for periodic increases in the potency of the Homeopathic remedy. Nothing had changed in her Physical Therapy, either.

She has been symptom-free ever since except after a misstep in a slippery sidewalk, some three months after she had started feeling well. This temporary setback brought about an episode of mild back pain that rapidly disappeared.

I have no idea why it took her so long to respond. Her Physical Therapist has no inkling, either.

Homeopathy can also help patients to consciously control their disease-syndromes.

Perhaps the most interesting patient, in this context, is a severely asthmatic little male, a 5-year-old *Nux vomica*. He received a few doses of the remedy at a potency of 200 C.

This child lives with his single mother in her parent's home. Both grandparents smoke—a lot.

To boot, I first saw this child early in winter. And my patient's mother didn't have the heart to ask her elderly parents to go outside to smoke and freeze to death there, so that her son could breathe cleaner air indoors. And, because of the cold, she didn't dare to take her son out whenever her parents would light up their cigarettes.

The little patient started to improve despite of it all.

Late one night, after several weeks of Homeopathic treatment, her mother heard him wheeze, and rushed to his room with inhalers ready.

Her son told her "Let me see if I can do it myself". Whereupon he controlled his incipient asthma attack.

His mother was still awed when she called to report the next day.

Homeopathy is no panacea, though.

In some patients it may fail to bring about balance.

In others, the nature of the disease is such that it may not permit remedies to act properly.

Malignant solid tumors are a case in point.

Dead tissues are another instance of the limitations of Homeopathy. The Vital Force cannot penetrate into dead tissues—nor can it regenerate structures that are absent.

An amputated limb will not regenerate, nor a decayed tooth will be made hale again by Homeopathic treatment. Nor will gangrene, that produces dead tissue, benefit from Homeopathic treatment. Many degenerative and ultimately destructive problems of the nervous system also belong to this category because cells of the nervous system, as well as those of the voluntary muscles, are unable to reproduce.

Insulin-dependent diabetes, hypothyroidism (poorly functioning thyroid gland in the neck) and other suchlike disease-syndromes of insufficiency, like hemophilia, will usually not respond to Homeopathic treatment. In these illnesses, patients do not produce enough hormones or other factors essential for a healthy life. The insufficiently produced principles (insulin, thyroid hormone, anti-hemophiliac factor, etc.), must be periodically administered if the patient is to remain alive and well.

Homeopathic remedies may indeed assist patients bearing these disease-syndromes, though. In insulin-dependent diabetics, for instance, Homeopathy may help stabilize their requirements of insulin. But these patients will generally continue needing the replacement of whatever their organisms produce in insufficient quantities.

In congenital defects, the effects of Homeopathy tend to be null, although there are exceptions. Let me describe one.

It has to do with two siblings, she 3, he 2 at the time of their first visit; both holding hands in the waiting room, both with that vacuous stare that one sees in the eyes of the blind. When the girl was around 2 years of age, their parents noticed that there was something wrong with her eyes. The boy started showing changes shortly afterwards. Ever since, these poor children had been becoming progressively blind. "A very rare ophthalmic genetic problem" Ophthalmologists had told parents in a famous Eye Center shortly after the diagnosis (I never received that Center's report despite of repeatedly asking for it). Nothing done in that Center helped either child. At the time of their first visit, both children could distinguish darkness from light, and have some idea of shapes. On examination, their eye grounds appeared pearly gray, instead of the normal red-orange color. I started treatment, he with *Calcarea carbonica,* she with *Phosphorus,* both at hefty potencies. I also added *Syphilinum* in both, because this appeared to be a degenerative process of their central nervous system. After three months of treatment their eye grounds had a more orange-reddish color. Parents decided to stop Homeopathic treatment at that point. This was the last I saw of these children. Three years later I phoned their home. Their father told me that they were going to School and that her vision was fairly good, although they had to aid it with strong eyeglasses. The boy has seizures, autism and ADD. They were still going periodically to the same famous eye Center. He didn't ask for a follow-up appointment.

Emergencies are almost always indications for Allopathic treatment.

This is so because it is usually impossible to predict how fast, or with what intensity, will a Homeopathic remedy act in a given acute patient. And also because of how difficult it is to find, in an emergency, an adequately trained Homeopathic Physician with all the necessary remedies at hand.

We must be very careful when considering the *best* form of treatment to be used in each individual patient.

An early malignant solid tumor, if not removed soon enough, will usually continues to grow and to spread into a slow and painful death. A gangrenous member, if not debrided or amputated in time, may likewise mean suffering and death. And a diabetic coma followed by death may also be the fate of an insulin-dependent diabetic patient deprived of insulin.

As mentioned before, it is convenient to associate Homeopathy to Allopathic treatment in patients with these kinds of problems.

But then, there are patients who are frustrating enigmas for Allopathy, but who do respond beautifully to Homeopathic treatment.

I remember a 39 year old post-graduate student, originally from a Third World country, who had been suffering for years from intense burning pain in his left lower abdomen at all times. This pain would temporarily ease when drinking steaming hot liquids. He was also tormented by severe anxiety and midnight insomnia.

He would wake up after midnight, full of anxiety and fear of death. He would need to pace the floor for hours, unable to fall asleep again. He was exhausted due to lack of sleep.

He was an impeccably dressed pack rat, had very solemn and unsmiling features and was punctiliously orderly and very parsimonious—the latter deduced from comments he made during the obtention of his History.

This patient had been thoroughly studied, and then treated with everything Allopathic, first in his original country and then in the most sophisticated Hospitals and Clinics in Europe and America, for he is a man of means. He carried with him a small but well stocked Pharmacy, full of everything he had been prescribed.

Nothing had brought relief. Finally, while studying in a Connecticut University, he decided to try something different. His sponsor suggested his coming to my office.

He was really a patient very easy to diagnose and treat, a textbook *Arsenicum album*. I gave him a 1 M potency, to be taken only once. He responded very rapidly. All his problems disappeared, together with his anxiety. He was exhilarated.

He returned to his native country three months after having started treatment. With our final handshake, at the end of his last visit, I asked him to please call if he ever needed me.

I didn't hear any more from him until years later, when his sponsor here in Connecticut also became my patient. The first thing I asked him was how my former patient had been doing. His sponsor replied that he had heard from him a few months before, and that he was doing fine.

The second easily cured patient was a 9-year-old girl. Her complaints were recurring urinary tract infections and bed wetting all her life.

She had burning during urination and could not hold her urine, not even in daytime. She had so many urinary tract infections since age 3 that her Pediatrician finally prescribed prophylactic antibiotic treatment in an attempt to prevent her infections. This girl had been taking antibiotics daily for the last two years at the time of her first visit, with no relief in any of her symptoms.

The patient was a sweet and loving, but also angry girl.

All her symptoms disappeared with a few doses of *Ferrum metallicum* 30 C, except for a very occasional episode bed wetting.

Her mother discontinued antibiotics because the patient stopped having urinary tract infections. Improvement continued despite of antibiotic withdrawal.

She was still wetting her bed, if less frequently, the last time I heard of her. Which, here too, was several years ago.

Another patient easily cured Homeopathically was an extremely dependent 19 year old female, suffering from tiredness and severe migrating muscle pains for several years—probably fibromyalgia.

She felt so insecure that there was no way she would leave her home without her mother, who much to her chagrin had to chaperone her everywhere.

This young lady had gone to see all kinds of Health Care Providers who had seen, tested, and treated her with no results whatsoever. One of the places where her distracted parents had taken her was some "Holistic Clinic", despite of her tears and protests. She had been admitted for several days and subjected to all kinds of weird tests, diets and treatments. The only result was that her parents lost a small fortune.

The patient's mother brought to my office a tray full of flasks of every source, form and description; all sorts of drugs, vitamins, natural, Homeopathic and Anthroposophic remedies that had been prescribed to her daughter. A veritable therapeutic *mélange*.

There was despair and distrust in the mother's features, as I went to the waiting room to greet them and usher the patient into my office. I couldn't blame her for being desperate and skeptical after so many unfulfilled promises and failures. Plus all the expense. Nothing had worked for her daughter, she said. She didn't know what else to do or where to turn.

She had come to see a Homeopathic Physician as the last straw.

The patient, a blonde, blue-eyed, attractive young lady, started to weep as soon as she sat down. It was an easy cry, like April showers. That would stop immediately, and be replaced by a sweet smile, whenever I would utter a few words of consolation. Crying would then recommence a few moments later, as the patient resumed talking.

She was a *Pulsatilla nigricans* textbook case. I gave her several increasing Centesimal doses.

Some 18 months later, this formerly very dependent young lady went to Europe on her own, with a student fellowship.

She met a nice young man after her return, married him and moved to the Midwest. Her parents remained in Connecticut.

Last thing I heard, she was doing fine. And was very happy.

There is also that 35 year old male, with pains in all his joints for several years. The pain would go from joint to joint and was very severe.

He had gone to many Doctors and other Health Practitioners, and was taking "a lot of [a strong over-the-counter pain killer]".

Laboratory tests for arthritis had been negative.

All had started 4 years previously, for no apparent reason.

I gave him one dose of *Abrotanum* 200 C.

He phoned me one week after his first visit to report that all his pains had disappeared with the remedy I had prescribed.

He didn't show up for the first follow-up visit, nor I have heard of him since.

Or that 27-year-old female with severe dysmenorrhea, or menstrual pain, for several years that, as well of all her other symptoms, would markedly improve when lying down. Here again, every Allopathic Medical treatment had failed.

She asked me if she could lie down as soon as she entered my office. Which she did immediately, in the examining table, as soon as I nodded acquiescence.

Then she started to recite her History—making me feel like a Psychoanalyst, sitting at my desk and scribbling down notes as she talked!

I gave her *Manganum* 200 C. All her symptoms started to recede.

The last time I saw her she was doing well.

The next patient is a 42-year-old male.

His arrival to my Practice was preceded by a very voluminous envelope full of Photostats of laboratory and biopsy results, copies of charts, memos and letters between Doctors of a very well known University Hospital. The patient had sent me that envelope. Everything inside very neatly ordered and classified.

His features were contorted with pain when I first saw him in the waiting room. He was holding his right wrist with his left hand above his head. I was to learn that this maneuver would ease somehow the agonizing burning pain he felt in his right hand.

Later on, during the Physical Examination, I had the opportunity to take a good look at that hand. The skin on the last four fingers was sloughing off, in the fashion seen after a very severe burn. Dark skin folds ware falling all over the front and back of his hand. The Doctors in the University Hospital had wanted to surgically clean up the debris on his hand, but the patient refused. The denuded area was blackish-brown and glistening, and would ooze a small amount of icorous, thin, yellowish-brown fluid. His fingernails were completely exposed, all the way to the very quick of their roots; to the point that they appeared to be loosely affixed to the tip of the fingers, as if ready to slough off. The hand was a claw and had no feeling. The fingers were almost paralyzed. There was only this unbearable, constant burning pain.

His left hand was showing the same ominous purple patches that, he said, had preceded the problem in his right hand.

He also had ulcers in his legs. Midway in the front. Covering most of the shins and, in the left leg, extending into the external aspect of his ankle. And burning with pain, like his hand.

The legs were well padded with gauze. The pads of gauze, as well as the bandage to keep them in place, were soaked with a thin, brownish-yellow, ichorous fluid, similar to that I saw in his fingers.

As soon as I removed the bandages and the pads of gauze, so that I could have a clear view of his legs, both ulcers slowly started to fill up with dark liquid, and to ooze. The fluid was soon dripping down his feet and onto the floor below. I asked him how long before coming to my office he had changed the dressings in his legs. "Oh, some half hour ago. Just before leaving home". The ulcers in his legs were large, flat, brownish-pink and torpid. No proud flesh anywhere, no other evidence of healing. The ulcers had been slowly but constantly expanding, he said.

His problem had started 5 years before, when he had noticed a blue decoloration and swelling in his right leg, from the knee down. Then Doctors had found a blood clot in his right knee and groin.

There was also a history of a blow to his right shin. After the trauma, an ulcer had appeared in the front of his right leg. Small at first, it didn't heal, but kept on growing.

Four years later a rash appeared on his left shin. That rash was followed by an ulcer very much alike that present on his left leg, that also went on growing and oozing, and burning with pain.

That same year the Doctors noticed an abnormality in his chest X Ray and ordered a CT scan. This study showed areas of calcification in his pericardium (or membrane that surrounds the heart), lymph nodes of the chest cavity and also in the spleen.

Three weeks before coming to see me his right hand began to bother him. Shortly thereafter the skin in his fingers had started to slough off.

This patient had been thoroughly studied in a renowned University Hospital. Doctors there had diagnosed as suffering from a recently described, rare disease-syndrome called *anticardiolipin antibody syndrome*. He was receiving Cyclophosphamide, an alkylating cancer chemotherapy agent loaded with side effects and toxicity. Also Prednisone and blood thinners. Plus, of course, strong pain killers.

The patient had been getting progressively worse along the past five years despite of all of these treatments. New manifestations of pathology kept on appearing.

I treated with patient with *Mancinella* and *Secale.*

One week later, the patient reported that the pain in his hand had lessened considerably, while his leg ulcers were oozing less and starting to close. On his first follow-up visit, three weeks later, the pain was gone, the ulcer in the right leg was almost closed, the one in the right was closing and his hands were considerably better. There was little or no oozing anywhere.

The patient canceled his next follow-up visit and didn't reschedule, now that he clearly saw he was getting better.

I phoned him some 3 months after he had first come to see me. I asked him how he was doing. His right hand was fine, he said, totally cured and with complete range of motion; "even though [his] fingers [were] a little shorter". His legs were fine. He was working again, very happy and totally free of symptoms. I asked him if he wanted to schedule a follow-up appointment. He declined. He stated he was being followed up at the Hospital, and that his Insurance covered all his expenses there.

That was the last I heard of him.

I would like now to describe briefly a 62-year-old non-smoker female with severe bronchiectasis[48]. Taking antibiotics, inhalers and decongestants that did little or nothing to help. In winter, she would frequently fall sick with bronchopneumonia, despite of periodic administration of flu and pneumonia shots; and would spend long periods of time in the Hospital as an in-patient.

She had been under the care of the same Pneumonologist for the previous 8 years.

This patient was a very sick woman when I first saw her, despite of the excellent care she took of herself, and of the many treatments she was constantly receiving. Her complexion was dusky and her breathing labored. I could clearly hear her wheezing across my desk. She was very short of breath. She had frequent bouts of a repetitive, difficult and mostly ineffective cough that would shake her whole frame and leave her exhausted.

I treated her with *Tuberculinum* 200, and with increasing potencies of *Phosphorus*.

Her Pneumonologist would send periodic progress notes to her Family Doctor (no reports were ever sent to me, despite of the patient's repeated requests). I will quote from one of those reports, written 3 months after the patient started taking her Homeopathic remedy, and that I received, together with a copy of the rest of her records, after the patient decided to continue her follow-up with a more accessible Pneumonologist "...Basically, she has been receiving Homeopathic therapy from Dr. Mullen, in Colchester [CT], who is treating her with some type of 'salts', but she doesn't know the name... She has had no fever, chills nor chest pain. She is not wheezing nor rising sputum. In fact, she is feeling much better. She is able to carry out her activities of daily living on a more regular and less limited basis".

The patient gradually discontinued all drugs and inhalers.

She went to visit one of her daughters, who lived in a mountainous area of a Western State. From there she sent me a postcard that read, in part "...I am enjoying a very healthy vacation. Doing things that...would have been a

---

[48] A chronic, very serious and progressive disease that destroys, widens irregularly and hardens the walls of the bronchial tubes within the lungs. In bronchiectasis, the bronchial tubes become uneven, too wide and too rigid, and cannot move up their secretions that stagnate and becomes infected. Breathing becomes impaired and labored. The patient is constantly out of breath, coughing and bringing up large amounts of old, foul and often infected expectoration with difficulty. As a consequence, he or she is often sick with all sort of infectious bronchopulmonary disease-syndromes.

chore. Walks at high altitude, etc. My daughter…cannot believe the change in me. And <u>no</u> [underlined in the original] coughing!".

She took her yearly flu and pneumonia shots as winter approached. She fell ill with pneumonia, nevertheless. None of the remedies I gave her helped her in the least at this point.

She was admitted into the Hospital, again treated with antibiotics, inhalers and decongestants; as well as with *Phosphorus* at high potency.

I started again to taper down her drugs and inhalers after she started feeling better. Recovery was complete. This again was a first. Prior to Homeopathy, her recovery from these episodes was wearisome, slow and incomplete.

She did wonderfully all spring, summer and fall.

Her cough increased the following winter. She had a mild instance of flu; and something that could have been either a bronchitis or else a very mild pneumonitis. It was short lived, with little fever, and responded very rapidly and completely to antibiotics.

Again, the following spring, summer and fall she was fine.

Next winter, the patient had only one mild instance of something that could either have been an upper respiratory congestion, or else mild pharyngitis.

She phoned the following Fall. She had been fine the preceding summer. She asked for an appointment. "I need you to winterize me" she said on the phone, with a chuckle. The patient was doing fine, though still a bit apprehensive about the winter to come.

She called me the following February to tell me she hadn't forgotten me, but that she hadn't called before because she had been feeling great.

The following Spring she moved West to live with her daughter. I haven't heard of her since.

The last case history I want to describe here, in this context of patients difficult for Allopathy, but responsive to Homeopathy, is that of a sixteen months old little girl.

I'll never forget the first time I saw her, she was so thin. She reminded me of the extraterrestrials of some Hollywood Sci-Fi movies. Her head was normal in size, but her neck was long, and so abnormally thin that her head looked too large, and as if precariously bobbing atop a delicate stalk. Her eyes were large, almond shaped and full of curiosity. Her hair was short, wispy and sparse. The trunk was very thin. Arms and legs were as skinny as toothpicks.

She was ethereal, almost transparent.

Her movements were slow and deliberate, as if attempting to save energy.

She had been diagnosed as suffering from "failure to thrive". She had no appetite whatsoever. She was also severely anemic.

And did she need love! Throughout the visit she was gently coaxing me through glance, voice and gesture. None of the kindness and attention I showed her were enough. I could as well have poured water onto the Sahara desert.

Her parents were hostile toward Homeopathy but, at the behest of a common friend, had consented in bringing their daughter to my office. They were scared of the treatments and tests that, according to specialists, this little girl would have to undergo. The Infantile Gastroenterologist had recommended a biopsy of her small intestine; that is, the introduction of a tube through mouth or nose, all the way down past the stomach and into the intestine, to then remove small bits of tissue there. This procedure was to be followed by forced feeding through a stomach tube.

The parents were very uncomfortable with Homeopathy, though. I still remember them at the office sitting close together, frowning and sullen.

The little girl became hungry almost immediately after receiving her dose of *Pulsatilla 1 M*. Her weight increased by 12 ounces ten days afterwards, in the Pediatrician's office scale. Our common friend later told me that the office Nurse had whispered to her mother, astonished after weighing her "What have you given her?"

After this visit to the Pediatrician, the patient's mother left a curt message in my answering machine. She was canceling her follow-up appointment. I called her back. I told her that her daughter's Homeopathic treatment had scarcely began, and that we still had a long way to go. I also told her I was very concerned about the child's evolution, and asked her to please bring her little daughter back for follow-up visits—or else to take her to another Homeopathic Physician of her choice if she wasn't happy with me. Her rather brusque answer was that both she and her husband had decided to stop Homeopathic treatment.

Through our common friend I learnt about her progress, of her increase in energy, and of her constant weight gain—and also of the astonishment in her Pediatrician's office.

I presume she is still doing well, and thriving, for I haven't heard of this little girl for quite a while.

As a side note, I would like to remark that timely Homeopathic treatment avoided this little girl the possibility of a serious, risky, delicate, expensive and uncomfortable procedure. In all likelihood, all those tests and treatments would have left this child emotionally traumatized, physically scarred and fearful of Doctors for a long time. Perhaps for the rest of her life.

The Infantile Gastroenterologist had ordered that battery of traumatic procedures, to be followed by force feeding via a stomach tube, because he or she didn't know what else to do with this little girl.

Most Allopathic Doctors are totally ignorant of Homeopathy, and many are still strongly prejudiced against it.

Patients would therefore do well in *asking an authorized Homeopathic second opinion before accepting a serious Medical and/or Surgical procedure.* At least until enough Allopathic Physicians are sufficiently enlightened regarding the usefulness, or lack thereof, when it comes to forms of diagnosis and treatment other than those they have been taught about in Medical School.

Some factors may diminish, even annul, the curative effects of a Homeopathic treatment.

Harmful medicinal influences, like those provoking suppressions, can thwart a Homeopathic cure.

Errors in living, such as a horrible marriage, a hazardous job, an extreme and protracted stressful situation can also annul or diminish the effects of a Homeopathic treatment.

Dr. Hahnemann stated that a Homeopathic treatment may fail if the patient yields to passions or doesn't lead an ethical and moral life (Hahnemann S., *Organon*. 6th. Edition. § 156). This paragraph places responsibility *on the patient.* The *passions* mentioned here by Dr. Hahnemann are indulgence in self-destructive behavior, such as in the instance of the patient with Chagas' disease, syphilis and alcoholism described at the beginning of this Chapter. Or else yielding to extreme, insurmountable and protracted grief after the loss of a very dear one. Or transforming a heartbreak into a prolonged tragedy. Or hatred, revenge, or envy; or haughtiness or ambition, or avarice, or ennui, or despair, or unforgiveness.

All these *passions* require much Vital Force to remain alive and growing. They leave little for day-to-day maintenance and healing. Furthermore, to indulge in these negative feelings or passions may produce such quality and quantity of venom as to oppose, and sometimes even annul, any beneficial action of the patient's Vital Force and its healing capacity.

Patients often ask regarding the therapeutic efficacy of a treatment in the disease-syndrome afflicting them.

The answer of a Homeopathic Physician will be different from that of an Allopathic Doctor.

Let us suppose that a strep throat-bearing patient asks a Mainstream Doctor about his or her possibilities of being cured. The answer will be that possibilities are excellent in patients treated with Penicillin or any other suchlike antibiotic. This is so because all strep throats are similar from an Allopathic standpoint, and consequently that all sore throats respond to the same treatment.

Which is generally true because Allopathic Medicine considers only what *all* patients have in common, rather than how *each individual patient* reacts to his or her individual disease-syndrome.

The result of this rather lopsided outlook is that lots of bacteria, including those profiting from that strep throat, will be massacred. While nothing will be done to control the weakness that allowed that infection to start in the first place.

But the same patient will receive a torrent of questions, instead of an answer, when asking a Homeopathic Physician about his or her sore throat.

Question such as,

Whose strep throat? What are the patient's symptoms? What side is affected? Is there pain? What kind of pain? Does it hurt when the patient swallows? Is there cough? What kind of cough? Is there pain when coughing? At what time are the symptoms worse? Are there chills, fever, sweating?, and so on and so forth. Questions that will continue until the Doctor understands how the sore throat and the patient integrate; or, to put it differently, what that individual *sore throat-bearing patient's* individual *profile* is.

Only then will the Homeopathic Physician have transformed an abstract sore throat in *the patient's* sore throat, and only then will he or she know what remedy to prescribe and have an idea about how that strep throat-bearing patient will respond to it.

One hundred patients with strep throat, treated by an Allopathic Physician, will likely end up receiving Penicillin, or else some other antibiotic if any of those 100 patients happens to be allergic to Penicillin.

One hundred patients with strep throat, evaluated and treated by a Homeopathic Physician, may well end up receiving one hundred different remedies, each remedy matching the profile of each different, individual and unique strep throat-bearing patient.

The cure of a psoric patient progresses from the emotional to the physical, from above downwards, from inside outwards, and from the most recent symptom to the most remote.

This progression is called *Hering's Law*, because Dr. Constantine Hering, the Father of American Homeopathy, was the first to describe it. It is interesting to note that Dr. Hering attributed this law to Dr. Hahnemann. He first described it in a scientific paper entitled *"Hahnemann's three rules concerning the rank of symptoms"*, that he published in The Hahnemannian Monthly, 1: 1-3, Aug. 1865..

When one drops a pebble into the center of a quiet pond, an eccentric tidal wave is produced.

The tidal wave starts where the pebble hits the water; to then proceed outwards from the point of impact.

In a similar fashion, when a Homeopathic remedy is administered to a psoric patient, its effect proceed from his or her center (i.e., the patient's emotions, level of energy and the like), outwards and downwards into his or her physical aspect, and towards the patient's past.

In a psoric patient, the Homeopathic treatment is a failure unless wellness progresses along these lines.

Say that a male psoric patient comes to his or her first Homeopathic visit wanting to get rid of pain and stiffness brought about by a chronic condition in the knee; and that, through the Homeopathic and Clinical History, the Doctor notices that the patient also suffers from sadness.

If, in the second visit, the patient states that his knee is fine but that sadness is intact, then the treatment is a failure; because the emotional sphere remained untouched by the treatment. Worse yet, the patient may be in serious danger, because this *local* improvement may well be the harbinger of a forthcoming suppression.

But let us suppose that in the second visit the patient states that his sadness has vanished, but that the knee is worse than before. Here the Doctor should rejoice, because the treatment is a success. *Even if the patient went to see the Doctor because of knee pain, and for nothing else.* The Homeopathic treatment is a success because the tidal wave that erased sadness will eventually decant, or reach outwards and downwards into the knee sooner or later.

Some old and probably forgotten symptom may surface for a short while, during a successful treatment.

Those old symptoms may reappear because sometimes the Homeopathic cure acts like an eraser on a slate, clearing up all diseases from the most recent to the most remote. Old disease-syndromes may become transiently activated before being deleted. The short and mild reappearance of some of those diseases may minimally trouble the patient for a short time.

To sum up,

In acute patients, a disease-syndrome appears when the Vital Force loosens its grip on some organ or tissue; due, usually, to some kind of insult. In chronic patients, a disease-syndrome is generally the consequence of an overall situation of imbalance.

Homeopathic remedies facilitate the reattachment of the Vital Force in acute patients and restore balance in chronic patients. Without side effects nor toxicity of any kind.

Allopathic drugs work by means of antagonizing the immediate cause and the symptoms of individual disease-syndromes, be those diseases acute or chronic.

The effect of drugs is not specific.

All drugs have side effects and often toxicity that produce new diseases and that can create, or intensify, imbalance in the patient.

Furthermore, drugs do not re-attach the Vital Force to ill organs and tissues and have no effect whatsoever on chronic patients' imbalance.

It follows that, when in need to treat a patient, be that patient acute or chronic, the reasonable thing to do is to consider Homeopathy as the treatment of choice. Allopathy should be used only if necessary and associated with Homeopathy.

This way, the Homeopathic treatment will be able to, in patients who must simultaneously be treated Allopathically,

a) bring about re-attachment of the patient's Vital Force wherever needed in acute patients,

b) bring about overall balance in chronic patients, and

c) contribute to neutralize the consequences of the inevitable side effects and toxicity of drugs used in the Allopathic treatment.

Chapter 14
TYPES OF HOMEOPATHIC REMEDIES

For therapeutic purposes, Homeopathic remedies can be divided into fifteen groups

- Polychrests,
- Small remedies,
- Constitutionals, also known as psoric or anti-psoric remedies,
- Complementaries,
- Locals,
- "Never well since" remedies,
- Nosodes,
- Acute,
- Sycosics,
- Syphilitics,
- Inimicals,
- Antidotes,
- Intercurrents,
- Detoxifiers, and
- Complexes.

POLYCHRESTS

A *Polychrest* is a thoroughly studied remedy. The changes it produces in most organs and systems has been repeatedly brought about in successive Provings. Its profile is well-known.

Lycopodium clavatum, For instance, is a Polychrest. Dr. Hahnemann found 1,000 symptoms for this remedy. In Dr. Kent's Repertory, Lycopodium can be found opposite to 463 symptoms.

Polychrests are tri-miasmatics, meaning that their range of action covers all three classic miasmas; meaning that *Polychrests* can be equally effective in psoric, sycosic and syphilitic patients.

SMALL REMEDIES

There are many remedies in which Provings have been incomplete, and in which the information from other sources is also scanty.

Our knowledge of those remedies is therefore limited, when it comes to their profiles or their range of action.

So-called *Small remedies* are generally used to treat *local* problems. They are also used as *Complementary remedies used to finish up some of the symptoms remaining after the incomplete action of a similar* (please see below, under *Complementaries*).

Allow me now to share with you an anecdote of my days as a student of Homeopathy. The protagonists were Prof. Dr. Bernardo Vijnovsky and myself. Dr. Vijnovsky is the author of an excellent 3-volume Materia Medica that unfortunately has not been translated into English. At the time of this anecdote, Dr. Vijnovsky was a frail, elderly man; kind, caring and tactful to a fault. He had a very keen sense of humor. Dr. Vijnovsky was extremely knowledgeable of Homeopathy, and therefore very humble. One day I was talking with this very dear and revered Teacher, and I mentioned something about a small remedy. He looked at me, his pale blue eyes asparkle, an amused smile playing on his lips. He said, "There are no small remedies, *doctorcito"* Doctorcito means little Doctor in Spanish. It is a term of endearment "there are only small Homeopaths".

CONSTITUTIONALS

Constitutional, or psoric, or anti-psoric Homeopathic remedies are used *exclusively* in the treatment of psoric patients.

If the Constitutional remedy matches *all, or almost all* of the psoric patient's symptoms; that is, if the profile of the remedy and that of the patient coincide perfectly or almost perfectly, the remedy is called a *simillimum*. The more a remedy is a *simillimum*, the more successful the treatment is going to be.

Constitutional remedies are usually *Polychrests.*

There is a catch here, though. A Homeopathic treatment with a Constitutional remedy is eminently *individual.* Meaning that, being billions of inhabitants in this Earth and only some 3,000 Homeopathic remedies, perforce once one of those inhabitants, or at most only a few, are going to find that the remedy they are treated with is their *simillimum.*

181

What can Homeopathic Physicians do with all the patients who do not match exactly a Homeopathic remedy?

Imagine a men's store that has 3,000 sizes of suits. These 3,000 sizes have to fit all clients.

Each client has a unique body. There is certainly many more body sizes than those of the suits the store has in stock. A few clients don't need any alterations. One of the 3,000 sizes will fit them perfectly.

The store clerks will sell all other clients a suit whose size is their closest fit, and then make the necessary arrangements.

Homeopathy has 3,000 + remedies to fit all but, alas! they cannot be brought to the each patient's size.

The profile of few of our patients fit a remedy like the men's store clients who fit perfectly in a suit. They are the ones that receive a simillimum, and all or most of their symptoms will disappear after its administration.

For the other, less fortunate patients we do a patchwork of similars, since there is no way in Homeopathy to arrange any remedy to fit a patient. So here new have no other choice than to administer a similar, then another and then still another until most or all of the patient's symptoms have vanished.

If the remedy we proffer a patient covers only *a part* of the patient's profile, then the remedy will be known as a ***similar***.

With a *similar* the therapeutic results, though evident, are bound to be insufficient and incomplete.

The *Constitutional remedy* is the heart, soul and center of the Homeopathic treatment of psoric patients.

It is to be administered, as the only treatment, for as long as its effect lasts——although his statement should be understood only as a *guide*, not as a *rule*.

COMPLEMENTARIES

For didactic purposes, Complementary remedies can be divided into three groups.

- Properly called Complementaries,
- Complementary remedies used to finish up some of the symptoms remaining after the incomplete action of a similar, and
- remedies that are Complementary because of certain characteristics

The first and second groups are based on the results of treatment, and the third on certain characteristics of the remedies.

Properly called Complementaries.

We are buffeted about as we age. We have to change and to adapt in order to survive. Each successive change can be compared to a coat of paint. Unlike those applied to a wall or to a door, though, these *coats of paint* become alive and part of ourselves.

The latest coat applied becomes the face, or the persona, or the profile that we show to ourselves and to the world—and to the Homeopathic Physician, at the time of the office visit.

The Homeopathic Physician treats with a Constitutional remedy the profile he or she perceives in the psoric patient. Put differently, the Doctor will treat the patient *as is*.

I recall a patient I saw years back. A 52 year old *Lycopodium*—almost.

For there was some unabashed tenderness towards his pet, a cat. Tenderness unusual in *Lycopodium* patients, who find it hard to display emotions. Makes them feel vulnerable, and *Lycopodium* hates to feel vulnerable. So *Lycopodium* patients will repress feelings so much, and for so long, that in the end they don't know, or have forgotten, how to express them. Consequently, they tend to appear cold and distant, even disdainful; a mien that does nothing to ingratiate them to those who surround them.

His family had grown weary, along the years, of his despotism and his need to control everything and everybody. His wife and children had been also badly frightened, all too often, by the violent, if sporadic, explosions of his chronically repressed rage—a rage that he would only discharge at home, with his dear ones; never, ever at his workplace. So his family did nothing to dissuade him when, one day, he left home in a fit of anger—he and his cat. *Lycopodium* people sometimes leave their families impulsively, and walk away. Then, their pride and rigidity may restrain them from apologizing for what they had done, and return.

He was a very successful man. His demeanor was courteous and he would dress impeccably. He was very reserved and tough in his dealings, as well as distrustful, cold and distant.

He was chronically stressed. His repressed fear of failure and lack of self-confidence were the likely causes of his high blood pressure. What brought this patient to my office was his hypertension and the side effects of Pharmaceutical drugs prescribed to treat it. Plus his tiredness, insomnia, lousy mood on awakening, forgetfulness of names, bloating after meals and frequent urination. Plus diarrhea and flatulence at the most embarrassing moments. In the evening, during his daily 4 to 8 PM slump, he would remember everything negative that had happened that day. He would feel angry, resentful and insecure. He would drown those feelings in alcohol and in some casual sexual encounter.

His Urologist had told him he had benign prostatic enlargement. This prostatic enlargement and hypertension were the only abnormalities I found in his Physical Examination, lab work and X Rays.

I prescribed *Lycopodium*. Soon he felt stronger and with a clearer mind to work. He started to sleep soundly and to awake rested and in a better mood. His bloating and flatulence disappeared, and he found himself able to control his bowels. He started to urinate at longer intervals.

The Urologist told him, a few months later, that his prostate had shrunk to almost normal size.

His blood pressure began to normalize. His Family Practitioner tapered down antihypertensive drugs. He was feeling well, happy, and grateful—and free of the drugs' side effects.

The 4 to 8 PM slump remained, but its pattern also changed. Memories of his family started to pop up, of specific beautiful moments spent with his wife and children. Sadness and loneliness began to creep in in lieu of his former anger and insecurity.

He started to drink in his apartment, alone. He would find himself exploding in tears unexpectedly; and it was unbearably embarrassing to find himself loosing control like that in public, in the fashionable bar where he used to hang evenings before going home.

He became more humane at work. He started to need and appreciate praise[49]. He also began to feel vulnerable, and feared that employees may be taking advantage of him.

Long repressed memories began to emerge. About his being at School when little. About his feeling forsaken and constantly in need to be loved. About his having been so sensitive and withdrawn and teary. How mercilessly, he recalled sadly, would his classmates bully and push him around, and made cruel fun of him in those days!

He started to oversleep, to arrive late to his office and to make mistakes at work. This had never happened before, and made him feel terribly embarrassed, bewildered and insecure.

His blood pressure began to rise. The Cardiologist re-started to treat him with antihypertensive drugs. I prescribed *Lycopodium* at higher and higher

---

[49] *Lycopodium* provers and patients tend to scorn compliments. Appreciation and admiration clash too painfully with the poor image they have of themselves.

potencies, but could do nothing to stop his free fall into despondency. He started to urinate more frequently, particularly at night.

I was much younger and inexperienced then, so it took me some time to realize that this man had become *Pulsatilla*[50]. I started to think that this patient might have started his life as *Pulsatilla,* after he shared with me his unhappy childhood experiences. I also realized he might have become *Lycopodium* later in life when he told me that he had been forced to "make [him]self of steel in order to be competitive and successful, and also to muster enough courage to start beating the shit out of [his] tormentors and competitors".

I prescribed *Pulsatilla* and obtained his permission to call his estranged wife. The whole family was sent to counseling. His blood pressure became normal again.

I haven't heard of him for years. Last thing I knew, he and his family—and his cat—were all back together and doing fine. And very happy.

This man obviously started out as *Pulsatilla*, and was buffeted around to the point of either breaking or else steeling himself up. He managed to anneal and to shield himself from his feelings. He became *Lycopodium* when he identified himself with the shield he had elaborated for purposes of self-protection.

Under *Lycopodium* treatment, the shield melted down; and his warm, loving and tender *Pulsatilla* profile, long repressed, started to emerge.

In this patient, *Pulsatilla* was a properly called Complementary remedy of *Lycopodium*. Which is why *Pulsatilla* became his Constitutional remedy after the usefulness of *Lycopodium* wore off.

Dr. Tomás Paschero, the great late Argentine Homeopathic Physician, coined the term *Biopathographic History*, to define and emphasize the need of obtaining the whole life history of each Homeopathic patient, and then plan treatment accordingly. The man described here is a good example of how useful this approach is in everyday Homeopathic practice.

Complementary remedies used to finish up some of the symptoms remaining after the incomplete action of a similar.

Consider a 32-year-old woman complaining of fatigue, menstrual cramps, migraine, dyspepsia and bloating. *Causticum* was the remedy that best covered most of her symptoms. It was not her simillimum, though, but her similar Constitutional remedy. It cleared up all the clinical picture with

---

[50] *Pulsatilla nigricans* is complementary of *Lycopodium clavatum,* and vice versa. Both remedies are *Polychrests.*

the exception of her dyspepsia and bloating. I treated those symptoms with *Gratiola.*

Gratiola is a so-called small remedy; mainly capable of producing, and consequently curing, symptoms related to dyspepsia and bloating, particularly in women.

As a complementary remedy, Gratiola finished the action of *Causticum* in this patient.

Remedies that are complementary because of certain characteristics.

These remedies were beautifully described by the late Dr. Alejandro J. Grosso, a brilliant Argentine Homeopathic Physician, in his *"¿Qué son los remedios complementarios?"*, in *"Páginas de Medicina Homeopática"*. Sociedad Homeopática Argentina, 1951. He considered that Complementary remedies are those that share the same symptoms, but with different modalities. For instance, both *Bryonia* and *Rhus Tox* may suffer pain, but *Bryonia* finds relief when resting and *Rhus Tox* when moving.

Remedies can also complement each other according to their area of action, such as *Lycopodium* and *Kali Carbonicum*. Both act on the stomach.

Laterality can also be considered in this context. *Lachesis* suffers more on the left side and *Lycopodium* on the right.

LOCAL REMEDIES

They are used for the treatment of *local* conditions, acute or chronic.

Polychrests, small remedies, nosodes, or complexes, all can be used as local remedies.

Local remedies are usually very successful as the only form of treatment in *acute* diseases, in otherwise well balanced individuals.

Examples of local remedies used in acute diseases would be *Capsicum* for the Homeopathic treatment of local acute mastoiditis, or acute inflammation of cavities in the temporal bone, immediately behind the ear. Or *Calendula Officinalis* in mother tincture, a few drops in one ounce of water, applied directly over a wound that is not healing properly or is infected.

In psoric patients, the administration of local remedies is a very delicate matter. There are several possibilities to be considered.

The first consideration is that it is not advisable to administer a local remedy to a psoric patient who is not receiving his or her Constitutional. There is a real risk of triggering a suppression.

If a local symptom, let us say heartburn, is present throughout the Constitutional treatment with little improvement, a remedy such as *Arsenicum album, Gratiola officinalis* or *Robinia pseudacacia* ought perhaps to be considered—although these remedies would be more Complementary than local in this context.

Or consider a psoric patient whose Constitutional similar remedy cannot be suspended, and who develops a local problem that does not respond to the Constitutional remedy.

Here I would probably consider prescribing an Allopathic treatment and/or a Homeopathic remedy, without discontinuing the administration of the patient's Constitutional.

"NEVER WELL SINCE" REMEDIES

There are patients who are unable to recover from misfortune or diseases. Or from traumatisms.

These events trigger crises that throw these patients out of balance. Eventually, their inability to recover may make their imbalance chronic.

Diseases afflicting these patients rarely respond even to well-chosen Constitutional remedies.

Sooner or later these patients will confess that they have never been well since a particular event or disease in their lives.

Often, in these patients, the administration of a remedy that corresponds to consequences of that event can dramatically improve and even cure them—or, at the very least, allow them to start responding to a Constitutional treatment.

Of course, this has nothing to do with the principle of Like cures like. Nevertheless, it proves the versatility, and also the range of usefulness of Homeopathy.

Under *Nosodes,* below, I am going to mention an 18 year old female, asthmatic since having had whooping cough in early childhood, who was cured by *Pertrussin.*

Other remedies for "never will since" patients are *Sepia* in patients never well since an exhausting pregnancy and delivery, *Aconitum* and *Opium* since frights, *Lachesis* since a difficult menopause, *Natrum sulphuricum* since traumas to he head, *Hypericum perfoliatum* since traumas to the spine, *Ignatia amara* since the loss of a dear one, *Cinchona officinalis* since a severe hemorrhage or any other important loss of organic fluids, *Cocculus indicus* since having taken care of a dear one, day and night, into exhaustion, etc.

NOSODES

Sensu strictum, a Nosode is any Homeopathically prepared substance secreted by an animal or a plant.

Most are used as remedies, such as in the case of ambergris *(Ambra grisea),* cow's milk *(Lac vaccinum),* musk *(Moschus),* thyroid gland *(Thyroidinum),* etc. Later on, I shall briefly discuss diverse forms and actions of several nosodes. But I would like to start discussing Nosodes directly related to the chronic miasmas.

When describing *"The Chronic Miasmas"* I compared a patient to a house and mentioned that, if the patient is a house, then the chronic miasmas are either a generally faulty foundation or else cracks within that foundation.

If the patient is a house, and the chronic miasmas faults in its foundation, then Nosodes are administered to *caulk* deficiencies or cracks in the *foundation* of the house that is the patient. *Nosodes* are Homeopathic remedies that mimic, up to a point, the diverse chronic miasmas. Constitutional remedies, on the other hand, are administered to treat the *whole* house, including the foundations.

There are two kinds of Nosodes: Nosodes proper, and remedies that can also act as Nosodes.

Nosodes proper are directly related to the chronic miasmas. *Psorinum* corresponds to Psora, *Medorrhinum* to Sycosis, *Syphilinum* to the chronic miasma Syphilis, *Tuberculinum* (of which there are several) to Tuberculinism, and *Carcinosin* and others to Cancerinism. There are also Nosodes proper related to a host of other diseases, such as *Petrussin* to whooping cough, *Morbillinum* to measles, etc.

Remedies that act as Nosodes are sundry. Even though all Polychrests are trimiasmatic, some tend to produce in the Provings symptoms that correspond to a miasma.

Aurum and *Mercurius,* and to a lesser extent perhaps *Arsenicum Album* and *Kali Carbonicum* among others, tend to exhibit, in their Provings, a profile reminiscent of the chronic miasma Syphilis; *Thuja, Natrum Sulphuricum* and others of Sycosis; *Sulfur* of Psora; *Pulsatilla* and *Phosphorus* of Tuberculinism, etc.

Nosodes can become very handy when the Constitutional treatment gets mired for no apparent reason.

Once the chronic miasma of the patient is known, the Doctor can administer the appropriate Nosode, and thus get things rolling again.

Nosodes can also sometimes be considered when the patient's current problem is rooted in an insufficiently or incorrectly treated disease in his or her past.

I remember, within this context, one of my first patients, an 18 year old female student with severe asthma. She was not responding to her Constitutional remedy, that had been prescribed by a very competent Homeopathic Physician. Her case was particularly sad because she loved sports, and would have given anything to participate. Yet, all she could do was to remain home and watch sport events on TV.

During History taking, I learnt that this young woman had had whooping cough when 18 months of age. The disease-syndrome had been poorly treated. She had been an asthmatic ever since.

So I give her one single dose of *Petrussin* 200 C. Petrussin is the Nosode of whooping cough. Her asthma disappeared. From then on, she was able to participate in all the sports she wanted.

Nosodes can also be used as preventives.

Influenzinum (the Nosode of influenza) can be used as preventive of the flu. Or the polychrest *Thuja*, when used as a Nosode, can prevent the bad effects of some vaccinations, etc.

Nosodes proper can also act as Constitutional remedies. I recall one such instances.

That of a 40 year old male who came to my office complaining of difficulty seeing, hot flashes with sweating, chronic low grade fever, chronic inflamed sore throat (actually very painful), enlarged lymph nodes in the neck, fatigue, depression, anxiety, headache, hoarseness and many digestive problems for the past several years. He had made the usual rounds of Allopathic Doctors, Clinics and Hospitals, all to no avail.

The patient's profile corresponded to that of *Tuberculinum*. The morning after taking it in a 200 C potency he awoke free of symptoms, except for some mild residual sore throat that disappeared in a few days. He has been well ever since. Once in a blue moon I have to hike the potency of his remedy, though.

Nosodes, when properly indicated as Constitutionals, can act like Polychrests; as Polychrests, or many of them at any rate, when adequately indicated, can also act as Nosodes.

It all depends, here as everywhere else in Homeopathy, in learning what the patient needs, and then figuring out how best to deliver.

Autonosodes.- These Nosodes are prepared with the patient's own secretions or excretions.

Patient's products are usually succussed to a 6 CH or another similarly low dynamization, and then administered by mouth to the same patient from whom they were obtained.

Autonosodes have been used for a variety of illnesses. Dynamized patient's urine, for instance, has proven to be valuable as part of the treatment of severe chronic cystitis, or inflammation of the urinary bladder, refractory to other forms of treatment; dynamized patient's blood as part of the treatment of frequent severe infections, etc.

Isodes.- Prepared with the substance that makes the patient sick in the first place. Dr. Hahnemann, in § 56 his *Organon*, defines this form of treatment as *Isopathy*.

An example of isode is a particular pollen, dynamized to a low potency and then administered to patients who may be allergic to it.

Sarcodes.- Homeopathic preparation of extract of *healthy* organs (nosodes proper are prepared starting from *pathological* organs or secretions).

ACUTE REMEDIES

All remedies can potentially be administered in an acute disease-syndrome, whether Polychrests, Small remedies, Nosodes, Locals, and/or Complementaries.

They must be given, like every remedy in Homeopathy, one at a time; if only up to minutes apart.

In Homeopathy there are two kinds of acute diseases: those that correspond to Nature gone mad, and that act upon well balanced individuals; and those acute diseases that affect patients who are chronically imbalanced already.

If it is indeed an acute disease in an otherwise well balanced individual, no more treatment will be necessary once the illness disappears.

If, however, the acute disease happens in a psoric patient *who is already under treatment with his or her constitutional remedy,* it will be convenient to suspend it in most instances, treat the acute problem, and then re-start the patient's Constitutional remedy as soon as the acute episode is over.

Every chronic, Homeopathically untreated patient suffering an acute disease, should be evaluated with extreme care.

Remember that to start a local treatment with Homeopathic remedies or Pharmaceutical drugs in an otherwise untreated psoric patient may put the patient at risk of suppression.

If the problem is surgical, or otherwise beyond the scope of Homeopathy, the patient should be referred to the appropriate Physician without delay while, at the same time, starting the patient in his or her Constitutional remedy.

No rules apply if the untreated patient has an acute problem within the reach of Homeopathic treatment. Each one of these patients must be evaluated individually.

The impression I get when treating an acute problem, particularly in children, is that of paddling a canoe in the rapids. It is the rapids that direct where one goes and not the paddling, however frantic.

All the Homeopath can do is to remain afloat, pray, push obstacles away, and somehow cope with events as they come—and as well as one can.

Professionals adequately trained in Homeopathy must closely follow up acute patients.

It is a pity that Homeopathy is currently *verboten* in most Hospitals. It is lamentable because it prevents Homeopathically treated patients—particularly acute ones, particularly children—from being able to benefit from a 24-hour a day care by professionally trained people, with immediate access to Allopathic treatment as needed. The clinical aspect of acute patients, and thus their therapeutic approach, can change very rapidly. And with each change, that the Doctor or Nurse must to be able to recognize immediately, may come a change in the remedy—or in the nature of the treatment.

One cannot just give a remedy to an acute patient and leave. That may work in chronic patients, but never in acute ones. The Doctor must remain with the acute patient until the acute situation is brought under control.

Homeopathy may be all that is needed to cure a formerly well-balanced patient suffering from an *acute bacterial disease*—but then again, it may not.

The Doctor must evaluate and follow-up these patients very carefully, and have antibiotics close at hand, particularly if the infection is severe. Here again the ideal, unreachable at the present time, would be to see and to follow up these patients in a Hospital setting.

In acute patients, something as innocent looking as a sore throat can be the earliest manifestation of meningitis. If that is the case, Homeopathy may indeed continue to be given; but the patient must be immediately started on antibiotics, preferably in a Hospital setting.
Which, nowadays, signifies the abrupt end of Homeopathic treatment and the onset of an exclusively Allopathic approach with all its limitations, side effects and toxicity.

Many *acute viral diseases* are serious. They may leave the patient deficient and even be life threatening.
Viruses enter the patient's cells after a short sojourn in the blood, and start to clone themselves there. Antibiotics can't reach viruses once they have found sanctuary inside our cells.
Allopathy has only some antibiotics to offer for viral infestations. These antibiotics have very limited effectiveness and lots of side effects and toxicity. Antibiotics, then, are out in acute viral diseases for all intents and purposes.
Homeopathy is the only hope for these patients. Treatment ought to be carried out in a Hospital setting if the viral infestation is sufficiently severe. In the course of the disease, the acutely infested patient may need intravenous hydration, or to be connected to a respirator, or to have vital signs constantly monitored by highly trained personnel, or to have the remedy changed every so often. None of which can be done at home. Nor in most Hospital settings, either, because of the obstinacy of the Allopathic establishment to take into consideration anything Homeopathic, no matter how useful—indeed, and no matter how useless what Allopathy has to offer may be.
Viral diseases can be prevented with Allopathically prepared vaccines, that have the potential of producing very serious side effects, and even

death, in patients who receive them[51]. Homeopathically prepared vaccines, on the other hand, appear to be ineffectual for purposes of immunization[52].

In Homeopathy, we also also have to deal with *acute exacerbations of chronic diseases* in psoric patients. Examples are a bleeding peptic ulcer, an acute myocardial infarction, acute adrenal insufficiency, diabetic coma, *status epilepticus*, etc.

Here, treatment has to be carried out in a Hospital setting—at least until the immediate situation of danger passes, and the patient becomes stable enough to resume his or her Homeopathic treatment.

Allopathic treatment may be needed for these and other acute episodes because Homeopathic remedies may take an unpredictable amount of time to start working, an interval that is bound to vary from patient to patient. Moreover, Homeopathic remedies are *specific.* Meaning that, if a wrong remedy is administered by mistake, that remedy will not work at all. This fact becomes particularly relevant when attempting to find the right remedy under pressure, or for patients who are unresponsive or unable to cooperate.

However, Homeopathy can very well complement the emergency Allopathic treatment. Or it could, rather; since it is banned from most Hospitals.

SYCOSIC AND SYPHILITIC REMEDIES

Used to treat the clinical consequences of the chronic miasmas Sycosis and Syphilis.

They will be described in some detail in Chapter 22, when discussing the treatment of genital warts, gonorrhea and syphilis.

INIMICALS

Remedies that are so much alike to each other that the action of one may interfere with, and even inhibit, the action of the other. The classical example is that of *Causticum* and *Phosphorus*.

---

[51] I strongly recommend reading a very objective, impartial and often disturbing paper regarding vaccinations, written by Kristine M. Severyn, R.Ph., Ph.D., entitled *"Immunization: a Pharmacist's View"*, published in the J. Am. Inst. Hom. 87 (2): 79-82, 1994.

[52] Fisher P., *Enough nonsense on immunization.* Brit. Hom. J. 79: 198-200, 1990. Burgess M., *Homeopathy and vaccination.* Lancet 344 (8930): 1168, 1994.

ANTIDOTES

Remedies and others that erase or neutralize the action of another.

For instance, *Lachesis muta* is said to be antidoted by *Calcarea carbonica*, which, in turn, is supposed to be antidoted by *Nux vomica*, etc.

In my experience, this antidotism of one remedy by another is a bit unreal. Ditto regarding the action of inimicals.

Sometimes I administered one remedy that should have been antidoted by the one the patient had been previously receiving—or that, conversely, should have antidoted the previous one. I've never seen this happen.

So I'm a bit skeptical in regards to antidotes and inimicals.

Potencies that are higher or considerably lower than the one a patient may be currently receiving can act as antidotes—antidotes of a particular *potency*, not of the remedy.

There are *universal* antidotes, such as the sniffing of camphor.

Or coffee. Although here the antidotal effect is not consistent. So far coffee has antidoted only a few of my patients.

I shall discuss antidotes more extensively in Chapter 15 *"Antidotes of Homeopathic remedies"*.

INTERCURRENTS

Suppose I am treating a psoric male *Natrum muriaticum* patient, and that the treatment is progressing satisfactorily.

Suppose now that this patient learns of the unexpected death of his father, to whom he was very attached, and suddenly becomes crushed with grief.

The *Natrum muriaticum* treatment shall be discontinued under this circumstance—basically because it will not work in a situation of acute grief—and be replaced by *Ignatia amara* until grief becomes manageable. At this point, treatment with *Ignatia* can be discontinued and *Natrum muriaticum* can be restarted.

In this example, *Natrum muriaticum* is this patient's Constitutional, and *Ignatia* the Intercurrent acute remedy for the duration of the patient's mourning.

Or take another patient, already under constitutional treatment with *Antimonium tartaticum*, who falls and hurts him or herself.

In all likelihood, the patient will receive *Arnica montana* to avoid bruising and to diminish the bad effects of the trauma.

Arnica, in this patient, will also be an Intercurrent remedy; for it will be administered while the patient is under Constitutional treatment with *Antimonium tartaricum*.

Intercurrent remedies, then, are those that are *intercalated* into a chronic treatment—usually Constitutional—when the need arises.

Treatment with the patient's Constitutional remedy can be continued as soon as the need for the Intercurrent remedy disappears.

DETOXIFIERS

They are usually derived from plant extracts, and are prepared in low dynamizations—low Decimals, usually.

Detoxifiers appear to be useful to cleanse diverse organs and tissues.

They are, among others, *Chelidonium majus* and *Carduus marianus* for the liver, *Ceanothus americanus* for the spleen, *Crataegus oxicanta* for the heart, *Hydrastis canadiensis* for mucosas, *Scrophularia nodosa* and *Solildago virga aurea* for lungs, *Berberis vulgaris* for the kidneys, *Helonias dioica* for the uterus, *Chimaphila umbellata* for the prostate, *Condurango* and *Ornitogalum* for the stomach, *Quercus glanduus spiritus* for the spleen, etc.

COMPLEXES

Complexes are admixtures of remedies, usually prepared to combat a particular disease-syndrome.

Anything and everything can be found in a complex. Mother tinctures, low dynamization triturations, hydro- or hydroalcoholic solutions and succussions, decimal and Centesimal potencies, etc.—you name it.

Any number of different remedies can be included in a complex—I have counted 45 remedies in one of them.

A treatment done with complexes is *not* Homeopathic. There is no possibility of Like cures like here.

Administration of complexes is a form of shotgun therapy delivered from a blunderbuss.

Even though one of the remedies in a complex may correct one or more symptoms, it is impossible to know which is the remedy that worked. This makes it impossible to modificaty potencies and to adequately follow-up a patient Homeopathically.

As we shall see later on, it very often happens that a particular potency wears off, and the Homeopath has to prescribe a higher potency to continue a successful treatment. This increase in potency can easily be brought about when the acting remedy is known to the Homeopathic Prescriber. But if the Doctor has no idea regarding which remedy in a complex is the one that is working, how is he or she going to increase the potency of up to *forty* or *fifty* or more remedies at a time?

Complexes, on the other hand, *may* be useful in short-lived, mild acute diseases—and then again, they may not.

This is because some remedies in the complex may antidote each other, rendering the complex useless.

Complexes are easy to obtain anywhere.

In their labels, it says what disease/s each complex is supposedly useful for.

Complexes may be dangerous for their self-medicating users, because they can be taken without adequate Professional supervision.

Most patients who medicate themselves, furthermore, are not sufficiently familiarized with diseases to be able to recognize what is afflicting them. What if their problem, mild as it may be, is actually the prodrome of a serious disease? Say that a patient is medicating him or herself with a complex for symptoms that correspond to a developing cancer, or to an insulin dependent diabetes mellitus, or to the gradual obstruction of a coronary artery in the heart. In these and other similar instances, the patient may needlessly be putting his or her very life at risk by using a complex instead of going to see a Doctor.

Chapter 15
ANTIDOTES OF HOMEOPATHIC REMEDIES.

I find Allopathic antidotism of drugs very easy to understand and to explain. It consists on the termination of the action of a drug.

In order to antidote Allopathically, all one has to do is to know how the chemical or molecule A *(the drug)* interacts with the cellular chemical or molecule B *(the receptor)*, located in most live cells. This interaction between A and B brings about a *therapeutic effect* if the drug A interacts with one or several receptors B located in the organ where the drug is supposed to act. In turn, this interaction brings about *toxicity and side and teratogenic effects* if the receptors B are located in organs or tissues where the drug A is not supposed to act, but where it acts nevertheless due to its lack of specificity.

Then one has to figure out how to block the interaction between chemicals A and B. Blocking the interaction between A and B does not allow the therapeutic effect, nor the toxicity and side and teratogenic effects to happen. The blocker of the interaction between A and B becomes the *antidote,* because it doesn't allow the action of A on B to take place.

Conversely, I find Homeopathic antidotism impossible to understand and to explain in most instances.

In Homeopathy, dynamized natural products guide the Vital Force either to correct chronic imbalance or else to re-attach itself firmly to organs and tissues.

Furthermore, there are no chemicals involved here.

The original substance in each remedy usually contains innumerable components, each with its own individual chemical formula, simple or complex. None of these components couple with any cellular receptor here, because those components are present in only infinitesimal amounts or absent altogether.

And there are no sub-cellular receptors to interact with, either. It is only the power or the dynamization of the remedy that guides the Vital Force where it is needed, or that produces an artificial disease stronger than the natural one ailing the patient.

Yet, Homeopathic antidotism does exist.

It annuls the effect of an otherwise successful Homeopathic treatment almost instantaneously. The antidoted patient starts again to feel as bad as he or she did before treatment—or worse.

Both acute and chronic patients can become antidoted.

In acute patients, the acute disease-syndrome returns with a vengeance. Chronic patients crash into their pre-treatment overall imbalance.

And, after the antidote has done its job, it takes an enormous effort to put the Homeopathic treatment back to work again; at least in my experience.

The subject of antidotisms is far from clear probably because, and with the exception of camphor in high material amounts, antidotism is found only in a few patients and in an apparently haphazard fashion.

I would like to divide antidotes into three groups, those that counter potencies, those that inactivate the remedies and those than annul the effect of Homeopathic treatment.

Antidotes that counter potencies,

Sometimes a Doctor may err by giving a patient too high a potency of the remedy. Often, when this happens, the patient may suffer an aggravation of his or her clinical picture before feeling better.

This aggravation can be neutralized by means of giving the patient a dynamization considerably higher or lower than the one that brought about the aggravation. For obvious reason, I always advice to give a lower potency.

This form of antidotism eliminates the aggravation, but not the action of the remedy.

Antidotes that inactive Homeopathic remedies,

SUNLIGHT.- It may inactivate a Homeopathic remedy after sufficient exposure. I don't believe anybody knows what "sufficient exposure" exactly means; which is why I recommend my patients to keep remedies away from sunlight.

This is also the reason why remedies must be dispensed in dark-colored glass containers, or at the very least in opaque plastic ones—*never* in containers manufactured with clear glass.

PERFUMES.- May have the capacity of inactivating remedies, if sufficiently concentrated.

Which is why I recommend my female patients never to carry remedies in their purses, but rather in the pockets; the reason being that perfumes used in lipstick, makeup and the like may concentrate and then linger in purses for a long time, even after cosmetics have been removed.

Perfumes here include also very odorous chemical substances, such as mothballs and the like.

DAMPNESS.- Of the kind found in most bathrooms, and therefore in the medicine cabinet. Remember that there is no places as damp and as odorous in any home as the bathroom's medicine cabinet—what with the after shave lotions, mouthwashes, make up things and so on and so forth.

In order to avoid dampness, and also perfumes and sunlight, I strongly recommend to keep Homeopathic remedies in *the white clothes drawer*. This drawer is usually a dry place away from the sun, perfumes, mothballs and the like.

CAMPHOR.- Camphor should be kept away both from the remedies and the patient. It is considered to be a *universal* antidote.

Fear of the antidotal effect of camphor is not fully justifiable nowadays. Yesteryear, people would use large amounts of camphor. In those days, considerable amounts would be placed all over the house and on people for every conceivable purpose, all the way from appeasing the sexual ardors of the young to ward off diseases. Often, particularly in times of epidemics, people would go around with a large block of pure camphor in a bag, or else hanging from a chain or a thread around their necks.

Nowadays, there are only traces of camphor in shaving creams and suchlike. I don't believe that the insignificant amount that remains in the face, after shaving, may bring about any harm.

To put it differently, I have never seen a therapeutic failure I could attribute to this factor.

However, there are certain ointments, used for purposes of decongesting, or of relieving joint and muscle aches, that carry hefty amounts of camphor.

My advice is to keep away from these products—and also to keep Homeopathic remedies as far away from them as possible. No matter how hermetically covered the containers of both the ointments and of the Homeopathic remedies may be. If you keep those ointments in one end of the house, please keep the remedies in the other. And don't allow any draft between both ends of the house.

MENTHOL.- Purified menthol must be kept away from remedies—far, far away, for the same reasons explained above, when discussing camphor.

This becomes particularly pertinent when it comes to toothpastes and mouthwashes, as I will discuss immediately below.

Antidotes of treatment.

TOOTHPASTE.- Both toothpaste and mouthwash can pose a problem of antidotism. The amount of purified mint extract, or menthol, tends to be considerable in both.

Which is understandable when one considers that the purpose of these concoctions is to mask bad breath or *halitosis.* The amount of menthol that remains in the mouth after teeth cleansing is so huge, and its scent so powerful, that it may well antidote the remedy if patients takes it after brushing their teeth.

Which is why I ask my patients not to use toothpaste or mouthwash before taking the remedy. Rather, I ask them to wet their toothbrush in a solution of baking soda in water to brush their teeth—or only plain water, if they are children—before taking the remedy. There is a good possibility that a remedy may become inactivated if placed in a strongly menthol-scented mouth.

Conversely, I don't feel there is any problem to brush one's teeth with paste, or to use a mouthwash *away from the times when taking the remedy,* such as the day after, or the morning of the day the remedy is taken, if the remedy is administered at night. The strong minty mouth odor will have dissipated by then.

COFFEE.- Coffee is a no-no in America. It is considered to be a powerful and universal antidote for all Homeopathic remedies. And yet, coffee apparently it poses no problem at all elsewhere.

Two Homeopathic students interviewed 26 Dutch Classic Homeopathic Physicians (that is, those who adhere strictly to Dr. Hahnemann's teachings and therapeutic approach), to ask whether or not they considered coffee to be an antidote. A full 75 % responded that neither coffee *nor* Allopathic remedies had, in their experience, interfered at all with Homeopathic treatment[53]. This lack of agreement with respect to coffee is quite interesting, as well as puzzling. In England I have heard it said that coffee may antidote of *Nux vomica*. And Dr. Hahnemann, in one of his writings (wish I could remember which!), stated that coffee can antidote *Opium*.

If, in effect, coffee would be such an powerful antidote, the word would have spread like wild fire, and its ingestion would have been banned everywhere—for, after all, who wants to risk ruining an otherwise successful Homeopathic treatment because of a cup of coffee?

I tend to agree with the outlook prevalent in Argentina, England and Holland regarding the lack of antidoting capacity of coffee, although with some reservations.

For example, Dr. Ignacio Lutzky started my own personal Constitutional Homeopathic treatment in 1980 in Buenos Aires, Argentina. Neither he, nor any of my Professors in the School of Homeopathy later on, warned me about coffee. So I continued having coffee and, being an M.D., in rather hefty quantities. My Constitutional Homeopathic treatment has been nevertheless successful.

However, I have found so far in my practice that 14 patients have been antidoted by coffee. Being so few and far between, I don't know who the 15th will be, nor when is he or she going to appear.

My attitude regarding coffee drinkers, therefore, is,

1. I request patient to stop having coffee and all other coffee-containing substances (i.e., cookies, cakes, ice-creams, liquor, etc.), *until feeling the first evident beneficial effects of the Homeopathic remedy.* Otherwise I have no way to know if the patient is or is not respond to treatment because of my choosing the wrong remedy, or if it is because of an antidotal effect triggered by coffee. The doubt posed here is not academic. Homeopathic remedies are very specific. If a patient does not respond to treatment because of not having given up coffee, and I wrongly assume that the patient is not responding because I prescribed the wrong remedy, I may change the current remedy for another. Something similar applies to potencies, in the sense that if I feel that a patient is not responding because the potency I administered was too low, when the patient was in actual fact antidoted by coffee, I may administer a potency far above the patient's needs. Changing remedies under these circumstances—and to a lesser degree, changing potencies—may spell failure in an oth-

---

[53] Dam K., *"Coffee and antidotes"*. Simillima 1(4): 29-34, 1993, read in Brit. Hom. J. 83: 102, 1994.

erwise well indicated and conducted chronic Homeopathic treatment.
2. I allow the patient to have a cup of coffee *after* improvement becomes evident;
3. if improvement vanishes, I ask the patient to immediately take another dose of the remedy and to stop having coffee; and
4. if improvement continues I allow the patient to continue having coffee to his or her heart content.

CERTAIN FOODSTUFFS.- Dr. Kent, in his *"Lectures on Homeopathic Materia Medica"*, in the Chapter devoted to *Bryonia*, states that, in *Bryonia* patients, sauerkraut may make disappear the wellness brought about by that remedy.

According to Dr. Kent, fatty foods may do the same in *Pulsatilla* and oysters in *Lycopodium* patients.

Once I took care of a 51-year-old *Natrum Muriaticum* patient whose clinical diagnosis was irritable bowel syndrome. She did very well under treatment, until eventually she became free of symptoms and started to taper down her Pharmaceutical drugs.

At that point she decided to travel south of the border. Once there, she ate something that triggered a very severe diarrhea. All symptoms of her irritable bowel syndrome returned. So much so that she had to start taking her Pharmaceutical drugs again.

There was no way I could help her Homeopathically upon her return. All symptoms would start to flare up as soon as she diminished her intake of Pharmaceutical drugs—even if by a tiny fraction.

Eventually she abandoned Homeopathic treatment.

I have no inkling of what happened with this patient afterwards.

Did that fateful meal triggered a suppression, or is this a *bona fide* case of antidotism?

Or was it that her bowel, still far from well after only a few months of Homeopathic treatment, couldn't put up with the onslaught of the meal that brought about her diarrhea?

BATHING.- Also in *"Lectures on Homeopathic Materia Medica"* under *"Certain foodstuffs"*, Dr. Kent mentions that bathing may also make the beneficial effects of *Rhus toxicodendrum* and *Calcarea carbonica* disappear.

Dr. Kent concludes that antidotal effects, like everything else in Homeopathy, have to be considered individual by individual. And that the only constant rule in Homeopathy is to administer a remedy as similar as possible to the profile of the patient.

I say Amen to that.

Antidotisms, in Homeopathy, can be a rather exasperating and perplexing catalog of do's and don't's.

If followed *verbatim*, some patients should be forbidden from even taking a bath!

Perhaps the only sensible conclusion here to follow Dr. Kent's advice, regarding the necessity of giving the patient a remedy as similar as possible.

As well as to be considerate with the patient, and to forbid as little as possible.

The patient is sufficiently restricted with problems inherent to his or her disease-syndrome and/or his or her chronicity to add still more limitations.

So let us forbid only the essentials, that is, camphor and purified menthol in large amounts and coffee—the latter only until wellness dawns.

Chapter 16

DR. HAHNEMANN AND THE HOMEOPATHIC PRINCI-
PLE OF "LIKE CURES LIKE"

The work of Dr. Hahnemann has been monumental.

Not only that. It was carried out in the midst of the thickest and most profound medical obscurantism—which means that Dr. Hahnemann had nowhere to turn for information and/or for guidance of any kind.

Allopathic discoveries came thick and fast after mid-19th Century.

The 18th Century, however, was rather stagnant in this regard. The only Allopathic breakthroughs worthy of note were Dr. Lind's findings in scurvy, Dr. Withering's discovery of the properties of foxglove or *Digitalis Purpurea* and Dr. Edward Jenner's—or was it Lady Montagu's?—discovery, or import, of the smallpox vaccine or inoculation.

The Scotsman Dr. James Lind (1716-1794) was the first successful Allopathic Researcher in History, as far as I have been able to determine.

Scurvy, also known then as "putrid gums", had killed over one million seafarers only in the 17th and 18th Century. To study how to control it, Dr. Lind chose 12 sailors with scurvy, and divided them into pairs. He gave one member of each pair orange juice, while the other member received seawater, vinegar or some other fluid. Only sailors who received orange juice were cured. Dr. Lind published his findings in 1742—a full eleven years before Dr. Hahnemann was born.

His discovery was recognized and accepted by the British Navy only in 1802. This acceptance, albeit belated, came very much at hand for the battle of Trafalgar, fought October 21, 1805. The crews of Napoleon's ships-of-the-line commanded by Admiral Villeneuve were stricken with scurvy. Villeneuve thought that British sailors were also prey of the same disease—which they weren't, thanks to the British Admiralty's timely acceptance of Dr. Lind's findings. The healthy British sailors, though vastly outnumbered by the French, were able to out maneuver their foe and win the day. I often wonder what the outcome would have been if Admiral Nelson's men had also been stricken with scurvy. Dr. Lind's finding very likely changed the outcome of Trafalgar and of World History as we know it.

It took two hundred additional years to elucidate the chemical structure of the antiescorbutic agent present in citrus fruits, the Vitamin C or ascorbic acid.

Dr. William Withering (1741-1799) heard of a medicine woman who claimed she could cure "dropsy" with a tea prepared with seven herbs. Dr. Withering found that, in effect, that tea was useful; so he tested each of the herbs individually.

He found that only one of the components, the leaves of the foxglove (or *Digitalis Purpurea*), could cure dropsy. Up to this day extracts of the whole leaf, or chemical derivatives of *Digitalis* are used in the treatment of the dropsy, or congestive heart failure.

In turn, Dr. Edward Jenner (1749-1823), a contemporary of Dr. Withering, noticed that cowgirls, when milking cows infested with cowpox, would develop pox lesions in their hands, but nowhere else. These lesions would disappear spontaneously after a time without a trace, and the cowgirls would never fall ill with smallpox afterwards. Dr. Jenner inoculated the discharge of infested cow udders in his patients. This is one of the stories regarding the discovery of vaccination.

Being the other that Lady Mary Wortley Montagu (1689-1767) saw in Turkey, in 1717, how healthy people inoculated with the pox would afterwards become immune to the disease. Back in England, she championed the procedure—before Dr. Jenner was born. By the way, vaccine comes from Latin *vaccinus,* that means related to cows and in turn from Sanskrit *vasa,* cow.

Dr. Lind's discovery of vitamin C, as well of Dr. Withering's of digitalis and Dr. Jenner and Mme. Montague of small pox vaccination were indeed momentous landmarks in the History of Medicine.

However, there were only the discoveries of only one preventive or therapeutic achievement per worker. Dr. Hahnemann, on the other hand, experimented with well over *one hundred* therapeutically useful substances during his lifetime.

Not only discoveries were scarce in the 18th Century. Everyday Allopathic practice at that time can only be characterized as atrocious.

Physicians would bleed patients within an inch of their lives—and not infrequently beyond[54]—with the aid of lancets, leeches and cups.

---

[54] Doctor James Craik assisted General George Washington during his final illness. The frequent and abundant bloodlettings he ordered are considered to have been the

Footnotes continue in next page

For *cupping,* short and shallow incisions, called *scarifications*, are made into the patient's skin with a surgical knife—*never* sterilized between patients, but just wiped clean with a cloth and sometimes even rinsed. Then a 2″ mouth glass cup is held over an open flame until very hot- or, alternatively, its mouth would be rubbed with purified spirits and then set afire. Afterwards, the cup's mouth is firmly pressed around the scarified area. As the cup cools down, vacuum inside the cup forces the patients' blood into it.

Setons were also used to produce and drain pus. A seton is a loop of non-sterilized thread or horse hair that is stitched through the patient's intact skin, in and out, along a length of around 2″ to 3″. Needle and thread are then removed. The pus produced by the inevitable infection, called *pus bonum et laudabile*, or pus good and praiseworthy, is then drained through the holes produced by the seton, or else through a surgical incision performed in between. *Pus bonum et laudabile* means pus good and commendable, because it was supposed to cleanse away toxins as it was discharged. It was called in this fashion to differentiate it from the watery and evil smelling pus that oozes from wounds that are decomposing.

Doctors would apply crushed Spanish fly ointments to blister the skin with the purpose of cleansing the blood through the liquid that would appear into the large blisters.

Powerful emetics and equally strong purgatives were routinely prescribed to make their patients vomit violently and to defecate till they collapsed—all in order, as they would say, to "purify the [patients] blood".

Antimony, mercury, arsenic, cyanide, strychnine, jalap and croton, administered at huge doses, were prominent drugs in the Pharmacopœia. Opium was prescribed in staggering amounts. Iodine was injected into the eyeball to treat retinal detachment. Smoke enemas were enthusiastically recommended for the treatment of certain diseases. As we shall presently see, electricity soon found a prominent place in this therapeutic chamber of horrors.

A Dr. Watson, in England, very famous in his day, wrote *"Lessons of Physic"* (John W. Parker, Ed., 2 vols. London, 1843), that became a standard textbook in many Medical Schools. In his book, Dr. Watson suggests to use veins other than the jugular, even if more difficult to find, to practice bloodletting in infants; for a pierced jugular can suck in air and kill the babies. Amongst many other abhorrences, he recommended to place as many leeches as possible around the patient's anus if the liver or intestines were found to be inflamed Leeches were used for bloodletting close to orifices,

cause, or at the very least one of the *main* causes, of General Washington's untimely death.

where cupping would be difficult to perform; even though leeches would often slither into organic cavities, thus creating "some annoying problems". Cupping was favored where the skin surface was flat enough to allow the 2" mouth of the cup to take firm hold. Phlebotomy, or cutting open a vein, was chosen where veins were available, particularly if they overlaid the organ or structure considered as diseased. In either instance, bloodletting was usually continued until the patient fainted-supposedly the only way to "really cleansing the blood". Then, in order to revive the victim, Dr. Watson highly recommended to make the patient smell a whiff of vinegar. This whiff was to be followed by the ingestion of sips of urine mixed with water.

Newly discovered scientific curiosities, such as electricity, were promptly put into clinical use.

Maria Theresa von Paradis, a talented young pianist and composer, was one of its victims. She lived in 18th Century Vienna and suffered from hysterical blindness, for which she was receiving a pension from compassionate Empress Maria Theresa.

The Empress' Physician, Dr. Heinrich Stoerk, very famous then, became interested in Ms. Paradis' plight and enthusiastically treated her with the Spanish fly, leeches, cauterization and purgatives for many years. When all proved fruitless to restore the patient's sight, Dr. Stoerk encased her head in plaster for two months. This treatment produced severe infections and seizures, but no improvement.

So Dr. Stoerk decided to try electricity, a curiosity in those days. Ms. von Paradis received a total of 3,000 electric shocks *on her eyes*—which became a bloated, bloody mess.

At this stage, Ms. Paradis very sensibly decided to try something else. She consulted Dr. Franz A. Mesmer, of animal magnetism fame. Dr. Mesmer did his mesmerisms and Ms. Paradis recovered her sight.

Once hale, this young woman lost her inspiration as a composer, her talent as a pianist and, to boot, her imperial pension; so her father became furious with Dr. Mesmer and threatened to sue him. But that is another story...

Maternity could not escape from this collective immolation.

The rate of obstetrical deaths and of woman left invalid after delivery due to infections was mind boggling. This was due to the fact that Doctors did everything with their bare hands in those days—surgery, autopsies, deliveries, etc., and would never bother to wash their hands afterwards. Wisely, most mothers would rather have their babies at home, assisted by midwives, instead of going to a Hospital and be cruelly mishandled there by the Staff Doctors, all of whom were male.

The Hungarian Physician Dr. Ignaz Philipp Semmelweis (1818-1865) worked for a time in the Obstetric Clinic of the famous Viennese *Allgemeine Krankenhaus*. As everywhere else, most women admitted in its Obstetric Clinic died of gynecological infections after having had their babies. Dr. Semmelweis was fired by his Chief, a Dr. Klein, for having the unconscionable effrontery of requesting his colleagues to wash their hands before assisting a delivery. Dr. Semmelweis died several years later, profoundly depressed by this injustice. By the by, in German, *klein* appropriately means small or little.

Some prominent Allopathic Doctors hated this horrible Medicine, though most clinged to it with remarkable tenacity.

Among those prominent Physicians was Dr. Thomas Sydenham (1624-1689). He was very partial to opium, though, and had it in very high regard as a the ultimate therapeutic agent. He despised all other forms of treatment. He used to say that, "if all medicines but opium were dumped into the sea, it would be a great disgrace for the fishes [sic], but an equally great blessing for Humanity".

The famous British Physician Dr. Thomas Addison (1793-1860), who worked at Guy's Hospital in London, would seldom prescribe. After seeing a patient, he would often sit down to write a prescription, then hesitate, put the pen down and leave, murmuring "What's the use!...".

In Vienna, again in the famous *Allgemeine Krankenhaus*, the renown Czech Prof. Dr. Joseph Skoda (1805-1881) would also abstain from prescribing, out of compassion and respect for his patients. The world renown Czech Pathologist, Prof. Dr. Karl Freiherr von Rokitanski (1804-1878), also worked there. People in Vienna would say that, in the *Krankenhaus*, Dr. Skoda's wonderful diagnoses would inevitably be followed by equally magnificent autopsies performed by Dr. Rokitanski.

Dr. Hahnemann and his prodigious and systematic work shines like a beacon in the barren, uninspiring and very often appalling 18th Century Medical landscape.

All by himself, Dr. Hahnemann created an entirely new Medical paradigm based on the principle that like cures like, discovered new and marvelous therapeutic uses of natural substances and conceived the idea of only one remedy per patient, instead of several drugs per disease—with no toxicity nor side effects, to boot.

He also devised an entirely new system for testing Homeopathically prepared natural substances. In other words, Dr. Hahnemann also created, single-handed, the first effective methodology for systematic Clinical Therapeutic Research.

Not only that. He also became aware of the importance of the Vital Force and of its relationship with the patient's balance and health. He created new definitions. He conceived a novel classification of miasmas, was able to discern between diseases and miasmas, etc., etc.

All after years of study, hard work, observation, and accurate interpretation of what he had observed.

His work has been as accurate as it has been colossal. Homeopathy was born complete and ready to work from Dr. Hahnemann's mind, in the same fashion Pallas Athena was born fully grown and armed from the head of her father Zeus.

The only tasks remaining to latter Homeopaths has been the study some new miasmas and remedies, the use of Homeopathy as part of novel forms of combined Allopathic/Homeopathic Research and the application of Dr. Hahnemann's principles, ideas and techniques in the benefit of generations of patients.

When one studies Dr. Hahnemann's work, and starts to capture glimpses of its author's personality, admiration knows no bounds—a fact that puzzles outsiders and beginners alike.

As I was puzzled the first time I saw a bust, as well as several engravings of Dr. Hahnemann in the Post-Graduate School of the Asociación Médica Homeopática Argentina. To the point that I wondered if by mistake I had entered the see of some sort of a cult instead of a Post-Graduate School of Medicine!

In time I learnt that this was not a form of hagiolatry. Rather, it is a manifestation of love, respect and admiration towards a giant of a man who was exceptional as a Human Being, a Physician and a Teacher—indeed, a Teacher from whom we all continue to learn 150 years after his death.

Now, a photo of Dr. Hahnemann presides my office. What Dr. Hahnemann did for me, for my life, for my family, for my outlook and way of thinking, for my development as a Human Being and for my health and the health of my family and of my patients certainly deserves this humble token of my gratefulness.

The principle of Like cures like embodies the essence of Homeopathy.

Meaning that, without "like cures like", also known as *similia similibus curentur*, there is no Homeopathy. All it other characteristics, such as the administration of only one remedy at a time for each acute disease, or per treatment of the Whole individual chronic disease-bearing patient, the dynamization of remedies, Provings, etc. are indeed important. Nevertheless, they are all but consequences, or by-products, of *similia similibus curentur*.

The principle of like cures like is the mirror image of the Allopathic "contrary cures contrary", that leads to the treatment of one disease at a time.

I don't believe Dr. Hahnemann really understood the rational behind "Like cures Like". And, according to what he wrote in § 28 of the 6th. Edition of his *Organon*, this ignorance didn't bothered him all that much, either. Furthermore, in his *Treatise of Chronic Diseases*, he states that "if facts contradict reason, then I will rather submit to facts" —which, as I have been repeatedly able to verify, is the acid test of courage for any University graduate.

The Spaniards learnt quite a few things from the natives they conquered together with their New World.

In Perú, for instance, they saw how the Incas warded off "intermittent fevers".

These fevers were known, in other insalubrious areas of the world, as "swamp fevers". Today we call those fevers malaria (from Italian *mal-* bad or evil, and *-aria*, air) or paludism.

In the early 1600's, the Count of Chinchón was the Viceroy of Perú. His wife, the Countess of Chinchón—or Chinchona—fell ill with the fevers. She suffered a great deal until she was cured with a bitter brew made with the bark of a tree that Linnaeus[55] would later call Chinchona because of the Countess; a term that was later changed to Cinchona.

Jesuit missionaries discovered that the bark of the Chinchona tree was much easier to transport once dried up and pulverized, while all its therapeutic virtues remained intact. Chinchona bark started to be used in Europe around 1650, variously under the names of "china bark" (thus its pharmaceutical name, *China officinalis)*, "Jesuit's powder" or "Countess powder" among others. It became a sensation.

It is hard for us to understand how totally powerless people were, in matters related to health, until the second half of the 19th Century. Something as useful as these powders was bound to produce quite a stir.

This commotion, in turn, brought forth a cascade of comments in the Medical literature of the time. Which, as well as every other form of com-

---

[55] Carolus Linnaeus (1707-1778). Famous Swedish botanist.

munication, had increased exponentially since Guttemberg had invented the printing press.

One of the best selling Medical writings of the time was William Cullen's *"Lectures of Materia Medica"* a book that had, among other topics, a description of Cinchona and its effects.

A copy of this book fell into the hands of a nomad who was barely making ends meet by means of translating Medical treatises and other works into German. The name of the translator was Samuel Hahnemann.

This translator was an itinerant Medical Doctor who once had a brilliant future ahead—a future that he squandered by disputing with his colleagues.

This cantankerous individual would constantly throw onto his colleagues' faces, and without mincing words, the claim that their methods were as useless as they were brutal, and would adamantly refuse to use them. Afterwards, the bone of contention with the Establishment became his daft idea that like cures like; an idea that, he claimed, could cure many people. So local Allopathic establishments would soon get furious at him, and kick him out of own town after another.

After roaming about for a long time, Dr. Hahnemann had reached an extreme of poverty. In order to make ends meet, and give his growing family a modicum of food and comfort, Dr. Hahnemann worked all hours of days and nights translating Medical treatises into German.

This Physician/translator heard of Dr. Cullen's textbook, and thought it would be a good idea to translate it into German. It was a fateful decision.

He became interested in the effect of Cinchona; interested enough to try it on himself.

To his astonishment, Dr. Hahnemann found that self-administration of Cinchona by mouth could produce the dreaded swamp fevers. He also found that Cinchona produced the fevers in *all* who took it, whereas the miasmas that came from the swamps would only make *several* of the exposed individuals ill.

Furthermore, Dr. Hahnemann found that, aside from the fevers, Cinchona would produce symptoms in many organs and systems, a phenomenon seldom found in patients ill with swamp fever—and that all changes would disappear when the administration of Cinchona was suspended.

From his studies, observations and experiments, Dr. Hahnemann concluded that the *"artificial disease"* caused by Cinchona was more powerful than the natural disease produced by the effluvia or miasmas in the swamps[56]; since the artificial disease would attack everybody and would produce more symptoms than the natural disease paludism.

He also observed how the *artificial disease* brought about by Cinchona could be started at will with the administration of Cinchona, and terminated also at will when discontinuing its administration—unlike the natural fevers that, once started, could not be stopped.

And so, two ideas germinated in Dr. Hahnemann's extraordinary mind:

The first was that a natural disease can be eliminated by the induction of a *stronger artificial disease caused by a remedy,* if and when that remedy *produces symptoms similar to those of the natural disease.*

The second, inevitable consequence of the first, was that *like cures like.*

The artificial disease caused by a Homeopathic remedy is more powerful than the natural one. It *displaces* the natural disease ailing the patient. Once displaced, the natural disease looses the supply of the patient's Vital Force it needs for its development. The natural disease consequently vanishes, because nothing can exist if devoid of Vital Force.

Then the artificial disease caused by the remedy is eliminated when the administration of the remedy is discontinued (Hahnemann S., *Organon*, 6th. Edition. § 26, 34 and others).

Dr. Hahnemann found that this sequence of event was consistently verifiable and repeatable with *all* Homeopathic remedies he tested and used in patients.

Only now did Dr. Hahnemann return to the practice of Medicine. In 1796 he published his first important work, the *"Essay on a new Principle"*.

It was the birth of Homeopathy.

Dr. Hahnemann's work, I may perhaps add, was not performed by some well paid Scientist assisted by his or her staff in some modern, state of the art laboratory or Hospital.

---

[56] These miasmas or effluvia had been considered to be the single cause of paludism, an idea that persisted during the 19th Century. The infestive parasites *Plasmodia* and their vectors, the *Anopheles* mosquitoes, were still undiscovered. Dr. Hahnemann theorized in one of his writings, some years after his work with Cinchona, that miasmas were likely to be composed by large quantities of living microorganisms, invisible to the naked eye—decades before any microbiologist set eyes on any of them.

Rather, it was done from 1785 onwards, at a time when the practice of Medicine was barbaric and when systematic Research was non-existent. Furthermore, it was performed by a man working alone and untutored. A man who was so poor that he could ill afford what he needed to start, let alone continue his experimental work.

He carried out his Research doggedly, besieged by poverty and uncertainty. Alone and against scorn amd overwhelming odds.

The temptation of returning to Allopathy must have been overwhelming in those days. All he would have had to do was to practice the same Medicine all other Doctors were doing. Nobody would have found fault in this—except, of course, his conscience. His roaming, poverty and uncertainty would have instantly became stability, respect and riches had he yielded. Plus a good life for his family.

How sorely must he have been tempted! How enticing those thirty pieces of silver must have appeared when he was seeing his family suffer as his colleagues prosper as he was besieged by the pangs of hunger! But he clung to his principles and stood firm.

Until eventually his admirable tenacity bore its fruits.

Dr. Hahnemann's first discovered that natural products can produce and annul artificial diseases according to the principle that like cures like. But many natural substances have side effects and toxicity, alas!

His next step was to find how to eliminate the ill effects of the substances he was studying. He started this phase of his work by diluting those natural substances but found that, after a certain dilution, the substances in solution would disappear—and also their beneficial effects (Hahnemann S., *Organon*, 6th Edition. § 56).

So he created *succussion,* that is, diluting or else triturating, and then shaking.

It never ceases to amaze me how Dr. Hahnemann conceived that, by means of something as simple as *diluting and shaking* dilutions, he could unlock hitherto unsuspected therapeutic capabilities.

I often wonder what made him aware of the usefulness of succussion. Could it have been perhaps a *dream*? For it is known that that some important inventors and empiricists found their greatest ideas during a dream.

Dr. William Kekule, for example, after a lot of frustrating work trying to figure out the structure of benzene, dreamt one night of six whirling ballerinas, each stationed in one of the angles of an hexagon.

Or take Walter Hunt, the American who invented of the tip-eyed needle sewing machine. After a lot of long and frustrating work attempting to device a useful needle, one night he had a nightmare in which he saw himself surrounded by savages, each aiming a spear at him—*all of which spears had a hole near the tip.*

Another explanation of how he discovered succussion has to do with the abominable state of the roads, and the inevitable shaking of the solutions he carried when going to see his patients. Dr. Hahnemann, always the keenest of observers, might have become puzzled at how much more powerful his remedies were after a home visit than after a visit in his office.

At any rate, this is the saga of what happened after Dr. Hahnemann and Cinchona met each other.

And how, as the consequence of such an encounter one man, during a lifetime of incredible work and realizations, first re-discovered single-handedly the concept of *"like cures like"*, and then applied it together with everything that came in its wake. Such as dynamizations, effective treatments for chronic patients, the concept of balance, the role of the Vital Force as a curative agent, etc.

With untold benefits for those who suffer.

I have had, and currently have under my care, several psoric patients who are receiving or have received *Cinchona* as their Constitutional remedy.

Many are doing quite well.

I always tell my patients that *Cinchona* is the very first remedy Dr. Hahnemann tested in himself and a few other provers, and then administered to patients over two Centuries ago.

I also tell them that Dr. Hahnemann, at the time of his first encounter with the china bark, was very poor, translating to make ends meet somehow; dying year in and year out to practice the quality Medicine he loved.

And I also tell my patients that the Jesuit's powder, when it met with that magnificent mind, produced this wondrous gift to Humanity that is Homeopathy.

And, as I tell my patients this story—and think, and write about it—I can't help it but to mull how History in its often quiet, discreet and wily ways, manages to bring things and events and circumstances and marvelous people together. And how, as the consequence of these in appearance fortuitous encounters, so many extraordinary things have come forth to assist, help, and bring solace to Humanity.

Chapter 17
ADMINISTRATION AND DOSAGE OF HOMEOPATHIC REMEDIES

Homeopathic remedies are usually administered by mouth.
They must be given *one at a time*, and *at adequate intervals*.

They can also be sniffed and rubbed, though little of this is done nowadays.

There is an amusing anecdote, apocryphal in all likelihood, regarding Dr. Hahnemann and one of his patients. It has to do with sniffing a remedy.

For a time, during his long and fruitful professional life, Dr. Hahnemann prescribed by means of asking his patients to sniff a flask containing their Homeopathic remedy.

So this patient comes to the office, is evaluated, and then Dr. Hahnemann asks him to sniff his remedy.

Once the patient sniffs, Dr. Hahnemann caps the flask and is said to have told the patient "You have been treated".

Whereupon the patient fetches his money purse, loosens up the strings, opens it up, and approaches the purse to Dr. Hahnemann's nose. "Please sniff" the patient supposedly said.

Dr. Hahnemann, caught by surprise, or perhaps in his innocence, did as told.

"You have been paid!" was the patient's Parthian shot as, smiling slyly, he turned on his heel and walked out of the office.

Remedies can also be administered percutaneously, that is, through the skin by means of rubbing. Dr. Hahnemann described this procedure in detail in the Preface to the Second Part of his *Treatise of Chronic Diseases,* in the section entitled *Antipsoric Medicines.*

For percutaneous administration, a watery solution of the remedy is rubbed onto one or more parts of the body where the skin is *free of pathology*, preferably one of the limbs.

Various areas may be used alternatively.

Dr. Hahnemann reported that, when a remedy is used both internally and percutaneously, its therapeutic action is considerable enhanced.

From now on, and until the end of this Chapter, I am going to refer exclusively to the administration of Homeopathic remedies *by mouth*.

In *Allopathic Pharmacology*, material quantities of drugs are placed into each pill, injectable or whatever.

If a pill contains, say, 100 milligrams of a certain drug, then two pills will contain 200 milligrams, three pills 300 milligrams, and so on.

The situation is entirely different when using Homeopathic potencies. Potencies are magnitudes that cannot be measured nor weighed.

From the 1 CH (that is, *one hundredth* or 10^{-2} of the original substance), to the 10^{-23} there is still material quantities of the remedy in each dynamization; if in considerably diminishing concentrations after each consecutive succussion. From 12 CH (that is, *one trillionth-trillionth*, or 10^{-24}) onwards there is no matter to weigh or measure.

Since there is no matter in dynamizations higher than 12 CH, if one imbibes one single lactose pellet with a 87% ethanol/water solution of, say, *Alumina* 30 CH, or 10^{-60} (that is, a *quadrillionth-quadrillionth-quadrillionth-quadrillionth);* and then one imbibes a bucketful of pellets with the same dynamization, then *each pellet,* as well as the *whole bucketful,* will have *Alumina* at the same 30 CH dynamization.

Meaning that if a patient takes one pellet imbedded with *Alumina* 30 CH, that patient is taking the same potency as another patient who takes a bucketful of *Alumina* 30 CH. That is, there is no change in potency associated with the quantity of pellets ingested. The only way of increasing the potency of each *dose*—or to decrease it, for that matter—is to imbibe another lot of lactose pellets with a *different* hydroalcoholic dynamization.

The exception here, as far as potencies, are the fifty-millesimal or LM potencies, when dispensed in solution, or *Plus.* Here the potency can be increased, prior to each take, by means of succussing the flask. This means that LM's Plus dynamizations can be taken every day without fear of provoking an involuntary Proving. This is because each day, and due to the daily succussion, the potency is a little bit higher than that of the day before (let me recall that, in order to produce a Proving, the potency—usually Centesimal—has to remain *the same* throughout the whole Clinical trial). The bad news is that, when succussing every day, the patient increases the potency by an *indeterminate* factor.

If one wants to know *exactly* how much a dynamization is increased (i.e., from a 30 CH to a 31 CH), then one has to dissolve one drop of the 30 CH dynamization into 100 drops of ethanol 87% or 96% in water, succuss the preparation and dissolve it in water, or else wet a new batch of lactose powder or of pellets with the newly prepared 31 CH dynamization.

Regarding *toxicity.*

Homeopathic remedies are said to be non-toxic. Which is true, with one exception.

Low dynamizations of poisons may still contain enough of them as to make them toxic.

It has been found that dynamizations of the order of 3 x (or one thousandth) to 12 x (or one trillionth) or *Arsenicum Album,* or white arsenic, still contain sufficient material quantity or amount as to make them potentially dangerous[57], particularly for children and for old and/or debilitated patients.

The same can be said of other substances that are poisonous in material doses—or that may induce an allergic reaction.

All potentially dangerous or poisonous Homeopathic remedies—and this includes *Apis mellifica* in patients allergic to bee stings—should therefore be administered in potencies of 12 CH (one trillionth-trillionth) or higher; that is, in potencies that have no original substance left.

As to *frequency, form and time of administration.*

As the result of the action of the Homeopathic remedy, the acute patient's Vital Force is liberated, or normalized, or attuned, or put in its healing mode. The Vital Force then grips firmly the acutely diseased area and makes the disease disappear.

In chronic patients, the remedy prompts the Vital Force to correct the imbalance. Once the patient is in balance, the Vital Force becomes attuned with its host and is able to roam at will, correcting everything it finds wrong and eventually curing the Whole chronic patient.

This sequence of events starts after the administration of *one single dose* of the right remedy.

The *speed* of this sequence of events is individual, and will not be accelerated by the administration of more than one dose, at least in my experience.

---

[57] Kerr, H.D., Saryan, L.A. *"Arsenic content of Homeopathic Medicines".* J. Toxicol. 24 (5): 451-9, 1986.

Consequently, remedies should be given one remedy and one potency at a time; usually to be repeated only when the action of the previous dose is waning.

Here again, as everywhere else in Homeopathy, this rule is riddled with exceptions. There are excellent Homeopathic Physicians who repeat the same low potency *every day* in chronic patients, for relatively prolonged periods of time, without any problems and with excellent results.

Waning of therapeutic action, in *chronic patients,* may take days, weeks or months, sometime years.

In *acute problems*, the adequate interval between potencies and/or remedies may be up to minutes apart, according to the patient's evolution. Here, waning of the therapeutic effect can happen very fast.

Homeopathic remedies are usually imbeded in pellets. To take one dose, several pellets are placed under the tongue and allowed to dissolve there.

When the remedy is dispensed in liquid form it is advisable to take it by drops or by the spoonfull.

In very small children in whom the remedy has been dispensed in pellets, it may be advisable to dissolve some pellets in a few ounces of water, stir and then administer a sip, or a spoonful at a time, at intervals considered optimal by the attending Physician.

Dr. Hahnemann recommended using a spoon made of horn for purposes of stirring and then administering the remedy in solution. Being these spoons so difficult to come by nowadays, I feel it is safe to use a new *plastic* spoon, thoroughly washed and dried. Never, ever, a metal spoon lest traces of metal may be administered to the patient unawares, traces that may become dynamized after stirring and that may interfere with the action of the remedy.

By the same token, the container where the remedy is dissolved in water should be made of *glass*, and have been thoroughly washed and dried beforehand. Never a paper cup, nor a plastic or a metal one. Pellets don't need dissolve completely in the water. Contents of the glass should be stirred, with the plastic spoon, only long enough to allow the active principle imbedded in the pellets to become soluble in the water of the glass. To completely dissolve the pellets in room temperature water takes close to forever and fulfills no useful purpose.

Acute patients should take the remedy whenever needed.

In *chronic patients*, it is recommended to give one single dose of the remedy at night, immediately before turning off the lights. Patients should brush their teeth with water and/or baking soda the night they take the remedy.

The remedy can also be taken in the morning, if the administration of the remedy at night brings about insomnia or excitement. If the remedy is taken in the morn, patients should be asked to set the alarm clock one half hour before usual waking up time, go to the bathroom, rinse their mouth with water, place the remedy under the tongue, return to bed and rest till their normal raising time. The patient should be instructed to brush his or her teeth with water and/or baking soda after breakfast and lunch, and then with whatever he or she chooses at night, before retiring.

Dr. Hahnemann recommended taking the remedy in the morning, and then relaxing for some time before starting the day's activities. Nowadays, and quite unlike what happened then, the world assaults us as soon as we wake up. Just to have an idea of the difference between then and now, let me recall that, in Dr. Hahnemann's day, when somebody was ill, servants would spread sawdust in front of the house to dampen the noise of passing carriages that could perturb the patient. *O tempora, o mores!*

There is no point in repeating a remedy while the patient's Vital Force is working; that is, as the patient is improving.

It will not bother the patient to receive another dose, and then another; provided this repetition is not too frequent or overextended in time, for fear of bringing about an involuntary Proving.

Also, an unneeded repetition will be as superfluous as to go on flicking and flicking the light switch of an already lit room.

As to the *dosage* of Homeopathic remedies

There is no way of knowing beforehand what the *correct potency* of a remedy will be for an individual patient.
There is no way to find out but by trial and error.

A potency should be increased when the effect of the previous dose is negligible, or else when it wanes after a short time. Conversely, the potency may also have be decreased if the Physician considers that the effect of the administered potency has been too strong, of if it has triggered an aggravation.

There are *five dosage schedules* or regimes in Homeopathy. Three use Centesimal potencies or CH's, one Decimal or X's, and one Fifty millesimal or LM's.

The first Centesimal dosage schedule increases by a factor of one Centesimal dynamization per step; that is, is starts with 1 CH, and then it continues with 2 CH, 3 CH, etc. until finally reaching 30 CH.

The second Centesimal schedule increases by a factor of 3. It starts in 3 CH, from there it goes to 6 CH, then to 9 CH and so on also until reaching 30 CH.

Both variances of this schedule have been called *Hahnemannians*, because Dr. Hahnemann was the first to use them.

The third schedule, also using Centesimal potencies, usually starts with 6 CH, and from there it goes to 30 CH, 200 CH, 1,000 CH (also called 1 M), 10,000 CH (or 10 M), 50,000 CH (or 50 M), and even higher. It is called *Kentian* because it was created by Dr. Kent.

The Decimal was the first dosage schedule Dr. Hahnemann experimented with.

He then abandoned it in favor of the Centesimals which he also left aside, late in his life, to start working with LM's.

In Fifty millesimals, or LM's dosage schedule, also discovered by Dr. Hahnemann, the remedy is usually administered by means of increasing one potency at a time, also when the usefulness of each potency has been thoroughly exhausted (i.e., LM 1, LM 2, LM 3, etc.).

LM Plus are always dispensed in liquid form, usually dissolved in water. The patient increases the dynamization by means of strongly succussing the flask prior to taking each daily dose. This way, the patient never takes the same potency twice.

It is said that the Hahnemannian schedule works better in *physical* problems, and the Kentian in *emotional* ones.

Like every other generalization in Homeopathy, this particular one is sometimes true, and others false.

The Physician has to consider each individual patient, his or her disease and his or her circumstance, and the relationship between all three.

If, after careful consideration, the attending Physician believes the patient is in need of a gentle progression, then he or she will probably favor either one of the Hahnemannians or else the LM schedule—probably in Plus.

If the Doctor wants to work faster, then he or she may use the Kentian.

As to the Decimal scale, I don't believe I have enough experience as to be able to comment about it, one way or another.

We do not only administer *one potency at a time*, but also *one remedy at a time*.

If two or more remedies are administered at the same time, one or more of them may neutralize, or antidote, one or more of the others.

These neutralizations or antidotisms, like everything else in Homeopathy, may vary from patient to patient; and may ruin an otherwise successful treatment.

I remember within this context a 16-year-old male I once treated. He came to my office with a very severe attention deficit disorder.

History revealed that there were no other abnormalities, and that the youth was *Sulphur*. His miasma was clearly tuberculinic. He was receiving Methylphenidate, the standard Allopathic treatment for this kind of problems.

I started treatment with *Sulphur,* and the patient's attention deficit disorder started to improve almost immediately. Administration of Methylphenidate was suspended within one month of treatment.

After two months of sustained improvement, and with the purpose of hastening the effects of *Sulphur,* I had the unfortunate idea of starting to treat his miasma at the same time. This, despite of the fact that *Sulphur,* like every other Polychrest, is trimiasmatic (that is, it covers all the chronic miasmas). I gave him one single dose of *Tuberculinum* in between two doses of *Sulphur,* that the patient was taking at monthly intervals.

His improvement disappeared almost immediately. His severe attention deficit disorder returned, and there was nothing I could do to help him from then on.

Older children and *adults* can receive remedies imbedded in pellets.

It is advisable to administer the pellets no later than one half hour before the child goes to bed. This way, pellets will have ample time to dissolve before the child falls asleep.

In *toddlers* and *bottle fed babies,* I recommend always dissolving the pellets in water, in a glass cup and then administering one teaspoon or less of the supernatant.

Only clean plastic spoons are to be used, here too, for purposes of stirring and to administer the remedy.

When treating a breast-fed infant it is advisable to administer the remedy *to the mother.* The mother will then pass the remedy to the baby with her milk.

Jose Miguel Mullen, M.D.

If the mother's remedy corresponds to that of the baby, the treatment will benefit both.

And, if the patient is the mother and not the baby, the remedy will also pass into the baby with her milk, but without affecting the infant in the least. This is so because each Homeopathic remedy is specific, and will act *only in the patient whose profile matches that of the remedy being administered.*

Pregnant women can also take Homeopathic remedies.

Remedies are specific and lack side effects and toxicity. They also lack ill effects on embryos and fetuses.

Expectant mothers and their developing babies will therefore never be affected negatively, in any way, by Homeopathic remedies.

Probably the only really dangerous, dramatic, and potentially irreversible problem in Homeopathy is that generated by an *involuntary Proving.*

Such an event occurs when a patient, who is taking the same remedy at the same potency every day, and usually without Professional supervision, continues its self-administration *beyond the point where symptoms of the Proving start to appear.*

Sometimes the results of these involuntary Proving can end up in *engrafting;* that is, changes that may become permanent and irreversible in the patient.

At the very least, consequences of involuntary Provings can be very serious.

I have already mentioned the problem of the Homeopathic Pharmacist who proved *Histaminum,* didn't stop in time, and had heartburn for the rest of his life.

I would like now to bring about two more examples of involuntary Provings and engrafting.

I once attended an 82-year-old female. She had heart failure, and also lung and kidney insufficiency.

She was taking a host of Pharmaceutical drugs, and would go about with one of those metallic valise- or suitcase-like reservoirs full of oxygen, with tubes ending up in her nostrils. Even so, her fatigue was noticeable. She also had high blood pressure.

This patient had been seeing an Acupuncturist for several months before coming to my office. I had no objection to her continuing Acupuncture treatment. Homeopathy and Acupuncture often complement each other nicely. Acupuncture had not helped this patient in the least, according to her daughter, a Nurse.

The patient started to improve with her Constitutional Homeopathic treatment, albeit slowly. She tapered down, and eventually stopped taking all Pharmaceutical drugs. She would go, for days at a time, forgetting to turn on the oxygen in her valise.

One day her daughter, who lived with her, phoned to report that her mother's heart was racing. She had taken her mother to the Gerontologist, who had studied her thoroughly and had found no reason for this phenomenon.

I saw and examined the patient immediately. I couldn't understand what was going on. At one point her daughter told me "You know, Doctor, that Acupuncturist my mother is going to? Well, aside from the needles, he has her on pills. He sells them to her. To take daily at home". "For how long has she been taking those pills?" I asked. "Oh, for months now".

I requested the patient's daughter to read me on the phone the ingredients in the pills as soon as she got home.

It turned out that this woman had been taking for months, every single day, four different complexes; each containing some *forty or fifty* different Homeopathic remedies in Decimal potencies.

She had been doing an involuntary Proving with 160 or more remedies simultaneously!

One of the remedies, in one of the pills she was taking, was *Digitalis*. When *Digitalis*, or any of its derivatives, is given in material doses as an Allopathic drug, it helps slow a weakened heart, thus making its contractions more powerful. But, if given in Homeopathic potencies, *Digitalis* can make the heart race.

I asked the daughter to immediately discontinue that ill-prescribed battery of Homeopathic remedies and, as a precaution, to quit seeing that Acupuncturist.

The involuntary Proving was reversible in this patient, thank Goodness. It hadn't gone far enough to produce engrafting. After one week her heart rate was back to normal.

Still, though, in a patient as delicate and as elderly as she was this episode, no matter how brief, could have ended up in and extremely serious disability, irreversible heart failure, and even death.

In another opportunity I received an anonymous phone call. A female voice. Didn't want to give her name.

The voice said that someone, another woman, was in a Mental Institution. She had forcefully been taken there after being arrested by the Police. She had wrecked havoc in a store for no apparent reason. Then she had resisted arrest.

The caller, who stated was her roommate, told me that the woman she was calling me about had been taken Homeopathic *Belladona* daily for months. Yes, at the same potency. No, it hadn't been prescribed by anybody, and she was not under anybody's supervision. She obtained her refills in some Health Food store.

The voice in the phone asked me if there was anything I could do to help.

I told her that one of two things could happen. Either the patient would be well after a few days of discontinuing *Belladona*, or else she wouldn't. And that, if she didn't get well, then the effects were likely to be permanent.

Belladona, when Homeopathically prepared, can bring about and therefore cure, among other things, episodes of destructive fury such as the one this poor woman had. Her current problem had been the consequence of an unsupervised, imprudent, long lasting and involuntary Proving of *Belladona*.

What to do when this alarming situation develops?

One can try a universal antidote such as camphor, administered by sniffing. However, not always can the effects of an excessively prolonged Proving be reversed.

My experience in changes caused by engrafting is not all that great. What I have seen is that, once it happens, the patient is not likely to fully return to normal. Despite of whatever treatment may be attempted to reverse the damage.

The moral here is:

Please, let us be extremely careful—and watchful—when administering any Homeopathic remedy, particularly when *frequently* and *at the same potency.*

When contemplating a treatment of any patient, the Physician, among many other questions, should ask him or herself the following:

* How much benefit am I aiming to obtain with this treatment?
* How much risk will I subject my patient to, in order to obtain that benefit?

These two questions are the basis for the assessment of the *benefit/risk ratio.*

If the benefit neatly exceeds the risk, the treatment may proceed.

But if the benefit and the risk are more or less equal; or, worse yet, if the risk is greater than the benefit to be obtained, then the Physician should abstain from using that particular form of treatment in the patient—the exception here being that a high risk treatment may have to be used in extremely critical situations, if nothing else less dangerous is available.

Every *Allopathic* form of treatment carry risks, whether allergy-inducing capacity, toxicity, and/or side- and teratogenic effects—all of which worsen as dosage and therapeutic effect increase.

Homeopathic remedies, on the other hand, have no risk whatsoever; since they lack allergy-inducing capacity, toxicity and side effects, as well as side- and teratogenic effects. Furthermore, their effectiveness increases with *decreasing* doses.

This complete lack of risk should make the consideration of Homeopathic remedies paramount, when outweighing different forms of therapy for a particular patient.

Chapter 18

THE HOMEOPATHIC AGGRAVATION

The Homeopathic aggravation can only be experienced by chronic patients receiving their Constitutional treatment.

One can attempt to describe the mode of action of Constitutional, remedies by saying that, when administered correctly, they ultimately *nudge*—or *guide,* or *usher*—the chronic patient's Vital Force toward the fulcrum of his or her imbalance.

The Vital Force can be compared to a dynamo, that provides energy for everything that happens within a Human Being (Hahnemann S., *Organon,* 6th. Edition. § 10).

Consequently, *it will be the Vital Force,* primed by the Homeopathic remedy, what will straighten up the chronic patient's fulcrum of imbalance. Once imbalance disappears the Vital Force attunes itself with the patient, and the patient's disease-syndrome/s will frequently disappear.

Dr. Hahnemann explains the Homeopathic aggravation in § 61 to 66 of his *Organon.*

He states that the *primary action* of a Homeopathic remedy may be one of aggravation, followed by a *secondary action* of improvement.

If the potency of the Constitutional remedy administered to the patient is *too high,* then the stimulus provided to the healing capacity of the *Vital Force* will be correspondingly great—as will be the action of both aggravation and improvement.

According to the *Law of Hering,* in a successful Homeopathic treatment, the healing capacity of the patient's Vital Force is first experienced in the emotional sphere, and then in the physical organism. Wellness will also progress—or appear to progress—from inside outwards, from above downwards, and from the most recent symptom to the most remote.

This concept can also be expressed as considering that the Vital Force acts everywhere at the same time and with the same intensity, but in such a fashion that its action is perceived according to the *density of the structures* on which it is working. Thoughts and emotions will show improvement first, being the most subtle, fluid and malleable. Then the effect of the remedy slows down as the density of structures increase. Therefore, bones, sinews, muscles and the like (particularly prevalent in the extremities), being the densest of all, will be the last to show any changes.

The *progress of the action of a remedy* can be compared to a tidal wave. Let me bring an example to clarify,

Imagine a pond in some forest, protected from the wind. Not a ripple alters the calm of its surface. Suppose there is a straw floating somewhere on it.

See yourself tossing a pebble into the pond. A tidal wave will form at the point of impact. The wave will spread outwards. Eventually, it will reach the point where the straw is floating, to then pass beyond it. The straw will wobble as the wave passes by, to then become still again.

Let us now say that the pond is the chronic patient, the straw his or her disease-syndrome, and the pebble the Homeopathic remedy.

The structures affected by the patient's disease-syndrome will wobble as the patient's Vital Force, unleashed by the administration of the remedy, reaches it. This wobbling may be perceived by the Whole patient as discomfort.

This uncomfortable feeling is the *Homeopathic aggravation.*

Say that the pond is a gouty patient. The straw here would be the gout and the stone we toss the *Decimal* or *Centesimal* potency of that patient's Constitutional remedy.

If what we throw is a *small pebble*, then the ripples of the tidal wave will be insignificant. If the ripples are small, then the wobbling of the straw is going to be negligible too.

In a similar fashion, if we give our gouty patient a low Decimal or Centesimal potency, both the ripples and the progress of the tidal wave will be gentle; and the commotion at the level of the disease-syndrome and the tissues that bear it will be insignificant.

Little commotion means little awareness of suffering on the part of the patient. In other words, there is going to be little or no *Homeopathic aggravation.*

If, on the other hand, we throw a boulder into that pond, then the tidal waves will be gigantic, and the wobbling of the straw ponderous—as will be that poor chronic gouty patient's suffering when a Homeopathic remedy is given in too high a potency.

The *Homeopathic aggravation* here can be very severe.

This example is not hypothetical.

I know of a gouty patient whose Doctor, in an attempt to cure him faster, started with a 10,000 CH, or 10 M of his Constitutional remedy. Almost immediately the patient started to howl with pain, and remained in extreme distress and pain for almost a week. Then his agony started to subside to finally disappear, and the patient became hale. He hasn't had a single symptom of gout ever since.

The suffering this poor man had to undergo was as extreme as it was unnecessary. A gentle administration, starting with a lower potency, and then increased it as needed, would have achieved the same result while avoiding his horrendous aggravation.

A Homeopathic aggravation usually means that the treatment will be successful.

I have never seen a Homeopathic aggravation in a baby or small child, no matter how high the potency used to start treatment.

I have no idea why children don't suffer aggravations.

The sequence of events described above, i.e., aggravation at the *onset* of treatment, is only valid for *Decimal* or *Centesimal* potencies.

Fifty millesimals, or LM's, specially when administered in *Plus* (that is, when succused prior to each take), can also elicit a Homeopathic aggravation. But aggravation here is experienced at the *end* of the treatment, and not at the beginning, as with Decimals and Centesimals (Hahnemann S. *Organon*, 6th. Ed., § 280).

One form of Homeopathic aggravation is the usually mild and short-lived *re-appearance of old and usually forgotten symptoms.*

This form of aggravation, that can frighten the patient, happens as wellness progresses from the most recent symptoms to the most remote.

Unlike what usually occurs with other forms of aggravation, reappearance of old and forgotten symptoms can be found even when treatment is started with low Centesimal or Decimal potencies.

And, to a greater degree than what happens with other forms of aggravation, the re-appearance of old and forgotten symptoms usually herald a successful outcome of the treatment.

Aggravation can also manifest itself as *discharges* of diverse nature, all the way from a rash to episodes of diarrhea. These phenomena usually happen early in the patient's treatment with Decimal or Centesimal potencies. Discharges tend to happen in areas affected by the patient's disease-syndrome.

I remember a man in his 60's with chronic bronchitis, in whom the first manifestation of improvement was a considerable—and uncomfortable—increase of his bronchial secretion for several days.

Or that other 52-year-old male, married to a very jealous woman.
He had been infected with gonorrhea years back, before getting married, and had been "cured" with some antibiotic.
The uretheral discharge returned shortly after starting Homeopathic treatment. His wife became furious and threatened to divorce the patient. It took me a lot of time and effort both to persuade the patient to leave the discharge untreated, and to convince his wife that this was but an innocent form of aggravation. The discharge disappeared after 3 days and the marriage was saved.

Frequently, chronic patients with sinusitis will complaint of a transient increase in the stuffiness of their sinuses; and/or of the appearance, re-appearance, or aggravation of discomfort in those areas; or of nasal discharge, post-nasal drip, etc.

Other patients may experience the appearance or re-appearance of vaginal discharges shortly before the onset of improvement.

When the patient develops a discharge, the Doctor must differentiate between a disease and an aggravation.

A Homeopathic aggravation usually means that *the Decimal or Centesimal potency administered has been far too high*—with the exception of temporary re-appearance of old and forgotten symptoms that, as already mentioned, can be found even if the potency originally administered is low.
More likely than not, a Homeopathic aggravation also means that a Constitutional treatment is going to be successful.
It is better to avoid it, though.
The gouty chronic patient, briefly described earlier in this Chapter, is a rather pathetic example to illustrate why aggravations should be avoided, if at all possible.

Sometimes patients should be forewarned regarding the possibility of an aggravation, particularly those in distress, particularly when treatment is going to be started with a high Centesimal dynamization. Here the Homeopathic Physician should spend some time, at the end of the visit, warning the patient about the possibility of an aggravation.

I don't believe there is an actual need to warn patients when treatment is started with a low Decimal or Centesimal potency. There is no point in needlessly worrying them. Chances are that they won't become aware of the aggravation, even if it happens.

Perhaps a patient about to receive an LM should be warned that he or she may have an aggravation at the conclusion of the treatment.

If, on the other hand, a male patient has had gonorrhea or any other suchlike disease at any time in his life, the Doctor should definitely discuss about the possibility and the nature of an aggravation.

I could have avoided a very unpleasant family situation, plus the risk of a divorce, had I done so with the patient with "cured" gonorrhea that I briefly described above.

There are some forms of aggravation that can actually be dangerous, even life-threatening.

Take for instance the ultra-rigid slavedriver of him or herself. The overachiever with a miserably poor self-image, who must accomplish the most impossible goals in order to derive some modicum of self-appreciation. And who falls into the deepest pits of self-directed fury and dejection whenever he or she fails. This kind of patient can become actually suicidal during these terribly somber and self-destructive moods. The remedy that both produces and cures this profile is *Aurum*, or gold.

This type of patient may well suffer an important aggravation when receiving *Aurum* at high Centesimal potencies at the onset of treatment. As the consequence of that aggravation, the patient may become depressed and even suicidal. And may even jump out from a window to his or her death[58].

Homeopathic aggravations usually do not happen when treating acute diseases.

By definition, acute diseases happen in well-balanced individuals. There is no chronic imbalance in well-balanced individuals.

---

[58] *Aurum* patients tend to commit suicide by means of jumping from high places. *Arsenicums* by hanging themselves, and *Pulsatillas* by drowning in the sea.

A local or acute remedy, injudiciously used, may provoke a *suppression* in acute patients, but not a Homeopathic aggravation.

Homeopathic aggravations are usually easy to control.

Crystals of camphor, and sometimes strong coffee, can be used. This drastic form of treatment, capable of erasing both the aggravation *and* the effect of the remedy, is to be considered only *in extremis,* in the most severe forms of aggravation.

A lower potency of the same remedy can be used in less dramatic circumstances. This method may control the aggravation, but without eliminating the therapeutic action of the remedy.

In order to allay the justified apprehension of a chronic patient regarding an aggravation, the Doctor should explain that this phenomenon is usually the first evidence of improvement and wellness.

And that its appearance depends both of the potency of the remedy and of the sensitivity of each individual patient.

In the event of an aggravation, the Doctor should make a mental note to go easy with the increase of potencies as treatment progresses.

The exception here is the re-appearance of old and forgotten symptoms that, as mentioned before, may appear regardless of the potency used.

There is something that superficially resembles a Homeopathic aggravation brought about by the administration of Centesimals, though it actually corresponds to the patient's collapse.

It happens in the very debilitated, that is, in patients with very little Vital Force at their disposal. This aggravation comes as the consequence of demanding the Vital Force to take care simultaneously of the day-to-day maintenance of the organism while, at the same time, healing the chronic disease or diseases afflicting the patient.

This form of collapse can be called the *no-return* form of aggravation.

I would like to bring up an analogy relating to plumbing, in order to clarify this form of aggravation.

In many bathrooms, when someone is taking a shower, and somebody else flushes the toilet, the person in the shower will scream as the shower water suddenly becomes unbearably hot.

This phenomenon happens when the cold water pressure in the pipes is only sufficient to either fill up the toilet tank or else to cool down the hot water in the shower. The pressure of the cold water will not suffice to satisfy simultaneously both the demands from toilet tank and from the shower. The toilet tank will fill up more slowly while someone will blister in the shower.

Something similar happens when a patient has not enough Vital Force available to cure and to satisfy the needs of everyday maintenance.

The choice a Homeopathic Physician faces with these very debilitated chronic patients is very tough.

They are indeed too weak to start Homeopathic treatment with Decimal or Centesimal dynamizations.

Treatment may be started in LM's—but this is something of a gamble. Remember that LM's bring about delayed aggravation. What if the patient has not gathered enough strength by then?

Often, the only viable solution is to refer these patients to an Allopathic Physician. An Allopathic treatment is not as thorough and effective as Homeopathy, and furthermore is fraught with complications, side effects and toxicity. But at least it will not trigger an irreversible aggravation in these severely ill and debilitated patients.

In a scale of severity, the mildest aggravations tend to be brought about by Homeopathic remedies prepared with plant extracts. Remedies obtained from the animal kingdom may produce more severe aggravations. Mineral Homeopathic remedies tend to produce the most severe and longer lasting Homeopathic aggravations.

Like everything in Homeopathy, this scale of severity is riddled with exceptions.

Let us always remember that the Vital Force is the *only* entity responsible for the everyday maintenance of chronic patient, and also for the cure of their imbalance.

In a successful Homeopathic treatment, *an adequate availability of* Vital Force provides the power necessary both to maintain chronic patients and also to straighten up their fulcrum of imbalance.

If, in a patient barely able to remain alive, a Homeopathic remedy asks the Vital Force to heal, there may not be enough Vital Force available to both maintain the patient alive and to cure. There will be exhaustion instead. The patient will worsen, often irreversibly.

Therefore, a Homeopathic Physician must ask him or herself the following questions before starting treatment: How much Vital Force does this particular chronic patient have at his or her disposal? Will this patient's Vital

Force suffice to carry on everyday maintenance activities while, *at the same time*, heal this patient?

I would like to briefly mention some differences between *aggravations* and *suppressions* to end this Chapter.

- An *aggravation* is the consequence of the tidal wave that brings the whole chronic patient into balance. A *suppression* plunges the patient into disease.
- An *aggravation* happens when the progression towards balance proceeds unhindered, if perhaps with too much momentum and force. A *suppression* happens when the patient, injudiciously treated on the way toward health, dives again into disease.

An *aggravation*, and the subsequent wave of improvement or cure, proceeds from the depth to the surface, from the most vital structures to the less important (i.e., from the emotional to the physical, from inside outwards, etc., according to Hering's law). A *suppression* proceeds instead from the most superficial to the deepest, most vital structures.

Chapter 19

FOLLOW-UP OF ACUTE AND OF PSORIC PATIENTS.

FOLLOW-UP OF ACUTE PATIENTS

Acute patients are easy to follow up.

Acute disease-syndromes generally appear as the consequence of some event that temporarily and partially detaches the patient's Vital Force from some organ or tissue. This detachment upsets the patient's balance and makes the affected organ or tissue scream for help.

The only purpose of treatment here is to neutralize whatever has caused the acute disease, and thus allow the Vital Force to re-attach itself again firmly to the afflicted organ or tissue.

Allopathic or Wholistic treatments can be used with similar success to eliminate the cause of this detachment.

Whenever possible, a Homeopathic treatments should be tried first, though. It is able to re-atach the Vital Force to the ill organ or tissue, it lacks side effects and toxicity, and is considerably less expensive.

If the injury is too severe or too frequently repeated, the patient's imbalance may become permanent. This is often how an acute patient may becomes chronic.

Acute *surgical* diseases pose a very unique problem. They will be discussed later on in this same Chapter.

FOLLOW-UP OF PSORIC PATIENTS

Psoric patients pose an entirely different challenge. Their Wholeness is chronically out of balance to start with.

This chronic state of imbalance frequently becomes evident as an acute or chronic localized disease that may affect any organ or tissue. There is not much point in treating only that particular localized disease, though. The Vital Force will no re-attach itself satisfactorily to the sick organ or tissue while chronic imbalance persists, even if the localized disease has been eliminated. Treatment here should be primarily directed toward restoration of balance in the Whole psoric patient.

I shall devote most of this Chapter to the evaluation and follow-up of *psoric* patients. *Sycosic* and *syphilitic* patients will be discussed in some length in Chapters 21 *"Pseudo-psora"* and 22 *"Treatment of gonorrhea, genital warts and syphilis"*.

If follow-up is important in acute patients it becomes *essential* in psoric patients.

Psoric patients are chronically imbalanced to start with.

It took them a long time to develop their imbalance. It follows that in most patients it will also take time for imbalance to disappear under Homeopathic treatment.

The only person qualified to follow-up a psoric patient's evolution is an adequately trained Homeopathic Physician, because each psoric patient will evolve in his or her individual and unique manner under treatment.

It is quite likely that a psoric patient may start treatment with some remedy, that may be effective for some time. Eventually, that remedy may have to be replaced by another, and then perhaps by another. Success cannot be achieved without the close supervision of a Homeopathic Physician.

I have already mentioned that Homeopathic remedies act by means of *nudging* the psoric patients' Vital Force toward the fulcrum of their chronic imbalance, in order to correct it.

Each dose of a patient's Homeopathic remedy gently *nudges* the psoric patient toward balance. The patient may fall again into imbalance, once the momentum of the nudge vanishes. Another dose may be indicated at this point.

Eventually, after a successful treatment, wellness will gel, and the patient will not need any more treatment. Until then, however, the remedy will have to be administered. Here again, the only person with enough knowledge, experience and criterion to determine when the next dose—or potency, or remedy—is due, is the Homeopathic Physician in charge of that patient.

In the patient's first visit, the Homeopathic Physician should clarify how essential an adequate follow up is for the success of the treatment.

> *Rapport is important during History taking. It becomes indispensable during follow-up.*
> *Each psoric patient evolves in his or her own individual fashion. Changes can sometimes be very subtle. Often, patients are unaware of those changes or don't know whether they are important*

or not. Or may be unable to express them. Sometimes, changes may frighten a patient.

Understanding the patient's evolution—and understanding is always consequence of a good rapport—is frequently the only guide the Doctor has to know regarding when to continue treatment, when to interrupt it, when to modify the potency and/or the remedy, and if and when to complement Homeopathy with any other form of treatment.

Follow-up begins after the first appointment. It may start with a telephone call or with the first follow-up visit.

In each follow-up visit, the Homeopathic Physician will have to find out *how the totality* of the psoric patient is evolving, and also do whatever is necessary to bring that patient into balance; or at least as close as possible to a situation of balance.

Rapport, important when obtaining a sound Homeopathic History, becomes *indispensable* during follow-up—indeed, each follow-up visit should be an opportunity to enhance and to strengthen such a rapport.

It is essential to create an atmosphere that makes the patient feel comfortable. If that takes some extra Doctor time, so be it. It is preferable to spend a few more minutes and build a sound rapport than to rush by and loose contact with the patient. All the more because, without rapport, the Doctor will be groping in the dark—no matter how much Homeopathy the Homeopathic Physician may know, or how assiduously he or she may consult the Materia Medica and the Repertory.

This is not Allopathy.

In Homeopathy, the relationship is *not* between a scientifically trained brain and a disease-syndrome; rather, it is a relationship between a compassionate and adequately trained Whole Human Being, and another Whole Human Being who is suffering and is in need of help.

To create and to maintain a rapport there must be two Whole Human Beings interacting, one of whom knows infinitely more about Homeopathy and Medicine than the other, granted. But both of whom *share a similar quality of common sense.* I personally like to frequently remind my patient that the "M.D." after my name means Medical Doctor, and not Medical *Deity.*

It is only at this level of Human-to-Human mutual understanding, mutual respect and common sense that a Homeopathically valid communication/relationship/rapport can exist and develop between the Homeopathic Physician and his or her patients.

The Homeopathic Physician should never *order* a patient to do this or that, or to follow such and such line of treatment after the fashion of the slave Doctors did in ancient Greece.

Through common sense, the Doctor must *appeal* to the common sense of the patient regarding what therapeutic approach is most appropriate for his or her individual instance.

Follow-up should proceed along successive clarifications and mutual agreements between Doctor and psoric patient—never through orders the patient may or may not understand, but must comply with, nevertheless.

Patients are apprehensive because they are psoric, and also because they are sick.

For many of them, Homeopathy is a new and totally heterodox form of Medicine—and, not infrequently, their last desperate hope.

Which means that the patient is trusting his or her future well-being to the Practitioner of a new and perplexing healing art.

The patient has therefore every right to be concerned, and Physicians have every obligation to appease that uneasiness.

And also to find the time and the mental disposition to answer questions, and to listen to the patient's advice and suggestions.

Homeopathic patients should always be able to reach the Doctor.

In Homeopathy we are dealing with Whole disease-bearing Human Beings. We have to communicate with their suffering Wholeness.

It won't do here to have an attendant answer telephone calls and then triage or filter them. *All* calls are important in Homeopathy. In each and every call, the Homeopathic Physician receives one or several bits of information. Each bit of information means a better understanding of the patient, and thus of the patient's imbalance and of the consequences of that imbalance.

Ease to reach the Doctor gives the psoric patient an enormous feeling of security and trust. Which in turn intensifies the rapport.

In Allopathy, the only communication necessary is between the Allopathic Doctor's mind and the patient's disease syndrome.

Take as an example the disease-syndrome iron deficiency anemia. It happens when a patient produces few red blood cells because he or she doesn't have enough iron in his or her system.

All an Allopathic Physician usually needs is a blood sample to make the diagnosis and start treatment. And then another blood sample some time afterwards, to evaluate the effect of the treatment.

Time spent with the patient under these circumstances becomes often a matter of courtesy, not of necessity.

Each psoric patient, on the other hand, must be considered as a unique Whole Human Being who will respond to Homeopathic treatment in his or her own unique individual manner. Neither the patient's response nor the pattern of that response can be predicted beforehand. Our previous knowledge and experience with "similar patients" is of little value, even chimerical. There isn't such a thing as "similar patients" in Homeopathy. Each individual complex psoric patient/disease/circumstance is unique.

The only guide a Homeopathic Physician has, when following up a psoric patient, is what the patient says and what the Doctor can find along successive and periodic Homeopathic and Clinical Histories and Physical examinations. As well as in changes recorded in lab results or displayed in X Rays, CT scans, MRI's and the like.

Homeopathic follow-up requires the patient's active collaboration.

Collaboration—or *compliance*—may be difficult to elicit in some patients.

For some, collaboration is difficult because they see very little point in complying. They have been sick for so long that they have forgotten what to feel well is like.

Others are so set in their habits that they simply don't want to change.

Other patients may have learnt how to obtain some kind of sick secondary gain from their disease. These patients may drag their feet, and "forget" to take their remedies—particularly when they perceive that the treatment is working.

Others may give up because of fear at their new feeling of wellness, or because they are unable or unwilling to abandon old habits.

Or because they may tire of a treatment they don't understand.

Or because they prefer to ignore the fact that they are sick, and like to act as if they were healthy.

Or because of fear.

Or distrust, or because of myriad other causes.

Take, as an example of fear, a 47-year-old female who suffered from severe restless legs syndrome for many years. She was desperate. The patient had gone everywhere, seen everybody, been treated with everything under the sun. All to no avail.

Soon after starting her History, I realized that this patient was a textbook *Zincum metallicum*. I interrupted the visit to prepare a tube of the remedy in a 200 CH potency. Then I returned to the office and asked the patient to put some pellets in her mouth. She complied and I continued History taking. To the patient's utter surprise, her legs started to quiet down after a few minutes, and were totally relaxed by the time I started her Physical Examination. There was fear in her features instead of relief. Every once is a while she would steal a frightened stare at the tube of *Zincum* pellets she was holding in her clenched fist, at arm's length. She paid and left in record time at the end of the visit. She did not schedule a follow-up appointment. I haven't heard of her since.

Patients may no comply because treatment interferes with their schedule or lifestyle.

Take a patient I recently saw, a rather obese female in her 50's, very set in her habits. Her complaint was many undefined digestive problems. This lady would swallow her food practically without chewing it. She stated that she did so because "[she] was too busy and didn't have enough time to waste eating". I told her, in the nicest possible tone of voice, that without her collaboration here it would be next to impossible to help her and explained why. She became annoyed, stated that Homeopathy was "hocus pocus" and left. I haven't seen her since.

Or take that busy—or rather frantic—hypertensive executive I once treated. He had high blood pressure for years, and was being treated with several Pharmaceutical drugs.

Visits to his Allopathic Doctor were as hectic as the rest of his life. He would go whenever his schedule allowed such an escapade.

Drugs he would indeed take at his wife's and secretary's constant behest, but he would seldom comply with the diet also ordered by his Doctor; due, as he would put it, to his many business eat-outs.

He was too busy to exercise. He would play golf, though, but he would use it for his business deals—many of which involved very heavy bargaining—so the exercise afforded by this sport did not provide any relaxation at all.

The man was scared when he came to see me for the first time. He had had an episode of mild constrictive pain in his chest two or three days before.

With *Nux vomica* his blood pressure eventually became normal, which in turned allowed me to taper down and then discontinue the antihypertensive drugs he was taking. For the first time, the patient was able to calm down and to put some order in his life.

After a few follow-up visits, as he was starting to feel well and to become balanced, this patient asked me if he could pop into my office whenever his many occupations would allow, instead of regularly returning for scheduled appointments. I explained such a thing would be impossible, due to the very nature of the Homeopathic follow-up. And also because, at this early stage of his evolution, he still needed my close supervision.

His secretary called a few days before his next appointment to cancel it. She stated her boss would reschedule soon. He never did.

Some two years or so later I heard that his hypertension had returned, and that he was on antihypertensive drugs again. And also that his life had regained its former frantic, breakneck pace. That was shortly before I left Argentina.

Some time ago, through a common acquaintance who was visiting America, I learnt that this executive had undergone some kind of heart surgery; probably a coronary bypass. The common acquaintance told me that my former patient wanted to know the name of a Homeopathic Physician he could see in Buenos Aires. I obliged.

I hope he complies this time.

Alcoholic and other substance abuse in psoric patients pose a serious problem for the Homeopathic Physician. It is impossible to reach a therapeutic success in an alcoholic patient.

The Doctor should order the patient to quit. And to start Counseling and/or join any of the excellent support groups in existence, many of which are free of charge.

The patient should be treated, of course, with the utmost kindness and consideration. But the Physician should be adamant when his or her patient considers continuing, or relapsing in his or her addiction[59].

What should the Doctor do when a new psoric patient is being *treated with Pharmaceutical drug/s* for his or her disease-syndrome, or when the

---

[59] Paracelsus used to say that a blend of love and sternness should be a Doctor's lifestyle. Compare with Jacob Böhme's (1575-1624) "Wisdom and love shine when sternness and compassion unite, darkness descends when sternness and compassion separate".

need arises of prescribing one or more Pharmaceutical drug during Homeopathic treatment?

The answer depends on the disease-syndrome, on the disease-syndrome bearing patient, on the patient's circumstance, and also on the drug/s the patient may need to take.

Physicians should never forget that the patient's welfare always comes first, whether that welfare is the consequence of a Homeopathic or of some other form of treatment.

The Old Masters were inflexible regarding Allopathic treatments. They would shun all forms other than Homeopathic, except for certain emergencies, surgical problems and the like (Hahnemann, S. *Organon*. 6th. Ed. § 29).

And they were right. Allopathic treatments were brutal then. To boot, clinical problem by clinical problem, Homeopathic treatments were vastly more helpful; aside from lacking side effects or toxicity of any kind.

Dr. Hahnemann strenuously denounced diseases brought about by Allopathic treatments with substances such as calomel, corrosive sublimate, mercury, Prussic acid (or potassium cyanide), sulphur, sulfuric acid, silver nitrate, iodine, opium, valerian, cinchona bark, quinine, foxglove and many others, often administered at extravagantly high doses. He also exposed the dangers of "perennial purgatives", blood letting "in torrents", leeches, fontanels, setons and the like. Three Centuries later, silver nitrate is still used topically, Podophyllum resin is still used locally for the treatment of genital warts, Iodine is currently used externally as a disinfectant and also internally for thyroid problems, though at doses vastly inferior to those used in Dr. Hahnemann's day. As to the "perennial purgatives", they are still around in full force, even if modern laxatives are much milder.

Dr. Hahnemann objected because those therapeutic atrocities would weaken patients, sometimes unto death (Hahnemann S., *Organon*, 6th. Edition. § 74). It is hardly surprising, then, that Allopathic Doctors hated the guts of this unruly and annoying colleague, all the more because he was obtaining results.

All the more because he was telling a truth they didn't want to hear.

Each individual psoric patient must be studied and treated individually.

Then, and according to each individual evaluation, each patient should be treated either with Homeopathic remedies only, or with Homeopathic remedies + other forms of Wholistic Medicine, or with Homeopathic + Allopathic treatment, etc.

241

Jose Miguel Mullen, M.D.

That is, with *whatever form of treatment that is best for each particular patient; done with whatever therapeutic tool may proffer the greatest benefit at the lowest possible risk*—although sometimes this ideal is impossible to reach due to lack of cooperation on the part of many Allopathic Physicians.

Take, for instance, a patient with *grand mal* epilepsy. She was taking Phenytoin sodium when I first saw her, years ago. Her electroencephalographic tracings remained abnormal, despite of treatment.

Was I to discontinue Phenytoin sodium and start administering her Homeopathic remedy (that, if I recall correctly, was *Cicuta virosa)?* Was I willing to risk the possibility of her having a seizure while crossing a street, or a dangerous and life-threatening series of seizures, what is called *status epilepticus*, before *Cicuta* kicked in? Or was I to put up with the toxicity and side effects of Phenytoin sodium until her electroencephalographic tracings became normal, and then slowly taper it down?

To put it differently, up to how much Allopathic *risk* (in terms of toxicity and side effects) was I willing to put up with, in order to reap a certain amount of *benefit?* Was it worth it to put up with the side effects and toxicity of Phenytoin sodium or not? I considered that, in this particular patient, it was best to continue the Allopathic treatment; and then start tapering it down when her electroencephalographic tracings became normal.

So I asked the patient to continue taking Phenytoin sodium. All her symptoms improved considerably with Homeopathic treatment, with the exception of her convulsions (she was having no seizures, due to the therapeutic action of Phenytoin sodium; consequently, I had no way to evaluate her improvement in this respect).

I suggested repeating the electroencephalogram after some time of treatment, and then perhaps start tapering down Phenytoin sodium if it was normal. The patient went to see her Neurologist to repeat her electroencephalogram.

The Neurologist refused and, to boot, frightened the patient into quitting Homeopathic treatment.

In my personal experience, administration of Pharmaceutical drugs does not interfere in any noticeable degree with Homeopathic treatment.

A good example of lack of interference between Pharmaceutical drugs and Homeopathic remedies is a 53 year old Teacher with long-standing rheumatoid arthritis.

He could hardly walk when I first saw him. He had been under the care of a Rheumathologist for years. He was taking Prednisone at hefty doses,

242

plus Methotrexate and Hydroxychloroquine sulfate (*Prednisone* is a power-ful depressor of the immune system, with severe side effects and toxicity practically everywhere, including the mind. *Methotrexate* alters the forma-tion of genes, can induce the formation of malignant solid tumors, lympho-mas and leukemias, is a very potent depressor of the immune system, and very toxic to every organ and system. *Hydroxychloroquine sulfate* is a strong anti-inflammatory drug with a host of side effects and toxicities).

The patient was unhappy with the results of his treatment. His disease was progressing despite of the combination of these very potent drugs, albeit slowly.

I evaluated him and his therapeutic schedule. I didn't dare taper the drugs down for fear of a flare-up of his disease. There would be plenty of time later, if and when the Homeopathic treatment kicked in, to taper down and eventually discontinue the drugs.

Natrum muriaticum was the remedy that best matched the profile of this particular psoric patient. His disease-syndrome had began immediately after a particularly nasty divorce, many years back. Improvement started within a few weeks, despite of his uninterrupted intake of Prednisone, Methotrexate and Hydroxychloroquine sulfate at the usual doses. Those drugs were ta-pered down carefully, one at a time, as the patient continued improving, un-til he was only taking a very small amount of Prednisone and Hydroxychlo-roquine sulfate. Despite of my pleas, he was afraid of completely discon-tinuing Allopathic treatment.

The patient was able to return to the teaching he loved so much, and that he had to quit because of his progressive disability. The first day he returned to work, as he later told me "I parked the car. I was afraid I wasn't going to make it to the classroom. I got there with amazing ease. I sat at my desk and started teaching. After a while I found myself so absorbed in what I was say-ing that I was walking from wall to wall as I was speaking—like in the old days, before I got sick! I stopped dead on my tracks when I realized what I was doing. Must have made a funny face, for some students were giggling. I grinned, too".

I saw the patient less and less, as it usually happens when patients get steadily better and better. Finally, I completely lost track of him.

He returned to my office after a few years. He was doing fine, though still taking Prednisone, if at insignificant doses. This time he agreed to taper Prednisone down slowly and to finally discontinue it. Again I lost touch.

He asked for another appointment some 2 years later. He was feeling drained out and irritable, and again in pain. He had quitted Homeopathic treatment on his own a few months after his last visit. He had quitted smok-ing and gained 40 lb. I re-evaluated him. He was still *Natrum muriaticum.* Treatment didn't work as rapidly this time. I asked him to start loosing weight. He had been portly when first coming to see me. Now he was grossly obese. I explained that his excess weight could very well be responsible for his tiredness, irritability and pain. I also told him that, by loosing weight, he would relieve the pressure on his back and legs and hence have less pain. He refused to even consider the possibility of getting slimmer. I replied that now it was going take much longer for the treatment to work, after his having been without treatment for so long and his refusal to loose weight. I also asked him to please comply and never to loose contact with me again, even after feeling fully well. Days later I found a message in my answering machine. He wasn't going to return. He had decided to quit Homeopathic treatment.

This patient is a good example of many things, including the necessity of an adequate follow-up.

He made the mistake of discontinuing treatment on his own, and of ending his communication with me when feeling well. His wellness hadn't jelled by that time, though. The patient started again to fall into imbalance when the nudge provided by the last dose of his Homeopathic treatment wore off. He took no new dose of remedy to check this new bout of imbalance. Symptoms inevitably returned, aggravated by his weight gain. Eventually, all the ground gained with Homeopathic treatment was lost.

It was only then that he thought of calling me. Unfortunately, and as it very often happens under these circumstances, it takes time, first to arrest the free fall into imbalance, and then to start correcting it again. Instead of complying, this patient became impatient when he saw no immediate improvement. He also refused to loose weight. He was obviously expecting Homeopathy to do everything to make him well—and soon!—without his collaboration and help. Finally, and completely disappointed, he quitted treatment.

IMPORTANT NOTICE

Treatments with Prednisone and similar drugs should NEVER be discontinued suddenly, no matter how well the patient may be faring.

After some time of administration, these powerful hormone-like chemicals replace cortisone secreted by the adrenal glands. The adrenals will subsequently stop working for all intents and purposes.

To discontinue Prednisone or any other derivative all of a sudden can become life threatening. Adrenal glands need some time to start producing enough cortisone and its derivatives to keep the patient alive and well. Meantime, the patient's organism will be deprived of hormones crucial to adequately manage stressful situations.

Hormone-like drugs should ALWAYS be tapered down slowly; watching carefully if, how and when the patient starts producing hormones again.

The process of tapering down should ALWAYS be done by an Allopathic Doctor, or under his or her direct supervision.

Who is to *discontinue* Pharmaceutical drugs, once the patient starts responding to Homeopathic treatment?

It necessarily has to be Health Care Provider sufficiently familiarized with both Allopathy and Homeopathy; that is, an Integrative Physician.

I would like to illustrate with two examples.

The first is that of a 42 year old man, besieged by feelings of inadequacy. Janitor of a building. With severe hypertension diagnosed 6 years before coming to my office. And whose blood pressure was refusing to come down, despite of the powerful Pharmaceutical drugs he was taking daily.

His blood pressure became normal some five months after starting Homeopathic treatment with *Lycopodium clavatum.* By that time, I had tapered down and discontinued his hypertensive drugs.

His feelings of inadequacy vanished, as well as all his other symptoms. This patient entered College—his most cherished dream—one year after starting Homeopathic treatment.

I haven't seen him for a long time now. Last time I saw him he was very happy and doing fine.

The second example corresponds to a 37 year old male executive who came to see me with a peptic ulcer, diagnosed both clinically and by X Rays. He had been suffering for several years. Despite of a strict diet, a life style considered as healthy, and adequate Allopathic treatment (he was taking several drugs for his ulcer), the pain was still present—as was his perpetual stress. His pain was constant, and so severe that this man was constantly kneading his upper abdomen and grimacing as I was obtaining his History.

The remedy that matched his profile was *Nux vomica.* Symptomatic relief was prompt and dramatic. X Rays done three months after starting Homeopathic treatment showed that the ulcer had disappeared.

Here again, I had to taper down the drugs he was taking, and eventually stop Pharmaceutical treatment altogether.

Homeopathic treatment may sometimes have to be temporarily *interrupted* in psoric patients for any number of reasons.

One interesting reason is when Homeopathic treatment may coerce the patient into unhappiness. Such a problem arose in the patient I am about to describe.

She was 45 and *Aurum* when I first saw her. The patient felt forsaken, had low self-esteem, a necessity to achieve impossible goals in order to give some sense to her life, implacable self-condemnation, crushing guilt, etc.

Her clinical diagnosis was chronic fatigue syndrome.

Her profile changed to that of *Natrum Muriaticum* after some time of treatment with *Aurum*. By then, her chronic fatigue syndrome was much improved, but still present.

Weeks later, my now *Natrum Muriaticum* patient complained about how difficult and unpleasant it was to continue treatment. Her infancy had been very unhappy. Many of the episodes she was recalling, as she was gaining balance, were extremely sad and often shocking.

I suggested suspending Homeopathy, after discussing the problem and gauging the severity of her distress. I suggested to do counseling, until again ready for Homeopathic treatment. Even if it meant a delay. The patient agreed.

Homeopathic treatment was eventually re-started some months later, and completed successfully.

Natrum Muriaticum patients are very sensitive, and tend to suppress memories with unpleasant or negative emotional contents. As these patients improve, repressed memories may come to the fore for a while before vanishing, and sometimes may considerably distress the patient. That is why I welcome the collaboration of a competent Counselor, capable of helping these patients understand those memories and their emotional content; and thus transform dismal remembrances into positive bits of knowledge and experience.

In Allopathy, the ultimate goal of any treatment is the elimination of the patient's clinical disease-syndrome. In Homeopathy, instead, and more so in the instance of psoric patients, it is to bring a Whole patient into balance— or, to put it differently, what Homeopathy seeks is to liberate the patient from the path of suffering he or she is enslaved to.

Homeopathy considers that disease-syndromes are but consequences or by-products of that psoric enslavement. Achievement of balance—or liberation from the *path,* or from the patient's *pathos,* if you prefer—allows him or her to develop and to become; and thus to harmonize with him or herself, those who surround him or her and Nature. From feeling hostages of Nature, cured psoric patients become first aware that they are free, and then that they are not any more hostages of Nature, but rather Lords of Creation. The disease-syndrome disappears as patients reach balance and become aware of their freedom.

In this *Aurum metallicum/Natrum muriaticum* patient briefly described above, to continue Homeopathic treatment would have been tantamount to forcing the patient to suffer, to interfering with her freedom of choice. Her resistance was understandable under the circumstances.

I couldn't coerce the patient into balance/ freedom. For, to say that someone can force someone else into freedom is to incur in an oxymoron.

There is also the very occasional patient who is *not eligible* for Homeopathic treatment.

I would like to describe here, in some detail, the only instance of this kind I have found in my practice.

A 68-year-old male came to see me bearing a long-standing Crohn's disease, a relative of ulcerative colitis that usually attacks the nether part of the small intestine. It produces ulcerations, scarring and much suffering.

His Constitutional remedy was *Sulphur.* The patient became balanced under treatment, started to feel well, and all his symptoms gradually disappeared. His visits became less and less frequent, until finally he stopped coming altogether.

Probably forgot to make a follow-up appointment. *Sulphur* people may do so. They tend to be absent-minded. Some are very bohemian, and like to live in a world of their own.

As I was to learn later on, the effect of *Sulphur* began to wear off in time, and symptoms of his Crohn's disease re-appeared, though considerably milder. He didn't call my office when this happened. Ill advised, the patient went to see another Health Care Provider, who prescribed some Homeopathically prepared remedy. The treatment didn't work. Worsening continued, and the patient panicked.

He consulted an Allopathic Doctor who prescribed Pharmaceutical drugs. Again no effect. The Doctor then referred the patient to a Surgeon. He was promptly operated upon. Several feet of small intestine were removed, with no benefit. He developed aseptic bony necrosis shortly after

247

surgery (*aseptic* means not infected, and *necrosis* death. Thus, non-infectious destruction of bony tissue). He was started on Prednisone.

The patient came to see me one year after Surgery. His condition was calamitous. He was taking hefty amounts of Prednisone, aside from a host of other drugs, nutrients and vitamins. He was very thin, a ghost of the man I had last seen. He came asking for "some Constitutional".

His aseptic bony necrosis was, in all likelihood, a suppression after the removal of a segment of intestine. Suppressions have been reported after Surgery.

I reevaluated the patient. He was still *Sulphur*.

Perhaps his aseptic bony necrosis would disappear if I were to give him *Sulphur* again.

But he could very well develop another bout of Crohn's disease in the meantime, however mild and transient, in what remained of his intestine, as a form of Homeopathic aggravation. The patient was in no condition of going through anything like that, on account of his feebleness.

Since his constitutional remedy was still *Sulphur*, the ONLY remedy capable of helping him was *Sulfur*. Yet Dr. Kent, in his *Lectures on Homeopathic Materia Medica*, explicitly warns that *Sulphur* and *Silicea* may worsen structural damage in several organs, unless given at very low potencies.

But I couldn't use a low potency. According to the law or Arndt and Schultz[60], a low potency could stimulate (meaning *worsen*) this man's aseptic bony necrosis. Could the Prednisone he was taking avoid or block this worsening?

This man was also extremely debilitated at this time.

Perhaps I could have asked him to sniff the remedy. Sniffing makes the effect of remedies milder. But then, what if the effects weren't mild enough in this extremely debilitated patient? LM Plus dynamization wouldn't have probably been of any help here either, since LM's can also produce aggravations, however delayed. Due to this man's extreme weakness, I had no way of knowing how long it would take him to respond to treatment, and whether or not he would be strong enough, later on, to withstand an eventual end-of-treatment aggravation. I wasn't willing to run such a risk.

---

[60] This law, one of the earliest of Pharmacology, was first enunciated in the second half of the 19th Century. It states that small doses stimulate, moderate doses inhibit it and high doses kill. For Homeopathic purposes, it can be translated as "small doses stimulate, moderate and high ones inhibit", because Homeopathic remedies have neither side effects nor toxicity and therefore cannot kill.

If none of the above happened, and if *Sulphur* was to work again, then *Sulphur* had to *command* this patient's Vital Force to straighten the fulcrum of his imbalance. In his severely weakened and compromised condition, he could undergo an aggravation, likely with no recovery afterwards.

I had no other choice but to refer this patient to an Allopathic colleague. I feared that a Homeopathic treatment could have actually been harmful for this man, due to his very unique and special situation of extreme weakness.

Probably any form of preparation, or any potency, are equally good to start Homeopathic treatment in a psoric patient—provided, of course, that the profile of the remedy matches the profile of the patient.

Some workers start with Decimals, and report good results.

Others start with Centesimals, or with LM's, and also report good results.

Or with high or with low potencies, and also report good results.

The only valid conclusion of this body of data is that, when the remedy is well indicated, all potencies achieve comparable good results; at least at the onset of treatment.

Symptoms may disappear rapidly or slowly.

With one remedy, or with several administered sequentially.

Broadly speaking, it can be said that children tolerate treatment better, and that respond more rapidly, and using less remedies, than adults.

And adults than seniors.

Like every rule in Homeopathy, this one is riddled with exceptions.

I have treated a 3 year old male with eczema. It took months for his eczema to disappear.

His Constitutional is *Sulphur*; although for a while he became *Pulsatilla* when his elder sister, to whom he was dearly attached, went to kindergarten while he had to remain home; and his heart went with her (an unquenchable thirst for love is at the core of *Pulsatilla* patients. No amount of love is enough for them. *Pulsatillas* are among the most forsaken patients of the Materia Medica Homeopathica. Love for *Pulsatilla,* complements for *Nux Vomica,* and gratefulness for *Lycopodium* are the royal roads to their respective hearts).

I was expecting a much more rapid resolution of his eczema, due to his age.

A 34 year old male once came to see me complaining of excessive and constant sweating of his hands, winter and summer. His hands were, in effect, soaking wet. No matter how often and thoroughly he would dry them up. His problem was intolerable as well as uncomfortable: he would wet everything he touched at home and at work, had to avoid shaking hands, etc.

He was desperate when he came to see me. Like so many patients seeking Homeopathy, he had also gone everywhere, seen everyone, and tried all forms of treatment to no avail. Finally he was referred to a Surgeon, who suggested cutting the nerves that control sweating in arms and hands. The patient was so shocked that he decided to consult a Homeopathic Physician.

His Constitutional remedy was *Ignatia.*

He took it at night, after seeing me. Next morning he awoke free of symptoms.

I followed him up for a few months. The problem never returned.

I haven't seen him for a long time now. I presume he is doing well.

A dour and cantankerous 72-year-old man came to my office for treatment of a chronic anal fissure of many years duration. An anal fissure is a crack, or superficial cut, in the anal margin. It doesn't heal. It is very painful, particularly at the time of evacuation. It may also ooze and become infected.

He had been advised to undergo Surgery as a last resort, but the patient wanted to avoid it.

His Constitutional remedy was *Nitricum acidum.* He was well, and free of symptoms, in a few days. His fissure closed, all by itself, a week or so later.

The patient developed a severe case of flu some months afterwards. I repertorized his disease, that came out *Bryonia.* He took a low potency at bedtime. Next day, he phoned to tell me that he had perspired profusely all night, and that he had awaken in fine shape.

I haven't seen this man for years now. So I presume he's also doing well.

The most puzzling and challenging problems in psoric patients, in my experience, are the ones I call *vicious circle diseases,* because they feed back on themselves.

Prominently amongst them, in my experience, are chronic bronchial asthma and chronic headache in adults.

In many patients, these problems disappears under treatment. In others patients it remains, no matter what.

In quite a few patients, vicious circle diseases behave like a wily fighter. The moment the Doctor has the problem cornered against the ropes, and is ready to deliver the knock-out punch, the darned thing slips away and starts dancing all over the ring.

In patients who respond, treatment may take a long time and a great deal of patience and perseverance. As well as oftentimes the collaboration of other form of Complementary Medicine like Acupuncture, Antroposophy, manipulative therapy and often Counseling.

Some of the most interesting and difficult everyday problems are posed by psoric patients who, for one reason or another, either feel uncomfortable when getting well, or else actually *refuse to get well.*
Let me give you some examples of each.
First of patients who feel strange when well.

Once I had under my care a 29 year old female diagnosed as having pseudotumor cerebrii, which is a disease-syndrome characterized by an increase of intracranial pressure and other symptoms and signs that correspond to a rapidly growing brain tumor, even though no tumor is present. Allopathic Doctors consider that there are two kinds of pseudotumor cerebrii, one that responds to drug treatment and another that doesn't. Neurosurgery is indicated in those patients who do not respond to drugs.
Her headaches were constant and frightfully severe. Her eyes were terribly painful, and the pressure inside them was so high that she was losing her sight. She was scheduled to undergo Neurosurgery one month after she first came to see me. She had been suffering for a long time, and all the clinical treatments she had undergone had proved unsuccessful.
This woman was a typical *Aurum* patient. A forsaken workaholic and compulsive overworker to give sense to her life and so gather any modicum of self-esteem. Plus crushing guilt and episodes of anxiety and profound and self-destructive depression if she didn't achieve her extravagant goals.
I had only 30 days to work. I prescribed *Aurum*, of course; although I also asked her to take *Syphilinum* for good measure, since she had a rather destructive Family History. I also requested her to start Osteopathic therapy. She responded favorably to treatment. Her headache, eye pain, increased eye pressure and other symptoms started to subside. Her anxiety and other emotional problems faded away. Surgery was postponed indefinitely.
As expected, her personality also started to change. She lost her compulsion to overperform. A totally alien feeling of peace replaced her forsakenness, guilt, anxiety and depression. She felt lost without her suffering!

As if her life had no meaning any longer, no object or no reason to be. She was actually *frightened* by her inner serenity and peace. She had to undergo Counseling to first understand, then adjust to and finally accept her new and wonderful state of being.

I also recall, a 9-year-old severe asthmatic male. He did well with *Phosphorus* as Constitutional and *Medorrhinum* as Nosode.

Yet, he felt strange when first well and free of symptoms. Particularly at School. Now he wasn't any more the kid with asthma to be pitied. Now teachers and the Nurse did not go out of their way to help him.

He felt fine but confused and his marks, as well as his behavior in class, started to deteriorate.

Minimal counseling brought things back to normal.

Regarding patients who refuse to get well. Or else who want to get well, but without abandoning the lifestyles that made them sick in the first place.

The weakened patient with Crohn's disease, mentioned above, who finally had to be referred to Allopathy, is a good example of someone not wanting to get well. He did fine with Homeopathic treatment. All his symptoms disappeared. Yet, when symptoms started to bother him again, he went to see another practitioner. When this provider's ministrations failed to help him he again chose wrongly, and ultimately underwent Surgery. *Knowing all the time that Homeopathy correctly done had helped him and that could, in all likelihood, have helped him again.* There was something in this man that impelled him away from the wellness afforded by Homeopathy, and into uncertainty and suffering.

In the instance of the frantic executive with hypertension and ulterior heart surgery also described earlier, the problem was his desire to maintain a demented lifestyle and, at the same time, to get well. In other words, to have his cake and eat it. For him, the important thing was his business. His health was a secondary matter.

And, in the case of the obese woman who refused to chew her food thoroughly, there was a complete refusal to change her lifestyle, even in that insignificant detail.

There are two astonishing psoric patients who pop into my mind whenever I think of not wanting to get well.

The first was 50 at the time of her first visit. She was referred by her employer, who stated he was going to pay for everything. My patient-to-be had been his secretary for many years and had recently retired. I thought nothing of this referral, since both her employer and his wife had been my patients, and had successfully been treated Homeopathically.

My new patient was suffering from multiple sclerosis, and wasn't doing well with her Allopathic treatment.

Through the Homeopathic History, I learnt that my new patient and her employer had had a love affair, and that he had promised to divorce and then marry her. His wife learnt of the intrigue in time, fought back and regained her husband. This botched *ménage à trois* filled my patient with an all-consuming hatred toward his boss; the kind of hatred that can only be sustained by *Natrum muriaticum* (resentfulness and its twin offspring, unrelenting sadness and unremitting hatred, are at the core of *Natrum Muriaticum).* Multiple sclerosis had made its *début* some months after the demise of her expectations.

How could this woman and her boss continue to work together after the latter had been rescued by his wife—and work together they did, and for some years afterwards—is something beyond my capacity to conjecture.

The patient started to improve under *Natrum Muriaticum* treatment. Her resentment and hatred began to simmer down—*so she quitted treatment!*

As she told me in her last visit "I am very thankful for all you have done for me, but I'm going to quit. I feel better. I am getting better. If I get better [he] will not suffer. I am hating [him] less, and I want to keep on hating him. I want [him] to suffer. I want him to suffer for what he did to me".

Nothing I said could dissuade her. That was the last I saw or heard of this woman. And also of her employer and his wife, for that matter.

The second astonishing patient who refused to get well—or rather, that I *presume* refused to get well—is also a woman.

I first saw her in the waiting room, sitting near her husband. They both had gray hair. They were in their 40's, though they looked much older. She appeared to be considerably more worn out, although she actually was some eight years younger than her husband. He was mousy and insignificant, sitting hunched forward, casting rapid glances this way and that, as if seeking some route of escape. She was very thin, would sit erect and was trembling all over. It became clear, even at first glance, that he dotted on her.

Her mouth and lips were dry. The latter were also chapped, and the patient constantly attempted to wet them with quick darting movements of her tongue. She was constantly grimacing. Her speech was slurred, urgent, hoarse, and unintelligible. I couldn't make heads or tails of what she was telling me. Her husband had to translate. The gist of her story was that she had been a successful executive. Three years prior to this visit, her husband told her that he wanted a divorce—he had found some other woman. The patient had two consecutive serious car accidents after this revelation, with concussion in both instances. Ever since she had become an invalid, under the care of a Neurologist and a Psychiatrist. The Psychiatrist had given her psychodrugs. These drugs probably accounted—at least in part—for her rigidity, grimacing, tremors and dryness of the mouth. The latter, in turn, could at least have been partially responsible for her tormented speech.

The Physical Exam was confusing. I couldn't get any Homeopathic symptom worthy of note, let alone a modalization. I phoned the Neurologist. He was as perplexed as I was, and told me the Psychiatrist was puzzled as well.

I started treating her with *Natrum sulphuricum,* one of the main remedies for patients never well after a concussion.

To my stupefaction, she showed substantial improvement in her first follow-up visit. Her husband's features displayed more deliverance than joy. Although the patient's mouth was still dry, she could give a more coherent account of her symptoms. Now I had enough information to consider her Constitutional remedy. She was improving with *Natrum sulphuricum,* though, so I didn't consider it prudent to change horses in the middle of the stream. In this first follow-up visit it also became apparent the ugly bond that united these two ill-starred Human Beings. He was crushed by guilt, and felt he was responsible for her wife's disease. The patient, meantime, was obviously exploiting her husband feeling of culpability to the hilt, both to punish and to keep him by her side.

A few days after this first follow-up visit I found a message in the answering machine. The call had been made at some absurd hour, well into the night. It was the patient's husband. The message was abrupt. They were canceling the next visit and were not going to reschedule. The patient had decided to quit Homeopathic treatment.

Regarding psoric patient who refuse to get well, I don't believe it is the treatment, or the personality of the Practitioner what may drive these patients amiss; but rather their discomfort in the new lifestyle and their lack of understanding of what is going on.

As well as, in some, a profound unwillingness to become hale. Despite of the establishment of a rapport, or of how exhaustively and clearly the Homeopathic Physician may have explained facts and events as they unfold.

Perhaps because, once well, these patients won't be able to elicit the secondary gain they were used to obtain when they were the victims of their diseases. Or because they can't find within themselves the courage or desire to actively change an obnoxious lifestyle. Or to stop justifying hatred, or anger, or pity.

Ultimately, I believe it is fear of the unknown that lays ahead of them; no matter how wonderful and exhilarating the allure of such a future may be. After the first moment of exultance becomes routine, these patients start missing their past, and gaze with foreboding at an ultimately advantageous future, free of the familiar ghosts that tormented them in the past.

Consequently, they freak out when feeling well for the first time in their lives, and thus needing to actively adjust to this new state of affairs.

It is a most frustrating situation for the attending Physician.

Success has been indeed achieved, or at least is dawning. The patient's disease-syndrome is fading away. The Homeopathic cure is making itself felt. Then, and often without any warning, the Doctor sees how the patient starts to drift back and away across his or her private Styx, eyes riveted onto the howling portals of the past—and nothing can be done to turn those unfortunate Beings back.

Then there is the problem of Surgery.

There are patients who come to the Doctor's office with a surgical problem, and unaware that their problem can only be solved by Surgery. There are others who have been told they need Surgery and consult a Complementary Health Care Provider in the hope of avoiding it. And still others may develop a surgical problem during treatment.

And then there are those patients who can successfully be treated Wholistically, but whose Allopathic Doctors insist that the problem they have can only be solved by Surgery. How can a Wholistic Physician convince a colleague, when that colleague has no idea regarding what Wholistic Medicine is about and, furthermore, feels he or she has knowledge and is prejudiced against it? Often, the Wholistic Physician has to end up by putting all the pros and cons of both procedures in front of the patient, and then inviting him or her to decide.

This ignorance is very real, often ludicrous and always a nuisance. A sizable chunk of many a Homeopathic visit time has to be wasted in disabusing patients of false notions planted in their heads by these opinionated ignoramuses. The following dialog is a by no means unique sample of this state of affairs.

Quite recently I saw a patient for the first time. She needed relatively minor Surgery. I suggested *Arnica* 30 CH, one dose before and another one after Surgery. The Surgeon became incensed when he learnt about it.

"You can't have Homeopathy before Surgery!" he blurted in a paroxysm of horror and indignation "It will interfere with your recovery!"

"But how?" asked the patient, horrified.

Jose Miguel Mullen, M.D.

"Because Chinese herbs can thin your blood. This thing will make you bleed"

The patient called me immediately after this absurd dialogue. She was very worried. I was able to clarify to the patient's satisfaction that Chinese herbs have nothing to do with Homeopathic remedies.

Fortunately, gone are the days when, in battle, bandages removed from soldiers who had died of gangrene were washed, hung to dry and then rolled up, usually by prostitutes, a.k.a. as "camp followers"; to be re-used afterwards in freshly wounded soldiers. These camp followers, by the way, were also a fresh reservoir of sexually transmitted diseases for the troops.

Also fortunately gone are the days when a prizefighter was a welcome addition to some Hospitals for his knock-out punch would effectively complete the action of opium and rum, the only anesthetics then available. Or the days when any sensible patient would write his or her last will and testament before going to Surgery.

Or when Surgeons would don, in the Operating Room, the same filthy cassock they used in the Autopsy Room—the stiffer with dry blood and gore the better. In those days, Surgeons carried the needles used for sewing surgical wounds in the lapels of those filthy cassocks, always threaded and ready for immediate use. Surgeons, furthermore, did not wear gloves nor washed their hands prior to surgery.

Those were the days when several patients were operated upon simultaneously in the same large communal operating rooms; each bound and tied in an operating table with thick leather straps. All half awake and groggy with alcohol and opium, all writhing and yelling with pain at the same time.

The speediest Surgeons were then the brightest stars in the Surgical firmament. They were in great demand because, in their hands, patients would suffer the same pain, but for a shorter period of time. The most famous of the lot was probably the Surgeon John Liston, a flamboyant, happy-go-lucky daredevil who worked in London during mid-19th Century. He was sought after and admired because of his unbelievable speed. For instance, he could disarticulate a human hip in less than 3 minutes. In one such feat, and in his haste, Dr. Liston also amputated one of the patient's testicles as well as two of his assistant's fingers. The unfortunate patient later died of surgery-induced gangrene, then far from uncommon. I haven't found any reliable information regarding the fate of the hapless assistant who lost his fingers during this memorable surgical procedure.

Those were also the days of that forgettable Surgeon who disdained the use of the recently discovered chloroform because "the touch of the knife is a stimulant. It is better to hear a man scream than to see him die silently".

Here again, and although things are still far from perfect, Surgery has made gigantic strides.

And, in many instances, benefits far outweigh risks—particularly in several disease-syndromes that, for one reason or another, are beyond the reach of any Wholistic form of treatment.

It is impossible to establish beforehand, or to make some rule of thumb, regarding whom should or shouldn't go to Surgery.

Each instance has to be considered individually, according to the benefit/risk ratio of each patient's Allopathic diagnosis.

There are a few problems where Surgery is clearly preferable to any other form of treatment.

Some acute problems, such as acute appendicitis, ruptured tubal pregnancies[61] and the like, must be rushed to the Operating Room.

It is justifiable to give these disease-bearing patients Homeopathic treatment, and to watch for results, if done while the Surgical team is scrubbing and the patient is being made ready for Surgery. These problems are too acute and potentially too dangerous to allow us to wait. All the more because a Homeopathic remedy—or any other form of Wholistic treatment, for that matter—may take an unpredictable amount of time to kick in. Indeed, a Wholistic treatment may even not even work at all. If the remedy starts acting before the patient is wheeled into the Operating Room, then perhaps Surgery may be avoided or delayed. But if the Surgeon is ready before the remedy acts, then Surgery must proceed without delay.

Early, localized malignant solid tumors have to go to Surgery. Homeopathy alone is usually only palliative here. And to Surgery must also go lumps, nodes, and moles suspicious of being malignant. Here a biopsy, and Surgery in time, can well mean the difference between life and death for a patient.

---

[61] The Human ovum is usually fecundated in one of the tubes that connect the uterus to the ovaries. These tubes are known as *Fallopian tubes.* The ovum then starts to divide while being propelled towards the womb, where it nestles and continues to divide, grow and differentiate until the time of delivery. In some instances, though, the fecundated ovum does not complete its journey into the womb but nestles in one of the Fallopian tubes and starts to grow there. It is then called a "tubal pregnancy". It becomes a surgical emergency because, when reaching a certain size, it invariably bursts the tube. This event causes sudden pain, so severe that it can easily lead to shock, and also blood loss into the abdominal cavity. This hemorrhage, if not controlled, can make the patient rapidly bleed to death.

The same goes for gangrene and other tissue-destroying diseases; since Homeopathic remedies are not likely to nudge the patient's Vital Force into dead structures.

But then, let me consider some other chronic problems that are considered surgical, but that often respond quite well to Homeopathic treatment.

Take ulcerative colitis as an example. It can produce bowel cancer and toxic megacolon, in which the large intestine may suddenly distend, burst, and spills feces into the abdominal cavity. This complication is often fatal, despite of intensive treatment. In these instances, the patient must go to surgery immediately. But, if there is no immediate danger of toxic megacolon, and there is no colonic cancer, then the patient should be treated Wholistically as the first choice—preferably with Homeopathy, sometimes aided by Acupuncture. Homeopathic treatment can work beautifully in ulcerative colitis-bearing patients. The main reason why Homeopathic treatment should be attempted in these patients is because their only Allopathic alternative is Surgery, sooner or later. Pharmacological drugs help very little here, and are generally useless in the long run. And Surgery for ulcerative colitis means removal of the *whole* large intestine, including rectum and anus; so that the patient is forced to live with a permanent colostomy thereafter—a situation all the more appalling when considering that the victims of this disease-syndrome are usually young.

I remember, within this context, a 26-year-old patient I first saw early in 1992.

She had been diagnosed as having ulcerative colitis in June 27, 1987. A flexible sigmoidoscopy, or introduction of a flexible tube through the anus into the lower large intestine in order to observe, study, and also obtain samples of bowel tissue, had shown "colonic mucosal changes typical of ulcerative colitis, involving the lower 20 centimeters of the rectum and sigmoid colon". Twenty centimeters (some 8 inches) is about as far as a sigmoidoscopic tube can go into the large intestine. The patient's problem had progressively worsened, despite of drug treatment and a strict diet.

In her first visit, she told me about the anger, sadness and resentment she felt toward her parents. She had married the man she loved in 1986, but her choice had far from pleased her dour parents, to whom she was devoted. Such were her annoyance and grief that she developed ulcerative colitis one year or so after her marriage. She was very weak when I first saw her, in chronic distress and severe pain. She had no appetite. Her pale complexion had a sickly yellowish tinge. She was abnormally thin and walked slowly and with hesitation, holding her abdomen with both hands. The jar of each cautious step would elicited a jolt of pain that would bring a grimace to her features and sometimes force a grunt, even tears. Her father would chauffeur her, for she couldn't have possibly driven in her condition.

She had insomnia, due to her abdominal pain and constant urge to defecate. She had many bloody bowel movements, day and night, that would exhaust her. Not only were these bowel movements very painful, but most times they were nothing but gushes of liquid blood. She had also developed pyoderma gangrenosa, a pathological skin condition associated with ulcerative colitis and similar disease-syndromes.

Her attending Allopathic Physician had recommended removal of her whole large intestine, rectum and anus by the time she came to see me. None of the drugs she was taking was having any effect. Her general condition was deteriorating.

Her remedy was *Natrum Muriaticum*. Improvement was rapid and dramatic. Her bowel movements diminished to two a day, and became normal. Her pain, weakness and insomnia vanished, as did her pyoderma gangrenosa. She started to eat well. She began to gain weight, and her complexion became healthy. She tapered down, and eventually discontinued, all the drugs she was taking. She started to eat what she pleased. Unfortunately, sigmoidoscopy was not repeated at this stage.

Eventually she moved out of State, and I lost track of her. Some months afterwards I heard she was doing fine.

I fear for her, though. This was an ideal instance for Homeopathy + Family Counseling. Homeopathy had indeed been successful. But I don't know for how long, because of her family situation. And unfortunately Family Counseling is out of the question here, due to the intractability and inflexibility of her parents.

The practice of Homeopathy is office based, and not accepted in most American Hospitals.

This state of affairs limits the practice of Homeopathy, for all intents and purposes, to acute and chronic ambulatory patients; that is, to patients not ill enough to need hospitalization.

Furthermore, most Allopathic Doctors will not refer patients to their Homeopathic colleagues except under very exceptional circumstances. This makes the goal of teamwork, essential in Integrative Medicine, almost impossible to achieve.

Take as an example of one of these exceptional referrals a note I received from an Allopathic colleague, dated May 24, 1995. I shall transcribe it verbatim, though greatly summarized. Names are omitted and will be represented by an empty space between brackets.

"Please evaluate my patient Mr. [ ] for chronic pain in back and left leg, secondary to recurrent disc L5-S1. Mr. [ ] has been involved in multiple accidents, especially a very severe one on (date). He was reinjured on (date). Mr. [ ] underwent lumbar disc excision L5-S1 on (date) at [ ] Hospital performed by Dr. [ ] neurosurgeon. Since that surgery, Mr. [ ] has developed recurrent pain. Mr. [ ] has a problem with dependence to narcotic pain medication, and I am hoping that natural remedies may control his symptoms without resorting to long term use of narcotic pain medication".

The patient never called to make an appointment—to my considerable relief. I phoned the referring Allopathic Physician some 3 months afterwards to report that his patient had not shown up in my office. He sounded rather disappointed at the news.

Most patients refer themselves to Homeopathic Physicians because they have read about Homeopathy, gone to lectures or because they have a friend or relative who did well with Homeopathic treatment.

Others go because Allopathy has exhausted its resources and has nothing more to offer (the acronym TEETH has been coined for these patients "tried everything else, try Homeopathy").

Still others because they have become allergic to drugs, because they don't feel well after Allopathic treatments or because they are plain tired at the impersonal treatment proffered by many Allopathic Doctors.

In a nutshell, Homeopathic follow-up of a psoric patient's, treated with Centesimal potencies, simply amounts to nudging the patient toward balance, with his or her Constitutional remedy, as often as necessary. A successful treatment ultimately produces the jelling of balance in the patient.

In most patients, the momentum toward balance elicited by the first dose of their Constitutional remedy ends sooner or later, and the patient relapses into imbalance. Another dose of the Constitutional remedy has to be administered at that point in time. And then the patient must be treated again and again, every time improvement peters out; that is, every time the swing toward balance looses its momentum. Until wellness finally jells, and the patients needs treatment no more.

Within this context, follow-up visits and telephone calls are so many opportunities to learn when to administer the next dose of that patient's Constitutional remedy, and also if and when to make changes.

Let me recall still again that each *Whole* psoric Human Beings will respond to Constitutional Homeopathic treatment in his or her own individual fashion.

Consequently, during follow-up, the Homeopathic Physician has no choice but to *play it by ear.* Meaning that, according to what the patient manifests in successive office visits and/or phone calls, the Homeopathic Physician may repeat or not the same potency of the remedy, increase or decrease it, add or change remedies, and/or refer the patient to other Allopathic or Wholistic Medical Practitioners for purposes of further diagnosis and/or treatment.

Follow-up visits and phone calls will also tell the Doctor when to discontinue treatment.

A Homeopathic treatment may be finished when the psoric patient's wellness jells, chronicity disappears, and consequently there is no need to continue treatment—or else when the Homeopathic Physician realizes that treatment is not helping the patient.

There is no way for the Homeopathic Physician to predict what is going to happen, how the patient is going to respond, or how long will it take for the patient to get well.

It is the patient who says how and when.

Which is one of the main reasons why excellent rapport and communication are so essential for success in the Homeopathic Doctor-patient relationship, particularly during the follow-up of psoric patients.

Long term follow-up of psoric patients can be very difficult.

Many patients leave when they are starting to feel well. Others get impatient and leave when they find no changes after a few weeks or months of treatments.

Still others are unable or unwilling to change harmful attitudes or lifestyles.

Or cannot continue paying, and are ashamed to continue seeing the Doctor under these circumstances. Or refuse to use their credit card.

The American Medical Association does not consider homeopathy a valid specialty.

Therefore, many Health Insurance companies don't accept Homeopaths or Integrative Physicians as Providers. This fact severely limits the population of patients who can afford to visit Wholistic Physicians, as well as the time those patients can remain under our care.

261

It is very difficult to learn how patients are doing once they leave treatment, unless news come via a friend referred by them or through some other circumsntance.

I remember once instance of the latter. I called one Government office for some business. As soon as I gave him my name, the man I needed to talk to said "Dr. Mullen, I'm Mr. [], []'s husband!" Ms. [], a very sick lady, had been a patient years and years back "I want to tell you how grateful we are! My wife has been doing great since she saw you!"

Patients may also ask for another appointment, sometimes years later, because the wellness afforded by the original treatment is starting to wear off, or has vanished altogether.

The usual pattern, as the psoric patient *evolves towards Homeopathic cure,* is that of a slow and gentle disappearance of symptoms.

I like to compare this form of disappearance with the gradual fading of a star as dawn approaches.

At first the star is twinkling brightly up there in the night sky.

Then the star becomes less and less distinct, as dawn progresses, until finally vanishes away.

Disappearance of symptoms tends to be so gentle, in fact, that psoric patients may fail to notice it.

As early as in the first follow-up visit, the patient may manifest that there have been no changes. Yet, as the Doctor reads up the History aloud, symptom by symptom, as given during the first visit, the patient will likely frown, and then grin. And finally reply, incredulous "Now that you mention it, that problem is gone!".

Or else the patient, feeling well for the first time, may fear that his or her disease-syndrome may return unexpectedly.

I call this fear the *waiting-for-the-other-shoe-to-fall* syndrome.

In time, the patient will forget his or her apprehension, and start feeling comfortable in his or her newly acquired wellness.

When all is said and done, in Homeopathy everything boils down to carefully evaluate *each individual* disease-bearing patient.

As well as *every instance each disease-bearing patient brings to our attention.*

And then to apply all our knowledge, experience and criterion to *each* instance brought up by *each* individual patient.

Chapter 20

EVOLUTION OF TREATMENT IN ACUTE DISEASES AND IN PSORIC PATIENTS

EVOLUTION OF TREATMENT IN ACUTE DISEASES.

Acute diseases may strike acute and also psoric patients.

Acute patients are in balance to start with. They become imbalanced when something hits them. Full balance is restored when the damaging agent disappears spontaneously or else under treatment, and the Vital Force regains a full grip on the affected area.

In some, the Vital Force doesn't regain a full grip. Balance is not fully restored after the acute disease subsides. These patients become psoric.

The only way of knowing if a patient is acute—or psoric, for that matter—is through a complete evaluation of that patient.

Therefore, the attending Physician must determine, as part of the patient's evaluation, if the acute disease-syndrome afflicting the patient is

- an acute disease affecting an otherwise well balanced individual,
- an acute exacerbation of a chronic disease, or
- an acute intercurrent disease in a psoric patient.

Treatment may vary according to each individual, and also to the acute disease-syndrome each acute or psoric patient may be bearing.

If the patient was in balance until before being stricken by the acute disease, then only the disease needs to be treated, *but in such a fashion that, after it is controlled, the patient's Vital Force may regain a full grip of the affected area.* That is, with Homeopathy associated or not with any other indicated form of treatment.

If the patient is psoric, and not receiving his or her Constitutional remedy, the treatment of the acute disease must be considered with extreme prudence and caution. Whenever possible, the patient's Constitutional remedy must be administered *before* starting treatment of the acute disease.

To act otherwise may invite a suppression.

If the patient is psoric, and under Constitutional remedy, then the acute disease must be treated by the best means available, Homeopathic, Allopathic or whatever other that may proffer the best possibilities for the patient.

If the patient is psoric, and the acute disease that appears is intercurrent, that is, bursting into an already present disease or imbalance, the intercurrent disease must be treated by the best means available.

If the patient is psoric, and suffering from an acute exacerbation of the patient's chronic problem, first the acute exacerbation has to be brought under control, and afterwards the underlying chronic disease and imbalance.

In this fashion, if the acute exacerbation is, for instance, a diabetic coma, then the diabetic coma has to be brought under control first. Then the treatment of the underlying diabetes mellitus has be to re-evaluated and re-programmed if necessary—as well as, in all likelihood, the patient's Constitutional treatment.

The acute disease must be neutralized in acute and in psoric patients, as soon as possible and with whatever means at hand. The patient must be proffered the treatment, or combination thereof, that combines maximum benefit with minimum risk.

The reason for this urgency is that, if not fully controlled as soon as possible, an acute disease may kill the patient, or else transform him or her into a psoric one. In psoric patients, in turn, an acute disease may considerably worsen their imbalance.

If Homeopathy is chosen as the only treatment, or as part of a more complex therapeutic approach, the frequency of administration of Homeopathic remedies and their potency will vary according to the type and degree of severity of the acute disease.

The usual strategy consists in administering one single Homeopathic remedy at a time, if only up to a few minutes apart.

Potencies to be administered vary. For instance, in a very acute *Arsenicum Album* asthmatic attack, the patient may receive a very high dynamization in a single dose. Usually, however, frequent administration of lower potencies tends to be favored.

The Physician must evaluate the patient immediately upon recovery.

No further treatment will be usually necessary if it was an acute disease affecting a well-balanced patient, and the treatment used was Homeopathic.

If, however, the acute disease was treated only Allopathically, or if the acute disease is an acute exacerbation or an intercurrent disease in a psoric patient, or if the formerly acute patient has become psoric, then the patient should be followed up, and treated, according to the guidelines described immediately below.

EVOLUTION OF TREATMENT IN PSORIC PATIENTS TREATED WITH DECIMAL DYNAMIZATIONS.

My experience here is very limited because, in my practice, I mostly use Centesimals and less frequently LM's.

I tend to use Decimal dynamizations only as a complementary treatment for problems beyond the reach of psoric patients' Constitutional treatment.

EVOLUTION OF TREATMENT IN PSORIC PATIENT TREATED WITH CENTESIMAL DYNAMIZATIONS
(a.k.a. The Second Prescription)

Allow me to recall here that, in psoric patients, and according to the Law of Hering, the direction of cure is from the emotional to the physical, from inside outwards, from above downwards and from the most recent symptom to the most remote; and that old and forgotten symptoms may appear at some time during treatment.

Psoric patients can respond in either one of the following manners, after being treated with *one single* Centesimal dose of their Constitutional remedies:

a) The patient gets well.
b) The patient shows a short improvement, then declines.
c) The patient worsens, then gets well.
d) The patient gets *stuck.*
e) Something happens during treatment.
f) The patient does not change.
g) The patient becomes progressively worse.

I shall briefly refer to each of these alternatives and their different variations.

Then I shall mention, whenever possible, the causes of each and the most likely solutions. Clinical examples will be brought up to illustrate, as needed.

a) The patient gets well.- This is, of course, the ideal situation. The most gratifying, both for the Physician and for the patient.

It usually means that the patient has a surplus of Vital Force; that is, enough to fulfill the tasks of everyday maintenance, and then ample reserves remaining to fulfill the requirements of the Constitutional remedy.

It also means that the patient has received his or her *simillimum.*

As a rule, never *change a psoric patient's Constitutional remedy as long as that patient's improvement lasts.*

a) i) The period of wellness, after each take of the patient's Constitutional remedy, starts to wane always after the same interval; say, after 5 months. This, and the variants that follow, happen when the patient has received his or her *similar.*

The solution here is to repeat the same potency of the Constitutional remedy when the period of wellness starts to wane.

a) ii) The period of wellness starts to wane, after taking the remedy, at intervals that grow longer and longer.

The solution is similar to that in **a)** i), namely, to repeat the administration of the remedy as the improvement starts to wane.

a) iii) The period of wellness becomes shorter after each take, i.e., 5 months after the first dose, 4 months after the second, 3 after the third, etc.

The usual cause is that the potency being used is exhausting its usefulness.

The solution consists in administering the next higher potency, observe results and then proceed as in **a)** i).

For instance, if the Physician is using the first Hahnemanian scale (i.e., 1 CH, 2 CH, 3 CH, etc.) and the exhausted potency is, say, 2 CH, then the potency should be increased to 3 CH. If the Physician is using the second Hahnemanian scale (i.e., 3 CH, 6 CH, etc.) and the exhausted potency is, say, 3 CH, the potency should be increased to 6 CH. If using the Kentian scale (i.e., 6 CH, 30 CH, 200 CH, 1 M, etc.) and the exhausted potency is, say, 200 CH, the potency should be increased to 1 M.

a) iv) The period of wellness becomes shorter and shorter, despite of increasing potencies of the remedy.

Either the patient is ceasing to respond to the remedy, or else he or she may be getting *stuck*. I shall briefly discuss possible solutions in **c)** and **d)** below.

a) v) After several doses, administered at approximately equal intervals, the effect of the last dose wanes after a much shorter interval.

a) v) i) The Doctor should check if there was an instance of stress, grief, disease, etc. after the last dose.
In this instance, treatment of the acute problem should be instituted. *Constitutional treatment is to be suspended during the treatment of the acute problem.* After the acute problem is over, the potency of the last dose of the patient's Constitutional remedy should be repeated.

a) v) ii) There is no apparent reason for this phenomenon.

a) v) ii) 1) The patient should be re-evaluated. Perhaps the phenomenon is due to a miasmatic blockage. If this is the case, the patient may need to receive his or her nosode (Please see **d)**, below). Then, the same dose of the Constitutional remedy should be administered again after improvement produced by the nosode, if any.

a) v) ii) 2) If the dose administered in **a)** v) ii) 1) is again too short acting, proceed as in **a)** vi), below.

a) vi) The period of wellness is too short.

a) vi) i) After a short time of improvement the patient's symptoms reappear.
It is possible that the potency administered was too low to start with.
Repeat the same potency and watch. Hike potency if wellness remains equally short-lived.

a) vi) ii) Improvement is short-lived, and takes time to become evident.

a) vi) ii) 1) Most of the potency's power may have been used to overcome the patient's *inertia*. Sometimes, starting a treatment is like pushing a stationary car. It takes a great deal of effort to overcome its inertia and start the car rolling, but once inertia is overcome, the car can be made to move faster and faster with considerably less effort.

The solution consists watching the patient, and repeating the same potency if necessary.

a) vi) ii) 2) It may happen that the potency administered was too low for the needs of the patient.

The solution here consists in administering the same potency as soon as the therapeutic effects of the previous dose ceases and watch what happens.

a) vi) ii) 2) a) If there is the same delay in the onset of the improvement, the reason may be that the potency is too low or that the Vital Force at the patient's disposal is too little. The differential diagnosis here is easy: if the patient is weak, then the likely reason is little Vital Force available and, if the patient is vigorous, then the likely reason is a low potency.

a) vi) ii) 2) a) I) If the reason is a little Vital Force, then the potency will have to either be maintained or else diminished. In these patients it is also important to consider the possibility of associating Homeopathy with Allopathy or other forms of Complementary Medicine.

a) vi) ii) 2) a) II) If the reason is a low potency, and the patient is reasonably robust, then the potency should be increased.

a) vi) iii) Improvement is short and also *partial.*

It may be due to the fact that the patient has received a local, instead of his or her Constitutional remedy.

The patient must be re-evaluated *as soon as possible.* The purpose of this re-evaluation is to find the patient's Constitutional remedy.

The administration of a local remedy to a psoric patient virgin of Constitutional treatment may bring about a suppression.

a) vi) iv) Improvement is short and, as it ends, *new* pathological symptoms appear.

The Physician must investigate the appearance of an intercurrent disease in these patients.

If, in effect, there is an intercurrent disease, and

a) vi) iv) 1) the disease-syndrome is *acute,* Constitutional treatment should be suspended and the treatment of the acute disease should be started. Constitutional treatment will be re-instated when the acute disease is brought under control.

a) vi) iv) 2) the disease-syndrome is *chronic,* or it is an *acute exacerbation of the patient's chronic disease.* Here the patient should receive a Wholistic, Allopathic or combination of both forms of treatment while continuing the administration of the Constitutional remedy. At the same time the patient should be re-evaluated, to see if his or her profile still correspond to that of the Constitutional remedy that he or she is receiving.

a) vi) v) Improvement is short-lived, and is followed by a severe and prolonged aggravation.
This situation here is extremely delicate. The patient's has very little Vital Force at his or her disposal. The Vital Force has exhausted its power while attempting to respond to the challenge posed by the Constitutional remedy. So much so that afterwards there isn't enough left to attend the patient's basic everyday needs.
What I feel should be done here is

a) vi) v) 1) To administer immediately another dose of a considerably lower potency of the patient's Constitutional remedy, or, is the aggravation is very severe

a) vi) v) 2) To administer immediately a very low potency of a *Complementary* and *milder* remedy (e.g., if the problem was caused by the administration of a metal, use a complementary plant, etc.). If there are no changes

a) vi) v) 3) Attempt to antidote with strong coffee. Camphor is more effective as an antidote, but I don't believe it is safe to try camphor in a debilitated patient. If antidoting doesn't work,

a) vi) v) 4) and the aggravation is severe, and does not respond rapidly to a lower potency, or to a lower potency of a milder Complementary remedy, or to an antidote, ask for immediate Allopathic assistance and/or send the patient to a Hospital.

a) vii) Mental and general symptoms improve, but local symptoms show no changes or worsen for a short time.

Good news!

In the treatment of psoric patients, Homeopathic cure progresses from the emotional to the physical, from inside outwards, from above downwards, and from the most recent symptom to the most remote.

In a successful treatment, therefore, mental and also general symptoms are supposed to disappear first. Everything else is bound to follow.

There is nothing further to do in this instance, but to sit, wait, watch—and enjoy!

a) viii) Mental and general symptoms improve or disappear, but local symptoms stubbornly refuse to go away or worsen consistently.

a) viii) i) The effect of a Constitutional remedy may be slower in some patients than in others, and may thus take a long time to progress from the emotional to the physical, etc.

The Doctor should wait and observe the patient.

a) viii) ii) It may also be the consequence of the fact that the potency administered was too low.

The solution here consists in hiking the potency. Please make hiking gradual, lest you may want to risk the possibility of a Homeopathic aggravation.

a) viii) iii) It may be due to unresponsiveness of the local symptom.

a) viii) iii) 1) If the patient receives a *similar*, instead of a *simillimum*, then the remedy will fall short of a complete cure. One or more symptoms are bound to remain after an otherwise successful treatment.

The solution here is to

a) viii) iii) 1) a) re-evaluate the patient in search of a simillimum and, if that simillimum cannot be found

a) viii) iii) 1) b) search for a Complementary similar or "small" remedy that may cover the non-responding or residual symptom/s.

a) viii) iii) 2) It may be that the non-responsive symptom/s is/are part of a disease-syndrome beyond the usefulness of Homeopathy; such as in the instance of cancer, diseases of insufficiency, gangrene or a surgical disease-syndrome.

Here the attending Homeopath must re-evaluate the patient, ascertain the nature of the symptoms that do not respond to treatment, find the disease-syndrome to which they correspond and then choose the correct treatment for that disease-syndrome—*although the patient should, at the same time, be treated Homeopathically whenever possible, both in order to bring his or her Wholeness into balance; and also to avoid the possibility of a suppression.* This instance can present itself early in treatment; or else after some time of Constitutional treatment.

a) viii) iii) 2) a) If early in treatment, the pathology is likely to have been present *before* starting Constitutional treatment. Aside from prompt diagnosis and referral to an Allopathic Physician for treatment if necessary, it is convenient to re-evaluate the patient, and so make certain the his Constitutional remedy is the correct one.

a) viii) iii) 2) b) Something is very, very wrong if diseases of this caliber appear months or years after onset of treatment. Here, and aside from a prompt diagnosis and referral to an Allopathic Doctor, the patient must be urgently re-evaluated. It is very unlikely that a patient may be receiving his or her correct Constitutional remedy and, at the same time, develop diseases of this ilk well into treatment.

a) viii) iv) It may be due to the fact that the psoric patient has changed profile, and that he or she may consequently need another Constitutional remedy. This possibility is extremely unlikely, because there has already been a mental improvement, and probably also improvement in other organs and systems. It must be taken into account only if not other explanation for the stubborn symptoms exists.

The solution here is to re-evaluate the patient, and then dispense the new Complementary remedy; associated or not with other forms of treatment.

a) ix) Symptoms improve, but old and apparently cured symptoms surface for a while.

Excellent news! Often frightening for the patient, though.

It means that the remedy is erasing the slate, from the most recent symptom to the most remote; with mild and temporary reappearance of some of some old and forgotten symptoms as the erasing progresses.

Here the Doctor should reassure the patient. Then congratulate him or herself for having chosen the correct Constitutional remedy. And afterwards sit back, relax and enjoy.

a) x) Improvement is seen in local symptoms only. None in mental or general.

Bad news. Often alarming. A local remedy has been administered by mistake, instead of the patient's Constitutional; and it has been administered *to a patient who, and due to an erroneous prescription, still remains virgin of Constitutional Homeopathic treatment.*

The remedy administered should be antidoted as soon as possible, and the patient should be URGENTLY re-evaluated.

After this URGENT re-evaluation, the patient should be dispensed the correct Constitutional remedy as soon as possible.

The reason for this haste is that there is a very real danger of suppression here.

a) xi) Improvement progresses from the periphery to the center of the patient, instead of the other way around.

This is a very serious situation, much more so than that described in **a)** x). It is an almost certain sign of an impending suppression.

Treatment should be suspended immediately. Patient should be instantly antidoted and then re-evaluated, and the Constitutional remedy should be started at once.

b) The patient worsens, then gets well.- Also known as Homeopathic aggravation.

The subsequent improvement, and its aspects, has already been described in **a)**, above.

The sequence aggravation → improvement is usually the harbinger of a successful treatment.

If aggravation is severe, it may be due to the administration of too high a potency, particularly if worsening appears suddenly or rather rapidly.

Aggravation can often be avoided by starting treatment with a low potency.

If the aggravation is too severe, and/or too long lasting—particularly when it becomes manifest immediately after the administration of the remedy—antidote with a considerably lower potency of the same Constitutional remedy.

c) The patient ceases to respond to treatment.- The patient has to be re-evaluated *immediately.*

c) i) The patient may have inadvertently antidoted his or her Constitutional remedy.

In this instance all, or at least most of the original symptoms will re-appear. Return of symptoms is usually *abrupt;* and there may be a History of exposure to, or ingestion of, an antidote.

The patient should be informed in regards to the antidote, and requested to get rid of it.

The Constitutional remedy should be repeated as soon as possible, at the same potency as before it having being antidoted.

The Physician should then wait a reasonable time for a response. The remedy is to be administered again at a higher potency if no response is elicited when repeating the remedy at the same potency.

c) ii) The patient may have *escaped* the effect of his or her Constitutional remedy.

Return of symptoms here is usually gradual and partial.

Not all of the initial symptoms are bound to reappear after an escape. New symptoms may emerge in their stead.

This may happen, for example, when the patient is changing profile as in the example of the *Lycopodium* patient who changed his profile into that of *Pulsatilla,* described in *Complementary remedies* in Chapter 13 *"The remedies".* In this *Lycopodium → Pulsatilla* patient, symptoms like emotional detachment, keeping one's distance, need to control, etc. disappeared; while others such as crying, and need of protection and love appeared in their stead.

The solution here is to re-evaluate the patient, and then to prescribe the new Constitutional remedy.

c) iii) Something may have happened to the patient, such an acute disease, sudden grief, an accident, etc.

The patient may be in need of intercurrent treatment, either Homeopathic, Allopathic or else some other Wholistic form of therapy.

d) The patient gets *stuck*.- The patient is receiving his or her correct Constitutional remedy.

Periods of improvement become shorter and shorter and are not as clear-cut, despite of periodic increases in potency. Finally, after some time, improvement ceases altogether, as the patient gets *stuck*.

d) i) This situation may be the consequence of the interference—or surge—of the patient's chronic miasma.

The Physician should consider using the *Nosode* that corresponds to the patient's chronic miasma. The *Nosode* should be followed, after a few days, by the Constitutional remedy.

The potency of the Constitutional remedy, when given after the *Nosode*, can be that of the last dose given before the administering the Nosode. However, I recommend re-starting Constitutional treatment at a lower potency, because with the patient's chronic miasma now presumably under control, the effects of the Constitutional remedy may be stronger, and thus capable of precipitating an unnecessary aggravation.

d) ii) It may be the consequence of changes in life style, such as new stressful situations in the patient's job, or the appearance of devastating emotional situations, such as loss of a dear one, a worsening marital situation, etc.

The Doctor may discontinue the patient's Constitutional remedy and prescribe an intercurrent remedy—such as *Ignatia* in the instance of the loss of a dear one—to then continue the administration of the Constitutional treatment once the crisis starts to fade away..

d) iii) It may be due to the appearance of a diseases-syndrome beyond the scope of usefulness of Homeopathy, such as, for instance, an acute appendicitis or a solid malignant tumor.

Here, Constitutional Homeopathic treatment must be continued while the patient is being simultaneously treated with Allopathy for his or her problem (Please see **e)** below, and also **a)** viii) iii) 2) above).

e) Something happens during treatment.- It can be anything, and it must be controlled as soon as possible, by any means at hand. If not controlled in time, the patient may loose all the ground gained with Homeopathic treatment—and then some.

It can be an accident, an extremely stressful situation, a disease, a suppression, an antidotism, or whatever.

There is an interval between the time when the treated patient starts shifting towards balance, and the moment when wellness *jells*.

If something, anything, happens before *jelling* takes place, then an acute exacerbation of the patient's disease-syndrome/s, or a flare-up, is likely to follow. Once wellness has *jelled* or affirmed itself, however, this phenomenon is less likely to occur and, if it happens, may be considerably milder and easier to control.

Flare-ups are generally gentler in patients who were not too ill at the onset of Homeopathic treatment.

Everything harmful that happens during Homeopathic treatment has to be taken care of. And *fast*.

Here, as everywhere else, the treatment chosen must be the one that assures maximum benefit and minimum risk for the patient.

How the problems are brought under control will depend on several factors: the Doctor's deftness, criterion and knowledge; the disease the patient is bearing, its acuteness, its type and severity; the disease-bearing patient; and, finally, the disease-bearing patient's circumstance.

But, again, whatever is done to control whatever interferes must be done as *fast* and as ***thoroughly*** as possible—no holds barred.

e) i) Suppressions and antidotisms can happen during treatment.

Suppressions have been discussed in Chapter 4 *"The suppressions"*, and antidotisms in Chapter 15 *"Antidotes of Homeopathic remedies"*.

e) ii) What to do if *fever* appears during a Homeopathic treatment?

Fever is a phenomenon that happens when the patient's metabolism is exaggerated—or needs to become exaggerated for some reason.

The center that regulates body temperature, located in the base of the brain, turns up its thermostat a couple of points when there is fever. The result is an increase of body temperature.

When that increased temperature reaches a certain point, or when fever is no longer needed, then the thermostat in the base of the brain turns itself down. The organism begins to cool. In order to cool itself, the body brings water out onto the skin in the form of perspiration, and then dissipates extra body heat by means of evaporating it. The transference of heat from the body to the water shed through the skin, plus the action of the center that regulates the temperature, are usually enough to cool down the body, and to bring it to its normal temperature range. Increase in body temperature, and the corresponding increase of the patient's metabolic rate, can happen for several reasons.

When caused by the invasion of foreign life forms (i.e., bacteria, viruses and the like), this increase in metabolic rate helps the organism to fight away the bacterial infection, or else the viral or parasitic infestation. When the body reaches a certain temperature, which is usually above 102° F or 38°8 C, fever can help destroy the stowaway viruses that are illegally lodging and cloning themselves inside our cells[62] (let us recall that, once inside a cell, viruses are sheltered from any adverse influence, including the action of antibiotics).

Fever, therefore, can be the only way of getting rid of many viruses. Without it, viruses can gradually transform our cells into breeding colonies while interfering with our cells' metabolism. Worse yet, when reaching sufficient numbers, they may strike if the patient's defenses plunge. Meaning that fever can be *good* in these instances.

In other instances, though, fever is *bad*; for it exhausts the organism for no useful purpose. The periodic bouts of high fever that accompany malaria are a good example of *bad fever*.

A *good fever* is generated so that invaders may be neutralized; consequently, its trend points towards health. A *bad fever*, on the other hand, needlessly exhausts the patient. It consequently tends towards death.

To treat a *good fever* means to suppress it and also to needlessly slow down or to neutralize the defensive capacity of the patient. To boot, this inopportune treatment allows viruses to continue proliferating undisturbed inside our cells. To leave a good fever alone, in turn, means to help the patient get well.

By the same token, not to treat a *bad fever* will help the patient worsen; and to eliminate it will help the patient improve.

Meaning that the attending Health Care Provider must carefully evaluate whether the fever is good or bad, before starting treatment. Here, as everywhere else, nothing can replace the Physician's knowledge, criterion and experience.

Homeopathy does not treat fevers.

If the fever corresponds to an *acute disease*, then the Doctor will treat the patient with the remedy that causes that particular kind of fever in Provings and in acute intoxications. The same criterion will be followed if the

---

[62] Prof. Wolff O., M.D. Personal Communication. Seminar on Anthroposophic Medicine. Argentine Society of Anthroposophic Medicine. Buenos Aires, Argentina. 1979.

Jose Miguel Mullen, M.D.

fever corresponds to the *acute exacerbation,* or to an *intercurrent infection* or *infestation in a psoric patient.*

If, on the other hand, the fever is a direct consequence of the imbalance of the Whole psoric patient, or is one of the manifestations of that imbalance, then the Doctor will treat the Whole disease-bearing patient with the corresponding Constitutional remedy.

f) The patient does not change.- The main reason is the administration of the wrong remedy.

A distant second would be the possibility of a mistake in the preparation of the remedy.

There is practically no third.

Some benefit is bound to be seen when the patient receives the correct remedy, even if the potency chosen is grossly below that needed by the patient or if a chronic miasma or something similar is hampering the capacity of the patient to fully respond.

The solution, when the patient shows no change after being treated, is the re-evaluation of the Whole patient.

And then perhaps a call to the Homeopathic Pharmacy, to inquire about the batch of the remedy dispensed, if the same remedy is chosen as the patient's Constitutional after re-evaluation.

g) The patient becomes progressively worse.-

g) i) Worsening may be due to the wrong selection of Constitutional remedy.

The patient should be re-evaluated, and then started in his or her correct Constitutional remedy.

g) ii) It may be due to the presence of a disease beyond the scope of usefulness of Homeopathy, such as insulin-dependent diabetes, hemophilia, a malignant solid tumor, etc. Or else to the existence of a surgical problem, such as acute appendicitis, an intrathoracic goiter, etc.

The patient should be referred to the Health Care Provider capable of helping the patient while, at the same time, continuing the psoric patient's Constitutional treatment (Please see **a)** viii) iii) 2), above).

g) iii) The cause may be the administration of the correct Constitutional remedy to a weakened patient; that is, with very little Vital Force to spare for curative purposes.

The patient should be re-evaluated.

g) iii) i) Treatment should be re-started with a much lower potency if the same remedy appears to the right one after evaluation.

g) iii) ii) If there is no response to **g)** iii) i) within a reasonable period of time, the patient should be referred to an Allopathic Doctor, or to another Wholistic Practitioner, according to his or her problem. Constitutional Homeopathic treatment can be either continued or discontinued in this instance.

g) iv) The reason may be the administration of too high a potency, causing such a severe initial aggravation that the patient is unable to overcome it.

The patient should immediately be given another dose of the remedy at a considerably lower potency; and then be re-evaluated.

EVOLUTION OF TREATMENT IN PSORIC PATIENTS TREATED WITH LM'S IN PLUS

This form of dynamization affords very little problems—at least during treatment—if the patient uses the remedy dissolved in water, and succusses the solution prior to receiving each daily dose; that is, if he or she receives it in *Plus*.

The only difficulty that may arise, in patients treated with LM Plus, is the aggravation at the end of the treatment. Such an end may be delayed indefinitely, by means of increasing the Plus potency by a factor of one when the effectiveness of the previous potency appears to be fading.

In LM potencies, increases are usually made in factors of one (i.e., from the first LM potency to the second, from there to the third, etc.).

Chapter 21

PSEUDO-PSORA

In well balanced patients (that is, a-psorics, or patients with latent Psora), sexually transmitted diseases tend to remain localized, and not to invade the patient's organism. In psoric patients, on the other hand, sexually transmitted diseases rapidly become generalized.

The chronic miasma Pseudo-psora *appears as the consequence of* local *treatments of sexually transmitted diseases.*

Pseudo-psora, so elicited, provokes the generalization of otherwise localized sexually transmitted diseases—or at the very least it makes them considerably more resistant to treatment.

In Chapter 5 *"The Chronic Miasmas",* Psora was described as a chronic, total and generalized state of progressive chronic imbalance.

Psora makes the patient vulnerable to the ravages of almost any acute or chronic disease-syndrome, whether it stems from inside or around the patient.

Aside from Psora, Dr. Hahnemann also described two other chronic miasmas.

Those two miasmas are Sycosis and Syphilis. He related the first to the disease-syndromes gonorrhea and genital warts, and the second to the disease-syndrome syphilis. Dr. Hahnemann called the latter "venereal disease proper".

Gonorrhea, genital warts and syphilis were the only sexually transmitted disease-syndromes known in Dr. Hahnemann's day.

Allopathy disdains the miasmatic theory.

From an Allopathic standpoint, the risk of becoming infected—or infested—is the same for everybody. Allopathy also believes that microorganisms are the only cause of *each and every* infectious disease-syndrome.

In Homeopathy, instead, we consider that diseases only attack those who are vulnerable to them—unless, of course, the attack is so massive as to overwhelm even well-balanced patients. In this fashion, only patients with Psora will develop sundry disease-syndromes, either localized or generalized; only sycosics will develop localized gonorrhea, genital warts or related diseases; only syphilitics will develop syphilis and related diseases; only tuberculinics will develop the disease-syndrome tuberculosis, etc.

Probably the truth about the origin of infectious diseases lies somewhere in between the Allopathic and the Homeopathic perspectives.

Indeed, the *external* causative agents of infectious disease-syndromes are microorganisms, each of which tends to produce identifiable changes in their hosts.
There is ample and undeniable experimental evidence in this regard.

Yet, it is equally true, and also endorsed by abundant Clinical experience, that not all who engage in unprotected sexual intercourse develop a sexually transmitted disease.
This is so because, in order to become infected or infested, the patient must have the miasma/s Sycosis and/or Syphilis.
Individuals who lack these miasmas will not develop sexually transmitted diseases, even after unprotected sexual contact—or, at worse, their diseases will remain localized.

In other words, sexually transmitted disease-syndromes become evident *only if*

- the patient suffers from the chronic miasmas Sycosis and/or Syphilis, and
- the microorganisms involved in the clinical manifestation of those disease-syndromes are present.

Dr. Hahnemann, in the Chapters devoted to Sycosis and Syphilis in his *"Treatise of Chronic Diseases"*, describes the evolution of sexually transmitted diseases that follows the "impure coition" that brought them about.

In patients who are psoric to start with, sexually transmitted disease-syndromes rapidly become *generalized.*
But in patients who are a-psorics, or in whom Psora is latent, those disease-syndromes will tend to remain *localized.*

If a *localized* sexually transmitted disease receives a *local treatment* only, then the patient so treated will develop the chronic miasma *Pseudopsora.*

Pseudo-psora will transform these *local* diseases into *generalized* ones. What's worse, this miasma is extremely difficult to eradicate.

Nowadays, only genital warts are still treated locally, that is, in the same barbarous fashion as in Dr. Hahnemann's days.

Most other sexually transmitted diseases are treated *systemically* with antibiotics and/or other drugs. Systemic treatment may not produce Pseudopsora because it is not local, and also because it is aimed exclusively at microorganisms.

However, antibiotics either cannot avoid, or else may produce Pseudopsora while treating the disease-syndrome gonorrhea; a phenomenon that will be described in the following Chapter.

Pseudo-psora superficially resembles the phenomenon called *suppression.*

Both pseudo-psora and suppressions come as the consequence of injudicious local treatments. Both play havoc with the patient. And both produce a disease far more profound and serious than that treated locally.

But similarities end here, while differences are profound.

Allow me to recall three of the main differences

- A *suppression* happens in patients with manifest Psora; whereas *Pseudo-psora* happens in sycosic and/or syphilitic patients in whom their sexually transmitted disease-syndromes remained circumscribed until treated locally.
- A *suppression* happens when the injudiciously treated diseasesyndrome originates from, or complicates, patients with Psora; while *Pseudo-psora* happens when the ill-treated disease-syndrome arises from the miasmas Sycosis and Syphilis.
- A suppression happens when a *psoric* patient's disease-syndrome— usually not sexually transmitted—is treated locally. Pseudo-psora appears when a localized sexually transmitted disease-syndrome, arising in patients afflicted with the miasmas *Sycosis* and *Syphilis,* is treated locally.

I don't know if the miasmas Sycosis and Syphilis appear in patients who are previously psoric or not.

With Homeopathic remedies, the chronic miasmas Sycosis and Syphilis can be made to disappear.

With the judicious *systemic* use of antibiotics, microorganisms other than viruses can be destroyed.

The judicious use of Homeopathy + antibiotic treatment will therefore be able to control most sexually transmitted disease-syndromes brought about by non-viral microorganisms.

In the case of viral sexually transmitted disease-syndromes such as genital warts, however, *only the use of Homeopathic remedies will bring about success.*

Conversely, local treatments will bring about the disaster called Pseudo-psora.

As mentioned before, sexually transmitted disease-syndromes, in patients without active Psora, tend to remain localized.

If sexually transmitted disease-syndromes in these patients are treated *locally*, then those disease-syndromes become generalized. This happens because of the appearance of Pseudo-psora.

Under the influence of Pseudo-psora the now generalized sexually transmitted disease, like a destructive flow, will turn against the patient and devastate everything in its path—even in patients apparently "cured" by the local treatment.

Psora usually damages the patient in a subtle fashion along many years.

Pseudo-psora may produce the same devastation—or worse—in a much shorter period of time, and in a much more thorough fashion.

Chapter 22

HOMEOPATHIC AND ALLOPATHIC TREATMENTS OF GONORRHEA, GENITAL WARTS AND SYPHILIS.

The term *gonorrhea* was first coined by Galen (130-200 AD) From Greek *gono*, semen, and *rhein*, to flow. Galen considered that gonorrhea was the flow of *abnormal* semen.

The term *syphilis* was coined by the Neapolitan Physician and poet Girolamo Fracastoro (1483-1553). In 1530, Fracastoro—also known as Fracastorious—wrote the poem *"Syphilis sive morbus gallicus"*, in which the disease-syndrome syphilis, as known today, is described for the first time. In Fracastoro's poem, the shepherd Syphilus (from Greek, *siphlos*, meaning maimed) dares to insult Apollo. The god, enraged, responds by afflicting Syphilus' genitalia with the *morbus gallicus*. Note that *morbus gallicus* means French illness. The French retributed in kind by re-naming syphilis *mal Napolitain*, or Neapolitan illness.

These diseases have been with us for a very long time. Regarding syphilis, the prevalent opinion is that Spanish sailors who had sexual intercourse with native women brought the disease to Europe. Díaz de Isla, a Catalonian Physician, stated in 1493 that, when asked, natives said that the *gallicus* had been afflicting them since time immemorial. Also see *Numbers* 25.

The ENVIRONMENTAL causal agent of the disease-syndrome gonorrhea is a bacterium called *Neisseria gonorrhœa*.

The ENVIRONMENTAL causal agent of the disease syndrome syphilis is a corkscrew-like microorganism called *Treponema pallidum*.

The ENVIRONMENTAL causal agents of genital warts, also known as condyloma acuminata, are the *Human papillomata viruses type 1, 2, 6, 11, 16 and 18*.

The INTERNAL causes of these sexually transmitted disease-syndromes are two very specific chronic miasmas, Sycosis and Syphilis.

These chronic miasmas allow the bacteria Neisseriæ, and/or Treponemata, and/or the Human papillomata viruses to enter into a patient's organism, to colonize and flourish there, and to produce clinical evidence of the disease-syndromes gonorrhea, syphilis and/or genital warts—localized at first in patients with latent Psora, but generalized to start with in Psorics and Pseudo-psorics.

Conversely, in the absence of the chronic miasmas Sycosis and Syphilis, neither microorganism will be able to invade the patient's organism even if present, and far less to colonize there; even after repeated unprotected sexual exposure.

Please remember the anecdote involving one of my Professors and the shantytown construction workers described toward the end of Chapter 5 *"The Chronic Miasmas"* in this context.

The chronic miasma *Sycosis*—the miasma of *aggrandizement*—is responsible for the imbalance that allows gonorrhea, genital warts and probably other disease-syndromes of the same ilk to become manifest in a patient's organism.

Syphilis—the miasma of *destruction*—in turn, is responsible for the imbalance that allows the disease-syndrome syphilis to become manifest, and also perhaps other similarly destructive ones.

From an Allopathic standpoint, the disease-syndromes gonorrhea and syphilis are considered to be caused by bacteria, that are sensitive to antibiotics systematically administered (i.e., by mouth, injections, etc.).

This happens because the causative microorganisms of these disease-syndromes can be killed by antibiotics. In turn, this is so because these bacteria have some structures, vital for their survival, that interact with the molecules antibiotics are made of.

Therefore, antibiotics are the mainstay Allopathic treatment for the sexually transmitted disease-syndromes gonorrhea and syphilis.

The disease-syndrome genital warts, on the other hand, is brought about by *viruses.*

Viruses are not sensitive to antibiotics. Viruses lodge *inside* cells; and live, thrive and clone themselves there. Antibiotics cannot enter into cells. To boot, most viruses have no molecules in their structures capable of interacting with antibiotics. The few strains of viruses sensitive to antibiotics can be killed only during the brief period of time they remain in the blood, in their sojourn to the cells.

Therefore, the Allopathic treatment for virus-induced sexually transmitted diseases continues to be

Due to the fact that it is only local, the current Allopathic treatment of genital warts is *injudicious, dangerous and creator of Pseudo-psora.*

The Allopathic treatment of the disease-syndrome syphilis remained local—and therefore creator of Pseudo-psora—until the

appearance of the first organo-metallic compounds, early last Century. These compounds were administered into the vein, and therefore systemically.

The Allopathic treatment of the disease-syndrome gonorrhea remained local—and therefore creator of Pseudo-psora—until the appearance of antibiotics in the 1940's.

The Allopathic treatment of the disease-syndrome genital warts remains local—and therefore creator of Pseudo-psora—to this day.

Inevitably, I must start by discussing the systemic administration of antibiotics, because antibiotics are the main Allopathic pillar in the treatment of most bacterial sexually transmitted diseases.

I will also discuss Pseudo-psora, the Sycosic and Syphilitic equivalent of the Psoric suppressions. There are people out there who believe that everything Allopathic is, per definition, suppressive. This is certainly not the case nowadays.

Pseudo-psora, as explained in Chapter 21, is the consequence of any local form of treatment that, when administered to sycosic or syphilitic patients who are have latent Psora, frequently bring about the generalization of their gonorrhea, genital warts, syphilis and probably also of many other sexually transmitted diseases.

The question now is, can systemically administered antibiotics produce Pseudo-psora when used to treat sexually transmitted disease-syndromes?

The answer is no, perhaps with some reservations that will be explained below, when discussing the treatment of gonorrhea.

The so-called *Herzheimer effect*, sometimes seen in the treatment of the disease-syndrome syphilis, is caused by the massive destruction of treponemata by Penicillin, and is manifested as a very serious aggravation or exacerbation of the symptoms of the disease-syndrome.

By extension, we call Herzheimer effect any reaction in which members of any bacterial strains are destroyed suddenly and in massive amounts. These ill effects may indeed become a nuisance or a hindrance, and may be even dangerous. They may slow the patient's swing towards health. But in no way can they be construed to be a suppression or a manifestation of Pseudo-psora.

The effect on antibiotics on *Neisseriæ* and *Treponemata*—the bacteria associated with the disease-syndromes gonorrhea and syphilis—far from being originator of Pseudo-psora, becomes a very important *factor leading towards the patient's health.*

However, let us always keep in mind that, although these very effective and powerful drugs *can indeed destroy the microorganisms causative of gonorrhea and syphilis,* **they cannot in any way alter or modify the miasmas that allowed those microorganisms to colonize and proliferate in the first place.**

> *Antibiotics, though extraordinarily effective to destroy the microorganisms that bring about clinical evidence of the disease-syndromes gonorrhea and syphilis, can do absolutely nothing to treat the patient's chronic miasmas.*
>
> *Thus, gonorrheic or syphilitic patients cured with antibiotics will be at constant risk of becoming ill again and again, until their chronic miasmas Sycosis and/or Syphilis are brought under control with adequate Homeopathic treatment.*
>
> *Homeopathy is the only form of treatment, either Allopathic or Wholistic, capable of eliminating chronic miasmas.*

Patients Allopathically cured of their sexually transmitted disease-syndrome/s are at risk of falling ill again with the same disease-syndromes. This is so because antibiotics are prepared and administered with the purpose of annihilating microorganisms, but *not of aiding patients gain balance.*

The chink in those patients' armors (or their susceptibility to these diseases, consequence of their chronic miasmas) closes only after the patient has regained balance. It will remain wide open despite any successful antibiotic treatment. Every time a *treponema,* or a *gonococcus,* or a *human papillomata virus* comes in contact with these patients, and finds the chink wide open, it will enter and produce its characteristic disease-syndrome all over again.

The only therapeutic approach capable of curing the Wholeness of sycosic and syphilitic patients—and not only their disease-syndromes—that is, of closing the chink in their armor through bringing these patients into balance, is still Homeopathy.

Furthermore, a Homeopathic treatment has also a *preventive* capacity. The chink in the patient's armor closes after a successful treatment. New batches of bacteria or viruses will find nowhere to enter. Consequently, chances are that these patients will not fall sick, even if again in contact with the microorganisms causative of these diseases.

In Dr. Hahnemann's day, the only identified sexually transmitted disease-syndromes were gonorrhea, syphilis and genital warts.

In this Chapter, I will limit myself to a brief description of the treatment of these diseases, as I interpret Dr. Hahnemann's thoughts and conclusions in the light of important modern Allopathic discoveries.

Genital warts are called this way because they resemble the warts that may appear elsewhere in the body.

As mentioned above, *gonorrhea* means discharge of semen, and it is usually manifested by a characteristic discharge from the urethra or the vagina, at least in its earliest stages.

The disease-syndrome *syphilis* is first manifested by a chancre, so called because of its similarity with a cancerous lesion. It is accompanied by an enlarged lymph node nearby (Cockburn, W (1669-1739) *"The symptoms, nature, cause and cure of gonorrhea" London, 1713)*. These lesions may disappear even without treatment. A long silent period ensues. It may last years. The only evidence of disease in this stage tends to be non-specific, skin rashes, episodes of unexplained fever, etc. Finally, in the third stage, syphilis becomes manifest by destructive lesions in the heart, great vessels and the central nervous system.

Needless to say, Allopathic treatments for sexually transmitted disease-syndromes, in Dr. Hahnemann's day, and for the next 120 years or so, can only be qualified as atrocious.

All treatments were *localized* in the genital area, with some frightening exceptions.

One such exception was in the treatment of syphilis. The patient's underwear was spread with a mercurial ointment—*calomel*, if my memory serves me correctly. The patient would be requested to don that underwear. He or she would then be led to a steam bath. Heat would facilitate the absorption of the greatest possible amount of mercury. This form of treatment was rapidly abandoned because mercury would indeed eliminate symptoms of clinical syphilis, but also destroy the patients' kidneys.

Many patients so treated—or rather, so horribly mishandled—would die several days later of kidney failure. Those lucky enough to save their kidneys would survive as chronically intoxicated mercury patients. This intoxication would become manifest as insanity, swelling of the gums, horribly painful ulcers in mouth and gums, loosening of teeth, etc.

After this mishap, mercury continued to be used, though locally, and only *after* the patient had taken a bath; thus assuring a more modest absorption of the metal. Treatment would often be rounded up with *Zittman tea,* rich in mercury. This poisonous tea had to be taken to the tune of no less than one pint twice daily.

Other favorite forms of treatment—or shall I say *mistreatment*—were the cauterization of the syphilitic chancre with caustics, hot irons, etc.

Systemic treatment of the disease-syndrome syphilis started early this Century, with the discovery of the first organo-metallic drugs or compounds; that is, compounds in which metals are united to an organic chemical structure. These compounds will be forever associated to the name of the great German Pharmacology researcher Dr. Paul Ehrlich (1854-1915), the first to synthesized them.

Dr. Ehrlich also coined the term "Chemotherapy" to design the destruction of a disease while sparing the patient. This Allopathic ideal, so deceptively close up to the 1980's, is dimming as more and more bacterial strains become resistant to antibiotics. Newer drugs, always a short step ahead of bacterial resistance, are considerably more expensive, have more side effects and toxicity and often considerably less clinical efficacy. With the exception of antibiotics, nothing even remotely close to the Chemotherapeutic ideal has been ever synthesized for the treatment of diseases.

The organo-metallic compounds were administered into the syphilitic patients' veins. Treatments lasted many years, even the whole remaining lifetime of the patient. Intravenous administration was very uncomfortable and often dangerous. The first metal used in these compounds was mercury, giving rise the caustic aphorism "one night with Venus, one lifetime with Mercury". The second metal incorporated into organic compounds was arsenic. Neither compound could completely eradicate the bacteria, even when treatment started in early stages of the disease. However, the biggest merit of these preparations is that they became the *finale* of local Allopathic treatments of syphilis.

Finally, Allopathic Medical Research proffered us the blessing called Penicillin. *Treponemata,* thank God, still remains sensitive to this antibiotic.

If gonorrhea is left untreated in sycosic males who have latent psora, the disease is likely to remain local. In those with manifest Psora or with Pseudo-psora, however, *Neisseriæ* will proliferate and eventually invade the prostate and testicles and, later on, joints and other more distant structures.

For gonorrhea, things started rolling in earnest as soon as it was discovered that the male urethra, that is, the tube that connects the urinary bladder to the outside, has a lot of redundant lining to provide for the stretching that occurs during erection. In order to accommodate all that redundancy, the urethra is full of microscopic creases when the penis is flaccid. Some of these creases are superficial, while other are deeper crevice- and rift-like structures.

Neisseriæ, the microorganisms responsible for gonorrhea, use these crevices to lodge and reproduce. The patient responds with uretheral inflammation that brings about pain and discomfort, plus the production of a characteristic and often painful discharge.

Doctors found many imaginative forms to treat gonorrhea locally. The one I am about to describe, probably the most sadistic and bizarre of them all, was described to me by an acquaintance much older than I, a man who happened to be one of its victims. This man became ill with gonorrhea, and was treated, in the early 1930's. In the city of Buenos Aires, Argentina, treatment was carried out at the *Asistencia Pública,* a long since torn down municipal Walk In of sorts. It occupied a full downtown city block.

Allopathic Doctors reasoned that, by means of flattening the uretheral mucosa, they could gain access to the crevices where *Neisseriæ* grew undisturbed. Once exposed, bacteria could be killed with a strong antiseptic. The patient would thus be cured—but only if the disease was caught in time; that is, before it invaded the patient's prostate and other organs.

A series of rigid curved metallic catheters became admirably suited for the purpose of dilating the urethra, and consequently of flattening the uretheral lining. These metallic catheters were originally devised to distend urethras narrowed by scar tissue—being that scarry tissue usually the consequence of gonorrhea. The artifacts were introduced into the male urethra at the tip of the patient's penis, and then all the way up into his bladder. Doctors would use progressively thicker and thicker metallic catheters for this purpose. The last one of the series was hollow and thicker than the little finger. Through this largest catheter, a fairly concentrated solution of silver nitrate was injected into the patient's bladder to overflowing. The catheter was then removed. My acquaintance told me that the introduction of progressively thicker and thicker metallic catheters was very painful, but that the pain at the time of voiding the silver nitrate solution was excruciating. The whole uretheral lining would be expelled a few days later with the patients' urine as a long, transparent tube. This acquaintance of mine swore to me that the screams of the gonorrheic patients under treatment could be heard blocks away.

This treatment was useless in women. In them, and unlike what happens in males, the urinary and the genital tracts end separately. In males both tracts end together at the tip of the penis, and remain together all the way up to just underneath the urinary bladder. In women, the uretheral and the vaginal outlets open separately in the vulva. *Neisseriæ,* being usually transmitted by coition, are discharged deep into the vagina. Consequently, there is no point in treating this type of infection with uretheral catheters. In sycosic women, or in those with latent Psora, *Neisseræ* likely remains in the vagina. In those who are psoric or pseudo-psoric, however, *Neisseriæ* propagates to the womb and from there into the Fallopian tubes and the abdominal cavity, articular joints and other distant structures. Feminine gonorrhea could not be treated in the old days. Silver nitrate or sodium permanganate douches were seldom useful, even if performed when the disease was its earliest stages.

Prognosis was ominous for women. First the painless, painful, itching and/or burning discharge and inflammation within and around the vagina. Then sterility, a chronic pelvic infection and finally perhaps peritonitis or formation or spilling of pus, or of bacterially contaminated material, into the abdominal cavity. Finally, inflammation of the joints and invalidity—oh, yes, plus blindness of their offspring, too; since *Neisseriæ* would infect babies eyes during birth and destroy their sight.

It is important to emphasize that the treatment of gonorrhea remained local until the early 1940's; that is, until the advent of the antibiotic era.

Genital warts are still treated locally by Allopathic Physicians.

Diverse hot, caustic and poisonous substances have been and are still used in a fruitless attempt to make warts disappear.

Therapeutic success has been always illusory. Warts may indeed disappear under Allopathic local treatment, but will unfailingly come back—with Pseudo-psora as an added bonus.

Nowadays, genital warts are still treated in the same brutal and dangerous fashion as in Dr. Hahnemann's day. Local poisons and caustics remain in use. Hot irons, however, have been replaced by more sophisticated forms of burning, such as electrocauterization and laser- and cryosurgery.

Some new systemic antiviral antibiotics, with a cost inversely proportional to their effectiveness, have been added to the current—and for the most part useless—therapeutic menu of horrors.

Therapeutic results of local treatments of genital warts are no different now than those obtained two or three hundred years ago.

Dr. Hahnemann, and every conscientious Homeopathic Physician after him, have always been dead against all forms of local treatments of sexually transmitted diseases.

All the more because those diseases are derived from the chronic miasmas Sycosis and Syphilis that, as mentioned above, seem to be only capable of producing *localized* disease-syndromes in patients who are not manifestly psoric or pseudo-psoric.

If local treatments are applied to early manifestations of these disease-syndromes, one runs the risk of transforming relatively manageable chronic miasmas, and their corresponding disease-syndromes, into a new and almost unmanageable monster that is *Pseudo-psora*.

Two hundred years experience have shown that Homeopathic remedies are indeed efficacious to treat sexually transmitted diseases.

Two hundred years of clinical observation have also shown how dangerous it is to subject sexually transmitted diseases to *local* treatments.

On the other hand, some forty years of Clinical observation have also demonstrated how useful antibiotics can be to destroy bacteria associated with these diseases.

Shouldn't we then consider the association of Homeopathy + antibiotics as the treatment of sexually transmitted diseases caused by bacteria?

Like everything else in Medicine, we must first study the equation benefit/risk for each treatment or combination thereof.

Sexually transmitted diseases are extremely serious. They can affect the lives, and the quality of life, of several people: the sick person, his or her sexual partner/s and his or her descendants.

Since Medicine is not an exact science, we cannot affirm that any individual form of treatment will cure 100% of all patients. For diseases of such a serious nature, therefore, it is advisable to use as many *systemic* forms of treatment as possible—the equation benefit/risk permitting—so as to approach that elusive 100 % as much as possible.

The equation benefit/risk of Homeopathic remedies is all benefit and no risk. That of antibiotics, when properly used, is mostly benefit and very little risk. Furthermore, there is no possibility of mutual interference between antibiotic and Homeopathic treatment. This is so because antibiotics work on bacteria, and Homeopathic remedies on the patient's imbalance caused by a chronic miasma.

Therefore, the ideal therapeutic plan in bacterial sexually transmitted diseases would be to combine systemic antibiotics (capable of destroying microorganisms) with Homeopathic remedies (capable of extinguishing the patient's chronic miasma *and* the disease) and so obtain the maximum of therapeutic effectiveness. Even if at the cost of *minimal* Allopathic side effect and toxicity.

Or else to use *Homeopathic treatment exclusively,* in the instance of infectious diseases of any kind, sexually transmitted or otherwise, *for which Allopathy has nothing but local treatments to offer*—as it still happens to be the case in the instance of genital warts.

HOMEOPATHIC AND ALLOPATHIC TREATMENT OF THE DISEASE-SYNDROME SYPHILIS.

In his *Treatise of Chronic Diseases*, in the Chapter entitled *Syphilis*, and in the section devoted to the *Cure of Chronic Diseases*, Dr. Hahnemann recommends the use of *Mercurius* 30 CH, as the only treatment of both the chronic miasma and the uncomplicated disease-syndrome syphilis.

Problem is, untreated syphilis is frequently complicated by manifest Psora, which means that the disease will rapidly become generalized. As Dr. Hahnemann put it "When a physician must treat an inveterate case of syphilis (i.e., that does not respond to *Mercurius* treatment. Parenthesis mine), he will frequently see that the disease is complicated by Psora, because this latter miasma is the most usual and fundamental cause of chronic diseases" (*Organon,* 6th. Edition, § 206).

Mercurius is to be administered only once, and then watch results.

It can be administered up to two more times, if the chancre and its satellite lymph node (called *bubo* in texts of Dr. Hahnemann's days) do not disappear.

The period of observation is bound to be much shorter when the patient is receiving Penicillin, the antibiotic of choice; and to which the *Treponema pallidum,* thank Goodness, is still quite sensitive.

As far as I can tell, treatment of syphilis with Penicillin alone does not produce any form of Pseudo-psora.

There is really no sound reason why Homeopathically prepared quicksilver should not be added to an antibiotic treatment with Penicillin in syphilitic patients; thus destroying *Treponemata* while, at the same time, treating the chronic miasma from which the disease-syndrome arises.

Mercurius—that is, Homeopathically prepared mercury—has absolutely no side effects and no toxicity.

Modern treatment of the disease-syndrome syphilis, therefore, should be carried out by means of associating *Mercurius* and Penicillin.

And, since there is no way of assessing whether or not the patient's Syphilitic miasma is complicated or not by Psora—because Penicillin treatment rapidly erases all clinical manifestation of the disease—the combined treatment *Mercurius*/Penicillin should be complemented by the administration of the patient's Constitutional remedy.

HOMEOPATHIC AND ALLOPATHIC TREATMENT OF SYCOSIC SEXUALLY TRANSMITTED DISEASES.

According to Dr. Hahnemann, in his *Treatise of Chronic Diseases*, the miasma Sycosis is manifested by two distinct disease-syndromes: *gonorrhea,* and *genital warts*—the latter also known as *"figwart disease"* in Dr. Hahnemann's days.

Gonorrhea, genital warts and syphilis were considered to be manifestations of the same disease by the Physicians or yore.

Homeopathic and Allopathic Treatment of Gonorrhea

Dr. Hahnemann advocated the use of *Thuja occidentalis* and of *Nitricum acidum* for the treatment of this disease-syndrome.

It's worth recalling how Dr. Hahnemann found the usefulness of *Thuja*. Once a seminarian, tremendously perturbed, went to see Dr. Hahnemann. He stated he had the urethral secretion characteristic of gonorrhea, but denied having had any kind of "impure contact". Through the patient's Clinical History, Dr. Hahnemann learnt that, while studying, this seminarian would amble about a garden where Arbor Vitæ, or *Thuja Occidentalis*, grew in profusion. Dr. Hahnemann also found out that, while strolling thus, this seminarian would pluck out a twig and absently chew on it. So Dr. Hahnemann obtained samples of Arbor Vitæ, prepared them Homeopathically, and proved them. Sure enough, amongst other changes, the provers found the appearance of a secretion similar to that found in gonorrhea in their genitalia.

According to Dr. Hahnemann, gonorrhea can be cured completely with *Thuja* and *Nitricum acidum*.

Treatment should be started with one single dose of *Thuja* 30 CH; and, when its action becomes exhausted after fifteen to forty days, administer one single dose of *Nitricum acidum* 30 CH.

The latter must be allowed to act as long a time as *Thuja* (Hahnemann, S. Chapter on *Sycosis*, Section on *Cure of Chronic Diseases*, in his *"Treatise of Chronic Diseases"*).

Nowadays there are extremely useful antibiotics to destroy the *Neisseriæ* that produces the disease-syndrome gonorrhea. Antibiotics are also useful against different sensitive microorganisms that give rise to sexually transmitted disease-syndromes of sycosic origin, such as *Chlamydia* and others.

Here again, there is no conceivable reason why antibiotics should not be complemented with Homeopathic *Thuya* and *Nitric acidum*, in patients afflicted by these disease-syndromes.

All the more because antibiotic-treated gonorrhea has been found to give rise to sterile gonococcal arthritis. A certain percentage of patients with gonorrhea, after having received an otherwise satisfactory course or courses of antibiotic treatment, complaint of painful swelling of one or more large joints after their genital symptoms have disappeared. Fluid obtained from those joints is free of bacteria (thus *sterile* gonococcal arthritis). This articular problem could very well be a manifestation of *Pseudo-psora* in patients deprived of Homeopathic treatment.

Therefore, if in the treatment of the disease-syndrome syphilis it is *convenient* to associate Homeopathy with antibiotics, in gonorrhea such a therapeutic association should become *obligatory,* because of the real risk of Pseudo-psoric articular disease in gonorrhea-bearing patients treated with antibiotics only.

Homeopathic and Allopathic Treatment of Genital Warts

Dr. Hahnemann recommended exactly the same therapeutic plan for genital warts as he did for gonorrhea; that is, *Thuja occidentalis* followed by *Nitricum acidum,* if treatment with the latter becomes necessary. Both remedies are to be administered by mouth, in a potency of 30 CH.

For genital warts resistant to the action of *Thuja* and *Nitricum acidum*, Dr. Hahnemann recommended the LOCAL use, on the genital warts, of freshly obtained, pure juice of *Thuja occidentalis*, or Arbor Vitæ. Pure juice obtained from fresh *Thuja* leaves is to be mixed with an equal volume of ethanol. Warts are to be wetted with this mixture. Afterwards, treated wart/s should be covered with a clean, dry lint dressing.

As mentioned above, antibiotics don't work on viral sexually transmitted diseases.

We are dealing with viruses in genital warts, not with bacteria. Antibiotics are totally useless in the treatment of most viral infestations, including genital warts.

Deprived of the use of antibiotics, Allopathy can only proffer local treatments for genital warts.

And these *démodé* therapeutic atrocities only bring about extremely limited and short-term benefits that must be outweighed against the risks of an almost inevitable local recurrence, plus the creation of Pseudo-psora.

Genital warts-bearing patients, treated locally, constitute the majority of the Pseudo-psoric patients I see in my practice. This is so because most genital warts-bearing patients go to an Urologist or a Gynecologist as their first choice. These Allopathic Doctors, totally ignorant of Homeopathy and Pseudo-psora, mistreat these poor patients with local caustics and cauterizations.

Unlike what happens in syphilis and in gonorrhea, there is no way for Homeopathy to complement Allopathy here.

Brutal local cauterizations and Homeopathic treatments are totally incompatible. It is as absurd to imagine that one can treat genital warts-bearing patients with local cauterizations + Homeopathic treatment as it is to attempt to treat Sycosis while creating Pseudo-psora.

Homeopathy should therefore be the only treatment of genital warts. To put it differently, *Homeopathic treatment should **replace** local applications in every genital warts-bearing patient*—and Allopathic local treatments should only be used as a very distant second choice, only if and when Homeopathic treatments fail.

As mentioned in the Chapter devoted to Pseudo-psora above, the treatment of pseudo-psoric patients is an extremely difficult, confusing, slow and frustrating enterprise. It often ends in failure.

The sad irony here is that Pseudo-psora would not appear if patients suffering from gonorrhea could receive antibiotics + Homeopathy; and if those afflicted with genital warts were to receive Homeopathic treatment only.

To sum up,

In the treatment of patients bearing the sexually transmitted disease-syndrome syphilis it would be very convenient to associate Homeopathy to the current Allopathic antibiotic treatment.

In the instance of patients bearing gonorrhea—and probably also in other sycosic sexually transmitted diseases of the same ilk—Homeopathic and Allopathic antibiotic treatments should complement each other.
This is so because there is a very real possibility of initiating Pseudo-psora if the disease-syndrome gonorrhea is treated with antibiotics only.

There should be *no* Allopathic, nor any combined Allopathic-Homeopathic treatments for genital warts.
Only Homeopathic treatment should be performed here.

In the treatment of sycosic diseases, Homeopathy should be administered according to Dr. Hahnemann's guidelines; that is, *Thuja* and *Nitric acid* by mouth in the case of genital warts and of gonorrhea and related diseases.
Associated with systemic Allopathic antibiotic treatment in the treatment of gonorrhea and associated bacterial disease-syndromes.

And, if the oral treatment with *Thuja* and *Nitric acid* does not suffice to cure genital warts, then the local application of freshly obtained juice of the leaves of Arbor Vitae mixed with ethanol in equal parts.
*But absolutely no Allopathic **localized** treatment whatsoever.*

Chapter 23

REGARDING RESEARCH

To research is actually to re-search; that is, to search several times. This is so because, as Thomas Edison so brilliantly put it, Research in 5 % inspiration and 95 % perspiration.

REGARDING PARADIGMS

This term defines, in scientific parlance, the enclosed area within which a worker can safely wonder about.

It is a virtual area, of course, since it exists only in the mind—or, rather, in the network of minds that choose to believe in the existence and validity of a particular paradigm.

It is also a hereditary thing, because it is transmitted from master to disciple.

Finally, it is a thing of Faith, for it is based on the firm belief that only within that paradigm will workers find adequate rewards for their toils.

The enclosure of a Paradigm, then, is virtual, hereditary and based on Faith.

For scientists other than Medical, a Paradigm is an area whose boundaries may be freely crossed if there is something particularly attractive beyond.

Take the Aeronautical paradigm, for instance. It is so successful that it has promoted progress in every kind of flying machine, all the way from space rockets to helicopters. There is an exception in that paradigm, though. It concerns bumblebees. These insects are not supposed to fly, according to the aeronautical paradigm.

Consequently, several aeronautical engineers, not only took notice of this fact, but also started actively to study the flight of bumblebees in order to learn how it happens. With the full consent and interest of their peers.

Things are different in Medical Research, alas!

Here, the limits of the Paradigm can be compared to the invisible fence one places around one's property to keep the dog in. The dog feels a nasty shock on his or her neck when approaching the invisible fence, and so becomes trained to stay away from it—all the more because to remain within the area delimited by the fence is pleasant and rewarding. In a similar fashion, Medical Research workers feel a nasty shock in his or her mind when approaching the limits of the Paradigmatic enclosure, and so becomes trained to stay away from the perimeter. To remain within, on the other hand, brings about a rewarding sense of camaraderie, status, frequently a satisfactory standard of living and in some instances even renown.

For Medical Researchers, their Paradigmatic area is considered to be the abode of Truth and a cornucopia of bliss and security for all insiders. It is also supposed and expected to be a great source of envy for those who have been left outside. It is the Garden of Eden where everybody can work, earn good money, obtain acceptable results and bask in the glory of plaudits, respect and recognition of other believers in the validity of that Paradigm; be those recognizers and applauders insiders or else members of the populace at large. There may be a pecking order within the paradigm, it may be based on everything but creativity and originality, there may also be unfair competitiveness and envy, misappropriations and jostling here and there—plus unbounded practice of the *droit du Seigneur* on the part the elders and the higher ups—but that is something that comes with the territory and that must be put up with.

Beyond this Nirvana of Wisdom, in the netherworld where *Lumpen* and renegade Doctors intermingle, there is wildness, howling and gnashing of teeth. The lumpen anxiously awaiting the Researchers' Panacea that will make one and all hale, happy and immortal. While the renegade Doctors—those ferine heretics—incomprehensibly remain skeptical regarding the Researchers' results, and insist in preferring the wilderness to the coziness of the Paradigm.

It is wise, for the blissful dwellers of the Paradigm, to leave the renegades alone. Apostates are a nuisance and a burden. It is licit to send a quackbuster expedition against them every now and then, if only to keep in check their numbers, the results of their crazy studies and their loud and obscene garrulousness.

Of course, when repentant, these defectors automatically become lost sheep and, as such, are welcome back into the fold—but only if and when they have not offended insiders, if they abjure their wicked ideas, leave their depraved proclivities behind, agree to start at the bottom of the ladder and heartily accept the mores, pecking order, *droit du Seigneur,* etc. prevailing within the boundaries of the sacred Paradigm.

There are several paradigms within the Healing Arts. I am going to mention only three here.

The major, wealthiest and most powerful of the three is the Allopathic paradigm. It is heavily scientifizised, has very clear and meticulously drawn limits and a punctilious pecking order.

Homeopathy has also its Paradigm.

It became so extreme that, one Century ago, it tore Homeopathy asunder into low potency and high potency prescribers—that, as Allopathy was massing up its resources and getting ready to strike.

The Homeopathic paradigm is much looser nowadays because modern Homeopathic Physicians tend to be less cohesive and more tolerant amongst themselves than those of yore.

There is another group of Healers that, of late, is trying to find its place under the sun. They are the Integrative Physicians.

Integrative Physicians are familiar with Allopathy, Homeopathy and also other forms of caring for the sick. They ignore paradigms. This way, they can comfortably roam an area considerable larger than those of only Allopathy, Homeopathy or of any other form of Medicine—which ultimately means that Integrative Physicians have more tools at their disposal to choose from when it comes to assist those who suffer.

REGARDING IGNORANCE ABOUT DISEASES AND THE IMPORTANCE OF RESEARCH

Each and every form and manifestation of disease, and also of untimely death, is not caused by bacteria, or by cancer or whatever—it is only caused by *ignorance.*

The disease-syndrome cholera, for instance, was once feared.

Vybrio choleræ, its microbial agent, when colonizing into a patient, brings about violent, watery and profuse diarrhea, high fever, dehydration, weakness, terrible muscle cramps and pain and finally death to most of its victims.

Homeopathy became the first effective form of treatment for that disease Its efficacy brought about its acceptance in Great Britain, where at first it had faced bitter opposition. But it gained wide public support, as well as Royal favor after its undisputed success during London's cholera epidemic of 1854. Patients stricken with cholera during that epidemic were mainly treated at St. Bartholomew's, Middlesex and the Soho Hospitals. St. Bartholomew's and Middlesex Hospitals were Allopathic, while Soho was Homeopathic. Figures of mortality were as follows: St. Bartholomew's 32.6 %, Middlesex 53.25 %, Soho Homeopathic Hospital, 19%.

If before Homeopathy nothing could be done for cholera patients, and Homeopathy saved many, this simply means that all the suffering and death was not caused by the disease cholera, but rather by *ignorance* regarding how to treat it.

There was once a Medical Journal entirely devoted to the disease-syndrome syphilis in its many clinical manifestations. Syphilis was incurable then, a universal scourge; except for the few who chose to treat it Homeopathically. It was called "the great impersonator", because it would mimic so many other diseases on its way to death. And it was so common!

Syphilis became a rare disease when Penicillin was discovered. The Medical Journal devoted to syphilis had to close due to lack of contributions.

Let me illustrate how rare it had become with an anecdote. In 1955 I was in a Hospital in Buenos Aires, Argentina, studying some Clinical subject or other in my last year of Medicine. Word got around that, in the Outpatient Department, there was a man with a syphilitic chancre. All who could left whatever they were doing and rushed to see that rarity. Doctors, Nurses and students jostled each other to get a closer look. The patient was a jockey. I'll never forget that young, short, gaunt man; pants around his ankles, pulling back his foreskin and looking around bewildered at all the excitement. Everybody wanted to take a look at that chancre and to feel its characteristic rubbery consistency. Ten or more years before, syphilis was so prevalent that nobody would have bothered to look at a chancre twice.

Since the beginning of times, Penicillin has been produced by a mold called *Penicillum notatum*. This mold is present almost anywhere.

Allopathic Doctors simply didn't know of its usefulness.

Ignorance, then, and not syphilis was the cause of all that misery. And it is knowledge what brought about the cure of the disease—although not of the miasma syphilis from which the disease-syndrome syphilis arises in the first place.

In one single winter, in 19th Century Vienna, *one out of every three children* died of diphtheria.

Since 1953, when I first started snooping into Hospital wards, until the present time, I have never seen a single case of diphtheria, a phenomenon largely due to the efficacy of the vaccination. I had studied the disease but never had a chance to see its dirty, pearly gray membrane in any throat; nor, thank God, one single child languishing, suffocating and dying from it. I find it impossible to fathom the depth of the shock and suffering of those children's parents, who had to watch the agony of their children, and then bury them one by one after suffering from diseases they could do nothing to control.

Its bacterial agent, *Corynebacterium diphtheriæ*, is still around, alive and well. What has changed is our knowledge about how to prevent the disease.

As a side note, allow me to add that although important to *prevent* the disease, Allopathy is practically useless to *cure* it. Homeopathy is much more useful here thanks to remedies like *Lac caninum* and others.

Ignorance, then, and not diphtheria, was the cause of death of those and of so many poor children whose parents choose Allopathy to treat their children's disease—a horrible death preceded by suffocation, heart failure and exhaustion.

Many natural substances, all the way from arsenic and mercury to gold, to amber, to plant products, to animal poisons, to secretions were somewhere out there all the time.

Many were considered useless, others were feared as dangerous.

Until Dr. Hahnemann discovered their hidden therapeutic value, and brought it forth through trituration and succussion.

Again here, knowledge is what cures many and saves countless lives.

With the exception of diseases nowadays labeled as "incurable", all others have been brought under control thanks to Research.

In turn, "incurable" diseases will also become curable because of Research, i.e., when our ignorance in regards to them ceases, to be replaced by knowledge.

To sum up, it is *ignorance* what brings about diseases, and *knowledge* what brings about their cure and disappearance.

Research is the only known and proven way of bringing about knowledge in regards to diseases, how to control them and how to promote Health.

Disease enslave us to our *pathos* or *path;* that is, to our fate.

Ultimately, then, it is Research what makes us, more and more, free and masters of our own fate.

Within this context, it is Research what transforms us, from hostages of Nature into the Lords of Creation.

Disease-syndromes are considered to be incurable *when our knowledge about them is insufficient.*

Disease-syndromes become curable *when we known enough to bring them under control.*

The only Medically sound way of obtaining adequate knowledge about illness, that is, of making them curable, is through Research.

The first step towards knowledge is to recognize our ignorance and our limitations.

This awareness is the only thing that makes us humble enough to start asking questions.

In Allopathy, questions are addressed to disease-syndromes one question at a time. This is so because, in Allopathic Research, only one aspect of whatever is being researched can be studied at a time. In Homeopathic Research, on the other hand, and as we shall see a bit further down, *all* the questions are asked simultaneously and the Researchers receive, also simultaneously, the answer to *all* their questions.

Questions are designed by Researchers. They are couched in a language, and using a technique, that can be understood by the subject under study. In turn, the answer to each question is interpreted by the Researchers, and then adequately evaluated.

The methodology used to prepare each question, and the interpretation of the answer to that question, is known as an *Experimental Protocol* and also as an *Experimental design*. In turn, the development of that Experimental Protocol is known as an *Experiment* or a *Trial.*

Research is the aggregate of all designs, experiments and interpretation of results.

I would like to discuss *Therapeutic*[63] Research here; that is, Research concerned with treatments.

Therapeutic Research can be divided into *Pharmacological*[64] and *Homeopathic.*

In *Pharmacological Research,* the question is addressed to a pure chemical formula *(the drug)* and to the sub-cellular element with which that pure chemical formula interacts *(the receptor in a cell).*

Pharmacological Research usually starts with the manufacture of a chemical formula.

This chemical formula is supposed to act on a subcellular element of cells sick with a disease-syndrome under study. Unfortunately, cells of all

---

[63] From Greek, *therapeúin,* to attend, to treat medically.

[64] From Greek, *Pharmacos* or *Pharmakos,* drug.

organs and tissues, diseased or not, tend to share the same key subcellular elements.

The prepared chemical formula and the sub-cellular receptors are supposed to interact with each other in a lock-and-key fashion. The outcome of that interaction results on either stimulation or inhibition of the receptor—a sub-cellular element that, again, is present in cells of most or all organs, sick and healthy alike.

There are two forms of *Homeopathic Research.*

In the first form, called *Provings,* the question is addressed to a succussed *substance* or *product* and to a group of *healthy Whole Human Beings.* The question asked is how, and in what fashion, the balance of these healthy Whole Human Being is altered when challenged by daily administration of the same potency of a newly succussed substance or product.

In the second form of Homeopathic Research, the question is addressed to a *well-known Homeopathic remedy* and to a *disease-syndrome*—so far, because this form of Research is quite recent. The question asked is how that disease-syndrome responds to the administration of that well-known Homeopathic remedy. And frequently also, how that response compares with that obtained after the administration of Pharmaceutical drugs.

> *Simply put, Research consists in asking questions to Nature in a language Nature understands; and then listening and interpreting Nature's answer to those questions.*
> *If no coherent answer is received, the Researcher should ask again the same question, but phrased differently; that is, using a different Research Protocol.*

Since the subjects under study in Pharmacological Research and the Provings are so dissimilar (i.e., a subcellular element vs. a Whole Human Being), and since the challenges presented are also so different (i.e., a pure chemical formula vs. a succussed natural product), the questions to be asked must also be different.

The means Researchers use to ask, understand and interpret respective answers, will also have to be different.

Let me consider one example.

Pharmacological Research can address its question to, say, a β-blocker drug and to a β-receptor in a *rat's* heart, and then decode the answer to that question. Rat and human hearts have similar receptors for β-blockers. Consequently, results obtained in a rat's heart may be extrapolated to the same subcellular fraction, this time located in a *human* heart.

But in no way can Homeopathic Research extrapolate results found in a *whole* rat into a *Whole* Human Being.

Ignorance and illnesses are interchangeable concepts.
Knowledge and cure are interchangeable concepts, too.
Consequently a Penicillin pill, as well as a pellet impregnated with, say, Calcarea Carbonica, can be considered as a Penicillin pill or as a Calcarea impregnated pellet, but also as knowledge in the form of a pill or a pellet.

REGARDING SCIENTISTS AND EMPIRICISTS

Years ago there was a humble Medicine man in Northern Argentina. He had learnt from his elders how to treat a disease he called "sweet piss", and his elders from their elders for Heaven knows how many generations.

This Medicine man would ask his patients to urinate out in the open. Diagnosis was positive if the urine attracted flies. Treatment of this disease consisted in the administration of dry pork pancreas dissolved in a local 100% proof brandy. He would ask patients to swish a mouthful of his potion several times daily, and then to swallow it.

Local Doctors despised this illiterate Medicine man, as well as his crude and primitive treatment. They would say that this man's success was due to the alcohol present in the potion (Personal communication by Pharmacist Luis Outon, Buenos Aires, Argentina).

Drs. Banting and Best discovered insulin in the pancreas of dogs.

They won the 1923 Nobel Price because of their discovery.

In 1910 or thereabouts, in an important Bacteriological institute, please don't ask me to divulge where, a Bacteriologist sent a request to the Director.

In the request, this Bacteriologist asked the Director to please paint his Lab as soon as possible. There was dampness on one of the walls, and mildew grew in those damp areas. Molds would fall from the damp wall onto his cultures and inhibit bacterial growth. Mildew was interfering with this Scientist's experiments. Grapevine has it that the note has been carefully preserved.

In the early 1920's, Dr. Alexander Fleming found that, in some discarded culture plates previously covered by a thick layer of bacteria, there were circular areas that showed no growth. He set himself to find out why there was no bacterial growth. There was dampness in the wall of his lab, and mildew grew there. Instead of requesting a paint job, Dr. Fleming found a mold, that he later identified as *Penicillum Notatum,* both in the ruined cultures and in the damp areas of his lab's wall. Eventually he learnt that the mold secreted a substance he called Penicillin, and that it was this Penicillin what had killed the bacteria in his cultures. The rest is History.

In these two examples we find individuals who are rigidly within the Allopathic paradigmatic enclosure and others who aren't.

In the first example I chose to show an Allopathic Medical Society, and its response to a lay Practitioner in Northern Argentina. In the second example, a Bacteriologist who was a worshiper of the Allopathic paradigm.

Outside the Allopathic Paradigm I have placed a lay Practitioner and Dr. Fleming. The Medicine man out of the Paradigmatic enclosure all his life. Dr. Flemming, trained within the Paradigm, but daring enough to cross its limits.

Those within the Paradigmatic enclosure are the *Scientists.*

Those outsiders, or daredevil enough to challenge the enclosure of the Allopathic paradigm, are the *Empiricists.*

Scientists work *by stages* and *in depth* within the confines of the Paradigm. A good example of Scientists are Cancer Researchers. For the past 80 years or so they have been working in depth on the fields of Pharmacology, cellular and molecular biology, immunology, genetics and virology—all sanctioned by, and well within the limits of the Allopathic paradigm.

Empiricists work *by leaps.* They don't respect or recognize boundaries. Their leaps open entire new fields of Research and knowledge. Empiricists, then, increase the *area,* rather than the depth of knowledge. Empiricists are usually motivated either by curiosity, by their desire to help others, or else by both.

Scientists' work increases the *quantity* of what we already know.

Empiricists produce new knowledge *qualitatively different* from what we already know. They create entirely new Paradigms.

Both are needed in order to increase our knowledge.

HOMEOPATHIC RESEARCH

Please see Chapter 8 *"The Provings, and the Homeopathic remedies' mode of action".*

PHARMACOLOGICAL RESEARCH

A Pharmaceutical drug is a *pure chemical formula*, usually designed and manufactured with the intention of interacting with another well known chemical formula, present in a subcellular fraction of sick cells and micro-organisms. Sometimes, as in the instance of Penicillin, the drug is not manufactured but obtained directly from Nature, and then modified to make it more active, more soluble in water, etc.

Pharmacological Research is interested in learning what happens when a *Pharmaceutical drug* is made to interact with a *subcellular fraction* present in microorganisms or in diseased cells. The purpose of this interaction being the elimination of that microorganism or of a disease originating in those cells. The interaction of the drug and the subcellular fraction is supposedly done in a key-and-lock fashion.

When the drug and the sub-cellular fraction interact, the subcellular fraction is either stimulated or inhibited. The effect of the Pharmaceutical drug is the consequence of that stimulation or inhibition.

Studies in bacteria or cells in culture.

The first phase of this experimental quest is done on *bacterial* and/or on *mammalian cell cultures*. Cultures grow in sterile nutritious media, in tubes, bottles, plates and/or dishes. They are kept in incubators at a constant level of temperature and humidity. *Cell cultures* are carried out using *individual* and *independently growing* mammalian cells; *tissue cultures* use instead little clumps of mammalian tissues. Among the two, Researchers prefer cell cultures because they are much easier to grow and to maintain than clumps of whole tissues. *Bacterial cultures* are favored over cell cultures whenever possible. Bacteria are much sturdier and easier to grow than mammalian cells. Experiments using bacteria are also considerably cheaper than those using cell or tissue cultures.

The drug is introduced into the media where bacteria or mammalian cells thrive. Bacteria and cells are studied to learn how they respond to the administration of the drug, and why.

If results are encouraging or positive, the next step in the experimental chain is carried out using *animals.*

Studies in animals.

These studies are aimed at learning how useful the Pharmaceutical drug acts in live, mammalian multicellular organisms.

Whole animals are used in the stage; usually rodents and dogs. Sometimes monkeys.

Animals used in early stages are usually *rodents;* that is, mice or rats. These poor creatures are preferred because of several reasons, namely

- They are relatively small, and therefore occupy a proportionally reduced space. They consume little chow, due to their size. They are tidy creatures—unlike guinea pigs, that can be quite messy. Mice and rats are also easy to handle, once the Researcher has learnt how to avoid their teeth. Rodents can bite in a flash. Their bites are deep, and can make the bitten finger or hand hurt and bleed a lot.
- They start reproducing early (8 weeks old females can get pregnant), do so swiftly (only three weeks gestation period), and plentifully (an average 6 or more offspring per litter).
- Their life span is about two years, so several generations can be studied during relatively short periods of time.
- They can also be genetically manipulated by means of breeding brothers and sisters, until a genetically and consequently immunologically uniform progeny is obtained. This process, called *inbreeding*, greatly reduces the individual variation of each of the rodents used in an experiment. *Inbreeding* allows Researchers to carry out experiments with fewer rodents since, and due to genetic and thus immunological uniformity, there is little individual variation in the results.

Inbreeding cuts both ways, though.

As we shall presently see, experiments are designed so that results obtained in a sample of only a few individuals may be safely extrapolated to most of the population from which those few individuals were obtained. There is no choice but to accept this compromise of studying only a few and then extrapolating the results obtained to all. This is so because we need to know how a drug affects the whole population that drug is aimed at; yet, and at the same time, it is impossible to test that drug on every member of that population.

When the sample of the whole population chosen for the experiment belongs to an *inbred* strain, results will tend to be quite uniform, since the animals used are genetically and thus immunologically similar. If the results obtained with an inbred strain are then extrapolated into a whole—and therefore *non*-inbred and diverse—population, an error (or *bias*) may inadvertently slip into the results.

This is so because the general population is not immunologically uniform. Consequently, there is a range of individual variations not found in the inbred animals used in the experiment.

A Pharmacological Experiment *studies how a certain disease-syndrome responds to the administration of a drug. Studies are carried out on a sample of the whole population because it is impossible to study the whole population. Results obtained in the sample are then extrapolated to the whole population.*

It is therefore critical to obtain a sample that is representative of the whole population afflicted by the disease under study. This is achieved by a procedure called "sampling". It is equally critical to accurately evaluate the results of the treatment, so that those results may then be safely extrapolated to 95 % or 99.5 % of the whole population afflicted by the disease. The latter is achieved by a procedure called "statistical evaluation".

A Researcher cannot work with large quantities of animals, particularly when those animals are inbred.

Inbreeding is an expensive and laborious procedure. Housing and budget are always limited in Research. Inbreeding was originally designed to keep the amount of animals needed per experiment at a minimum.

The quantity of animals to be used in this Research stage is therefore *limited;* that is, the Researcher is forced to make do with only a *sample* of the whole population—and an inbred sample, to boot.

Researchers are interested in how the animals in sample respond to treatment, but only insofar the results obtained in the sample may be safely extrapolated to *most of the population* from which the sample was originally obtained.

When studying a new cancer drug, for instance, what Researchers want to know is how the *whole* rodent population ill with cancer will respond to that drug. However, in order to obtain that information, Researchers have no choice but to study the drug in a minuscule inbred sample of that population.

The limitation in the number of animals used in an experiment, and the need to subsequently extrapolate its results into the majority of the population, is what makes the need for *sampling* both obligatory and inevitable.

Sampling are several Statistical procedures designed to select at random certain individuals from a given population, following a method such that the individuals so selected can be considered as *representative* as possible of those of the population under study. Here is the first pitfall. *Selection at random* is an oxymoron. *Selection* and *random* mean totally different things. If one selects there is no possibility of randomness, and vice versa.

Characteristics to be studied *must be shared by all the individuals of the population under study.* A Researcher can study, for instance, the effect of a certain drug on a subcellular element present in all individuals, or the quantity of red blood cells (all individuals have red blood cells), or the height of those individuals (all individuals share height)—that is, characteristics or elements present in *all* the individuals of the population under study. The experiment is carried out on individuals sampled from that population, and results of the study carried on the sample are then extrapolated to the population from which the sample was obtained.

Let me illustrate with an example.

Say that I am interested in learning what is the average height of the *whole* healthy adult American male population, and also how much I stretch that average, in plus and in minus, until I include 95 % or 99.5 % of the whole adult American male population. I can carry out this study because what I intend to study is height, one of the characteristics all healthy adult American males share.

I cannot possibly measure the height of *every healthy adult male* in the whole American population, so what I will have to do is to select a *reliable sample* of that population in which to conduct my study. In order to obtain or select a sample I can rely upon, I will have to use one of the several *sampling procedures* available. There are quite a few of these procedures. They can be found in any good textbook on Statistics. They make *very* tedious reading.

Once I obtain my sample,

a) I will first find out what is the *average height* of the individuals who constitute that sample, and then

b) I will calculate how far I can extend the limits of that average height, in plus and in minus, so that I can include under that umbrella either 95% or 99.5% of the sample, afterwards

c) I will consider if such a spread can be safely extrapolated onto 95 % or 99.5 % *of the whole healthy American adult population.*

These estimations are accomplished by means of using one of several methods of *Statistical evaluation.*

The first thing I must be concerned about is where I am going to look for my *sample.*

If the sample is obtained from, say, a population of professional basketball players, then the average height will probably be around 6', 6" or more; and the 95 % or the 99.5 % of the sample will be found to be in individuals probably measuring between 5' 9" and 7' +. More important still, data obtained from this sample will be representative of the average height of professional basketball players, but not of the *general* healthy American male population. Meaning that the results I will obtain in my study will be *biased* due to defective sampling.

Only if the *sampling* has been correctly carried out, and if the *statistical evaluation* is reliable, will I be able to safely learn what the height of the 95 %, or else of the 99.5 % of adult American males is in the sample I have studied. With such and assurance, I will now be able to extrapolate the results obtained in the sample onto the 95 % or the 99.5 % of the whole adult male American population. The remaining 5 % or 0.05, that is, the excessively tall and the extremely small, will be left out. This is so because statistical techniques can only be considered reliable up to either the 95 % or the 99.5 %, according to the statistical method chosen to evaluate the data obtained from the sample. Therefore, it is possible that there may be an element of error beyond that 95 % or the 99.5 %. Which is the reason why, in statistical jargon, 0.05, or 0.005 are called the experiment's margin of error, or "p".

Thus, a margin of error or $p \leq .05$ (where $\leq$ is a combination of =, equal to, and <, smaller than. Thus, $\leq$ means equal to or smaller than) in a study of the height of the healthy adult American male population means, in essence, that the results obtained in the study of the sample can be safely extrapolated onto the 95 % of the *whole* healthy adult American male population. By the same token, a $p \leq .005$ would mean that results obtained in the sample can be safely extrapolated onto the 99.5 % of the whole healthy adult American male population.

Again, studies of this kind can be done if and when Researchers are only studying and/or comparing one *single* characteristic *shared by the whole population*—such as the height of healthy adult American males—because height is a feature all healthy adult American males share. One can study only *one parameter or characteristic at a time,* if one uses sampling and statistical methods to evaluate results.

Such a study is totally impossible if we attempt to group together objects, subjects, individuals or characteristics that have nothing in common.

If I get one pebble, and another pebble, and still another pebble, I will end up having a *population* of three pebbles. This happens because pebbles are pretty similar to each other. In the same fashion, I can put together characteristics all animals or all Humans share, like height, sex, a particular disease-syndrome, a certain organ or subcellular fraction, etc. If I add up those common characteristics I will have a *population* because all the elements in the sample *share similar characteristics.* This is the reason why populations can be created in Allopathic Research. Samples can be obtained from populations of cells, fractions of cells, etc. that share similar characteristics. These populations can then be sampled and processed statistically.

If, on the other hand, I attempt to add a book, an apple and a space ship, I cannot possible have a population—or a sample thereof—because each object is totally unlike the others. In a similar fashion, in no way can I sample Whole Human Beings. Each individual Human Being is so unique as to be wholly different from every other Whole Human Being—which is ultimately why it is impossible to carry out statistical studies in Provings of Homeopathic remedies, as we shall presently see.

It is important to briefly discuss *GIGO,* or *Garbage-In-Garbage-Out* within this context.

GIGO means that any Statistical test *is as accurate or as inaccurate as the data poured into it.*

In themselves, Statistical tests are shapeless things. They are like a sweat shirt. Both the Statistical tests and the sweat shirt will take the shape of whoever or whatever fills it.

That is why, readers should first peruse "Materials and Methods" in any paper, in order to learn how the experiment was designed, performed and evaluated.

If the study was poorly planned, executed, or evaluated there will be GIGO; because garbage has been poured into the Statistical method, and consequently garbage will also come out of it. Meaning that the results of the whole study will be null and void.

Which is still another of the reasons why a Statistician is such a vitally important member in any Research team.

The *unicellular stage* of Pharmacological experiments does not need a Statistical study.

In effect, the quantity of bacteria or mammalian cells growing in culture is so mind boggling—zillions upon zillions—that the almost infinite number of individuals in the sample under study is very close to the almost infinite mammalian cell or bacterial population. So there is nothing extrapolate from sample to population here and thus no need for sampling or statistical evaluation. The characteristics under study in those almost infinite bacteria or cells in the sample is likely to be similar to the characteristics of the almost infinite population of unicellular beings.

Studies done in animals are basically concerned with *effectiveness of the drug under study against disease,* and its *toxicity and side effects.*

Effectiveness is evaluated using animals made sick with the disease-syndrome the drug is expected to control.

Toxicity and *side effects* study the interaction of the drug with subcellular fractions of tissues *other than* those the drug has been designed to work on. Toxicity is called *teratogenesis* if the tissues under study belong to embryos and fetuses. These parameters are studied on *healthy* animals of both sexes— rather than in ill animals, as it happens in studies done to determine therapeutic effectiveness.

Some of the females used in these assays are made pregnant before starting the experiment. This is done so that Researchers may determine whether or not the drug under study produces alterations in embryos and/or fetuses.

Drugs are administered at diverse dosage levels, some of which are purposefully very high. One of the parameters to be determined here is the LD_{50} or lethal dose 50; that is, a dose sufficiently high to kill half the animals used in the experiment. This determination is important, later on, to calculate dosage in other animal studies and in Human Beings.

In every experiment, animals are randomly divided (again the oxymoron!) into *controls* and *treated.*

In studies of effectiveness against disease, both groups are made ill with the disease the new drug has been manufactured to combat. The control group will not receive the drug under study, but treated animals will.

In experiments of toxicity and side effects, animals in both control and treated groups are healthy to start with. Here too, only the treated group receives the drug under study.

Control groups are used to determine whether or not results are due to the drug administered (in which case *only* animals in the treated group will respond); or if, in effect, the results are due to some other factor (in which case animals in *both* the control and treated groups will show similar changes).

Drugs are administered by several routes (orally or by mouth, intravenously or into the vein, subcutaneously or under the skin, intraperitoneally or inside the abdominal cavity, etc.).

Animals may be sacrificed before, during or at the end of the experiment, in order to study the effect of the drug in all organs and systems.

Animals may also be left to die and then studied; but this modality is not usually favored. Say that a mouse dies at 9 PM, in a cage located in a room where the temperature is held constant between 22° and 26° C, and the autopsy is done the following morning at 9 AM. Twelve hours will have elapsed between death and autopsy in an environment that is not refrigerated. Post-mortem changes present in tissues will make autopsies difficult or impossible to interpret adequately. Another hazard is that rodents tend to devour their dead, no matter how well fed they may be.

Through these experiments Researchers learn

i)   what changes the drug produces in diverse organs and systems. If these changes are present in the target organ (i. e., the organ bearing the disease the drug was designed to combat), changes will be known as *therapeutic effects.* Changes will be known as *toxicity* and/or *side effects* if found in organs other than the target organ, and *teratogenesis* if seen in embryos and fetuses.

ii) whether or not the sample used in the experiment is representative of the whole population, and,

iii) therefore, whether or not the results obtained in the experiment can be safely extrapolated into 95% or 99.5% of the whole population. For the evaluation of this aspect of the study, the Research team uses one or more of several statistical evaluations.

A *Statistician* is an essential member of the Research team.

He or she will help design the experiment, approve or veto any changes while in progress, and statistically evaluate the results after it is finished.

One of the loose cannons in every experimental design is the use of inbred animals—in fact, this is the first serious flaw of Pharmacological Research. Because results obtained using inbred animals *cannot* be safely extrapolated to the *whole, non-inbred* population of any animal species or strain.

Nor to the Human population that, by definition, is non-inbred, but rather immunologically and genetically diverse; aside from being different from any rodent strain.

The design of an experiment is extravagantly strict in matters relating to interferences that may produce *variables*.

A variable is anything, other than the drug being tested, that may influence the results of an experiment. The experimental design must eliminate as many variables as possible. In point of fact, the ideal experimental design is the one that eliminates *all* variables, and leave only what will be under study.

Chow, water, caging, temperature, age, sex, timing of light and darkness, disease under study, dosage of the drug, etc.; everything has to be as standardized as possible in order to avoid variables.

Animals used will preferably be inbred, in order to eliminate the ultimate variable of genetic and immunological diversity.

If the animal phase of the study is successful in rodents (i.e., good therapeutic effect and relatively mild side effects, toxicity, and teratogenesis) the next step is to study that drug in other animals, usually *dogs* and sometimes also *monkeys,* the latter preferred for the study of antiviral medications.

Studies here are generally related to toxicity, dosage and the like.

This completes the *experimental* stage of the study.

The drug under study is ready for its Clinical phase if it can pass this wringer and still show promise.

If not, the drug is discarded or its structure is modified—and the study is started all over again, in bacteria and/or cell cultures, and then in animals.

The next step of a so far successful drug is its *clinical stage*. It is carried out in *Human Beings.*

Studies in Human Beings.

Broadly speaking, there are two types of studies done with Human Beings.

In one of them, the still experimental drug is tested in *healthy* volunteers at risk of becoming sick with the disease under study. Tamoxifen citrate, for instance, is under study as a possible preventive of breast cancer, in healthy adult women who fear may be at risk. I fear that this study is at least partially flawed by defective sampling. Women participating in this study have enough fear of cancer as to participate in it. Meaning that, once the studied is finished, we will only know about the incidence of breast cancer in women who fear it. Another parallel study should be carried out using two groups of *untreated* women, one with fear of cancer and the other without, in order to find out how this fear influences the incidence of breast cancer in women. In my experience, fear frequently increases both the incidence of cancer and the speed with which it grows and spreads.

In the other type, by far the most prevalent, volunteers are *sick* with the disease the experimental drug is expected to control—sick and also usually resistant to Allopathic treatments currently in use or else incapable of tolerating them.

We will be dealing with this latter type of Clinical Pharmacological Research from now on.

Clinical Research in ill volunteers is usually carried out along three stages.

In the first stage the drug, fresh out of the animal stage, is studied in few individuals whose disease is advanced and usually non-responsive to treatments currently in use. What is mainly studied here is tolerance to the new drug, its toxicity and its side effects.

In the second stage, done in a larger number of patients suffering with the disease under study, Researchers' interest is focused both in toxicity, side effects and response of the disease to the drug.

In the third stage, carried out in a still larger number of patients, the matter under study is mainly the efficacy of the drug.

The quantity of patients used, particularly in the early phases of the Clinical Stage, is perforce limited.

All volunteers must have a *positive pathological diagnosis* of the disease under study. The pathological study of the diseased tissue is usually done under the microscope by a Pathologist—another essential member of the Research team.

Follow-ups are usually carried out in state-of-the-art Hospital centers.

The evolution of the experimental treatment is studied by Clinical Medical Researchers, mainly by *indirect* methods such as X Rays, blood work, etc., and sometimes also by sequential biopsies (or obtention of pieces of tissues that are afterwards studied by a Pathologist under the microscope).

Needless to say, there is obviously very little possibility of standardizing variables such as age, sex, immunological and genetic variation, etc.

Here, and since at this level the experimental subjects are Human, every effort is made so that the relationship between the Researcher and the experimental patient is as *impersonal*—or *objective*—as possible.

One of the most frequently used precautions is the design of so-called *double blind* studies, in which neither the Researcher nor the patient know what is being administered; if an inactive substance or if the drug under study. In this fashion, any subjective effect due to interpersonal relationship or other causes is supposed to be neutralized.

I often wonder how much a double blind study, or any other suchlike experimental subterfuge, can really avoid this interpersonal bias. Not necessarily because of the drug being tested, but because of the relationship that inevitably develops between the Clinical Researcher and his or her experimental patient in a day-to-day basis. Studies have shown that plants, for instance, when lovingly talked to, or stroked, or being taken care of, are stronger and grow more luxuriantly than those treated impersonally—indeed, even the mood of a person present in the room has been found to have an effect on how plants thrive. And if this happens with plants, how much more intense will the effect be in a patient who is aware of how desperately sick he or she is, and who sees his or her Clinical Researcher, that is, his or her Doctor, every day! There is no way that a relationship based on care, faith and hope can be totally avoided or neutralized. Nor is there any way of knowing how it may affect the ultimate outcome of the clinical experiment. All the more if the Clinical Researcher is also a caring person.

Many drugs that show promise in the experimental stage are weeded out in the Clinical Stage.

The most frequent cause of rejection is prohibitive toxicity and/or severe side effects that could not be detected in animal models, but that becomes evident in Human Beings. Some of these effects appear soon, in the earliest stages of Clinical Research. This happened with 5-bromouracil, that showed great promise as an anticancer drug in animals. But had to be withdrawn because, in early Human trials, it produced severe psychiatric disorders. These effects could not be observed in animals because of the obvious differences between the brains of rodent and of Human.

In other drugs, serious side effects and/or toxicity may become manifest after the hurdles of the early Clinical trials have long been successfully overcome, and the drug is being sold to the public. Perhaps the most catastrophic example is that of thalidomide in the 50's. This drug was first tested in animals and Human volunteers who were not pregnant. In Humans, thalidomide was found to be a wonderful remedy for insomnia. But it also proved to have devastating effects in the development of Human embryos and fetuses. Many babies of mothers who had used thalidomide during their pregnancies were born without arms or legs. Of course, the drug was immediately removed from the shelves—although too late, alas!

All drugs act on subcellular elements *that are present in cells of the diseased or target organ, as well as in cells of every other organ and system of the patient, whether born or unborn.*

Consequently, when using any Pharmaceutical product fresh out of clinical trials, a Doctor should consider very soberly the possibility of a therapeutic disaster.

Despite of its many pitfalls and biases, though, the benefits this form of Research has brought to Humanity are as unquestionable as they are impressive.

To sum up,

Pharmacological Research aims at curing diseases by means of interacting with sub-cellular fractions.

In order to achieve this end it develops drugs.

Drugs are pure chemical formulas designed to act on chemical structures present in subcellular fractions of sick organs and tissues, and also on subcellular fractions of invading organisms such as bacteria and the like.

Drugs are designed to work only on subcellular fractions of sick organs and tissues. Problem is, though, they also interact with similar subcellular fractions present in healthy organs and tissues. Consequently, and for all intents and purposes, Pharmaceutical drugs act on many if not all of the patient's organs and tissues. This circumstance is the cause of their toxicity, side effects, allergic reactions and damage of embryos or fetuses, as well as of their therapeutic effects.

Pharmacological drugs are studied first in bacteria and/or mammalian cells in culture, and then in experimental animals. The purpose of these studies is to determine how effective the drug is, how serious its side effects and toxicity, and what is the safe dosage range.

Once these data are known, the drug is tested in Human Beings, ill with the disease the drug has been designed to eliminate or to control.

And, when all these stages are successfully completed—at the cost of many lives and suffering, years of work, and millions upon millions of dollars spent—the drug is made available to the Medical profession at large.

It is then prescribed by Doctors, and dispensed in Pharmacies.

SOME DIFFERENCES AND SIMILARITIES BETWEEN ALLO-PATHIC AND HOMEOPATHIC RESEARCH

Differences are many and considerable.

The first and most basic difference between Pharmacological and Homeopathic Research is one of *aim.*

In chronic patients, Homeopathy aims at preparing remedies that work by means of directing the patients' Vital Force to the fulcrum of their imbalance. Then the Vital Force attunes itself with the patients and makes both the chronic imbalance and the disease-syndrome/s afflicting the patients disappear.

In acute patients, a correctly prescribed remedy directs the patient's Vital Force to the area assailed by an acute disease-syndrome, and makes that acute disease-syndrome vanish.

All of which will happens according to the principle of *"like cures like".*

On the other hand, Pharmacological Research aims at manufacturing pure drugs that interact directly with sub-cellular fractions and, through this interaction, fight and destroy disease-syndromes, or else cure sick organs or systems, following the principle of *"contrary cures contrary".*

All the other differences between Pharmacological and Homeopathic Research derive from these basic differences in aim.

The second difference is one of *procedure.*

Pharmacological Research aims at the interaction of drugs with subcellular elements present in microorganisms, ill and healthy organs and tissues of patient, and tissues of embryos and fetuses. These sub-cellular elements are *shared by all, or almost all cells of different kingdoms and species.* Therefore, *the action of a Pharmaceutical drug on a subcellular fraction can be studied in, and is equally effective on, uni- and/or multicellular organisms.* Thus, and with the exception of several antibiotics, results obtained by a drug on a subcellular fraction present in one species can be safely extrapolated to any other species with which it may share that particular subcellular fraction.

Essential to the procedure is the use of *ill* Human Beings in the Clinical stage.

Also essential is the whole *Statistical* structure; by means of defining a sick population, obtaining a sample that may adequately represent the whole population, evaluating results, and finally safely extrapolating those results to the 95 % or 99.5 % of the sample and then of the whole ill population.

The *final evaluation* of the Experimental and Clinical Stages of Pharmacological Research is based on an accumulation of extrapolated data corresponding to cells of very diverse creatures belonging to the vegetal and animal kingdoms and to the Human species.

The procedure is completely different in Provings.

In chronic patients, Homeopathy challenges each patient's Vital Force's healing capacity to work on the fulcrum of *each individual* patient's imbalance. The fulcrum of each chronic patient's imbalance—as well as the Vital Force—belongs *only* to that individual and unique patient. It cannot be extrapolated into any other Human Being, far less into animals, bacteria or cells.

Homeopathic Research is carried out only in *healthy* male and female Human volunteers. The idea here is *to provoke a temporary state of imbalance* in healthy Human Beings and then to study its characteristics.

Each individual Human Being is unique, and so is each healthy prover. The uniqueness of each prover's individuality cannot be shared, nor lumped together with the unique individuality of other provers. To say "Whole unique individual" and "population" in the same breath is a contradiction, because population implies uniformity and uniqueness diversity. Consequently, one cannot create populations in Homeopathy. Without populations, one cannot obtain a sample of that population nor carry out a statistical evaluation on that sample. Therefore, the whole statistical set-up, so essential in Pharmacological Research, it totally inapplicable here.

Let me recall that Homeopathic remedies have no side effects, toxicity nor teratogenic effects. This characteristic eliminates the need for toxicity studies, indispensable in Pharmacological Research. The dose or potency, as well as the frequency of administration of Homeopathic remedies, vary from patient to patient, and have to be found in each individual by trial and error. This is unlike what happens in Pharmacological Research, where dosage is learnt in rodents and dogs, usually in milligrams or micrograms per kilo of body weight, or per square meter of body surface; and then used as the starting point to evaluate dosage in ill Human Beings.

And so, for Homeopathic Research purposes, the whole stage of Pharmacological Research performed on animals can safely be done away with—a wonderful thing indeed, when considering how much misery Pharmacological Research signifies for the poor creatures used and abused in these studies.

All that is needed in the Provings is something that resembles the Clinical stage of Pharmacological Clinical Research—though infinitely less complex and causing very little discomfort to Provers.

The third and the fourth differences relate to *infrastructure* and *cost.*

The infrastructure necessary for Pharmacological experiments is mind-boggling, as well as extravagantly expensive. State-of-the-art chemical laboratories to first synthesize and purify the drug, and then to produce it in sufficient quantities for both the Experimental and Clinical Stage. Specially built warehouses for experimental animals. Cages. Chow and water. Recipients. Cleansing facilities. Accommodations for disposal of blood, excretions and cadavers. Sterilizing equipment. Sterile environments and media. Incubators. Diagnostic facilities, etc., etc.

Plus state-of-the-art wards in Hospitals, to carry out studies in Humans.

Add to this specialized personnel, all the way from lab technicians to Bacteriologists to Vets to Statisticians to specialized Nurses to Medical Doctors.

For a Proving, all that is needed is a natural substance; mortars, pestles and spatulas. Enough lactose, both as powder and pellets. Enough ethanol. Flasks. Personnel specialized in preparing Homeopathic remedies. Homeopathic Physicians to coordinate, evaluate and often participate in the study. Human volunteers. Writing materials. Period.

In Homeopathic Research, furthermore, the expense for each Proving is minimal. To boot, no Provings ends up in a failure, for all remedies will produce some kind of a profile; and that profile may be useful for some patient.

The fifth difference resides in the *mode of interpretation of results.*

The Pharmacological Researcher must make sure that there are no errors in the experimental design, nor in the observation, nor in the recording and interpretation of results. The most insignificant error can unleash variables capable of vitiating a whole experiment.

In Pharmacological Research, and because of the very nature of its experimental design, *only one thing can be studied at a time.* If the experiment wants to explore, say, the effect of a drug on a cell's membrane, that study will have to be conducted on only one single element of that cell's membrane at a time. Consequently, a complete experimental study can take very close to forever.

321

Elements for statistical evaluation must be scrupulously selected beforehand. The number of experimental subjects, both control and treated, has to be adequate and determined prior to the onset of the experiment. The experiment has to be airtight and repeatable, in order to rule out any possibility of an erroneous observation and/or interpretation that may mar its results. All experimental variables, with the exception of the one under study, have to be reduced as close to Zero as possible in order to avoid confusion in the interpretation of results. And the correct sampling and statistical method must be used in order to be certain that the results obtained are not due to chance, and that those results can be safely applied or extrapolated into at least 95 % of the whole population.

In Pharmacological Research, results must be *objectively* recorded and evaluated, and then transformed into *subjective* knowledge in the mind of the Researcher. Extreme precautions must be taken to keep the transfer of objective evidence into subjective knowledge free of the danger of individual distortion, or *bias*. This hazard is forever present because, in Pharmacological Research, everything happens *outside* the Researcher; and then all that external evidence has to be transferred *inside* the mind of the Researcher in the form of knowledge. It is very easy, at the delicate juncture senses-mind, to peg a bias to information obtained in the experiment—be it an emotion, previous knowledge, the Researcher's beliefs or whatever. Subjective knowledge, and the subsequent interpretation of results, can go haywire if contaminated by the Researcher's bias.

Only after scrupulously following all rules can the Researcher be reasonably sure that the experiment has been properly performed, and that he or she has not fallen victim of some *bias* that may have distorted its results. Bias, then, has to be eschewed like the plague. Experimental evidence has to become unpolluted information, and then untarnished knowledge not contaminated by any bias—or distortion—whatsoever.

Things are quite different in Homeopathy—although the difference cannot be fully appreciated unless the Researcher performs at least one Proving in him or herself.

In Homeopathy there is no objectivity whatsoever. *The whole experiment is subjective from beginning to end.* A prover does not observe what happens outside him or herself, nor has to transform any objective evidence into subjective knowledge. Rather, the prover *feels* within him or herself, and simultaneously, all the changes that happen while the remedy is acting, *understands* those changes, *becomes aware* of them, *lives* them all *subjectively from beginning to end.*

Remember the first time you got tipsy. You don't need to design an experiment to objectively determine what you felt under those circumstances, sensation by sensation. *You knew what it was and how you felt it, in each and every one of its aspects or facets at the same time.* And, when you compared notes with others who underwent the same experience, you became able to *understand,* and be aware of, the gamut of sensations, thoughts and feelings that make up the *whole profile* of a mild alcoholic intoxication. And, consequently, in the future, you will be able to recognize, or diagnose, someone with a mild alcoholic intoxication in someone when you see him or her.

If you were a smoker, and became a quitter, you *understand* how it feels to kick the habit. And, as you recall what happened when you were quitting, then you are aware of how it affected you; all those sensations at the same time. Then, if you ask other quitters to compare experiences, you will have a broader *understanding* of the *profile* of *your own personal experience* of quitting smoking. And you will able to recognize someone who is trying to quit without much difficulty.

The first time you held your first born child in your arms in the Delivery Room you felt a constellation of sensations and feelings, special and unique, all at the same time. If you compare what you felt with what other fathers felt in the same situation, then you will *understand,* have a clear *awareness* of what the *profile* of holding a first born is like. Only then you will be able to understand how a guy feels in that marvelous moment of his life.

If you volunteer for the Proving of, say, *Hepar sulphur,* you will feel the changes brought about by the Proving in yourself, all at the same time, all within you. And if after proving *Hepar* you discuss what you felt with other provers, or read in the Materia Medica Homeopathica about *Hepar sulphur,* then you will become *aware* of the whole profile of *Hepar Sulphur.* And, what is more important, you will be able to recognize that same profile in any patient needing *Hepar sulphur.*

Homeopathic Research is a form of learning through *understanding* and *acquisition of awareness.*

The prover—who is at one and the same time Researcher and experimental subject—*experiences* the remedy's profile within him or herself. Bias, that big bugaboo of Pharmacological Research, is not feared nor rejected here—it simply doesn't exist. There is no outside → inside journey of evidence into knowledge. The Researcher/prover becomes immediately and pristinely aware of *all* the changes brought about by the experiment he or she is carrying on in him or herself. Experimental evidence/knowledge/awareness is one and the same thing in Homeopathic Research, because it all happens at the same time inside the prover.

Provings, then, are an understanding- and awareness-based form of experimentation; as opposed to the objective evidence → subjective knowledge pattern required by Pharmacological Research. Provings make the ap-perception of what has been experienced within oneself perfectly clear and accurate in all its aspects and facets, as well as immediately perceivable by the prover.

Put differently, Homeopathic experiments have been designed to be *subjective* from beginning to end. And results are acknowledged after being *felt* and *understood,* rather than after having been observed and acknowledged.

Pharmacological and Homeopathic Research have two things in com-mon, though—even if here, too, differences are considerable.

The first is the use of healthy subjects, so that no illness may interfere with interpretation of results.

Pharmacological Research uses mainly healthy dogs and other animals for toxicological studies.

Homeopathic Research uses only healthy volunteers for its Provings.

Both Allopathy and Homeopathy use Human Beings in their experi-ments.

Pharmacology uses ill Humans to put the final frosting to a long chain of experiments.

In Homeopathy we are interested in is learning what changes a dynam-ized natural product may bring about in the Wholeness of *healthy* Human volunteers. Provings, then, are not the last link of a chain of Research that starts in cells or bacteria, but the sole source of information and knowledge, the only experiment needed. The purpose here is to find out how those healthy and well balanced volunteers become *reversibly* unbalanced—or ill—under treatment, and what changes that particular form of induced im-balance brings in its wake.

In Pharmacological Research, the Researcher—who is *not* an experi-mental subject at the same time—is only interested in finding out only one aspect of how a drug and its sub-cellular receptor interact, how effective the drug is to fight a particular disease-syndrome, what is the correct dosage, and what the toxicity and side effects it may elicit.

In a Proving, the Researcher—particularly when that Researcher is also a healthy prover—is interested in *every change* the natural product may bring about in him or herself and other provers, whether such as change is considered normal or pathological by Allopathic Medicine. This is so be-cause the only purpose here is only to find the *profile of a remedy.*

In Pharmacological Research, *experiments are carried out outside the Researcher. Experiments yield objective evidence. Objective evidence must then enter the Researcher's mind through his or her senses and so become subjective knowledge. Most precautions and safeguards when planning and designing an experiment (sampling, statistical evaluation, etc.), are but ways and means to assure that results are consistent and reliable, and that transition from objective to subjective proceed with as little distortion—or bias—as possible.*

In Homeopathy, *on the other hand, every experiment is subjective from beginning to end. All the evidence happens inside the prover. The prover becomes aware, within him or herself, and at the same time, of all the changes brought about by the remedy under study. There is no possibility of distortion or bias here.*

This absence of bias in Homeopathic experiments probably explains why, along the past 200 years, there has been such a steady progress in a straight line. And no need whasoever of altering or correcting in the least results obtained in, or interpretations gathered from previous experiments or Provings—something that can hardly be said of Pharmacological Research.

HOMEOPATHIC-PHARMACOLOGICAL RESEARCH

A new and potentially very exciting form of combined Therapeutic Research has been emerging of late—slowly, though, probably because of the inevitable discordance between the Homeopathic and the Allopathic paradigms.

Unlike what happens in Homeopathic Research, experiments along these lines can also be carried out in animals and even in unicellular organisms. And, unlike what happens in Pharmacological Research, these experiments are carried out using Homeopathic remedies instead of a Pharmaceutical drugs.

The aim of these studies is to evaluate the effects of the administration of *well-known* Homeopathic remedies to *ill Human Beings, or ill laboratory animals, or bacteria or mammalian cells in culture.* Homeopathic-Pharmacological experiments study the effects that *well-known* Homeopathic remedies bring about on *a particular disease-syndromes,* and on *the changes that particular disease-syndrome may elicit in unicellular organisms, or else in organs and tissues of ill animals and Human Beings afflicted by it.*

Let me recall, for purposes of comparison, that Provings are done to learn about the profile an *unknown* Homeopathic remedy by means of administering the unknown remedy *exclusively* to *healthy Human volunteers* with the purpose of *producing a temporary imbalance* and, through that imbalance, learn the profile of that new Homeopathic remedy.

There is abundant literature describing the alterations Pharmaceutical drugs bring about when interacting with sub-cellular fractions present in ill organs and tissues.

This plethora of knowledge is the consequence of the great deal of serious Pharmacological Research carried out at a cellular, sub-cellular, enzymatic, micro- and ultramicroscopic, genetic and immunological levels.

Homeopathic remedies work by ultimately attuning the Vital Force with the patient through the action of the correct remedy. Little to nothing is known regarding what changes this attunement bring about at a cellular, sub-cellular, enzymatic, micro- and ultramicroscopic, genetic and immunological level. Experimental work here hasn't even started to skim the surface.

It will be very exciting to learn what changes Homeopathic remedies— or rather, the healing capacity of the patient's Vital Force, guided by the remedies—brings about at these levels, and even more fascinating to compare these results with those elicited by Pharmaceutical drugs.

Imagine, within this context, a comparative Pharmacological/Homeopathic study performed on, say, the intestinal lining of patients afflicted with ulcerative colitis; to mention one disease-syndrome that responds consistently to Homeopathic treatment.

Imagine dividing ulcerative colitis-bearing patients into Pharmacological and Homeopathic groups, instead of into control and treated.

In such an experiment, the Pharmacological group would receive Mesalamine, Sulfasalazine, Olsalazine and/or Prednisone; that is, the standard Pharmacological treatment for this disease-syndrome. And each patient in the Homeopathic group would receive his or her own Constitutional Homeopathic remedy (because all patients suffering from ulcerative colitis are chronic to start with).

Imagine a comparative evaluation of results in both groups.

And imagine obtaining serial biopsies of the colonic mucosa; and studying the tissues macro-, micro-, and ultramicroscopically; as well as learning about the enzymatic, genetic and immunological changes encountered in the colon of Pharmacologically vs. the Homeopathically treated patients.

Another important study, among many, would be the assessment of the comparative usefulness of Homeopathy vs. Chemotherapy in the treatment of advanced cancer patients.

Cancer Chemotherapy is extravagantly expensive and extremely devitalizing for the patient. It brings about severe forms of toxicity and side effects, including exhausting vomiting and diarrhea, damage to the bone marrow, heart, lungs, liver, kidney etc. Except in patients bearing feminine choriocarcinoma, Wilms's tumor, neuroblastoma, Ewing's tumor of the bone, seminoma and dysgerminoma, its therapeutic results have consistently been nil to insignificant in malignant solid tumors. Indeed, if we consider Cancer Chemotherapy from a benefit/risk standpoint, it is almost all risk against insignificant benefit for most cancer patients.

What can Homeopathy offer these unfortunate Human Beings? How do its results compare with those obtained by Cancer Chemotherapy? This point requires urgent clarification. If Homeopathic/Pharmacological experiments show that results are similar in both groups, then the terribly mortifying and expensive cancer chemotherapy could perhaps be replaced or else complemented by the gentleness of a Homeopathic treatment—and all the more if therapeutic results with Homeopathic remedies prove to be better.

An increasing number of parents is concerned regarding the ill effects of many injectable vaccinations for viral childhood diseases, such as mumps, measles and the like. These ill effects may range from a mild local inflammation to irreversible brain damage and death.

Why not study and compare the results obtained in Homeopathically treated, non-vaccinated children who suffer viral childhood diseases vs. the ill effects of vaccines in children vaccinated against them?

A study of this kind would clarify, once and for all, if the very real risks and benefits posed by vaccinations can compare with those suffered by those found in children who suffer those viral diseases and are treated Homeopathically.

Comparison of results would allow parents to take an intelligent stand, either for or against, regarding vaccinations and/or Homeopathic treatments.

Such a study would carry little risk for the children who fall ill because they didn't receive vaccinations. Childhood diseases respond very nicely, in most instances, to Homeopathic treatment. And without ill effects of any kind.

I could continue this list on and on, describing one possible experiment after another.

The quantity and quality of studies of every kind that can be designed and carried out in this virgin field of Pharmacological/Homeopathic Research is mind-boggling. Furthermore, this form of Research could become an excellent source of hard experimental data regarding how to prevent and treat many disease-syndromes.

In order to succeed, this composite form of Research has to somehow intermix

- the *individualization of treatment,* a key element of Homeopathy, and,
- the effect of treatment on a particular *disease-syndrome*, a key element of Pharmacological Research.

Clearly, a compromise has to be reached.

In order to do so, one must retain the characteristics of each of the two systems that are useful for an experiment of this kind, discard those that are unsuitable or useless, and ultimately harmonize what remains.

The *Experimental Stage* of Pharmacological Research has to remain, if these experiments are carried in unicellular organisms or in animals.

The Allopathic design of the *Clinical Stage* must remain if experiments are done in Human Beings.

Studies in bacteria or cells in culture.

Here, criteria to be followed should be identical to that described above in *Studies in bacteria or cells in culture,* under the heading *Pharmacological Research.* The Research Director should be a culture Researcher, supervised by a Homeopathic Physician knowledgeable of cell, tissue and bacterial cultures

Studies in animals.

The Research Director in this stage should be a Veterinary Homeopathic Physician. This is so because, in any study of this kind, the profile of the Homeopathic remedy administered has to match the profile of each individual animal.

Except for this difference, I believe that the steps described in *Studies in animals,* under *Pharmacological Research,* can be safely followed.

Studies in Humans.

Criteria for selection of the patients (or *sampling),* determination of clinical and pathological diagnoses, evaluation of results and statistical/pathological assessment, as done in the Human stage of Pharmacological Research, will have to remain for purposes of standardization, evaluation and interpretation of results.

The disease-syndrome under study in each experiment should be *the same* for all patients, whether that disease-syndrome is acute or chronic.

Everything else Homeopathic will remain, such as the obtention of Homeopathic and Clinical History and Physical examination, flexibility regarding selection of the remedy according to the patient's—or acute disease's—profile, the follow-up of the acute or chronic patient. The adequate potency, dosage and frequency of administration will not be fixed beforehand, but attained by trial and error. Several remedies administered sequentially, and several potencies, may have to be administered to each patient. The need for nosodes and complementary remedies must also be taken into consideration. There is no room here of the fixed *single drug* and *single dosage* used in Pharmacological studies.

An individual patient will not respond unless the correct Homeopathic remedy is administered. Or, to state it with propriety, the disease-syndrome under study will not respond to treatment unless the patient's Vital Force becomes properly attuned, due to the action of the correct remedy—a remedy that is specific and that cannot be individualized before evaluating and re-evaluating each individual patient. Ditto for the potency of that remedy, although here the latitude may be greater.

The profile of the patients under study may also change during the experiment, so more than one remedy per patient may potentially be needed. Ditto for the potency.

The bottom line here is that, *even though the disease-syndrome to be studied is only one, one or more Homeopathic remedies, and one or more potencies, may have to be used.*

The *experimental design* has also to be taken into consideration.

Before starting the experiment, all patients should have diagnosis of disease, obtained preferably both clinically and pathologically. This means that all patients entering the study must be evaluated, and followed up, by Clinical and Homeopathic Histories and Physical Examination, ancillary studies, and biopsies studied by a trained Pathologist.

The criterion for selecting patients, drugs and schedules should also be agreed upon beforehand, as described above, in *Pharmacological Research.*

But...

- In each experimental patient, the Homeopathic diagnosis/treatment will be arrived at after *each patient* is individually evaluated and re-evaluated by the Homeopathic Researcher as needed, and then

- each patient should be treated with *one single Homeopathic remedy, and one single potency* at a time. The remedy to be used will be chosen after the patient is Homeopathically evaluated. The single remedy and the single potency are to be used for as long as therapeutic effects last. The experimental patient is to be re-evaluated as often as necessary and, if needed, the remedy or the potency, or both, may have to be changed. Nosodes and complementary remedies may have to be administered at some time during the study. Allowances are to be made in the Research Protocol for changes in remedy and in dosage schedules as needed, and for eventual administration of nosodes and complementary remedies.

This is in complete discrepancy with Pharmacological Research, where drug and dose are agreed upon and fixed beforehand.

The Research Protocol must also be as airtight, and must foresee as many contingencies as possible, as well as diverse ways and means of dealing with those contingencies.

In these experiments, Researchers collect *objective evidence,* that they then must transform into subjective knowledge, as free of biases as possible; as it happens in Pharmacological Research.

In order to succeed, Researchers should follow all the precautions described in Pharmacological Research regarding variables and biases.

The Homeopathic Researcher.-

There is one extra precaution that must be taken. I consider this precaution essential for success in this kind of experiments.

It concerns *the Researcher* responsible of the Homeopathic diagnoses and everything Homeopathic that follows; namely, identification of the correct remedy/ies to be administered, the correct potencies and frequency of administration, and of the follow-up of the experimental patients.

For all intents and purposes, then, this means that the Homeopathic Researcher, as well as the rest of the Research team, will have to rigidly comply with the Research Protocol only as far as the obtention of the correct pathological diagnosis, the follow-up the patients and evaluation of results; but not in regards to the remedy/ies and potency/ies to be used.

In a Clinical Pharmacological study, and with everything clearly and meticulously planned beforehand, even a relatively unskilled Medical Doctor can conduct the experiment. This is so because, if perplexed or facing a problem, all the Researcber has to do is to consult the Research Protocol and/or the whole Research team for an answer.

This means that the Clinical Researcher is not, by far, the pivotal member of the Pharmacological Research team. Everything has been planned and designed for him or her. All the Clinical Researcher has to do here is to treat, evaluate, and follow up the experimental patients according to a Protocol fully agreed upon by all beforehand.

In a Homeopathic/Pharmacological experiment, on the other hand, the Homeopathic Researcher is the *most important* member of the whole team.

In Homeopathic/Pharmacological trials, *a correct Homeopathic diagnosis, as well as the choice of the correct Homeopathic remedy and an adequate Homeopathic follow-up, will be exclusively the consequence of the skill of the Homeopathic Physician* that evaluates, and follows up, each individual experimental patient.

The percentage of successes depends on the skill of the Homeopathic Physician present in the Research team, every bit as much as the timely and adequate observation and interpretation of results.

Which is why, when planning a Homeopathic/Pharmacological experiment, and in order to keep errors of diagnosis/treatment to an unavoidable minimum, it is *indispensable* to choose the participating Homeopathic Researchers among the *most capable and experienced* Homeopathic Physicians, with a well-known track record of successful diagnoses/treatments.

> *A good, experienced and well integrated Research team, with easy and full communication among its members, is the essential ingredient in a successful Pharmacological trial.*
> *A group of motivated and conscientious volunteer provers is the essential ingredient in a successful Homeopathic Research trial, or Proving.*
> *A top Homeopathic Physician, with outstanding diagnostic skills and experience, is the essential ingredient in a successful Homeopathic/Pharmacological trial.*

The Statistician.-

A competent Statistician should assist in the design, follow-up and interpretation of results of every Homeopathic/Pharmacological experiment; and, in daily meetings, the whole team should report every change to, and consult every move with the Statistician.

This is important because, even though Researchers must have some latitude during an experiment, that latitude shouldn't veer too far off; lest it may create variables capable of confusing results, and/or of tarnishing the experiment by means of creating totally avoidable biases.

There are only two ways of knowing how far to roam.

Either to have extensive knowledge regarding how to conduct Research, or else by means of being oriented by someone experienced in organizing it; that is, a competent Statistician.

All the steps described above must be strictly adhered to when designing and carrying out Homeopathic/Pharmacological experiments.

There is no other way to assure that Homeopathic diagnoses/treatments will be accurate and that follow-up will be adequate, correct and easy to interpret. And consequently that therapeutic results will be reliable and trustworthy.

The Pathologist.-

If biopsies are performed, and necessary to study the follow-up, a Pathologist must form part of the team here also.

Last but not least, correct and sound planning and execution of these experiments will allow us to start to learn—for this is still an almost totally virgin field—how the healing capacity of the Vital Force acts on cells of sick organs and tissues.

Ultimately, how the Vital Force cures patients.

The publication of results

A finished Homeopathic/Pharmacological experiment is usually followed by its publication in a Scientific Journal. Let us not forget here that Medical Journals are read by all kinds of Physicians, mainly Allopathic Doctors.

We must therefore endeavor to make the text as readable and understandable as possible by all, whether Homeopaths, Allopathic Physicians or whatever. The only way of achieving this goal is to write the paper as a standard Clinical Pharmacological Report.

The paper submitted to the Journal should have a Title, followed by the name/s, title/s, specialty/es, affiliation/s and mailing address/es of its Author/s. It should be clearly stated who is/are the Homeopathic Researcher/s, who the Statistician/s and who the Pathologist/s; the latter necessary to verify the diagnosis prior to the onset of the study, to confirm if the diagnosis of the disease-syndrome shows verifiable changes under treatment, and to study biopsies and/or autopsies in the patients under study.

Immediately afterwards, the paper must list keywords used in the text. Then must come the paper's summary, Introduction, Materials and Methods, Results, Comments (be very careful with potentially biased interpretations here!) and Bibliography.

Authors must understand that this form of report is quite unlike those Allopathic readers are used to. Consequently, a sizable part of the Introduction should be devoted to explain the differences between Homeopathic/Pharmacological and Pharmacological trials, and the reasons for those differences. Also, in Materials and Methods, it should be clearly explained how the Allopathic diagnosis was arrived at, how many patients were studied, whether the disease under study is acute or chronic from an Allopathic standpoint, what criteria were used for selection of patients, evaluation and evolution of both the disease-syndrome under study and the patients' improvement or cure, what statistical method was used and why, and what constitutional, nosode, complementary and/or acute Homeopathic remedies were used in each patient, at what potencies, and why.

333

It is not easy to design and carry out this kind of Research. Many things must still be ironed out.

It can be very hard on Researchers because of the hybrid methodology that needs to be used.

Allopathic Doctors find it easy to think in terms of disease-syndromes and ways of destroying them using drugs or other means. Homeopathic Physicians, on the other hand, find this approach very difficult to work with, since they are trained to think in terms of a Wholeness and harmony that includes, but is not limited to, the control of the disease-syndromes patients may be bearing.

Some very interesting and exciting papers on Homeopathic-Pharmacological Research have appeared in the Literature, despite of all of these difficulties.

The British School is the undisputed pioneer in this field.

To sum up the *purpose of these three forms of Research.*

The purpose of *Pharmacological Research* is to develop and then test drugs that, by acting on subcellular fractions, may help bring disease-syndromes under control. Also, these experiments can be used to find new usefulness of already known drugs, or to compare usefulness of some drugs with others of similar chemical structures, characteristics and/or therapeutic actions, the effectiveness of a single drug vs. that of several in combination, etc.

The purpose of *Homeopathic Research* is to study dynamized natural products in healthy male and female Human volunteers, and so learn the profile of newly Homeopathically prepared natural substances. Once the profile of these new triturated and/or succused substances becomes known, they will be administered to patients bearing acute diseases or chronic imbalances with profiles similar to that of the remedy, according to the principle of *like cures like.*

Finally, the purpose of *Homeopathic/Pharmacological Research* is to learn how the healing force of a patient's Vital Force, attuned by the Homeopathic remedy, acts in cells of organs and tissues that are devitalized by specific disease-syndromes; and how the Vital Force's action compares with that elicited by Pharmaceutical drugs.

Chapter 24

VACCINATIONS, ALLERGY SHOTS, AND HOMEOPA-THY

Superficially, allergy shots and vaccinations seem to act in a manner similar to that of Homeopathic remedies.

Allergy shots administer the same stuff that produces allergies, and vaccinations the same substances that cause infectious diseases (sounds a lot like *Like cures like,* doesn't it?). To boot, allergy shots inject the allergy-inducing agent in infinitesimal amounts into allergic patients.

There is even talk of Homeopathically prepared vaccinations, and their administration with the purpose of immunizing patients.

Small wonder the subject is confusing!

A person falls ill with an infectious disease when invaded by microorganisms. Changes that happen at that time are not brought about by invading microorganisms, but rather by the patient's response to that invasion.

An infectious disease-syndrome, then, is the sum total of mechanisms a patient puts together to rid him or herself of those invading microorganisms. These mechanisms become manifested as malaise, fever, lack of appetite, pain, increased pulse rate, labored breathing, etc. As a rule, the most vigorous and robust the patient, the more intense the response is bound to be.

Consequently, when we say that a microorganism "makes us sick", what we are actually saying is that what is making us feel sick is our reaction to the invasion of a particular strain of microorganisms—a reaction that is frequently very uncomfortable and sometimes even dangerous.

Usually, only a part of the invading microorganism is responsible for the patient's reaction.

In some instances, what triggers the patient's reaction are components of the microorganism's body. In this case, we say that the microorganism's body contains the *toxin* that makes the patient sick. In others, the patient's reaction is triggered by substances *secreted* by microorganisms. Bacteria and the like are very tiny. They don't have room inside for a digestive system like ours. They consequently must secrete their digestive juices into their surroundings, digest their food outside themselves and then absorb the nutrients already digested—problem is, when they invade us, their surroundings and consequently their food is *us!* In other words, what is their *digestive juices* is our *toxins.*

These strains of microorganisms don't need to invade. Their digestive juices/toxins are absorbed into the patient's bloodstream (usually via the patient's lymphatic system) and then taken everywhere. Toxins are so poisonous that just the minutest amount can cause enormous harm. Toxins may remain active even after the microorganisms that secreted them have been killed with antibiotics or whatever.

We have an immune system for the purposes of first identifying invading microorganisms, and then producing substances capable of neutralizing, as soon as possible, the body parts or digestive juices of the microorganisms that are harming us.

In immunological lingo, the part or the secretion of the microorganism that makes us sick is called an *antigen,* and the stuff the immune system prepares to neutralize an antigen is called an *antibody.* Anything produced by microorganisms, then, and that makes us sick, is called a *toxin.* A toxin is called an *antigen* when it triggers a response of the immune system, often in the form of *antibodies.* In other words, a toxin is always a toxin, but it becomes and antigen only when it elicits the response from its host's immune system.

The immune system takes some time to first identify an antigen and then to design and prepare antibodies in sufficient quantities to neutralize that antigen.

By then, in diseases such as tetanus, the patient will likely be dead.

Vaccinations are ways of making the immune system instantly prepared to successfully combat disease-syndromes in which microorganisms are involved.

Vaccines achieve this purpose by means of proffering the immune system something that is harmless, but so similar to an actual antigen as to trigger a full-blown immune reaction against it. The only purpose of this deception is to stimulate the immune system to produce antibodies, plus the templates necessary to produce them, *in the absence of disease.* Then, if and when the actual disease happens to strike, there will be sufficient antibodies available without delay.

The stuff used to prepare vaccines is obtained from microorganisms.

Vaccines are quite specific. For instance, the tetanus vaccine will only trigger production of antibodies capable of neutralizing the tetanus antigen; that for typhoid fever will trigger the production of antibodies capable of neutralizing only the typhoid antigen, etc.

Specificity is another point of coincidence between vaccinations and Homeopathy. *Lycopodium clavatum,* for instance, will only act on patients with a *Lycopodium* profile, *Natrum muriaticum* in those who exhibit a *Natrum muriaticum* profile, etc.

Vaccines can be administered as they are produced from Nature. They can also be prepared by attenuating or killing microorganisms or else by altering the molecular structure of their digestive juices/toxins/antigens.

An example of a *natural vaccine* is that used for smallpox, obsolete now because the disease-syndrome smallpox no longer exists.

This vaccine was made with the pus—and viruses therein—present in udders of cows sick with cowpox. The cowpox virus is not dangerous for Humans, but is similar enough to the smallpox virus as to make the immune system produce antibodies that work on both cow- and smallpox.

The pus obtained from cows infested with pox, later to be used for purposes of vaccination, is freed from contaminants, homogenized and preserved in a suitable fashion prior to its administration.

Attenuated vaccines are prepared with live microorganisms that have been tamed or calmed down, so to speak, before administration.

The tuberculosis vaccine BCG (or *bilis*—or *Bacille—Calmette Guerin,* originally prepared by French Bacteriologists Drs. Albert L. C. Calmette (1863-1933) and Alphonse F. M. Guérin (1817-1895)) is a good example of an attenuated vaccine. It is prepared with the live *Mycobacterium* that causes tuberculosis in cows, but not in Humans. This particular microorganism is then *attenuated*—or tamed, if you wish—by means of culturing it, through several passages, in a medium prepared with bile.

The polio vaccine created by Dr. Albert Bruce Sabin, and that is administered by mouth, is also prepared with live attenuated viruses.

Over 100 years ago Bacteriologists found that they could attenuate microorganisms by means of passing them from one culture media to another. Conversely, microorganisms become increasingly dangerous when passed from one mammal to another.

Vaccines can also be prepared with *killed* bacteria. This procedure is favored when their toxins are either *within* the bacterial body, or else *attached* to their membrane.

The antityphoid vaccine is prepared in this fashion.

There are bacteria that spew their toxins into their environment—that is, into the patient. These toxins are complex molecules. About a Century ago, Researchers found that toxins secreted by these particular bacteria has two fractions, one that actually causes the disease-syndrome and another that is only a carrier. Translated onto ballistics, the carrier fraction would be the propellant module of a rocket, and the dangerous fraction the nuclear warhead.

The vaccine is made only with carrier fraction, that has no punch whatsoever. The patient's immune system, however, is duped into believing that the carrier is the *whole* toxin, and will start producing antibodies to neutralize it.

During an actual infection, it often happens that the immune system doesn't have sufficient time to first identify the toxins (or antigens) secreted by bacteria, and then to produce enough antibodies to neutralize them. The patient may therefore succumb before enough antibodies are ready.

When only the harmless carrier is administered through a vaccination, and the immune system wrongly identifies it as the whole antigen, then the immune system will be able to prepare all the antibodies needed to neutralize the *whole* toxin molecule at the time of a future actual infection. More important yet, the template used to prepare the antibody will remain in the immune system's memory for a long time to come.

Examples of toxin-secreting bacteria are those triggering the diseases tetanus and diphtheria, and examples of vaccines prepared only with the carriers of their toxins are the antidiphtheric and antitetanic.

Vaccines prepared with whole dead bacteria or viruses, or will live and attenuated bacteria or viruses, will also dupe the immune system into believing that those organisms are the real infection.

The immune system will respond, here too, by manufacturing templates that will produce antibodies in abundance to be used at the time of an actual infection.

Vaccinations have only a *preventive* capacity. Their purpose is to lure the immune system first into producing, and then into having enough antibodies at hand *while the patient is healthy;* and so be ready to neutralize antigens as soon as an actual infection starts.

There are also patients who have fallen ill with some of these infections diseases, and who have cured themselves and survived without their needing to be vaccinated beforehand. The immunity thus acquired may be permanent; as it happens for example in survivors of typhoid fever.

Here it can be said that these patients have become vaccinated with the *whole* toxin molecule—needless to say, at great risk for themselves.

An infectious disease-syndrome is the normal reaction of an organism when it feels invaded by dangerous microorganisms, whereas an *allergic reaction* is an insane response of the immune system when the patient's organism is invaded by substances that pose no risk or danger whatsoever.

Here the *aller*gen (or *aller*gic anti*gen*) can be a simple or complex molecule, live or not.

There are plenty of allergens out there. Pollen, dandruff, molds, hair of diverse animals, dust mites and what not.

In some patients, their own organs and tissues may act as allergens and trigger an allergic reaction against them. Such events can end up with the destruction of organs and tissues.

The *normal* reaction to an overabundance of allergens like pollen, dust, etc., generally manifests itself through congestion, increased nasal and bronchial secretion and the like, perhaps a bit of reversible wheezing, and/or by the development of some kind of rash and itching somewhere in the skin. For a short time. Plus perhaps some complaints of discomfort and malaise.

The patient's organism may also boost the production of certain elements designed to ward off allergens.

In some individuals, though, exposure to an allergen will actually bring forth unpleasant reactions, all the way from severe nasal congestion to asthma to severe eczema; to mention only three allergic responses or reactions—three of the *mildest*, actually.

Allopathic Medicine has several ways to deal with the symptoms brought about by allergic reactions, such as the prescription of decongestants, adrenaline injections, the administration of adrenal cortical hormones or their chemical derivatives, etc. The beneficial effects of many of these substances tends to disappear almost as soon as the patient stops using them.

In certain instances, such as when using decongestants, there is usually a rebound effect; congestion almost inevitably returns with a vengeance as soon as treatment is suspended.

There are also **allergy shots**.

Allergy shots are used to desensitize the patient; that is, to make him or her tolerant to the substance that triggers an allergic reaction. As far as I know, this is the only long-range treatment Allopathy has to offer to allergy patients.

First the allergic patient is studied in the usual fashion; that is, through a Clinical History, Physical Examination, etc.

Then the patient receives intradermal injections, or else has patches applied onto the skin. The patient's forearms are generally used for this purpose. Each of the patches and/or injectables contain a minute amount of a particular allergen. The skin reacts where an allergic reaction takes place. This is how the Allergist learns what the patient is allergic to. Then the patient starts receiving *allergy shots.*

Allergy shots consist in administering frequently by *injection, minute* but *increasing amounts* of the substance the patient has been found to be allergic to in the skin tests.

This purpose of this progression of shots is to make the patient *less and less sensitive and less and less reactive* to the allergen that triggers the reaction.

A treatment is considered successful when the patient stops developing an allergic reaction—that is, when he or she becomes non-responsive—to the allergen formerly capable of triggering it.

Allopathy has not been designed to consider *how foreign substances manage to enter the patient.* Nor, of course, to take the necessary measures to close the ports of entry to those foreign substances.

In imbalanced individuals, that point of entry is usually a chink in his or her armor, or else a damaged area in the boundary that stands between the patient and the environment.

There is nothing Allopathy can do to correct overall imbalance; and subsequently to close chinks, or to repair boundary damage, either.

Since nothing is static in Nature, this inability to close the port of entry will make the imbalance greater and greater, and thus that portal of entry larger and larger in time. Through it, foreign matter will keep on entering in increasing quantities.

All Allopathy can do for these patients is to attempt to neutralize the action of foreign molecules once inside the patient by means of *deadening the patient's response* to them.

In the Allopathic treatment of allergy, to my knowledge at least, *therapeutic success is the consequence of anesthetizing the patient's capacity to* react to a foreign invasion and to respond, however abnormally, to that invasion.

Allergy shots are a rather poor way of tackling allergic reactions.

An allergic reaction happens when there is a chink that allows foreign substances to enter an allergic patient and triggers a reaction that, daft as it is, *it is still the only way that allergic patient's immune system reacts against certain alien substances.* What is more rational, then, to anesthetize the immune system or else to bring the patient into balance and consequently close the allergen's portal of entry? This, of course, if and when the allergen comes from the outside.

When an allergic reaction is triggered by components any of the patient's organs or systems, the only form of successful treatment is to bring the Whole patient into balance.

Because, if the patient is brought into balance, then the immune system will learn how to respond in a healthy fashion. Furthermore, the chink in the armor that allows foreign substances to enter will close as the patient recovers balance. From then on, what has to be out will remain out, and what has to be in will remain in—without needing to interfere in the least with the patient's immune system patterns of response.

Both vaccination and allergy shots act directly on the immune system, not on the Whole patient.

Vaccinations overstimulate the immune system, in order to bring about a faster and stronger response when an infectious diseases strikes.

Allergy shots benumb the immune system, in order to deaden its reaction towards the molecules that trigger an allergic reaction.

Vaccines and allergy shots either overstimulate or benumb the immune system. Meaning that they upset the balance of the immune system and consequently of the Whole patient.

The priority of Homeopathy is to bring Whole disease-bearing patients into balance.

Consequently, vaccinations and allergy shots are antithetical to Homeopathy.

If we compare allergy shots and Homeopathic treatments we will find that both allergy shots and Homeopathic remedies are administered in infinitesimal amounts.

Allergy shots are the *same actual substances* that cause an allergic reaction.

Homeopathic remedies are the same actual substances that bring about a selective form of imbalance in the Provings.

Homeopathic remedies are administered *dynamized,* that is, diluted and shaken.

Allergy shots are administered *diluted,* not dynamized.

Allergy shots work by means of weakening a patient's allergic reaction.

Homeopathic remedies by bringing the Whole patient into balance, which in turn normalizes the patient's immune reaction to allergens.

Therapeutic success with allergy shots is usually the consequence of injecting stronger and stronger concentrations of the allergen; increasing concentrations that, in turn, elicit weaker and weaker allergic reactions.

Success of Homeopathic treatment is often the consequence of administering higher and higher dynamizations; that is, lower and lower material doses.

With allergy shots, therapeutic success is achieved when the patient is injected the same substance that causes the allergic reaction.

With Homeopathic remedies, instead, success is achieved when the patient receives the remedy that is similar to the Whole patient's profile, not the substance that provokes the allergic reaction.

The effectiveness of both allergy shots and vaccines is studied and evaluated according to the Protocols described in Chapter 23 for Pharmacological Research.

The effectiveness of Homeopathic remedies is studied through Provings, clinical observation, evaluation of intoxicated individuals and some times, with a great deal of caution, from clinical observations.

Homeopathic remedies are prepared with the totality of a natural product, be it mineral, vegetal, etc.

Allergy shots are also produced with the totality of the allergen. In turn, vaccines are usually prepared either with the whole microorganisms or else with parts of them.

A Homeopathic remedy is considered to be a stronger disease that displaces a weaker one, and so brings the patient into balance. A vaccine is an element, originally infectious, that stimulates the patient's immune system. A vaccine is always a *decoy*, prepared to lure the immune system into action against an imaginary infectious disease-syndrome. Homeopathic remedies prevent infections by means of bringing the Whole patient into harmony with him or herself and with Nature.

Vaccinations are administered in *material* amounts.
Homeopathic remedies in *infinitesimal* and/or *immaterial* amounts.

Microorganisms used to prepare vaccines may or may not be those that actually make Human Beings ill.
In the case of smallpox vaccine, it is the virus of a *different* disease, the cowpox, which is scratched—or *scarified*—onto the patient's skin. In the BCG, the *mycobacteria* corresponds to a disease of a different species, namely *bovine* tuberculosis, suitably weakened prior to being administered by mouth or by injection to Human Beings.
In the instance of the polio vaccine and others, it is the same virus that produces the disease in Humans, but *attenuated*. And, in the instance of the antidiphtheric and antitetanic vaccines, patients receive only the carrier of the toxin produced by actual and live infecting bacteria.
The antityphoid vaccine and others, instead, are prepared by the same actual bacteria that causes the disease, but dead.

Any number of microorganisms can be used to prepare allergy shots, harmful or not to animals and Humans.
The only requirement for their use is their capacity to produce allergic reactions.
They are used in increasing quantities, dead and infinitesimally dissolved.

Homeopathy also uses microorganisms, but *dynamized.*
They can be microorganisms that produce diseases is species other than Human, such as in the instance of *Tuberculinum bovinum* and others. Or else they can be microorganisms harmful to Humans, such as *Bacillinum, Syphilinum, Petrussin* and others.
These dynamized microorganisms are used as *remedies* in patients whose profile is similar to that brought about in the Provings of those microorganisms.

343

Or else, as Nosodes, dynamized microorganisms are used in patients whose chronic miasmas make them vulnerable to diseases brought about by those microorganisms.

As mentioned before, vaccines have only a *preventive* capacity or usefulness. They are not administered when the patient is suffering from the disease the vaccine is supposed to prevent.
Allergy shots, on the other hand, are supposed to be *curative.*

Homeopathic remedies have both *preventive* and *curative* properties.
Take *Influenzinum*, for instance. It may help prevent the disease-syndrome flu and, in acute patients with an adequate profile, it may also contribute to cure it.

Most vaccines and, of course, allergy shots, are administered by injection; whereas Homeopathic remedies are usually administered by mouth—exceptionally by sniffing and rubbing.

In essence, vaccinations and allergy shots are only concerned either with *stimulating* a patient's immune system in the instance of vaccines or else with *appeasing* it, or making it *more tolerant*, or *deadening* or *numbing* its response, in the case of allergy shots.
Homeopathic treatments aim at normalizing the patient's immune system indirectly, by means of bringing the Whole patient into balance.

Allergy shots and vaccines either bring about or else worsen patients' imbalance. Vaccines by means of overstimulating the immune system and allergy shots by numbing it.
Exactly the contrary is what happens after a successful Homeopathic treatment, that aims at establishing balance and harmony within the patient and between the patient and his or her environment.

To think that vaccinations make a patient healthier, or that allergy shots can cure an allergic patient is tantamount to deceiving oneself.
A patient can be considered as cured only when his or her balance has been restored. And there is no possibility of restoring a patient's overall balance with vaccines and/or allergy shots, that worsen the immune system's—and thus the Whole patient's—imbalance by means of exaggerating the defensive, or else the tolerant response to antigens or allergens.

When all is said and done, then, after a vaccination, or at the end of a successful series of allergy shots, all that has been achieved is a worsening of the patient's imbalance. Even if the patient becomes immune to a certain infectious disease or if he or she is cured of an allergy.

Overstimulating a patient's immune system with vaccination is tantamount of commanding *"Defend yourself and attack!"*. Anesthetizing it with allergy shots is the equivalent to ordering it *"Tolerate and accept!"*.

There is still no way of knowing how this set of powerful contradictory orders—often commanded to the immune system of same patient—may affect the immune system's correct response to everyday challenges, nor what the long term consequence of these contradictory orders may be.

Vaccines have side effects, some of which can be very severe. And it makes sense.

It is never good practice to overload or overstimulate any one of our systems; whether it is the digestive, sexual or mental systems, for instance.

By the same token, is may well be risky to overload our immune system with impunity—particularly when overloading starts in hours-old babies, in whom the immune system is still far from adequately developed.

All the more when many of the vaccines infants receive contain toxic elements, such as Thimerosol, an antiseptic incorporated into many vaccines. 49.6 % of Thimerosol is mercury. Mercury is very toxic, particularly to the central nervous and the immune systems, and also to the kidneys. Its half-life in the human body ranges between 40 and 50 days (Clarkson T.W. *"Mercury: Major issues in environmental health"*. Environmental Health Perspectives 100: 31-38, 1992).

This state of affairs moved the American Academy of Pediatrics and the Public Health Service to issue a joint statement July 7, 1999. The statement said that infants who receive Thimerosol-containing vaccines might be exposed to more mercury than recommended by Federal Guidelines for total mercury exposure. Since, the onset of childhood vaccination was postponed from the first day of life to the 6th month.

A recently published paper (Creticos, P.S., *et al.* *"Ragweed immunotherapy in adult asthma"*. NEJM 334(8):501-506, 1996) points out that allergy shots are very expensive and may have side effects, some severe.

The paper also remarks that allergy shots may also be useless in the treatment of asthma.

And that, even though successful in hay fever, the effects of allergy shots tend to vanish after 2 years of treatment.

Vaccinations may contain residues of the culture media used in their preparation (that cannot be removed completely), plus added antiseptics (to prevent the vaccine from spoiling), stabilizers, etc.

And so, when vaccinated, the patient may receive, aside from the vaccine itself, variable amounts of elements such as aluminum, formaldehyde, Thimerosol, gelatin, ammonium sulfate, neomycin, polysorbate 80, sorbitol, chick embryo tissues, glycerol, hydrolysate of casein, yeast, MR 5 proteins (residue from medium), human diploid cells (originating from human aborted fetal tissue), polyribosylribitol, polymyxin, gentamycin, streptomycin, monkey kidney cells, lactose, calf serum, phenol red, MSG (monosodium glutamate), potassium monophosphate, potassium diphosphate, fetal bovine serum, amphotericin B, EDTA (ethylenediaminetetraacetic acid), etc. (PDR (Physicians' Desk Reference) 53rd Ed, 1999).

Who should receive vaccinations, and when?

A comprehensive discussion of this subject would exceed the scope of this book. Furthermore, such a discussion would be loaded with very strong emotional charge when it comes to the vaccinations of one's children.

Yet, I don't believe it is fair to leave the reader without some orientation in this respect.

Perhaps the best thing would be to learn about vaccinations, their pros and their cons and their benefits and their risks, and so become able to reach an understanding regarding their usefulness, dangers and limitations. And then decide what to do based on that knowledge and that understanding.

My advice would be to contact,

- the Center for Disease Control, in Atlanta, GA, and
- the National Vaccine Information Center, founded in 1982 by parents of vaccine injured children (www.909shot.com, or 800 909 SHOT); and to read
- the excellent Chapter on vaccinations in *"How to rise a healthy child...in spite of your Doctor"*, written by Robert Mendelsohn, M.D., a brilliant Board Certified Pediatrician with decades of experience (Ballantine Books, 1987). In point of fact, the whole book is extraordinary. I enthusiastically recommend parents to read it from cover to cover; and
- a paper written by Kristine M. Severyn, R.Ph., Ph.D., entitled *"Immunization: a Pharmacist's View"*. It has been published in the

Journal of the American Institute of Homeopathy, 87 (2): 79-82, 1994.

A final word.
Regarding the so-called Homeopathic *vaccines*.

To start with, to say *Homeopathy* and *vaccine* in the same breath constitutes an oxymoron. These two terms oppose each other as it has become, I hope, abundantly clear above.

Vaccines work by means of proffering the immune system material amounts of a product that is supposed to overstimulate it. One needs a minimum of that stimulating matter in order to bring about an immune reaction. Below this minimal amount, the immune system will not be able to acknowledge the presence of the vaccine or react to it.

A Homeopathic vaccine has been succused until what remain is only infinitesimal amounts of the vaccine used to prepare it—clearly not enough to trigger an immunity reaction.

It has been claimed that these so-called Homeopathic vaccines work as well as real vaccines, but without their side effects and the like.

Authoritative scientific reports, however, have shown that Homeopathic vaccines are *not* effective for purposes of vaccination (Fisher P., *Enough nonsense on immunization*. Brit. Hom. J. 79: 198-200, 1990. Burgess M., *Homeopathy and vaccination*. Lancet 344 (8930): 1168, 1994).

These products may become useful Homeopathic remedies once their profile is known, though—after all, *everything* that has been succussed and tested in Provings, develops a profile that can find its usefulness in the treatment of some particular imbalanced patient.

Chapter 25

THE NEED TO INTEGRATE HOMEOPATHY AND AL-LOPATHY

Allopathy and Homeopathy are both useful. There is plenty of evidence in this regard.

Both, however, have limitations.

Many of the limitations of Homeopathy are nicely covered by Allopathy and vice versa. Meaning that each approaches complements the other.

There are currently only a handful of Physicians knowledgeable in Integrative Medicine, that is, in Allopathy, Homeopathy and other forms of Complementary Medicine.

This small number of Doctors has little impact on the big picture.

Sooner or later, though, Allopathy and Homeopathy will have to integrate; in the same fashion that Clinical Medicine gradually integrated with Surgery and then with other specialties along the past two Centuries.

Clinicians despised Surgeons before Clinical Medicine and Surgery integrated.

Surgeons had started humbly as barbers, bleeding patients and performing other suchlike messy and undoctorlike tasks, aside from cutting people's hair and shaving their beards. In point of fact, the post one still sees in front of many barbershops today, painted in white with a red strip spiraling around it stems from a tradition dating to those days. Barbers announced that the did bloodletting by means of rolling a bloody strip of white cloth around a post, and then displaying it in front of their shops.

Clinicians would consider Surgeons inferior and unworthy to be called "Doctors". Indeed, to this day, in Great Britain, Surgeons are called "Mister" while all other Physicians are called "Doctor".

It took a long time of jostling to have Clinicians and Surgeons finally working together.

Something similar happened when the Medical/Surgical establishment was challenged by the X Ray people. Again, after some pushing and pulling, Radiologists and Radiotherapists were also accepted into the fold.

It is interesting to note that, in all of of these instances. the paradigms of the diverse specialties was respected.

In the first instance, Clinicians recognized that there were things Surgeons could perform that they couldn't, and that what Surgeons did could benefit patients—although such an assertion is only valid after antiseptic techniques made their appearance in Operating Rooms. Before that, Surgery was but a repetitive massacre.

After integrating, both Clinicians and Surgeons recognized the usefulness of Radiologists and Radiotherapists.

In other words, in every instance, and after some inevitable shoving and elbowing, diverse specialists integrated and reached an *entente cordiale* that allows them to complement their efforts to benefit patients through recognizing their respective possibilities and limitations.

There is no reason why such integration will not happen between Allopathy, Homeopathy and other forms of Complementary Medicine.

But it will take time.

As mentioned before in this book, integration will likely need a new *generation* of Doctors rather than a new *attitude* of those currently in practice, if History is anything to judge by. Take, for instance, modern scientific Medicine. From the 1870's onwards, it proved undeniably that it was infinitely more useful than bleeding, purging, blistering, cupping and the like. Yet, this new form of Medicine was fully accepted by Allopathic Physicians, and incorporated into their practices, only between 1900 and 1910.

Consider the following, regarding how important it is to integrate all forms of Medicine.

I am acquainted with a very nice man, a staunch believer of Wholistic Medicine. He despises Allopathy.

He phoned me one Friday morning. He asked if I could see his 13-year-old daughter that same day. When I asked why, he gave me a fairly clear clinical picture of acute appendicitis.

He also told me that, since the previous Monday—that is, for the past five days—the patient had been treated by a Wholistic Practitioner with *Bryonia*. This man told me that his daughter got worse and worse as days went by, that he had repeatedly called the Practitioner, and that the only answer he had received was to continue the treatment with *Bryonia* at increasing potencies.

I replied that what he was telling me sounded a lot like a very acute appendicitis, and asked him to take his daughter to the Hospital without delay.

He flatly refused. He insisted on my seeing her, so I gave them the last appointment of a very busy day, late in the evening.

They didn't show up.

His wife called me the following Monday, full of apologies. She told me that, on the way to my office, her daughter had cried with pain every time the car hit any insignificant irregularity on the road—a characteristic of *Bryonia*. Worried, she had taken the girl directly to the Hospital.

The patient was immediately operated upon. Her appendix had ruptured. She had peritonitis.

Thank Goodness, her youthful constitution and modern Allopathy this young lady got well—but not before having to stay a full 10 days in the Hospital. Mostly febrile, desperately ill and in pain; with tubes into her veins and into her stomach, plus drainage tubes into her abdomen.

She was left with a large and unsightly scar, instead of the small one that would have remained if she had been operated in time.

The second patient I would like to briefly describe is a 25 year old female.

Extremely anxious. A live wire. Pale, with dark circles under her eyes and very, very thin. Feeling weak and sickly all the time.

She was also about to get married but her fiancé, seeing her so thin and weakened, had started to drag his feet; a fact that contributed in no small measure to her anxiety.

This patient had gone to see her Family Doctor a few years back because of chronic low back pain. The Doctor X Ray'd her lumbosacral spine and found some intervertebral disc displacement.

He referred the patient to a Neurosurgeon after an unsuccessful course of muscle relaxants, tranquilizers, pain killers and antiinflamatory drugs.

The Neurosurgeon operated on her spine.

The pain persisted, so she underwent Neurosurgery a second time.

The pain was still there after the second intervention, but apparently the Neurosurgeon considered he had done enough. He did not attempt any further surgery.

Some time later, this patient developed Crohn's disease. The ulcers and scarring in the nether part of her small intestine, characteristic of this disease-syndrome, caused her a great deal of pain and misery.

Her Family Doctor first treated her with drugs and, when he found no results, sent the patient to a Surgeon.

The Surgeon removed all the diseased area of the intestine and then some, in order to be able to sew healthy gut to the large intestine. But Crohn's disease re-appeared in the stump.

More Surgery, and still more small intestine removed. Her Crohn's disease stubbornly re-appeared in the new stump.

No more surgery was performed because, as things stood, she had already very little small intestine left. To remove still more might have thrown her into severe malnutrition, for she wouldn't have had enough small intestine surface left to adequately absorb foodstuffs.

It was then that she came to see me.

Her abdomen, that was painful and tender to palpation, was streaked with scars. The backache was very bothersome. There were surgical scars and stiffness in her back, too.

I gave her *Calcarea Carbonica*, that I considered was her Constitutional remedy. I warned her that Homeopathy may be very slow to act, due to all the Surgery.

She stopped seeing me shortly after starting Homeopathic treatment.

I haven't heard from her since. I hope she's faring well, though I strongly doubt it.

I chose these two patients, from several I have seen and heard of, to highlight a problem that is as unfortunate as it is prevalent. A problem that appears, only too frequently, when a patient goes to the wrong Health Care Provider in search of assistance.

Most Health Care Practitioners are usually knowledgeable in their chosen field of practice, but many are ignorant in—and often prejudiced against—other form of diagnosis and treatment.

The result of this lopsided outlook is that patients are proffered either only Allopathic treatment if they go to an Allopathic Physician, or else only some form of Wholistic treatment if they go to a Wholistic Practitioner. Whether they may benefit from that unilateral approach or not.

All of this means that the choice of Allopathic or Wholistic treatment for a particular patient has nothing to do with the patient's needs. It is only related to the scope of knowledge and, frequently, of the intensity of the prejudices the Health Care Professional has.

The results can be disasters like the ones described above in some detail.

This mutual intolerance between Allopathic and Homeopathic Physicians, by all means justifiable up to 150 years ago—when it was either Homeopathy or else a gruesome catalogue of atrocities—should have ceased after the advent of modern Allopathy.

Yet, this obsolete and unavailing attitude, fed by moldy distrust and prejudice, remains alive and strong.

There are Wholistic Practitioners who still consider that all Allopathic treatments are suppressive and very dangerous, and state they have nothing useful to offer—or else that whatever usefulness they may have is so fraught with perils that it's better left alone. It is as if Allopathy wouldn't have advanced at all in the past 150 years, as if it would still be using leeches, jalap, the Spanish fly and all other therapeutic brutalities of yesteryear.

Patients who visit these Health Care Practitioners will be treated with Complementary Medicine *only.* Whether or not they may also need Allopathic treatment for their disease-syndrome/s.

On the other side of this absurd no-man's-land, many Allopathic Doctors still cling to the belief that all forms of Wholistic treatment are charlatanry or worse. A total waste of time, a scam, something only worthy of a scoff and a sneer—even though they have seen, or at least heard of, instances in which patients were cured or at least considerably relieved by Wholistic treatments.

Most Allopathic Doctors won't bother to look around to see if perchance there is something better elsewhere. They will continue prescribing drugs, performing surgeries and radiating tumors—or doing nothing.

For instance, in Argentina there was a terrible epidemic of poliomyelitis in 1956—ironically, the year when the Salk vaccine became widely available in America for the first time. Argentine Homeopathic Physicians gave all their patients the remedy *Lathyrus sativus* every 15 days as a prophylactic measure. It has been known for a long time that *Lathyrus* is useful both to prevent and to treat polio. Allopathic Doctors, who at that time had nothing to prevent or to treat polio with, could have availed themselves of *Lathyrus,* but they didn't. They did nothing to prevent the appearance of polio in their patients. *Lathyrus* was way beyond the boundaries of the Allopathic paradigm and therefore *verboten.* The result was that every single Homeopathic patient survived the epidemic unscathed whereas a host of the Allopathic Physicians' patients—and their relatives, too—fell sick. Of them, many became paralyzed, or died, of the disease.

Both forms of treatment, Allopathic and Wholistic, have been growing side by side along the past two Centuries—indeed, the principles of *contrary cures contrary* and that of *like cures like* have coexisted throughout Medical History.

The Greek philosopher Empedocles (490-430 BC) first enunciated the principle of *like cures like* that, 2,300 years later, was to become the foundation of Homeopathy. This principle was afterwards appropriated by Hippocrates (460-360 BC), who incorporated it in aphorism # 42 of his classic masterpiece *"Places of Man"*. In the same aphorism, Hippocrates also included the principle of *contrary cures contrary*, later to become the cornerstone of Allopathic Medicine.

Everybody demands better quality Medicine, and rightly so.

When thinking about good quality Medicine, one generally envisions well-equipped Hospitals, better trained Doctors and Nurses and the like.
Which is true, *but only insofar as Allopathy is concerned*.
Wholistic Medicine should not be ignored in this context.

Good quality Medicine starts with Physicians who are proficient, or at the very least knowledgeable, in diverse forms of Medicine.
And good quality Medicine continues with the patient's full participation in the design of a therapeutic plan designed for the control of his or her disease-syndrome. Participation can only be achieved by means of discussing *all* therapeutic lines with each patient, all options, possibilities and alternatives—until, at the end, both Doctor and patient agree on the best course of treatment.

Discussion between Doctor and patient should include an assessment of the benefit/risk of each possible treatment as well as an estimate of how much suffering, money and time the patient is willing to spend in each of the options or combination of options.
Only then will the patient be in a situation of making an intelligent decision regarding what therapeutic course to follow.
At worst, this frank discussion between Doctor and patient will assure a better compliance on the part of the patient, and help create an atmosphere of mutual respect, cooperation and trust.
At best, the patient will leave the Doctor's office feeling the satisfaction of having been treated as someone endowed with intelligence and common sense, someone whose decision as to what to do with his or her own life is seriously taken into account, and respected.

Good quality Medicine consists on studying and treating the Whole disease-bearing patient, and not just of the disease a patient may be bearing.

Jose Miguel Mullen, M.D.

> Good quality Medicine doesn't surge from gleaming state-of-
> the-art equipment in Allopathic offices and/or Hospitals. Nor from
> cozy, all Natural Wholistic Centers—the locale is not important
> here.
> Good quality Medicine stems from the minds and the hearts of
> Caregivers sufficiently acquainted with both Allopathic and Wholis-
> tic Medicine.
> This is so because Integrative Physicians can proffer their pa-
> tients a full range of therapeutic possibilities, both Allopathic and
> Wholistic. That is to say, Integrative Physicians, using many
> sources of knowledge, can plan a treatment that combines maximum
> benefit with minimum risk, according to the needs of each individ-
> ual patient.

Aside from the few Caregivers knowledgeable in both Allopathy and
Wholism, most Practitioners are trained to treat patients with either one
form of Medicine or with the other.

Which means that, nowadays, only patients under the care of Integrative
Physicians have the possibility of receiving the form of Medicine, or combination thereof, most adequate for their needs.

Integrative Medicine, today the privilege of a few, will become everybody's patrimony when Wholism and Allopathy *integrate.*

Integration, however, necessary as it is, should never be reached at the
cost of lowering the standards of quality Medical care.

Quality Medical care consists on knowing, for instance, when to ask for
what diagnostic procedure after obtaining a sound History and Physical Examination and when not to. When and how to maintain or discontinue a certain Allopathic treatment the patient may be receiving. When to send the patient to a specialist or to the Hospital, when and how to replace an Allopathic treatment with Homeopathy or any other Complementary treatment,
when and how to associate a Wholistic or an Allopathic treatment to whatever the patient may be currently receiving, etc.

We are still far from that ideal.

Many Medical students are still influenced into disdaining Wholism,
and discouraged from having anything to do with it.

In turn, many students of Complementary Medicine are taught only a
smattering of Allopathy and related subjects.

Results of this divorce between Scientific and Complementary Medicine are often calamitous.

At best, patients may end up receiving only part of the treatment they need; at worst, their future well-being, if not their lives, may be placed in jeopardy.

Take the legion of young men and women left with a permanent colostomy after Surgery for ulcerative colitis, an intervention performed by Surgeons totally ignorant of the usefulness of Homeopathy and Acupuncture in the treatment of this disease-syndrome.

Or the diabetic patient who visits a Wholistic Practitioner insufficiently trained in Allopathy—and who may also have an inwrought irrational distrust regarding "chemicals" and/or "drugs". The diabetes will continue undiagnosed and the patient will receive Wholistic treatment instead of Insulin. The patient may well end up decompensating into diabetic coma. If this catastrophe happens when somebody is around, then that patient may be rushed to a Hospital and saved—but that patient can also die, if decompensation happens when he or she is alone.

Or take all those toddlers whom, by age of 2 or 3, and after being saturated with antibiotics—and becoming resistant to all and allergic to many—end up by having tubes thrust through their eardrums.

Or the myriad of babies with skin rashes that are made to disappear with some local treatment or other, and who later on develop asthma that will last for the rest of their lives.

Or all those women who want to have children but can't, and who end up with multiple pregnancies after having been subjected to the diagnostic procedures and treatments currently *en vogue*. Here also, Homeopathic treatment is very effective, comfortable and safe. It balances both parents, and usually brings about *one* healthy baby per normal pregnancy.

I don't see too much of a point in having Homeopathic Hospitals any more.

They were a needed Haven at a time when being admitted to an Allopathic Hospital often meant to leave it either dead or disabled; unless the patient had sense enough to escape in time.

As it happened to a patient of the eminent British Physician Dr. John Elliotson, of St. Thomas Hospital in London. The patient had severe neuralgia in one finger. Taking into account that "one does not storm a castle with only four constables" Dr. Elliotson vigorously treated that poor man and his finger with morphine at high doses, potassium cyanide, carbonate and sulfite of iron, ether, strychnine—also at hefty doses— tartar emetic and arsenic. The good Doctor manifested his disappointment when the patient signed himself out of the Hospital three weeks later, "looking as ill as when he first came in". (Elliotson, J. *"Clinical Lecture"*. The Lancet 1: 323-325, 1832-33).

Those days are fortunately gone with the wind. Things have changed a lot since the 19th Century.

Hospitals have become more and more complex and sophisticated institutions of diagnosis and treatment where, and despite of numerous shortcomings, a considerable number of lives are saved, and the health of many is at least partially restored.

In some cities of Europe, as well as elsewhere in the world, Homeopathy is nowadays done in General Hospitals, on patients who are too ill to be ambulatory. Often, these patients may undergo drug treatments or Surgery simultaneously with Homeopathy.

Under an integrated outlook Homeopathic Hospitals would indeed be a needless—and very expensive—duplication of efforts.

Clinical diagnoses are needed by both Allopaths and Integrative Physicians to determine what has to be treated by whom, when, how, what with and in what sequence. This kind of work can easily be carried out in an integrated General Hospital.

Integration between Allopathy and Homeopathy, for Medical Doctors, should start in Medical Schools and continue through their Post-Graduate Hospital training. In Medical Schools, Wholistic Medicine should be taught as a specialty, allotting to it the same time granted to subjects such as Ophthalmology, Otorhinolaryngology, etc.

In Hospitals young graduates, if they so choose, should be allowed to train in an Integrative Medical residency.

For students in Schools devoted to Wholistic Medicine, integration should start by placing more emphasis—*positive* emphasis—in the pre-graduate teaching of subjects related to Allopathic Medicine. Graduates should then be allowed to do post-graduate training in Hospitals—despite of the inevitable conflicts and other forms of turbulence integration may bring in its wake.

Conflicts are always at risk of happening among Doctors with diverse outlooks, anyway. Once in 1956 or '57, for instance, I witnessed an Internist and a Surgeon as they almost came to blows in the corridor of a Hospital because of their divergent opinions regarding the treatment of a peptic ulcer-bearing patient. This episode was, of course, extreme; but I have seen, and occasionally participated in or protagonized other discussions, if in a considerably more polite, gracious and urbane fashion.

The existence of conflicts, inevitable when opinions diverge, should therefore not be considered as a deterrent for integration.

A handsome benefit of integration would be a very considerable reduction in the costs of hospitalization.

Patients eligible for Homeopathy or other forms of Wholistic Medicine can be treated at an insignificant fraction of the cost incurred by Allopathic treatments.

Just consider, in this context, the young lady with the spinal disc problems and then Crohn's disease mentioned at the beginning of this Chapter. Consider how much expense—and suffering—would have been averted is she had received adequate Wholistic treatment.

In addition, Homeopathy and other forms of Wholistic treatment can oftentimes improve results of Allopathic treatments, and reduce the length of Hospital stay.

Last but not least, in these days of dwindling Hospital clientele and receding Hospital revenues, integration would give many patients a good reason to return to Hospitals.

According to common knowledge and well documented information, an ever increasing number of Americans are using diverse forms of Wholistic Medicine nowadays. Many of those patients have vowed never to return to a Hospital again.

Most Hospital defectors drift into the care of Wholistic Providers many of whom, however undoubtedly proficient in their respective fields, have little knowledge about Allopathy, have been taught to distrust it, and likely will not recommend it even when needed.

I am sure many Hospital defectors would be much less remiss to request Hospital care if they knew they could be seen, in a Hospital setting, by an Integrative Medical team.

For instance, I am certain that people like the father of the girl with appendicitis, in this Chapter, would have had no objection to go to an integrated Hospital as the first choice.

Chapter 26

THE CASE FOR AND AGAINST HOMEOPATHIC SELF-MEDICATION

Over the counter (OTC) Homeopathic or Allopathic prepara-tions have been designed to treat common disease-syndromes.

OTC preparations can often successfully control mild acute disease-syndromes in otherwise well-balanced patients. The cure of psoric patients, on the other hand, presupposes their being brought into balance through the use of a Constitutional Homeopathic rem-edy.

A Constitutional remedy can only be prescribed after a meticu-lous assessment of the chronic patient's profile by a Homeopathic Physician—meaning that a self-prescribed remedy can never re-place the administration of the Constitutional remedy in a chronic patient.

In chronic patients, self-medication can only treat local dis-ease-syndromes. In chronic patients virgin of Constitutional Ho-meopathic treatment, local treatments may well trigger a suppres-sion.

An individual can medicate him or herself Homeopathically by means of purchasing, and then taking, any remedy *not* prescribed by a Homeo-pathic or Integrative Physician.

Most health food stores carry a comprehensive stock of Homeopathic remedies, usually at low potencies.

Many Homeopathic remedies can also be found in shelves of the over the counter (OTC) floor area. Medical Doctors or Osteopathic Physicians, however, must dispense some of them.

OTC Pharmaceutical drugs are usually displayed in the same floor area, but in separate shelves.

OTC Homeopathic remedies are sold as mother tinctures or as dynam-ized preparations; as single remedies or as a combination of several (the lat-ter also known as *complexes*).

In their respective labels, OTC Homeopathic remedies clearly spell out what they are made of, as well as the potencies of their respective compo-nents. Elsewhere in the same label it is also stated what disease-syndrome/s each single remedy or complex is considered to be useful for (i.e., nausea, headaches, rheumatic pains, etc.).

This listing of what remedies are useful for is unreliable, as purchasers of OTC remedies have found to their chagrin. Let me recall that, for a Homeopathic treatment to be useful in a disease-syndrome, its symptoms have to be *modalized* as exhaustively as possible. This modalization is what accurately points toward the correct remedy, rather than the *bare* symptoms or the disease-syndrome. Disease-syndromes listed in the labels of Homeopathic remedies are not in the least modalized, thus the uselessness of those listings.

Remedies and complexes are usually sold imbedded in pellets, with the exception of cough syrups and the like, that are commonly sold as solutions.

Many—though by no means all—OTC remedies are prepared by large, well-known and reliable Homeopathic Pharmacies.

Of late, more and more Practitioners are directly selling natural products to their patients.

In most instances, those products are not Homeopathic but rather vitamins, antioxidants, essential fatty acids, plant extracts and the like.

OTC Homeopathic remedies can indeed bring about relief in many acute diseases. That is what they have been designed for. This relief may be all that is needed in acute patients. This is so because acute patients return to full health and balance when their Vital Force is re-attached to the diseased organ or structure. This re-attachment, consequent to a successful Homeopathic treatment, makes most acute diseases vanish.

In chronic patients, though, relief is likely to be only partial—at best.

If a chronic patient suffers an acute disease, modalizes its symptoms properly and takes the correct Homeopathic OTC remedy, that remedy may indeed alleviate his or her acute disease or else make it disappear altogether. Such a treatment, though, will not alter the progression of that chronic patient's real disease, namely, his or her overall imbalance.

OTC Homeopathic remedies usually behave like *local* remedies or like Pharmaceutical drugs, although without sharing the latter's side effects and toxicity. However, and like any other *local* treatment, OTC remedies may trigger a suppression or else Pseudo-psora in chronic patients.

This doesn't mean that actual acute diseases should be left untreated in chronic patients. Far from it. What it means is that the chronic imbalance should be treated first and, if any of the acute disease's symptoms persists afterwards, then a local treatment can be safely used.

There are many books dealing with self-medication. These books usually advice which OTC Homeopathic remedies to use for diverse disease-syndromes.

They are usually designed like cookbooks.

In cookbooks, dishes are usually listed in alphabetical order. *Vis-à-vis* the name of each dish there is a list of the necessary ingredients, their proportions and the procedure to be used in order to cook them.

In the case of most books devoted to OTC treatments, disease-syndromes are listed in alphabetical order. Opposite are Homeopathic remedies and/or complexes useful to combat them.

These therapeutic cookbooks also contain instructions regarding schedules of administration, warnings, etc.

Medicating oneself can become actually dangerous if the patient's acute disease-syndrome is severe, as in the instances of a coronary attack or acute appendicitis. Self-medication here usually means a delay in diagnosis, and consequently of a vigorous professional treatment that can be life-saving.

Self-medication of a symptom can also pose a risk for patients suffering of a dangerous chronic disease. Just consider the OTC Homeopathic treatment of a cough brought about by lung cancer, for instance.

The correct thing to do, when dealing with a serious or severe acute disease-syndrome—or *if in doubt*—is to consult a Doctor as soon as possible.

Sometimes, and after the OTC treatment fails, a patient may consult a qualified Health Care Professional.

Here the course of treatment is bound to differ if the patient is Allopathically or Homeopathically oriented.

Take an Allopathically oriented middle-aged patient suffering from long-standing aches and pains, say in his or her hands. The patient goes to the OTC area of the Pharmacy and purchases some analgesic/antiinflamatory agent such as Acetaminophen, Acetylsalicilic acid, Ibuprofen or any other.

Jose Miguel Mullen, M.D.

If these drugs don't relieve, the patient will go to a Medical Doctor. The latter will evaluate his or her joints and, in all likelihood, prescribe an analgesic/antiinflamatory drug that is more powerful—and also laden with more and more toxicity and side effects. These potent drugs may bring about some degree of relief in the patient's pain and limitation of movements, but at the cost of having to deal with their various toxicities and side effects. All of which will contribute to the acceleration of the chronic imbalance of the patient.

As a Greek present, the patient may also receive a suppression in the bargain.

Take now a middle-aged chronic Homeopathically oriented patient suffering from the same problem.

Instead of an OTC analgesic/antiinflammatory drug, that patient will chose an OTC Homeopathic remedy or complex to treat the problem. Let us now suppose that the remedy or complex doesn't work or that it has stopped working after a while, and that hopefully hasn't provoked a suppression in the meantime. The patient will feel compelled to go to a Homeopathic Physician.

The Homeopathic Physician will not prescribe a more powerful remedy or complex for the pain and inflammation, but rather will study the Whole patient. The Doctor will then prescribe the remedy designed to bring the patient into balance and, in the process, to make the pain and the inflammation vanish. If the pain and inflammation persists, the Doctor will prescribe a Complementary or local remedy afterwards.

All of which means that, when a patient is *chronic*—that is, when the disease-syndrome ailing him or her is the consequence of progressive imbalance—*that patient may indeed find some degree of relief by treating the problem with OTC Homeopathic remedies.*

However, this OTC treated patient *will not profit from the main beneficial effect of Homeopathy; namely, from its unique capacity of correcting a chronic state of imbalance*—and consequently of making the disease-syndrome ailing the chronic patient improve or disappear as an added bonus.

Furthermore, by medicating him or herself, instead of starting Constitutional treatment as soon as possible, a chronic patient is *maintaining and perpetuating a condition of chronic imbalance that is constantly worsening.* And consequently favoring the appearance of one disease-syndrome after another, as imbalance inevitably becomes more and more pronounced.

To sum up.

The case *for* OTC Homeopathic treatments is that, in the instance of *mild* acute disease-syndromes, they can correct the disorder without side effects and toxicity, and at a minimum cost.

The case *against* OTC Homeopathic treatment focuses on its use in the treatment of *severe* acute disease-syndromes, as well as in illnesses arising as the consequence of chronic imbalance.

In the case of severe acute disease-syndromes, because OTC treatments may delay a life-saving treatment—sometimes until it is too late.

In the instance of chronic imbalance-induced disease-syndromes, OTC Homeopathic preparations may cure one disease-syndrome after another, but will do nothing to correct the relentless progression of the patient's chronic imbalance.

Moreover, let me recall that, in many instances, an acute disease-syndrome is the means through which the Vital Force temporarily hooks the patient's imbalance to some organ or tissue with the purpose of slowing down the progression of the patient's imbalance. The "cure" of a disease-syndrome, under these circumstances, is tantamount of accelerating the pace of that patient's imbalance. This uncontrolled imbalance will, in time, become incompatible with life.

To boot, and by treating each disease individually, chronic patients may trigger the appearance of suppressions.

Chapter 27

SOME SIMILARITIES AND DIFFERENCES BETWEEN HOMEOPATHIC REMEDIES AND PHARMACEUTICAL DRUGS.

HOMEOPATHIC REMEDIES	PHARMACEUTICAL DRUGS
Follow the Principle that *Like Cures Like.*	Follow the Principle that *Contrary Cures Contrary.*
Act on the Whole chronic disease-bearing patient. In acute patients, only on the disease-syndrome.	Act on the diseased organ or structure (the so-called *therapeutic effect).* When acting elsewhere, their action is described as *toxicity, side effects* or *teratogenesis.*
Use mainly natural substances, as found in Nature, that are Homeopathically prepared by succussion.	Use only pure chemical formulas.
In chronic patients, the site of action is the fulcrum of imbalance. In acute diseases, it is probably the disease itself.	Their site of action is a subcellular target in the patient's cells; or else of bacteria, viruses or parasites.
In chronic patients, remedies work by means of bringing the Whole patient into balance.	Drugs work by means of blocking, stimulating or inhibiting subcellular targets.
Usefulness of remedies is learnt through experiments performed exclusively in healthy human beings.	Usefulness learnt through experiments carried out in bacteria, cell cultures, laboratory animals and sick human beings.
Correct *potency* determined by trial and error, in each individual patient.	Correct *dose* determined first in laboratory animals, and then refined in sick human beings.
Act by means of bringing chronic patients, through cure, into health and balance. Which, in turn, usually improves the quality of the patient's life.	Act by means of curing the disease-syndromes ailing chronic patients.

HOMEOPATHIC REMEDIES	PHARMACEUTICAL DRUGS
Lack side effects, toxicity, teratogenesis and allergy-inducing capacity.	Have side effects, toxicity, teratogenesis and allergy-inducing capacity.
The patient's Vital Force, primed by the Homeopathic remedy, is the *only* element that brings about the shift into balance, and subsequently health.	The administered drug, sustained by the patient's Vital Force, is the *only* element that brings about the cure of the patient's disease. Drugs have no effect on the patient's overall imbalance.
Aggravation usually due to excessive stimulation of the patient's Vital Force.	Aggravation usually due to massive destruction of bacteria, or of direct action on the patient's tissues. May also be due to the drug's toxicity and/or side effects.
Increasing effect related to a *decreasing* concentration of the active principle in the remedy.	Increasing effect related to *increasing* dose of the drug.
Only one remedy, called *Constitutional,* will act in the Whole disease-bearing psoric patient.	Several drugs may work equally well on the same disease.
Diagnosis and treatment are *one* and *the same thing.* The profile of the chronic patient, or that of the acute disease, must match the profile of the remedy.	Diagnosis is related to the pathological entity that ails the patient, and treatment to the drug/s or procedure/s necessary to fight the disease.
Presence of the Physician *necessary* during *both* the Homeopathic Clinical History and Physical Examination.	Presence of the Physician important during the patient's Physical Examination. The Clinical History may be obtained by an Assistant.
For diagnostic purposes, the Doctor must know, and be able to correctly interpret what ails the patient. But he or she must also *understand* the patient.	For diagnostic purposes, it is sufficient for the Doctor to know and to adequately interpret what ails the patient.

Jose Miguel Mullen, M.D.

HOMEOPATHIC REMEDIES	PHARMACEUTICAL DRUGS
Rapport *indispensable* in the Doctor-patient relationship	Rapport *unnecessary* in the Doctor-patient relationship.
Large amounts of a dynamized remedy can be administered in one single dose without problems.	Large amounts of a drug in one single dose can be very dangerous and even fatal.
Danger of an involuntary Proving if *the same* low potency is administered daily for long periods of time.	Possibility of only mild side effects and toxicity if the same low dose is administered daily for long periods of time.
Preventive capacity achieved by means of bringing about balance and harmony within the patient, and between the patient and his or her environment.	Preventive capacity achieved by means of overstimulating the patient's immune system, and also by means of tampering Nature.
Diseases are considered to be the *consequence* of the acute or chronic patient's imbalance.	Diseases are considered to be the *cause* of the patient's imbalance.
Symptoms are defined as *all* the manifestations, *both normal and pathological*, of the *Whole* acute disease, or of the *Whole* chronic disease-bearing patient.	*Symptoms* are defined as the *pathological* manifestations of the patient's disease-syndrome.
Full *cooperation* of the patient indispensable.	*Compliance* of the patient necessary.
The Whole psoric disease-bearing patient must first be brought into balance, through the action of the Vital Force challenged by the Constitutional remedy. Only then will the patient's Vital Force attune itself with the patient and cure any disease-syndrome ailing him or her.	Allopathic treatments may cure a patient's disease. However, since those treatments have no effect on the patient's Wholeness, they can do nothing to direct the Vital Force to correct that patient's imbalance. Paradoxically, imbalance progresses and worsens as the patient becomes cured of his or her disease/s.

HOMEOPATHIC REMEDIES	PHARMACEUTICAL DRUGS
Ultimately, the Homeopathic remedy interacts with the patient's Vital Force, and then the Vital Force with the Whole patient.	Ultimately, one molecule (the Pharmaceutical drug) interacts with another molecule present in some sub-cellular fraction.

Chapter 28

HOMEOPATHY AND THE LIFE BELL

Please imagine a bell-shaped curve—well, sort of, because its top has to be flat like a plateau instead of curved.
Please draw the bell on a blank sheet of paper.

Start drawing from the bottom left. Slope up, up, up until you reach the plateau. Now I would like to ask you to go flat for a spell and then slope the line down, down, down to the bottom of the sheet of paper on your right.

Now I would like to ask you to write the word "birth" where you started drawing the curve at the bottom left. "Childhood" and farther on "adolescence" as you go up, "maturity" on the plateau, "old age" in the downward slope and "death" where the downward slope ends on your right.

Consider this bell as how the lives of folks who consider themselves healthy should look like.
According to this model, life goes upwards, full of vitality, from birth through childhood into adolescence and early adulthood. It is horizontal during maturity to then slope gently downward onto death.

The fact of the matter is that it is very improbable that the life bell of folks considered as healthy will look as neat as in the drawing. Childhood and adolescence may slope upwards like shown in the curve, with some wavering here and there.
During maturity's plateau, though, chances are that the line will be anything but straight. It will likely swing up and down, more and more markedly as it approaches the downward slope of old age.
And the slope that corresponds to old age is prone to be jagged, with sharp ups and downs, and becoming more and more steep as it approaches an untimely death.

Here is why.

Let's imagine a baby. Let us say that he or she was born a-psoric even though, in all likelihood, that baby was born from a psoric mother, hopefully not from a sycosic or a syphilitic one.

The baby receives the hepatitis B shot shortly after birth; that is, the vaccine itself plus with a hefty mélange of chemicals. Aside from the vaccine proper, the hepatitis B shot contains, among other substances, aluminum, complex and potentially allergy-inducing molecules like gelatin, toxic antibiotics like neomycin and also poisons like formaldehyde and Thimerosol, the latter a mercury-containing antiseptic.

At this stage the baby's immune system, as well as the organs that have to dispose of everything else in the hepatitis B shot, are not sufficiently developed. They will reach an adequate degree of maturity only at around 8 months of age.

The overstimulation of the immune system, plus the overwork of liver, kidney and other organs of metabolism and excretion, brings about imbalance.

In the process of accommodating to the environment, and provided that the infant has survived successfully the earliest period of life, it is quite likely that he or she may develop some diaper rash, particularly during teething.

Mom will worry and take baby to the Pediatrician. It is quite possible that the Pediatrician may prescribe some cream or similar to successfully treat (please read *suppress)* that innocent rash.

As often as not, this early suppression may blossom into asthma later on.

The hopefully still a-psoric baby may also develop otitis or tonsillitis.

This means that the grasp of the Vital Force on the baby's ears or throat has loosened due probably to some environmental upset. As the consequence, one or more of the 200-odd strains of microorganisms populating the baby becomes active above and beyond its call of duty. In other words, the baby develops otitis or tonsillitis.

The Pediatrician prescribes an antibiotic that decimates the invading bacteria and that, in the bargain, ends the *entente cordiale* that existed between the diverse strains, makes the surviving invaders resistant, and perhaps also triggers an allergy to that antibiotic and others chemically related to it.

Symptoms disappear and baby is happy again. This treatment, however, does nothing to re-attach the Vital Force to the devitalized areas. It will be a stroke of luck if the Vital Force re-attaches itself to the patient's middle ears or the throat after an antibiotic-treated infection. And even if it re-attaches, chances are that its grasp will be weaker than before the infection.

This weakness will likely allow another invasion, which will again be decimated with another antibiotic treatment, and then still another and another until finally tubes are placed into the child's ears or else his or her tonsils are removed. None of these treatments will be able to re-attach the Vital Force to the devitalized areas, simply because none of those drugs have been designed for that purpose.

Something similar will happen if, instead of otitis, or aside from it, the child develops pneumonitis, a urinary tract infection or any other suchlike disease, so frequent during childhood.

The child will likely develop fever during the infections. Fever increases the metabolic rate, necessary to better ward off infections and facilitate the Vital Force's re-attachment to the diseased areas. The fever is likely to be aborted with acetaminophen.

The partial detachment of the Vital Force from the diseased organs or systems causes the onset of imbalance in the Whole patient.

The child is, in effect, becoming psoric.

Simultaneously with environmental onslaughts, the child receives lots of vaccinations against several diseases—most of which, by the way, can often be brought under control, and cured, with Homeopathic treatment.

The child's immune system responds by putting itself in overdrive to produce an immune reaction towards the vaccine itself, and an allergic reaction towards the gelatin and other complex molecules present in the injected fluid.

Aside from the immune system, the liver, kidneys and another organs are also put to work on the double to first neutralize and then excrete many the niceties that come attached to the vaccines.

All these factors stimulate the development of the child's psora.

The baby may be also suppressed due to the skin conditions that have been treated locally. These early suppressions don't show symptoms because the patient's chronicity, at this stage, is only budding.

The upward slope of this child's life bell, probably smooth at first, is likely to start wavering as childhood progresses.

Please remember that nothing is static in Nature. This child's psoric imbalance is not static either. It continues to worsen as time goes by.

Chances are that the child won't notice this progressive increase of imbalance. A tremendous surge of vitality will cover it very effectively throughout infancy, adolescence and into early maturity.

Psora will continue advancing, nevertheless.

The patient is likely to be in a state of *latent Psora.*

And so the child's life bell reaches the point of adolescence and then a young adulthood.

The prevalent feeling in those carefree years is one of omnipotence and invulnerability. Youth considers that to be hale is an inherent and inalienable right that will last forever.

Many future patients abuse themselves with feats of power. They may overeat, drink to excess, stay up all night in hovels filled with deafening music and foul smoke and indulge in many peccadilloes. Add the inevitable stress associated with studies and when starting to work in this big, complex and confusing world.

All of which, together with the stuff used to treat hangovers, indigestion, exhaustion, and insecurity and, with any luck, perhaps no sexually transmitted diseases, becomes the direct cause of still greater imbalance.

Of course, all of the above doesn't matter then. Vitality is at such a boil that adolescents and young adults hardly notice any of the consequences of their excesses. They may treat their illnesses with this or that, to then impatiently go back in search of yet more fun and still greater challenges.

The young person may feel as fit as a fiddle despite of his or her increasing imbalance. The grip of the Vital Force is so firm—yes, even on those organs and structures where it has weakened by imprudent treatments earlier in life—that chronic progressive imbalance is effectively masked.

The patient's latent Psora may only be manifested perhaps by some mild asthma, an attention deficit disorder at School, a flu in winter now and then, perhaps some menstrual pain or irregularity, difficult pregnancies and deliveries, a miscarriage, tiredness, episodes of transient joint discomfort and suchlike afflictions.

Other factors that contribute to the progress of latent Psora are the ill effects of drugs used to treat the above-mentioned problems, anticonceptive pills and all the additives, colorants and the like present in the junk food and drinks young people ingest.

Things start to settle sometime after the life bell reaches adulthood. The patient's exuberant vitality evens out.

Now the weakened grip of the Vital Force in some organs and tissues, that started at some point or points during the ascending slope, start to become evident. Not only that. As age and imbalance progresses, the Vital Force continues loosening its grip in one organ after another, mildly at first, then more markedly. Each devitalized organ screams for help. Each cry is felt as distress by the patient and interpreted as a disease-syndrome by the Doctor. The patient's pathology becomes richer and more severe.

Add the ill effects of chronic stress brought about by a lousy job, a poor marriage or a bad relationship with one's kids, heartbreaks, looses of dear ones, etc.

And, last but certainly not least, add the toxicity and side effects of all the drugs necessary to control each of these problems.

Manifestations of chronic imbalance become more evident as the life bell reaches the slope of old age. Illnesses happen more frequently and tend to remain as new problems appear.

Problems like cataracts, prostatic enlargement, osteoporosis, a difficult menopause, adult onset diabetes, arthritis, congestive heart failure, malignancies, infections, sundry neurological problems and a host of other illnesses start to appear and to pile up. Not only that, diseases hit harder and the patient is never left as well or as strong as he or she was before falling sick. Each illness is like a sharp plunge into the void underneath the slope of old age. And, after the illness is hopefully gone, the curve never picks up where the patient left it before falling ill, but several notches below.

Of course, this means more and more visit to the Doctor, and more and more drugs, surgeries and the like; each with its retinue of side effects and toxicities.

We can observe the depressing results of this pattern in most of our Senior Citizens, kept alive by means of taking drugs by the shovel full and of having their organs removed piecemeal. Yet, most feel worse and more and more limited as time goes by. They live in and out of the Hospital in a drug-, surgery- and radiation-induced artificial state of increasingly precarious wellbeing.

The now deeply serrated declining curve of the bell becomes steeper and steeper as progressive and unchecked imbalance first stretches and then snaps the cordage that maintains the Vital Force and organs and structures held together.

Until finally the grasp of the Vital Force and the patient becomes too tenuous to maintain the Whole person alive.

And far too soon, alas! And after far too much and too unnecessary uncertainty and suffering the Vital Force finally snaps away, and the patient dies an untimely death.

What can Homeopathy do to avoid and/or correct this dismal panorama? Plenty, actually.

First of all, in Homeopathy we believe that diseases are the consequence, and not the cause, of the Whole patient's imbalance. Therefore, we concentrate on the patient's imbalance and less so on the patient's diseases.

Homeopathy considers that diseases happen when the Vital Force loosens its grip in some organ.
This loosening happens because of imbalance.
The dispossessed organ screams for help and often becomes vulnerable to offensive environmental influences.

Homeopathy has been designed to detect and to control imbalance, be it the one that happens in acute disease-syndromes, or the one that underlies any chronic disease, problem or condition.
Once imbalance is detected, Homeopathy has the means to correct it.
With very few exceptions, diseases disappear after the patient's balance has been restored.

And, of course, there are 200 years of experience that show that this approach is correct.

The only aim of Homeopathy in a patient's life is to maintain balance and to restore it if lost.

This role of maintenance/correction ideally starts at the time of conception.
It then continues during and after birth and into childhood, adolescence and early adulthood.
During this time, the role of Homeopathy is mainly that of vigilance and immediate correction of whatever imbalance may happen, before that imbalance has a chance of becoming chronic.
Whether that imbalance is something that came with the patient since before birth, or the consequence of negative environmental influences, vaccines and treatments.

The therapeutic aspect of Homeopathy becomes more and more necessary as adulthood progresses. This is so because this is the time when more and more people start showing pathological evidence of chronic imbalance, often interspersed with acute diseases or with acute exacerbations of their chronic condition.
Homeopathic treatment has two very beneficial effects here. For starters, Homeopathy very often brings these patients into balance, thus making their

illnesses disappear. And then, the patients' newly acquired balance usually prevents them from acquiring severe diseases in the future and, consequently, also allows them to avoid the consequences of the inevitable side effects and toxicity of drugs that would be needed to treat those serious conditions.

Allow me define healthy old age, before I start discussing the role or the purpose of Homeopathy in elderly people who are out of balance.

In the same fashion that childhood and adolescence are the preparation for life, old age is the preparation for death.

As balanced people traverse old age, the Vital Force loosens itself from organs and tissues *gradually, softly, slowly, harmoniously, evenly and more or less simultaneously.* In this fashion, the slope of old age is long and smooth. At its end, death is satisfactory felt like falling asleep after a long and fulfilling journey.

The purpose of Homeopathy here, therefore, is to keep elderly patients in balance and thus make the slope leading toward death as long, as smooth and as fulfilling as possible. This goal is not difficult to achieve when the person entering old age is in balance.

The situation is quite different when the elderly patient has been out of balance for any length of time.

In these patients, the Vital Force does not loosen away gently from organs and tissues as imbalance worsens. It does so in *jerks,* forced by the patient's increasingly strong chronic imbalance.

A healthy way of life, exercise and an adequate diet may certainly delay this snapping away from one organ after another, but won't be able to stop it.

It is this jerky loosening of the Vital Force what makes diseases of old age so serious, and it also explains why, after each disease ends—and few of them do—the patient's recovery is so incomplete and so slow.

Homeopathy can certainly be helpful here. Its results, however, will be commensurate with how much Vital Force the patient has at his or her disposal, and also with how strong the attachment of the Vital Force to organs and tissues remains at the patient starts Homeopathic treatment.

There is a new Medical specialty called *Anti-aging Medicine.*

I find it quite useful. I often prescribe it in my patients starting in mid- to late adulthood. Its purpose is precisely to make the slope of old age as long and as smooth as possible

Consequently, Anti-aging Medicine agrees very nicely with, and very often enhances, the results of Homeopathy.

I have seen, in my limited experience of combining Anti-Aging Medicine with Homeopathy in patients out of balance that its results are not as good as in well-balanced patients.

For Homeopathy, death is as natural a phenomenon as it is to be born.

It is something to be *respected.*

Again here, in balanced patients there is little a Homeopathic Physician has to do to assist the person. At the very most, some advice and counseling if they become alarmed at the increasing weakness that often happens shortly before death ensues.

And, for those who reach this moment while still out of balance, Homeopathy has remedies that can help a lot.

Chapter 29

TO CONCLUDE...

Homeopathy is extremely ductile. It adapts to most situations, many disease-bearing patients, and all stages of life.

It works nicely, often beautifully, either alone or else associated with other forms of treatment, and is also useful in acute and in chronic disease-bearing patients.

Much as I am used to it by now, I still frequently feel awed at what Homeopathy can do.

Those old enough to remember CinemaScope will recall that, in one of its first movies, only the usual screen was on sight as the lights dimmed. Straight ahead, center stage.

In this particular movie, the screen displayed a rocket about to be launched. Its engines roared modestly from a single loudspeaker behind the screen.

Curtains lifted and parted silently at that point. Two enormous lateral silver screens came to life as that in the front enlarged. All three screens fused and formed a huge arc in front of the theater. The rocket, that had hitherto occupied most of the screen, was now suddenly a small, almost insignificant part of the majestic landscape that filled all three screens with one single image. A powerful hi-fi system exploded with a roar of thunder all around the theater, as the craft slowly started to climb toward the heavens.

The moviegoer, for the first time in the midst of all that magnificence, found him or herself dumbfounded, immersed in a new and astounding sea of light, color and sound.

Or when, in Joseph Haydn's *Creation*, the chorus sings the phrase *"Und es ward..."* in a *pianissimo,* almost a whisper until *"...Licht!"* explodes, and fills the listener with a cataract of ineffable sounds and voices that grips the throat and fills eyes with tears.

I have been practicing Allopathic Medicine from 1953 (if I count my earliest snooping into Hospital wards) to 1982, and Homeopathy afterwards.

When I attempt to compare one form of Medicine with the other, I find that the difference comparable to that between a regular and a CinemaScope movie, or between the beginning and the end of the phrase *"Und es ward Licht!"* in Haydn's *Creation.*

This is not an exaggeration but a statement of fact.

As I have often mentioned all along, Allopathy is concerned with disease-syndromes and, up to a point, with the repercussions such disease-syndromes may have on the patients who bear them. Diseases is all that counts to reach Allopathic diagnoses.

For Homeopathy, instead, the disease a patient is bearing is only *one third* of what is necessary to reach a Homeopathic diagnosis. Being the other two parts the patient and the patient's circumstance or surroundings. In Homeopathy, the disease the patient is bearing is as important as one of the three legs of a tripod. It is impossible to reach a correct Homeopathic diagnosis without including in it a sound modalization of the disease, as it is impossible to attempt to reach a diagnosis without taking into account the Whole patient and his or her circumstance. A Homeopathic diagnosis must stand firmly on all three legs. It is impossible to make it stand on only two— far less in only one.

This said, let us not forget that a correct Allopathic diagnosis will permit the Doctor to determine whether or not the disease the Whole patient is bearing is or is not treatable by Homeopathy alone.

In Homeopathy we visualize each Human Being in his or her Wholeness, majestically developing and expanding between Heaven and Earth. And growing, and integrating this Greatness and Freedom into the Universe.

And becoming an irreplaceable part and voice in the Harmony of the Whole—while standing on feet of clay that are o! so fragile, so brittle, so vulnerable. A vulnerability that often makes that marvelous masterpiece loose balance, and crash helplessly into the torment of his or her own Pathos.

Allopathy visualizes Human Beings from another and much more limited perspective.

It progresses from disease-syndrome to organ to cell to molecule. That is, from the Whole to the part and from the part to the particle. It thus proffers Allopaths the means of assisting patients at a molecular level.

In this context, I find very pertinent the thought of the French mathematician Jules Henri Poincaré (1854-1912) *"Would a scientist who has never studied an elephant, except through the microscope, consider that he has an adequate knowledge of the creature?"*

377

In Homeopathy, instead, the only infinitesimal thing we deal with is the amount of matter present in the remedies we administered to our patients—infinitesimal or absent altogether.

In Homeopathy, Physicians are afforded the possibility of studying and treating patients at their superb, supremely exquisite level of Wholeness.

A level where a patient can tell me, when in balance, with these or similar words "I am well now, and aware of myself. I am ready to start to enjoy, and to grow, and to develop, and to become, and to integrate".

How different is this cry of freedom and triumph from the fearful moan I used to hear when practicing Allopathy "I am not sick now, but I fear I may fall sick again. I fear that this time bomb that is my body may be getting ready to play still another of its dirty trick on me".

There are still too many people out there, trapped in their Psora, who believe disease is the inevitable consequence of what they vaguely refer to as "our human condition". How mistaken they are! Our Human condition is one of development, fulfillment, health, harmony, freedom and joy. The feeling that our bodies—our most obedient servants—are time bombs can only be the consequence of our awareness of being out of balance, something that makes us constantly vulnerable and prey of every disease.

It is only after acquiring knowledge of both Allopathy and Homeopathy that one fully appreciates how truly rewarding Homeopathy can be to its practitioners.

I vividly recall the day I started my studies of Homeopathy, in the Post-Graduate School of the Asociación Médica Homeopática Argentina, early in 1982.

A Faculty member gave us rookies the Asociación's welcome. Among other things, he said that Homeopathy was "going to give [us] great satisfactions".

I was very skeptical then. I was there only to find out if Homeopathy was, in effect, charlatanry or not—and in those days, I was heavily biased into thinking that indeed it was a hoax. I consequently dismissed this welcome as only a pep talk. Little did I realize then that I was going to become a Homeopathic Physician, and that the practice of Homeopathy was indeed going to give me satisfactions beyond my wildest expectations.

Training was hard.

I had to learn the incomprehensible peculiarities of Homeopathy, so different from everything I had considered to be factual truths until then. Including concepts such as the principle of like cures like, of only having to dilute and shake to make any remedy active, the increasing power of diminishing concentrations in a remedy and many others. But I had no choice but to accept these incongruences when starting to see how many and astonishing therapeutic successes could be achieved by the judicious application of those ideas.

That was not the hardest part, however.

The thing that was really difficult was to radically change my mind's wiring, and my way of thinking, in order to understand Homeopathy.

Homeopathy is based on *synthesis*, that is, on going from the parts to the Whole. This pattern of thinking is the exact opposite than the one my mind had been trained for. I had been trained to learn through *analyzing* everything from kindergarten onwards; that is, to go from the general to the particular, and from the particular to the minute. This way of thinking was cemented in Medical School, because Allopathy is based on analysis, not on synthesis.

Homeopathy made me realize that there is more than diseases and syndromes and vaccines, and molecules interacting with other molecules, and Surgery and radiations. No matter how enticing Allopathic explanations, and treatments based on those explanations might be.

Homeopathy also made me aware of the fact that, for us Humans, our Whole is indeed more—infinitely more—than the sum total of its parts.

And, as an added bonus, I also started to realize how extraordinarily useful and safe this Medical approach could be.

I soon learnt that Homeopathy is capable of directing the patient's Vital Force into healing many acute and chronic disease-bearing patients; if and when those acute and chronic patients, and the disease or diseases they may be bearing, are within the reach of Homeopathy.

Provided, of course, that those patients also embrace a healthy way of life and that the Homeopathic Physician finds the *simillimum* or at least the correct sequence of *similars,* accompanied perhaps by the patient's nosode. And that patients comply, and consent to be followed up adequately until their newly found wellness gels.

In the Chapter dealing with Homeopathy and the bell of life I described, rather succintly, the usefulness of Homeopathy.

I would like to broaden my description here.

Homeopathy facilitates *normal* conception in many women previously unable to become pregnant, instead of proffering them the risk inherent multiple induced pregnancies. It thus helps the individual since before being conceived, because the ovum is fecundated, and the implantation takes place in a balanced environment; free of the inevitable side effects and toxicity of drugs and hormones.

The balance afforded by Homeopathic treatments will also make future parents more tolerant, understanding and loving. Innumerable marriages have been saved by the emotional balance afforded by Homeopathic treatments—leading to a harmonious home where their children are conceived and born.

Homeopathy is precious during pregnancy.

All the more because, unlike Allopathic drugs, Homeopathic remedies have no side effects, toxicity or ill effects on the mother nor on her embryo or fetus.

Homeopathy may prevent and also cure many instances of morning sickness, itching, varices, liver problems, backache, fears, etc., that often appear during pregnancy.

It can prevent and may actually arrest threatened abortion.

It makes vaginal delivery faster and easier, and helps immensely in the post-partum period of both mother and baby.

Afterwards, it can increase, or decrease, the mother's flow of milk.

Infants have an excess of Vital Force when they are born, and then for months afterwards. Which is understandable, when one considers how powerful their Vital Force must be to live all their years ahead.

Babies remind me, within this context, of the gas rangettes one takes to picnics. The ones connected to gas tanks that are too full. When applying a match, the flames appear a fraction of an inch away from the burner. Flames will flicker, and the slightest breeze will blow them away.

In a similar fashion, the Vital Force in babies is often too powerful for the body that hosts it. This is why babies need so much care and why they are so vulnerable—indeed, why in some of them life may be blown away for no apparent reason.

Homeopathy can harmonize the Vital Force and the baby, and thus help them survive this delicate stage of their life without problems.

Homeopathy helps maintain and regain health in childhood.

Countless sickly children had been made well, and weaned off antibiotics and other suchlike drugs they had used for years in some instances.

Failure to thrive is very often corrected.

Otitis with or without effusion, pharyngitis, tonsillitis and pneumonitis will very often disappear and not return after successful Homeopathic treatments.

Homeopathy often works very well in problems such as attention deficit disorder, autism, infantile asthma, eczema, enuresis, and a host of other disorders.

It has also to be very seriously considered when there are problems brought about by vaccinations. It acts as a *preventive* of those problems.

Homeopathy is effective in the treatment of many diseases children are currently being vaccinated against. There are two Centuries of experience behind this assertion. The catch here is that some children ill with these diseases may need hospitalization in order to be successfully treated Homeopathically; and that Homeopathy is currently *verbotten* in most Hospitals nowadays.

Since it is so effective, so inexpensive, and so lacking in side effects and toxicity, Homeopathy should be the first therapeutic choice in most Pediatric problems.

Furthermore, the balance afforded by Homeopathy allows the child to live a healthier and more fulfilling life, both during childhood and also later on.

Homeopathy is also excellent for most problems that appear during adolescence.

It can help maintain, and/or regain health throughout adult life; as attested by the examples strewn along this book—a few among many, and described only for purposes of illustrating some particular point in the text.

Homeopathy may avoid the need for Surgery.

At the very least, it can considerably ease problems associated with operative procedures and their concurrent hospitalization. I remember, within this context, a woman who assisted one of my lectures.

She said that her adolescent son had had a bad motorcycle accident, and had to be admitted in a Hospital. This woman mentioned the stupefaction of the Orthopedic Surgeon at how fast her son was recovering.

"I wouldn't have told the Doctor, of course" she concluded, with an impish grin "that I was giving him *Arnica* on the sly!"

Many feminine problems are either relieved or else cured with Homeopathic remedies.

All the way from delayed menarche, to PMS, to irregular, excessive and/or painful menses, to anorgasmia, non-malignant tumors, inability to conceive, menopausal and post-menopausal problems, etc.

Many manifestations of male pathology can also be either helped or cured in many instances.
Problems like anhedonia or lack of desire, erectile difficulties, premature ejaculation, and benign prostatic enlargement, to mention only a few.

Homeopathy works very consistently in patients with urinary problems. It can prevent the formation of kidney stones. It can also bring under control inflammation of the kidneys, cystitis, etc.

In sexually transmitted diseases it is *convenient* to associate Homeopathy to antibiotic treatment in syphilis.
It is *necessary* to make this association in gonorrhea and similar disease-syndromes.
In the case of genital warts, Homeopathy should replace the current local Allopathic treatments, and be the *only form of treatment.*
In genital herpes, Homeopathic treatment is, in my experience, at least as effective as any current antiviral treatment. It would be very interesting to do a comparative Homeopathic-Allopathic Research study of this disease.
As far as AIDS, there is still not enough evidence to assess how useful Homeopathy can be in the treatment of this disease-syndrome.

Homeopathy has proven useful in many collagen and allergic diseases, such as eczemas, allergic nasal problems rheumatoid arthritis, lupus and the like.
It can also correct disorders of the immune system caused by overall chronic imbalance.

Many digestive problems can also be relieved or cured by Homeopathy, such as indigestion, peptic ulcers, bloating, diarrhea, liver problems, Crohn's disease, ulcerative colitis, hemorrhoids, anal fissures, etc.
Every patient with ulcerative colitis and Crohn disease should consider Homeopathy, associated or not with Acupuncture, *as the first therapeutic choice. Always,* unless there is colonic cancer or the possibility of toxic megacolon (a rapid and severe bloating of the large intestine, that flattens the blood vessels that feed its wall. The intestinal wall then dies and the intestinal contents spill into the abdominal cavity). The appearance of these two extremely serious and life-threatening complications, as well as the failure of Homeopathy and Acupuncture, should be the *only* reasons for con-

templating the possibility of drug treatment—and, indeed, of Surgery—in these patients.

Homeopathy is very useful in the treatment of stress related problems, and is also in the many manifestations of fatigue.

Homeopathy should be seriously considered in many infectious bacterial diseases, associated or not with antibiotics, according to the individual needs of each individual infectious disease-bearing patient.

Viral diseases respond very poorly if at all to antibiotics or other forms of Allopathic treatments. Homeopathy, instead, has proven to be valuable in many viral disease-bearing patients.

Homeopathy is an ideal complement of Counseling and Psychotherapy in many conditions related to neurosis and mild depression.

There are reports that it can also be very useful in psychotic states. In point of fact, Homeopathy could offer a very interesting alternative to anti-psychotic drugs, if it could only be used in Psychiatric Hospitals and Institutions.

Homeopathy is infinitely preferable to Allopathic treatments for problems derived from difficulties in the sphere of love.

Instead of prescribing psychoactive drugs, balance-altering hormones or gross sexological techniques, Homeopathy offers gentle natural remedies for problems associated with lack of love, fear associated with love, distrust, exhaustion, etc.

As well as for perversions such as exhibitionism and the like.

It is very useful in the elderly—indeed, in many instances it is probably the *only effective form of treatment* for Human Beings who are reaching the sunset of their lives.

It should be considered as the first line of treatment, together with Allopathic drugs as needed; all the more because much of the pathology of elderly people is the consequence of a chronic imbalance that, having been left untreated, has progressed and worsened throughout their lives.

Old age precedes death. Death happens when the Vital Force and the material body separate.

This separation can be harmonic or chaotic.

When harmonic, the Vital Force separates from every organ and structure at approximately the same pace. The aging person perceives this balanced separation as increasing tiredness, and as not unpleasant and progressive limitation of his or her activities. More important, separation is gradual and gentle and causes no pain, fear or anxiety. Needless to say, this form of separation happens only in well balanced individuals.

This process of separation is chaotic in patients who are chronically out of balance. Homeopathy is of supreme value to ease the death throes and agony of these Human Beings about to end their journey, and pass away.

Homeopathy offers remedies, frequently as useful as morphine and the like for pains associated with disease-syndrome such as cancer and others; but without the stunning side effects, or addictive potential, of those powerful pain killers.

As it happens in every branch of Medicine, there are patients who respond to treatment, and patients who do not; some who will respond rapidly and others who will do so more slowly.

Unlike what happens in Allopathy, though, there is no risk here of side effects, toxicity or teratogenesis.

As mentioned several times along the text, there are disease-syndromes that Homeopathic remedies are often unable to cure.

I have mentioned that Homeopathy may have a very limited usefulness in malignant tumors, in tissue destroying diseases and in problems that destroy the nervous system, be it central or peripheric, all the more if this destruction is complicated by old age.

And yet, and yet...

I remember, within the context of destruction of nervous tissue and advanced age, an 82 year old male I once took care of. He had been diagnosed as suffering from Alzheimer's disease. It had started—or become clinically manifest—over ten years before I first saw him. His disease-syndrome was very advanced by the time his wife and daughter brought him to my office.

The patient was lethargic—he slept throughout the first few office visits—and his memory was entirely gone for all intents and purposes. For instance, he would easily get lost in the suite he had been occupying for years in a classy Nursing Home with his wife.

Through the information afforded by his wife and daughter I felt that his Constitutional remedy might be *Lycopodium clavatum*.

Under treatment, the patient became oriented in his suite he became able to recognize which was the cold and which the hot water faucet in the shower. His attention span became considerably longer. He was again able to play cards, and his lethargy disappeared. One day he found his way, all by himself, from the Nursing Home's Park to his apartment—and remained contentedly there while family members and Police frantically searched all over, believing he had gotten lost.

Improvement, though, did not progress any farther.

Homeopathic remedies generally cannot replace hormone administration in hormone-deficient syndromes, such as insulin-dependent diabetes mellitus or hypothyroidism. Nor can they usually stimulate the appearance of factors in diseases such as hemophilia.

But they can help stabilize the daily requirements of thyroid hormone in patients who do not produce enough of that hormone and may also diminish and stabilize the requirements of of insulin in insulin dependent diabetes mellitus patients.

As far as malignant solid tumors, Surgical removal of the tumor remains by far the first choice in early, resectable cancers. Removal of the tumor in time can cure cancer patients.

Homeopathy can help a lot in patients whose tumors are beyond the possibility of removal. Clinical studies are urgently needed to asses how useful Homeopathy can be in these patients, either alone or else combined with Radiotherapy and/or Chemotherapy.

Homeopathy has gone a very long way since its inception, 200 years ago. We have learnt a lot about its possibilities and its limitations.

Perhaps, and still more important, we have some idea regarding when to use it alone, when to associate it with other forms of treatment, and when not to use it at all—although a lot of Research work is still needed here.

Either way, the value of Homeopathy is indisputable. Aside from also being considerably safer, gentler and incomparably less expensive than its Allopathic counterpart.

Some time ago, after one of my lectures, one of the listeners approached me. His features were aglow with the amazement one feels after having discovered something of importance.

"But then" he told me, all excited "Homeopathy is the Medicine of Understanding!".

I pondered his words over for a while. I had never thought of Homeopathy under that light until then.

This man was right.

Not only that; what he had said is probably the most succinct, as well as the best definition of Homeopathy I had ever heard or learnt about in my life.

I smiled and nodded.

"You're right!" I answered.

I thought of ending this book with his commentary:

"But then" he said, all excited "Homeopathy is the Medicine of Understanding!"

BIBLIOGRAPHICAL REFERENCES

I shall list here only those references written in, or translated into English, that I consider essential for a knowledge—and understanding—of Homeopathy in some depth.

Most have been either published by several Editorial companies, or have had several editions, or both.

In three of the references, however, I believe it may be important to mention the Editorial house and perhaps also the year of publication. Those references are the 6th Edition of Dr. Hahnemann's *Organon,* as translated by Künzli, J. *et al.* that I consider uniquely valuable; the latest Edition of Harris L. Coulter's *"Divided Legacy",* Dr. Sankaran's *The spirit of Homeopathy,* and also that of Dr. T. M. Cook's *"Homeopathic Medicine Today".*

Regarding other references, I shall only write down the name of the author/s and that of the book.

HAHNEMANN, S.
Organon of Medicine, 6th. Edition. Trans. by Künzli, J., Naudé A., Pendleton, P. J. P. Tarcher, Inc., Los Angeles, 1982.
Treatise of Chronic Diseases.
Lesser Writings.
Materia Medica Pura.

KENT, J. T.
Lectures on Homeopathic Materia Medica.
Lectures on Homeopathic Philosophy.
Lesser Writings.
Repertory of Homeopathic Materia Medica.

ALLEN, H. C.
Keynotes of the Materia Medica with Nosodes.
Materia Medica of the Nosodes.

ALLEN, J. H.
The Chronic Miasmas. Psora, Pseudo-Psora and Sycosis.

ALLEN, T. F.
Boenninghausen's Therapeutic Pocketbook.

ANSHUTZ, E. P.
New, Old and Forgotten Remedies.

BARTHEL, H., KLUNKER, W.
Synthetic Repertory.

BOERICKE, W.
Pocket Manual of Homeopathic Materia Medica with Repertory.

BORLAND, D. M.
Children's Types.
Homeopathy for Mother and Infant.
Homeopathy in Practice.

BOYD, H.
Introduction to Homeopathic Medicine.

CANDEGABE, E.
Comparative Materia Medica.

COOK, T. M.
Homeopathic Medicine Today. Keats Publishing Inc., New Canaan, CT, 1989

COULTER, C.
Portraits of Homeopathic Medicines.

COULTER, H. L.
Divided Legacy, A History of the Schism in Medical Thought. Wehawkehn Book Co., Washington, D.C. 1977.

EIZAYAGA, F. X.
Clinical Homeopathic Algorithms.
Treatise on Homeopathic Medicine.

FARRINGTON, E. A.
Clinical Materia Medica.
Comparative Materia Medica.

GUERNSEY, H. N.
Obstetrics.

Keynotes to the Materia Medica.

HERING, C.
Condensed Materia Medica.
Guiding Symptoms.

KNERR, C.
Repertory of Hering's Guiding Symptoms.

NASH, E. B.
Leaders in Homeopathic Therapeutics.
Leaders in Respiratory Organs.
Regional Leaders.

ROBERTS, H. A.
Sensations "as if".
Principles and Art of Cure.

SANKARAN, R.
The spirit of Homeopathy. Ed. Homeopathic Medical Publishers, Bombay, 1991.

SANKARAN, R.
The substance of Homeopathy, Ed. Homeopathic Medical Publishers, Bombay, 1994.

TYLER, M. L.
Homeopathic Drug Pictures.
Pointers to Common Remedies.

Jose Miguel Mullen, M.D.

INDEX

Decima, 75
Decimal, 81
Decimal potencies, 228
Decimals, 249
DECIMALS, 81
decongestants, 173, 174
decoy, 343
defecate, 259
dehydration, 300
delayed menarche, 382
delivery room, 122
dementia, 67, 68
denominator, 133
dependency, 63
depression, 189, 251, 383
Dermatologist, 121
desensitize, 339
design, 332
desire/fear, 59
despair, 176
destruction, 57, 69
Destruction, 59
destructive diseases, 69
DETOXIFIERS, 195
develop, 247
diabetic coma, 120, 193, 355
Diagnostic facilities, 321
diarrhea, 39, 105, 183, 202, 229, 300, 382
diet, 239, 245, 258
differential diagnoses, 118
Digestive problems, 382
Digitalis, 86, 223
Digitalis Purpurea, 204
Dilantin, 242
dilution, 75, 79
diminishing concentrations, 379
diphtheria, 301, 338
disability, 243
discharge, 291
disease-bearing patient, 100

disease-syndrome, 1, 22, 247, 255, 334
disease-syndromes, 257
disposal, 321
dissatisfaction, 60
distention, 103
Distention, 103
distress, 56, 258
distrust, 59, 383
diuretics, 154
dogs, 315, 320
dosage levels, 313
dosage range, 318
doses, 88
double blind, 317
Dreams, 105
dropsy, 205
DRUG, 1
drug affinities, 98
drug alleys, 58
drugs, 173
dry cough, 109
dryness, 106
dynamizatio, 42
dynamization, 42, 216
DYNAMIZATIONS, 79
dynamized, 359
dynamized natural products, 334
dysmenorrhea, 45, 170
dyspepsia, 185
ear infection, 25
ear infections, 25
ears, 61
ECOSYSTEM, 4
eczema, 40, 45, 46, 249, 381
efficacy, 88
Ehrlich, 289
Einstein, 3
Elastic tissue, 13
elbow, 142
electric shocks, 207
electricity, 207

ill volunteers, 88
imbalance, 23, 125
immune system, 243, 336, 338, 344
immune systems, 345
immunity, 338
immunological variation, 308
impersonator, 301
implantation, 380
inability to conceive, 382
inability to get pregnant, 21
inadequacy, 245
inbred animals, 308, 314
inbreeding, 308
Incas, 210
Incubators, 321
indigestion, 382
INDIVIDUAL, 5
individual variation, 308
induced diseases, 28
inertia, 269
Infantile Gastroenterologist, 176
infants, 58
infection, 338
infinitesimal, 378
Influenzinum, 189, 344
infrastructure, 321
inhaler, 37
inhalers, 41, 173
injectable, 216
insane, 288
insecure, 184
insecurity, 55
insomnia, 168, 183, 259
instability, 61
insulin, 167, 385
Insulin, 355
insulin-dependent diabetes, 69, 278
Insulin-dependent diabetes, 166
insulin-dependent diabetes mellitus, 385

integrate, 378
intercurrent disease, 124
intercurrent treatment, 274
INTERCURRENTS, 194
interdependent, 12
intermittent fevers, 210
Internal Medicine, 119, 143
interpretation, 329, 332
interpretation of results, 321
interrelation, 13
Interruption, 122
intestines, 206
intoxication, 105
intradermal injections, 340
intraperitoneally, 314
intrathoracic goiter, 141, 278
intravenously, 314
Introduction, 333
involuntary Proving, 222
iodine, 241
Iodine, 206
Ipeca, 86
Ipecacuanha, 86
iron deficiency anemia, 237
irregular menses, 382
irritabilit, 60
irritable bowel syndrome, 202
Isopathy, 190
Italic style, 101
itching, 380
jalap, 206, 352
Jenner, 204
Jesuit's powder, 210, 214
job, 62
joints, 289
jugular, 206
jugular veins, 155
kah, 3
Kali bromatum, 109
Kali Carbonicum, 103, 126, 186, 188
Kekule, 213

Pharmacies, 196, 318
Pharmacological drugs, 318
Pharmacological Experiment, 309
Pharmacological Research, 304, 320
Pharmacological trials, 88
Pharmacological-Homeopathic Research, 332
Pharmacology, 129
Pharmacopœia, 206
pharyngitis, 174, 381
Phlebotomy, 207
Phosphoric Acid, 102
Phosphorus, 102, 132, 188, 193, 252
Physical Examination, 129, 153, 184, 340
Physical Therapist, 165
Physics, 79
Physis, 3
Phytolacca, 109
pil, 216
placebo, 155
placebo effect, 317
placenta, 14
Places of Man, 353
Plain Style, 101
plant products, 302
Plato, vii, 237
Plus, 216
Pneuma, 3
pneumococcus, 24
pneumonia, 24, 61
pneumonia shots, 173
pneumonitis, 61, 129, 158, 174, 381
Pneumonologist, 37, 173
polio vaccine, 337, 343
politician, 63
pollen, 9
Pollen, 339
Polychrests, 181, 188, 190

polyps, 140
porcelain, 78
portal, 24
position, 62, 125
post-menopausal problems, 382
post-nasal drip, 229
post-partum, 380
post-partum discomfort, 380
post-partum pelvic infection, 142
potassium cyanide, 356
potencies, 216
Potencies, 194
potency, 216, 229, 231, 320
POTENCY, 79
pounding, 79
power, 63
Prednisone, 129, 142, 172, 242, 243, 244, 248
Preface, 98
pregnancy, 380
Pregnancy, 105
pregnant women, 222
premature ejaculation, 382
premenstrual pain, 37
pre-menstrual pain, 37
premenstrual pains, 37
pre-menstrual pains, 37
preventive, 338, 344
prison, 60
prize fighter, 256
Proctologist, 140
PROFILE, 101, 102, 103, 130, 323
progress, 227
progressive, 21
prostate, 289
prover, 322, 325
Proving, 129, 216, 223, 224, 322
Provings, 50, 86, 101, 102, 104, 118, 132, 188, 342
Prussic acid, 241
Pseudo-psora, 67, 235, 295, 296
PSEUDO-PSORA, 60

soldiers, 256
Solildago virga aurea, 195
sordes, 101
Spaniards, 210
Spanish fly, 207, 352
spatula, 78
spatulas, 321
specialization, 12
spirits, 76
spleen, 154, 155, 172
sporadic, 19
sputum, 173
square meter, 320
St. Bartholomew's, 300
Staff, 119
Stages of Life, 105
standardization, 329
staphylococcus, 24
starboard, 10
statesman, 63
statistical assessment, 329
statistical evaluation, 309, 311
Statistical procedures, 310
Statistical structure, 320
Statistician, 314, 332
status, 62
status epilepticus, 193, 242
sterile gonococcal arthritis, 295
sterility, 291
Sterilizing equipment, 321
stimulants, 56
Stoerk, H., 207
store, 83
STRANGE, RARE AND PECULIAR
   symptoms, 112
stress, 65, 245, 383
Stress, 56
strychnine, 206, 356
stuffiness, 229
Styx, 255
sub-cellular, 4
subcutaneously, 314

subjective, 119, 120
substance dependence, 69
succussion, 213
SUCCUSSION, 79
succussions, 83, 84
suggestions, 237
suicidal, 230
suicide, 58, 69
sulfite of iron, 356
Sulfur, 103, 132, 188, 247, 249
sulfuric acid, 241
Sulphur, 109, 241
summary, 333
sunlight, 84
superimposition, 129
support groups, 240
suppression, 38, 41, 107, 202,
   231, 275, 282, 293
Suppression, 43, 276
suppressions, 41, 43, 286
suppressive, 352
suppuration, 207
Surgeon, 250, 257, 350
Surgery, 37, 38, 43, 143, 146,
   251, 256, 257, 381
suspicious, 59
Suspiciousness, 59
swamp fevers, 210
sweat, 61
sweating, 189, 250
sweating at night, 61
sycosic, 54
Sycosic, 55
Sycosic patients, 235
Sycosics, 58
Sycosis, 54, 60, 67, 69, 70, 188,
   280, 285
Sydenham, 208
Sympathetic, 102
Symptoms, 89, 132
syncytium, 12
synthesis, 379

ABOUT THE AUTHOR

José Miguel Mullen graduated as a Medical Doctor from the Medical School of the University of Buenos Aires, Argentina.

He spent the next four years in America.

The first two at St. Vincent's Hospital, Erie, Pennsylvania; doing his Rotating Internship and one year of Surgical Residence.

He was then a Pathology Resident for one year in the George Washington University Hospital, and also Assistant to the Chair of Pathology in the George Washington School of Medicine, Washington, DC.

During his last year in America, he trained in Clinical Cancer Chemotherapy and Clinical Pharmacological Cancer Research, in Massachusetts General Hospital, Boston, Massachusetts, and the Lemuel Shattuck Hospital in Jamaica Plains, Massachusetts. All with a Fellowship from Harvard Medical School, Boston, Massachusetts.

The following year was spent at the Chester Beatty Research Institute and the Royal Cancer Hospital, in London, England, training in Clinical Cancer Chemotherapy and Cancer Research in cell cultures.

At that time he designed, and started, his first Research Project that involved Human hormones and cells from Human feminine breast adenocarcinoma *in vitro*.

Dr. Mullen then returned to Argentina and started his private Oncology and General Medical practice that he continued until 1982, when he became a Homeopathic Physician.

As an Oncologist, he also worked at the Hospital de Clínicas, University of Buenos Aires, Argentina, until 1972, doing Clinical Cancer Research. At that time, he felt that his Research work would be more useful at a Laboratory level.

From 1972 onwards, in the Institute of Pharmacology, National Department of Health, Buenos Aires, Argentina, Dr. Mullen developed several of his own Research ideas, using for that purpose inbred BALB/c mice and Sarcoma 180.

Dr. Mullen took several Post-Graduate Courses during his years as Cancer Researcher.

Courses were Cancer Chemotherapy, at the Sloan Kettering Research Institute, New York, NY; Use of Radioisotopes in Biology, National Atomic Energy Commission, Buenos Aires, Argentina; Calculus and Biostatistics, Hospital de Clínicas, University of Buenos Aires, Argentina; and Genetic Toxicology, University of Texas in Galveston, Texas.

Dr. Mullen was awarded three traveling fellowships.

The first from Unio International Contra Cancro, Geneva, Switzerland, to assist to the IX International Cancer Congress in Tokyo, Japan. At that time, Dr. Mullen visited Cancer Research Laboratories and Centers in the University of Tokyo.

The second Fellowship was from the Deustcher Akademischer Austauschdient, Bonn, West Germany, to visit the Medischinische Klinik, University of Köln; Innere Klinik für Tumorforschung, Essen; Deutsches Krebsforschungszentrum, Heidelberg; Medischinische Klinik, University of Tübingen; and finally Univ.-Frauenklinik, Hamburg-Eppendorff, in Germany.

The third Fellowship was from the Panamerican Health Organization, Washington, DC, to visit the National Institutes of Health, Bethesda, Maryland; Food and Drug Administration, Washington, DC; Fredrick Cancer Research Center, Fredrick, Maryland; Johns Hopkins Hospital and School of Public Health, Baltimore, Maryland; National Institute for Toxicological Research, Jefferson, Arkansas; Department of Medical Genetics, University of Southern Alabama, Mobile Alabama; Department of Preventive Medicine, University of Texas Medical Branch, Galveston, Texas; and the Cancer Institute of the University of Southern California, Los Angeles, California.

By the late 1970's, Dr. Mullen became aware of the fact that cancer, as well as every other disease, has more to do with the Whole Human Being than with only ill organs and systems; and also that the Allopathic Medicine he was familiar with had no way of dealing with such a perspective.

This awareness made Dr. Mullen begin a quest that would ultimately conduct him to Homeopathy.

Before finding Homeopathy, he took Seminars and Workshops dealing with Gestalt, Reich techniques, Psychocybernetics, Sexology, Nutrition, Natural and Folk Medicine, Hydrotherapy and Massage.

He also took a course on Acupuncture, in the Asociación Argentina de Acupuntura, Buenos Aires, Argentina; and two seminars on Anthroposophic Medicine in the Sociedad Antroposófica Argentina, conducted by Profs. Drs. Otto Wolff, M.D. and Michaela Glockler, M.D., Pediatrician, both of the Herdecke Krankenhouse, Schlichten, Germany.

In 1982, Dr. Mullen was accepted as a student into the accredited Post-Graduate School of the Asociación Médica Homeopática Argentina, Buenos Aires, Argentina, where he formally studied for 3 years, and where he also took two Post-Graduate courses on Materia Medica Homeopathica.

He was granted the title of Homeopathic Physician in Argentina after successfully passing two exams.

Dr. Mullen has been doing Homeopathy ever since.

In 1987 he came to America with his family.

He took, and successfully passed, the Examination for Foreign Medical Graduates, and also the FLEX (to be allowed to practice Medicine independently) in 1988; as well as the Connecticut State Board Medical Examination for Homeopathy in 1989. In 1997 he took and passed the Homeopathic Medical Board Examination of the State of Arizona, and was granted a Homeopathic Medical license in that State.

He is currently devoted full-time to the practice of Homeopathy in Colchester, Connecticut.

He resides in Colchester, Connecticut, with his family.

Dr. Mullen has been appointed by the Governor of the State of Connecticut as a member of the Homeopathic Examining Medical Board, Department of Health, State of Connecticut in 1994.

He is an associate member of the Faculty of Homeopathy, Royal Homeopathic Hospital London, England, since 1994.

And, since 2000, he is also Adjunct Faculty of the Desert School of Classical Homeopathy, Phoenix, Arizona.

Dr. Mullen has written several scientific papers on subjects related to his Cancer Research work.

He is a professional free-lance writer; and has published articles about Political Philosophy in the *Correo de la Semana,* Buenos Aires, Argentina.

He has also written and sold several stories. On fantastic realism to *Atlántida* magazine, Buenos Aires, Argentina and on *Science Fiction to Analog, Science Fact/Science Fiction,* New York, New York.

79 Norwich Avenue, Building C,
P. O. Box 387,
Colchester, CT 06415, USA
Phone (860) 537-3699.
Fax (860) 537 6985.

Website www.homeopathyandyou.com